DISTRIBIA

A SOCIETY FREE OF TRIBALISM

ALI CHEAIB

Distribia: A Society Free of Tribalism.

ISBN-10: 1732446539

ISBN-13: 978-1732446533

DEDICATION

I dedicate this book to everyone around the world who fell victims to tribal systems that make people torture, abuse and hate one another.

To those born as slaves to an unforgiving economy that leaves people no decent choice but to rent themselves out for money just to survive.

To those condemned to starvation by a fraudulent monetary system controlled by international bankers and their debt-based papermoney.

To those left homeless in a cynical society that recognizes landownership and legitimizes landlords.

To all those who fell victims to such ruthless concepts and were chained by loans or debts and oppressed by wage slavery.

ACKNOWLEDGMENT

Writing this book has been a life-changing decision that has educated and enlightened me beautifully in so many ways along the way. I truly hope that it will have the same wonderful effect on you too.

I have always been a critical thinker but was unfortunate to have lived most of my life in cultures where criticism isn't tolerated and where critics are routinely and systematically oppressed. I spent a lifetime stuck in silence afraid I would say something wrong. I am very fortunate to be living today in a free and open society like the United States because living in this liberal nation finally allowed me to write critically and share my thoughts without fear of oppression or retaliation.

Criticism is a virtue, which I hold dearest. The path to enlightenment is paved through criticism and analytics, which are the keystones of the process of thinking. Therefore, everything and everyone should be self-critical and accept criticism or else the path to enlightenment would be lost.

It takes remarkable strength to swim against the tide and similarly it takes stamina and courage to challenge the status quo and be controversial. I choose dissidence over obedience and controversy over conformity.

It was emotionally and mentally brutal journey against the tide, but I am thankful for finally seeing this illuminating work of literature published and shared with the world.

TABLE OF CONTENTS

PROLOGUE

Humanity has come a long way from dwelling in caves and the hunter-gatherer way of life. Humans have been on Earth for a relatively short time compared to the billions of years our planet has been orbiting its star in the vastness of space and existence. In that short period, we have dreamt up and produced fantastic innovations from the moment someone bashed a rock on the ground to make the first sharp-edged tool, to the development of spacecraft and the Internet. Whether it was the first use of fire or the discovery of the wheel, innovation has always been the primary catalyst behind humankind's evolution. Some of these breakthroughs brought about immediate change, while others humbly laid the groundwork for essential developments down the road.

Humanity's primary defining feature is our ability to design systems, but at the same time, such hallmark is our downfall because systems have the potential for enslaving and destroying humanity. Although nature blessed us with remarkable intelligence, it cursed us with flawed thinking. As a result, the designs that people introduce are reflections of that flawed human mind that we all share. A system is a good servant but an evil master. Not realizing the dangers that lurk within systems, humanity foolishly enslaved itself under ghoulish concepts. Citizens of the world allowed an authoritarian social class system in which a ruling class of people ruled everyone and made all the critical decisions on behalf of the masses as if such a system is natural. This authoritarian world order consisted of only two classes: the working class and the ruling class. The ruling class rules while the working class does all the work for them. It was a slavery system consisting of masters and slaves. The masters designed a world that was so misarranged that the only way of living it was by destroying other lives. They cultivated tribal civilizations that had the capacity for horrors in terms of what one tribal culture could do to another or, even worst, what one tribal society could do to its own people.

1

The ruling classes of the world designed a horrific global social system in which slavery is systematic and is passed down from one generation to the other. The laws that they wrote were enslaving, the innovations they introduced were inefficient and wasteful, and the societies they engineered were dysfunctional and abusive. They developed speed for themselves but shut everyone else behind walls and national borders. They freed themselves but enslaved the people. They built machinery that could produce in abundance but left most of humanity in need. They made remarkable discoveries that could cure all diseases and illnesses but made others that could destroy humanity and wipe it off the surface of the Earth. They designed an indoctrination system to institutionalize and indoctrinate young generations in the service of nation-building, teaching children blind obedience to the authorities and reinforcing class and race prejudice. The political systems of all republics around the globe naturally fostered corruption, and instead of ensuring liberties they strangled them at birth and became self-absorbed authoritarian regimes that repress the public and abuse power.

The monetary systems that a minority of people designed enslaved humanity with debts and created disparities in society. They created a snowball system in which the rich get richer while the poor linger. Money became the master instead of a servant of humanity. They created economic systems that reduced entire populations to slavery through wage labor in abusive hierarchical institutions. A cruel global economy controlled by bankers and large corporations that treated people as deplorable objects and shamelessly called them *"human resources."* It was a cynical culture where people rent themselves out in droves for a worthless paper that they call money. A sadistic culture of slaves and lords.

Humanity desperately needed to eradicate its abusive ruling classes and their dysfunctional systems. A need emerged to tackle the threat of flawed systems and designs that complicated human relationships and worsened human behavior towards the natural environment. And so, this condition initiated a theory introduced by unknowns for designing better systems after recognizing how systems have become masters of humanity instead of assistants to it. To mitigate the impact that systems can have on humanity and to

2

prevent a minority from conceiving flawed designs and policies that could regiment the lives of the majority, a school of thought was born for the *"distribution of everything."*

The method, known as *distribia* and means *"the distribution of all"*, provides a principle for measuring the correctness of humankind's plans through the convention that the more distributed a system is to its fundamental elements, the more accurate it becomes. Representation, delegation, intermediation, centralization, and segregation are paradoxical to *distribia's* school of thought and are always avoided at all costs. Put simply, DISTRIBIA IS THE LIBERATION FROM THE TYRANNICAL CONCEPTS OF REPRESENTATION, DELEGATION, INTERMEDIATION, CENTRALIZATION, AND SEGREGATION.

Distribia formalizes a standard and a measurement of the correctness of any system designed by society. One can apply it to any human-made design such as the economy, society, commerce, education, government, agriculture, energy production, or the monetary policy. The systems that *distribia* delivers naturally have no central command or dependency on other parts within the same system because every single part is self-sustaining and functions independently.

Distribians (those who live by the system and philosophy of *distribia*) were most interested in applying their school of thought to society because they saw the immense value and benefit awaiting people worldwide from adopting *distribia*. They believed there would be no more conflicts, wars, hunger, lack of education, poverty, houselessness, unemployment, lack of safety and wellbeing, and all other problems that humanity struggled with at their present time when tribalists ruled the planet. Such a theory generated the belief that the world would become a far better place and that people everywhere would finally be treated equally with equal access to all facets of life. Humanity could subsequently attain world peace, freedom, and happiness for everyone.

Throughout history, technology has always been the real instigator of social progress and mostly in a sane way. *Distribia's* solution to the middlemen problem came in the form of technology that has

3

distribution, trust and anti-intermediaries built into it. It is called the blockchain, and it was the underlying technology of a cryptocurrency called bitcoin. A group of unknown *distribians* under the name of Satoshi Nakamoto conceived this marvelous technology with the desire to annihilate all tyranny on Earth especially the financial kind. It was a technology engineered to liberate humanity from the cruelty of the banking elites and the fascism of their central banks. The blockchain created a domino effect where piece by piece all aspects of the way of life gradually evolved through the innovative solutions and discoveries of *distribians*. It led to the reconstruction of all telecommunication hardware used to connect people, transforming the internet into a peer-to-peer web within an ad-hoc mesh network that has no central server or administration.

Inspired by the blockchain's ability to solve the double spending problem without requiring a trusted authority, a group of American university students designed a program as an online peer-to-peer legislature, called *Unipublic*. It's an opensource blockchain-based technology that allows everyone anywhere in the world to act as a legislature to write or vote for the laws they wish to see in the world. This legislature is a public ledger recording identities, petitions, laws, and votes in a peer-to-peer network of people who act as independent legislatures, allowing everyone in the world to participate in writing laws of any kind and vote on them to become the laws of humanity everywhere.

The word *Unipublic* comes from the root Latin word *unus* (which means one) and the English word *public* (which means of or concerning the people as a whole). Together they mean *"one public."* The name is meant to remind everyone that the class system is over; that there's only one public now for humanity and that the people now have the power and can make direct decisions free of representatives or middlemen. *Unipublic* allowed early *distribians* to vote on crucial decisions that changed the world forever, and eventually, it conceived several systems and laws that allowed *distribia* to grow into a governing social system. The brutal regimes of the ruling classes everywhere could finally be challenged and overthrown. The unelected systems that became masters could finally be tamed to be servants of humanity as they should be, and humankind could eventually liberate itself from the chains that enslaved generations after generations of human beings around the globe by a handful of people.

Not long after the birth of the global legislature, a distributed artificial intelligence called *Ve* was born to secure people's identities and information. Most importantly, *Ve* became people's virtual self and the channel for a global legislature, where laws are written and selected based on the consensus of the entire human population. Voting became seamless and casual through regular discussions between a person and his/her *Ve*. By the completion of this vital infrastructure, the inevitable finally happened and the citizens of the United States of America revolted against their ruling parties and peacefully dismantled their government paving the way for pure democracy for all humanity. The fall of the U.S. created a ripple effect that sprawled within days to all other republics of the American continent and then to the independent nation-states of the EU and soon later to the entire world.

With the fall of the governments of the United States and the EU, the totalitarian regimes of Russia, China, and the Middle East had no reason to exist, and their citizens rebelled as well but at great cost. Citizens of every country on Earth ignited leaderless protests demanding leaderless governments. They burned their national flags, passports, and national IDs. They destroyed their national borders in favor of global citizenship and the freedom to work and live anywhere and for as long as they desire. Representative democracy and all other ruling systems collapsed, and replaced by *distribia's* direct democracy, which is democracy in its purest form, leading to the unification of people from all corners of the world under one universal citizenship but free of a centralized government or leadership. All national borders gradually disappeared, and *distribia* became global. When *distribia's* pure democracy became a global reality, marvelous innovations started to surface around the world. Flags, national borders, armies, and weaponry were abandoned and became mere artifacts in multiple museums serving as an unpleasant reminder to future generations of these horror tales of the past when tribalism ruled humanity.

Representation in all its forms and intermediaries or middlemen were renounced and illegalized. Instead, humanity decided that *Ve* is the only legal intermediary and representative of humanity.

A new generation of the internet became an open space for unchained content, accessible and manageable from any software and not centralized or restricted to one or few servers. All operating systems became open source allowing programmers and software engineers worldwide to innovate new technologies, produce and share the profits through fair partnership programs.

Law and justice became uniform and borderless free of designated buildings or authorities allowing the public of the world to collectively elect the laws they wish to live by in a global society and directly enforce these laws without requiring middlemen or central courts. Simply put, the people write their own rules and practice them in a peer-to-peer fashion without representatives or delegates such as lawyers or judges.

Distribia localized electricity production and storage to every building followed by completely shutting down all centralized power plants. They also restricted the generation of drinking water and its storage as well as greywater and blackwater treatment to every building and stripped off all the foolishly designed centralized municipal sewer systems.

Humanity decided that cattle and all animal life confinement is illegal and elected a universal meat production system to regulate such food. They produced a meat tax to protect animal populations from pouching and averted from slaughtering animals for their meat in favor of lab-grown meats or plant-based meats that mimic the taste of traditional meats. As a result, all slaughterhouses, which were traditionally tucked away far from sight and lost to memory, shut down completely. Food is no longer canned or packaged, and no longer comes from the dead bodies of the animals that were caged, grown artificially, tortured, and exhausted until they biologically malfunctioned. Food is no longer designed for profit, but for health. *Distribia* introduced a same-day-consumption policy on edible products and banned the use of preservatives and long-distance shipping in favor of a quick consumption policy of local produce. Now, every city is self-sustaining. Food is grown, harvested, packaged, sold, delivered, and consumed within the same city. Companies aren't allowed to ship their edible products to other cities, but consumers can buy them in one city and take the food with them somewhere else.

Distribians built a new generation of the subway, a skyway and a waterway as a distributed and shared global transport network for people and freight connecting all residential blocks of all cities worldwide together and replacing traditional methods such as pavement highways, trains, and centralized airports.

A universal architectural standard reshaped all cities worldwide, landscaping communities as a chessboard of residential blocks surrounded by squares of green parks, drastically minimizing urban invasiveness in nature and maintaining a naturalistic way of living.

They freed education from the grasps of institutions and made it online and public transforming universities and schools into research facilities or open meetup places for knowledge-seekers and scholars designed to stimulate creativity in the minds of attendees. They produced a type of education that tests students' critical and analytical capacity, not their memory. It is a type of education that invariably involves open-book tests in any field of study. An evolving form of education formulated, maintained, directed, and delivered by teachers alone directly to their students without any middlemen such as schools or universities or institutes.

They composed a universal voting system along with a social incentive program that focused on a person's merits as the ultimate measurement of human quality leading to generations of enlightened people living in peace with one another, enriching life and defining a meaning for it together.

The financial system became unrecognizable, and the salary-based income was finally replaced by a profit-sharing partnership program converting employees/employers into partners and creating equality in the economy. Under such program, the corrosive corporate hierarchy or the arrangement of individuals within a corporation according to power, status, and job function was finally eradicated from the human society. The salary system or the hourly wage, which is a temporary form of chattel slavery revolving around renting out oneself for money, became illegal. No more bosses and employees. No more blue-collar or white-collar workers or men in fancy suits in high castles. No more masters and slaves.

Guaranteed income, education, healthcare, and housing became a reality for everyone. These necessities became available to every human being no matter where they live or how much they earned through a universal basic income. Poverty, houselessness, illiteracy, and lack of access to medical treatment all became nothing more than a dreadful memory in the grievous past of humanity's history.

Like dominoes, piece by piece the defective systems fell, making way eventually to a globally distributed system of living after all the offshoots of tribalism collapsed forever. The change happened randomly around the globe and progressively across several decades, but it was a swift change in comparison to how long humanity took to evolve from one ruling social system to another across the centuries.

It started by countries splitting apart from within into hundreds of thousands of fully independent city-states. San Francisco became independent from the state of California and the federal government. Same goes for Los Angeles and every other city in the United States of America. Some communities around the globe did it politically through citywide referendums, others achieved it through mass protests, and the rest realized it through armed rebellions. These city-states then decentralized further into independent self-protected neighborhoods that operate under international laws, which are nominated and elected by humanity collectively.

Blockchain and cryptocurrencies were the first instigators of this wonderful decentralization of governance. They acted as the first infrastructure that supported the birth of the global peer-to-peer economy. After this vital foundation was ready, central banks and commercial banks collapsed when their fiat currencies lost their value and after people rushed to secure their wealth in cryptocurrencies.

In this book, we tell the story of a monstrously oppressive system called tribalism, which propagated two classes in society and sustained one in abusing and enslaving the other for thousands of years until the inevitable rise of *distribia*. Travel with us on a journey in time to a wonderful world free of tribalism. To a nonauthoritarian society free of representation, delegation, intermediation, centralization and segregation to discover the beautiful way of life of *distribia's* fascinating nonhierarchical society.

THE PEER-TO-PEER LEGISLATURE

The tale of delegating decision-making and power in the hands of the few on behalf of the many is as old as the first human civilization. As the case with everything human, any behavior or practice always begins with a "*need*," which can be explained in biological terms. Why do humans have needs? We have needs because the human body is designed to be inseparable from its natural environment and we cannot survive without the elements outside our skin. What we call needs are in fact external nourishment that our bodies lack to sustain an inadequately designed biological system. We grew out of this planet in the same way apples grow on apple trees and just how apples continuously need the tree for nourishment, we are destined to have never-ending needs to countless things in our world. Humanity is intended to be one with Earth, and this aim is most evident in how our bodies are structured. Our bodies are destined to be naturally dependent on outside elements and continuously demand nourishment from these elements for mere survival. We cannot hold our breath for too long or stop eating or drinking because we are dependent on these elements to persevere. We need food and water among many other things, and our survival will always be contingent on them. We need to build shelters to protect us from the elements and predators or otherwise we will perish. Our continuation as a species is reliant on a vast number of things, and for as long as this dependency lingers, we will remain vulnerable and we will continue to have needs.

There is a limited number of things that one person can accomplish on one's own. You might be a gifted hunter, but you might fail at building a proper shelter or protecting yourself from predators. You cannot live alone in a forest somewhere because the chances are high that one day you might get sick or injured and this shortcoming will prevent you from securing your food and water, which would eventually kill you. Moreover, we need others to be there for us on our worst days, and in return, support them on their worst days. The *need to trade* with others is a necessity in the human way of life because of humanity's natural vulnerability to the elements and dependency on outside nourishments. The urge to trade is hard-wired into our DNA, and it is what brought people together and inspired them to form communities and build cities.

Trade Created Society

Society would not exist if humanity did not need to trade. Everyone is good at something but in need of something else, and we need other people to provide us with the things we can't get on our own. You might be a skilled potter but a horrible farmer, and you need to trade your products for food with someone else to put food on your table. So, you'll naturally thrive when you are able to trade with others. And just how you would typically thrive when you trade goods and services with others, the community in which you live prospers proportionally. Civilizations of yesterday flourished because they were able to conduct agreements to get what they didn't have from other people in return for what they did have. In such way, if a civilization plants a lot of grain but not so much rice, and if its people like to eat both, it can supply some grain to the rice-growers in exchange for some rice to enjoy both foods.

Whether it started by cavemen exchanging animal coats and hunting tools with one another, or later when humanity learned to domesticate cattle and trade them as a commodity, trade is the founder of the human society. The need for trade drove people to live in proximity to one another forming ever-expanding communities so they can readily and efficiently transact with one another.

Laws Are Inevitable Byproducts Of Society

As explained earlier, a single person cannot live prosperously on his/her own without help from others. A person needs to be part of a social group to enhance his/her chances of survival or experience a better quality of life. But there's a problem with living in a society, and it is the *"need for laws."* Obviously, you wouldn't need laws if you're living alone on a deserted island because you're not disturbing anyone and there's no one around to offend or disagree with at all. You could just do whatever you feel like doing, and you wouldn't be self-conscious of anything you do because there's no one around to judge you or your behavior as right or wrong. Anything you do on that island will be your way of doing things, and you'll be entirely free to live in any way you desire because you won't be at odds with another human being.

Humanity introduced laws (the concept of right and wrong or good and bad) because we cannot live in a healthy community without them. You need to find a way to tell the other person in your community that it is not okay for him or her to act in a way or to do certain things. You will naturally judge the behavior of someone else in your community as good or offensive to you, which will create problems and you'll find yourself needing to find a way to tell that person to stop. It is not okay for members of a community to kill one another for example or just take whatever they want. And so, rules are inevitable if we wish to live in a society. The concept of right and wrong evolved so we can explain to other people what they can or can't do and so everyone can live peacefully together in a successful community. In other words, the social convention of morals, which are a person's standards of what is right or wrong, evolved so that the people of the community can all agree on the way of life in which they wish to partake.

However, not everyone could or would play by a rulebook faithfully, especially if there's a possibility to commit wrongdoing and get away with it undetected or unchallenged. Problems quickly emerged within such early forms of the human community because, even though there's a common understanding of what is right or wrong, who will be the authority that enforces the law when it is violated? In other words, who will be the prosecutor, the judge, and the law enforcer? Admittedly, they can't all be the same person or otherwise there'll be chaos. Everyone can accuse anyone of a crime and proceed to implement the punishment without answering to anyone, and no one will ever know the truth behind any claim. And so, a need emerged to safeguard the people of the community from each other. People needed an authority to inspect disputes and enforce the laws of society. And thus, the concept of tribes was born when they learned to write their rules and consolidated the authority of enforcing these laws in a handful of people.

As people continuously traded, they accumulated more assets that needed safekeeping. The concept of land ownership arose giving some people the exclusive right to do anything they wanted over a specific piece of land, demarcated geographically. And so, the authorities in the community needed to keep a record and safeguard everyone's assets and properties. As soon as people started drawing lines in the dirt declaring ownership of what goes behind the lines and defining borders on a map, multiple tribes began to emerge in many locations.

Each tribe's authority, of course, needed to establish a system which registers everyone who belongs to the tribe so that they can better protect the tribe and its members from each other and from everyone else who doesn't belong. It didn't take long for the concept of *"you are not one of us"* to perpetuate in each tribe, and they became enclosed social bubbles with a sense of unique tribal identity. And with that, the tribe's authority took ownership of the tribe in the same way parents own their children and hold power over them. In a family, parents are the ultimate authority, and they more or less own their children whereas the ruling class of a tribe entirely owns and masters its citizens.

And so, tribalism disrupted the ancient understanding that *"we are all one human family"* and divided humanity into distinctive groups tucked away behind borders and setting them in endless conflict with one another. People no longer share a common heritage as human beings, or at least they stopped recognizing it that way. Now, the real heritage is the one passed down by the tribe to its citizens from one generation to another. Anyone who does not belong to the tribe is an alien and is not to be trusted.

It began with small tribes scattered around the globe competing for local resources. Each tribe was a community of people linked by social, economic, religious, or blood ties, with a standard culture and dialect, and typically having one recognized leader. And most importantly, each tribe had a *ruling class* that made all the critical decisions, controlled all the money and power of the tribe, and ruled over another category of people called *the working class*.

The ruling class was in charge while the working class just followed orders and did what they were told. The ruling class was the shepherd while the working class was the sheep. And just how a shepherd steers his sheep in any direction he desires, and the sheep simply obey and follow the orders hoping that the shepherd will treat them nicely for as long they conform, the working class followed the same approach. Just how sheep think that the shepherd is protecting them from wolves and out of fear of the wolves they continue to obey, the working class also submitted to their ruling class out of fear of other tribes.

The ruling class of every tribe never failed to envision and immortalize the image of the big grey wolf to the sheep-like public, so it forever remains vivid in their clueless minds. Like parents telling horror stories to their children about monsters that will come and get them if they misbehave, the ruling class always reminded the working class of the dangers the lurked behind the fence and why they must always submit to their rulers. Fear, as a tactic in the hands of the ruling class, always works because it is a powerful instinctive emotion and human beings are helpless against it.

Each ruling class in every tribe taught its working class the tribal doctrines, ways of life, and of course most importantly the inherited sense of tribal identity. The workers learned to support their rulers and fight other clans whenever the workers were commanded to do so. Every tribe on every side of the fence had sheep-like public, which was terrified of the wolves and voluntarily submitted to its ruling class thinking they would protect them. Never knowing that there never was a big bad wolf on the other side of the fence but just more sheep-like public who were also terrified of that same imaginary wolf.

Tribes were destined, by design, to fight one another, and they learned to be always prepared for war.

Tribes Are Destined To Fight One Another

It is not a question of why tribes must fight, but it is a question of who the next tribe to fight is and when. The primary reason for this problem is the practice of segregating humanity into exclusive isolated groups, which naturally yields all sorts of differences between the people on each side. These differences will eventually grow and become the basis for further discrimination and perpetuate an additional sense of distinction between the public of different tribes. When tribes set up unnatural borders to separate human beings from their brothers and sisters in other regions, distinguishable traits start to surface on each side of the border including accents, skin or hair or eye colors, height, facial patterns, manners, practices, and attitudes. It then becomes relatively straightforward for the ruling class on each side of the border to bolster the *"us vs. them"* mindset due to how different cultures tend to be whenever humanity in zoned that way. Most importantly, tribalism is inherently a hostile system. Those who practice it or endorse its principles will sooner or later find themselves following an approach to the world based on hostility that will put them at odds with everything and everyone.

The ruling class of any tribe must always have an enemy because historically the sheep-like public would sooner or later question the need for the authority of the ruling class if there was no such threat as the big bad wolf. The public conforms better if they know that the evil wolf is out there somewhere behind the fence and they even perform extra favorably when they realize that the wolf is attacking them. Therefore, it was useful for the ruling class of every tribe to start a new war every now and then only to preserve their authority and to maintain a tractable public. Much of such wars were utterly useless and had no significant or strategic aim whatsoever. Nonetheless, battles or conflicts were highly beneficial for the business of government, and it helps keep the public under control and gives the ruling class a valid reason to continue to collect taxes. After all, someone got to be paid for all the hard work of protecting the tribe and keeping its people safe.

If there were none around to start a war with, a typical ruling class would invent an enemy nonetheless because it is imperative to have one. And if the neighboring tribes did not wish to fake a new conflict and play the war-game, sometimes a tribe turns on its own public and stage an internal conflict or civil war. Sometimes they would target a minority within the tribe and turn the public against them to start a conflict. When people of the same nation turn on each other, they eventually seek a moderator to put an end to the madness, and it is in such dark times that the ruling class can prove its usefulness to the public when it intervenes to solve a problem which they originally staged or secretly invoked. And so, the ruling class would come out of such scenarios as the savior or the protector while at the same time solidifying its presence or necessity to the human society.

In other times, the ruling class of a nation would develop a completely imaginary figure or group which they would blame for several orchestrated events to start a witch hunt that usually never ends. Of course, large masses of innocent people were brutally murdered in an orderly fashion in such conflicts and wars, but that never bothered the ruling class because they genuinely despised the public and unanimously regarded them as ignorant peasants that must occasionally be sacrificed to keep their numbers in check.

The ruling class genuinely and utterly loathed the public in principle and intellect with particularly remarkable hatred dedicated to the underprivileged. The ruling class would never lift a finger to help the poor, and they consistently blamed the needy for their misfortunes. Their open disdain for the wide variety of groups they ruled over should surprise no one because such contempt was combined with a sense of political entitlement and the coercive power of government. They saw it as the natural order of things - the powerful govern and are justified in everything they do while the weak linger in their misery. It is the survival of the fittest kind of ideology. A lion doesn't concern itself with the opinion of sheep and, likewise, the ruling class perpetually regarded themselves as superior and entitled by the natural order of things to command and sacrifice the sheep-like public whenever needed.

Aside from the sheer sadistic joy of commanding legions of slaves working for them and fulfilling their every desire, the ruling class would never lift a finger to help the impoverished because it would be against their own interests as rulers. A necessity that all tribal governments needed to persevere is, of course, poverty or poor living conditions for a significant portion of the local population. Rulers must always maintain a substantial segment of their society under miserable living conditions and must keep them wretched, exhausted, miserable, and in need. It is not of any ruler's benefit at all if everyone in the nation is happy or doing well. Otherwise, who would work all those daunting or dehumanizing chores that the ruling class wants to be done, and who would risk their lives or the lives of their own children to fight someone else's bloody wars or the shallow ideological conflicts?

If you have a decent roof over your head, a beautiful person in your bed, delicious food on your table, and if all your basic needs are satisfied, why would you bother yourself with following someone's orders? Why give yourselves to uniformed brutes, who regiment your lives, diet you, treat you like cattle and use you as cannon fodder? Why would you submit to unnatural men who despise you, who wish only to enslave you, to regiment your life and tell you what to do or what to think or what to feel? Why go to war to risk death or make a murderer out of yourself by killing a complete stranger you never even seen before? Why worry at all by putting yourself in harm's way to fight someone with whom you never had any quarrel? Surely, you wouldn't go anywhere and would alternatively choose to stay put enjoying life while you still can and surrounding yourself with all the wonderful people you love. If, however, you are poor, you might willingly decide to enroll in the army just to earn a living. Either poverty will make you stand in line like a sheep with a gun on your shoulder or when your rulers remind you again of the big bad wolf lurking outside the fence with evil intentions. And therefore, poor livelihood and misery persisted in all tribal nations even in the wealthiest ones thanks to the ruling class and their governments. Such predicaments continued not because they couldn't be easily solved within a year or more, but because they were necessary for the business of government.

No One Rules Alone

A single person never runs the entire tribe, and it always involves the exclusive contribution of a small group of people with different roles in different positions of authority - a ruling class of people. Tribalism, as a system, was never practiced entirely by the ruling class alone because sooner or later everyone in the tribe - the public included - learned to practice its doctrines. In this book, we are referring to those who lived in the era that predates *distribia* as tribalists. A tribalist is one who loves his/her tribe or nation and is indoctrinated by tribalism. Tribalists could be part of the ruling class or just ordinary citizens who endorse and exercise the principles of tribalism either subconsciously due to successful brainwashing or willingly in the forlorn hope that they might join the ruling class one day.

"No one rules alone" is a concept that the ruling class understood very well, and they constantly needed each other to maintain control over the public. They did compete among themselves to consolidate as much authority and power in the tribe as possible, and usually, there were no restrictions on who and how many people could join the ruling class for as long as they played by the rules. As a standard in every tribe, the most dominant and influential tribalists in the ruling class (called key tribalists) avoided driving public attention at all costs while they sat back in the background pulling the strings of the tribalists beneath them and influencing decisions.

The people of each tribe were beholden to their tribe with loyalty and devotion. From these two values proceeded racism, fear, hatred, and intolerance to other tribes. These humanistic emotions are the fuel the ruling class used to legitimize their authority over their tribe, perpetuate the institution of tribalism, and inevitably plunge their people into bloody tribal warfare. On each side of every national border, a ruling class of people engraved their system and its symbols in each member of their tribe to ensure complete obedience. It came in the form of anthems, flags, rituals, and most importantly through schooling and the teachings of the tribe's values to children. It was vital for each person to be fully institutionalized into his/her tribe and brainwashed by its doctrines because he/she must be willing to kill himself/herself fighting other tribes for the ruling class—for the king or queen or flag or country or glory or whatever hollow concept that the public foolishly thought they were fighting for—when the inevitable day comes. In the same way sheep owe their lives to the shepherd, citizens owed their lives to the state (to the ruling class specifically) and they learned that they must forfeit their existence whenever needed. They must serve without any guarantee of any personal reward. They must forever follow the government, bow to the authority and do what they are told. Obedience without question. Loyalty until death comes.

A national flag never represented the sheep-like public behind the fence, but it signified the ruling class and their governments. Same goes for the notions of *"tribe"* or *"state"* or *"country"* or *"nation."* Nonetheless, the public foolishly thought or believed that such concepts represent the populace and that soldiers were actually fighting for the people within their own nation while, in fact, they were only serving the ruling class the whole way along.

The ruling classes of the world, of course, knew that they must always invent new tactics and tools to cement their ownership of the tribe and keep it under control. They hacked the human language and used it as a weapon against those who speak it. *"Words are mightier than swords"* is a concept that tribalists understood thoroughly and that's why they invented the tactic of *languagewashing*. They needed to control what the people think, feel, and believe to get a tractable public and for that reason, they invented tribal belief systems, which we now know today as religions. They camouflaged their laws with spiritual beliefs to efficiently consolidate the power of the people in the hands of a few rulers to wage wars and establish empires. They desired becoming the *All-Seeing Eye* that they envisioned through their tribal religions to regularly know what the populace is doing and thinking and, therefore, they developed the *Big Brother* tactic. They resorted to secrecy in government to hide their mistakes, atrocities and hostile intentions to the world. Through secrecy, they produced a blind public that never knows how any path started or where it is heading. They hacked the economy's medium of exchange and created a type of money that corrupted the human mind and was the root of most of the tribal conflicts and bloodshed in history.

Religion Is Fiction

There is no better way for authoritarian regimes to legitimize their ownership of the tribe than to convince everyone that a godly power authorized it. To control the tribe, every dictatorship naturally invents a religion, which is nothing more than their laws masquerading as commandments from a higher power.

Each religion customarily comes with a built-in philosophy that reinforces blind obedience to the authorities and legitimizes the powers of a ruling class leading inescapably to a totalitarian form of control. Through religious indoctrination, the ruling classes of the world practiced social control and steered their tribe to any course they desired to take it. Tribal authority presides over a nation unchallenged for as long as the people maintain that their religion is divinely revealed and inspired or that it is the genuine word or will of the divine. The public continues to submit to voluntary servitude for as long as they believe that their religion is God-made and not man-made.

The ruling classes of the world used religion as a tactic or a tool to consolidate power from the public, manufacture consent, and control their citizens. They also used it as a weapon to wage wars against other tribes and build their empires. But how did they accomplish this and how did they invent such a mind-controlling weapon? To answer this, we must probe back in time.

The word *religion* as used today does not have an obvious pre-colonial translation into non-European languages. Although the etymology of the word *religion* is doubtful and controversial, some philologists agree that it comes from the root Latin word *religare,* which means *"to bind,"* and another Latin word *religio,* which means *"bond"* or *"obligation."* One analysis of the meaning behind these two root words is that the system we identify today as religion, binds people up or restrains them with a false obligation to put them under control. In any way, the root of the word is not important because what matters most is what the word actually stands for or the concept it represents.

What we have objectified under the name *religion* is a people-hypnotizing man-made social invention which historically played the most vital role in transcending tribes into empires and farmers into conquerors. Religion, in fact, is an empire-forging social system consisting of the following 7 fundamental elements:

> ➤ A set of beliefs, or more accurately, several ideas or opinions or theories which one judges as correct. A belief is simply an idea that you believe. So, instead of saying *"I have an idea that I believe in,"* one says, *"I have a belief."*
> ➤ Faith, which is a sincere and blind belief. It involves profoundly believing an idea without holding any doubts

about it and refusing even to question it. So, instead of saying *"I have an idea that I blindly trust as true,"* one says, *"I have faith."*

➢ A ritual, which is a ceremony consisting of a series of actions performed according to a prescribed order. It is a standard sequence of activities involving gestures, words, and objects. The ritual can be performed privately or publicly with a large mass of people.

➢ Worship, which is to display rooted respect in a way to surrender entirely without holding anything back. Worship, according to this system, is an act directed towards a deity.

➢ Novels that revolve around a creator or creation. As a standard, the novels are always older than the religion itself by several generations and conveniently occurred at a period in history when everyone who witnessed the events in these novels is already dead so that such alleged incidents can never be verified.

➢ Laws or rulebooks, which is the most critical element in this system, and it is really the whole point of religion and the entire purpose behind it for the authority that invented it. This element of religion is what weaponizes a belief and turns it against humanity.

➢ The exploitation of the natural flaws or weaknesses in the human mind such as how we think and our humanistic emotions. This crucial aspect of the system is as essential as rhythm to music, and it is employed in all 6 elements of the system we listed above. Without it, the system will never be able to hypnotize the human mind efficiently, and the entire system will fail. Some of the emotions that the system exploits are fear, egocentricity, amazement, guilt, grief, admiration, loathing and rage. Such emotions are institutionalized in the system's beliefs, the arrangement of the rituals, the content of the fables that the system revolves around, and the design of the system's buildings of worship.

Starting with the religious novels, why do they all revolve around characters who lived and died a long time ago or around events that began and already ended in the past? It is done that way because an author can invent dead men in the past but never living ones in the present. And since the past already passed and no one will ever have

21

the means to go back in time to validate the existence of such dead men, people in the present will accept such mythical characters who, in fact, never existed. And once the act of forgery is forgotten, such fictitious characters would exist just as authentically and with the same historical evidence as other historical figures of the same era. In other words, such men exist only in words written about them a long time ago. For example, there's no historical evidence whatsoever that the so-called Jesus of Nazareth existed outside the 4 Christian novels (the 4 gospels of Matthew, Mark, Luke, and John), which were written a long time ago by unknown authors about such a man. Everything and anything that Christians know about Jesus came exclusively from these 4 novels. Such novels come in an equal level of authenticity as the stories about Thor (the hammer-wielding God of thunder in Norse mythology) or Zeus (the sky and thunder God in ancient Greek religion) or Ra (the sun God in ancient Egyptian religion) or Indra (the God of thunder and weather in Hindu religion) or Perun (also the God of thunder and lightning in Slavic mythology) and so on. Therefore, historians say that if someone thinks that Jesus existed, then such person should also accept that Thor existed because the historical evidence that both men are real is identical. And such proof exists exclusively in the novels written about them and nowhere else. Put differently, assuming that such characters indeed existed merely implies a personal opinion and a decision to accept the novels as true.

Nonetheless, *all fiction is rooted in truth*, and some novels might revolve around real people in the past, who indeed lived in that period, but greatly exaggerate and amplify their life stories or the course of events like *making a mountain out of a molehill*. The fictitious character of Santa Claus, for example, was inspired by the life story of a man known as Saint Nicholas (also called Nikolaos of Myra or Nicholas of Bari), who was the Bishop of the ancient Greek town Myra (known as Demre today in the present-day city of Antalya). He was a Christian saint who lived in the third and fourth centuries. This wealthy man was famous for his habit of secretly gift-giving poor children and putting coins in the shoes of those who left them out for him. He wasn't an obese bearded man on a magical sled with flying reindeers and living in the North Pole - this, of course, is nothing more than a fabricated work of fiction. Nicholas's ritual, which was addressed exclusively to

22

underprivileged children, changed centuries later to be a purely commercial ritual of wealthy families of greedy children and became the bedrock for perpetual lies and fallacies revolving around the idea of a fictitious character with an *All-Seeing Eye* lodging somewhere out of site in the North Pole. Similarly, Jesus's cross, which originally was the symbol of the suffering of impoverished families, became the symbol of the soldiers' armors of all-powerful empires and the oppressive regime of *Big Brother*.

No man has seen God. Think about this for a moment because it deserves to be thoroughly understood. No human being, including those who received their religion at its conception when the authorities first promulgated it, ever saw or met or spoke to God. Absolutely no one living on Earth today has ever seen God either. Christians, Muslims, Jews, Hindus, and all other religionists in the tribal era thought their religions are real just because their parents convinced them so at an early age using the religious novels. And their fathers received the doctrine on their forefathers say so, who also inherited it from their ancestors, and the brainwashing goes back in history until the time the novels were first written.

Storytelling is compelling and captivating. Little children specifically are most vulnerable against the practice because their minds absorb all the stories they hear without scrutiny and with little capacity to differentiate between truth and fiction. When they hear a story about an old man who talked to God on the top of a mountain or inside a cave, they believe it actually happened. *A lie told often enough becomes the truth.* And if enough people in society received the same fallacious indoctrination, fiction becomes truth and ancient novels become historical scriptures.

Beliefs cannot be reasoned with because they are mere ideas that lack tangible proof. Otherwise, if measurable or logical evidence transpires, beliefs become facts. The system that we call *religion* encompasses several beliefs bundled up together that target particular flaws or weaknesses in the human mind. One of these flaws, for example, is egocentricity. Humans are intrinsically self-centered but in different degrees according to personal circumstances. So, by proposing a belief that the universe revolves around humans and that we are the center of the world, such claim will always sound plausible by a lot of people. Such a theory is readily marketable because people will naturally love it and subconsciously choose to endorse it. Additionally, proposing an idea that one kingly God or a small group of divinities rule over the entire cosmos will also sound very plausible to people because it is in their nature to be self-centered and, therefore, accept the idea of a world centered around one or more supreme beings.

Another flaw is fear, which also exists in people in different percentages. One person's shortcoming is another person's strength, and likewise, some people chose to induce fear among other people to produce a desirable performance or steer them onto a particular path. Fear, therefore, is a very effective tactic for controlling other people. Parents practice it on their children, and likewise, rulers exercise it upon the parents. All human emotions can be hypnotizing, and since fear is the strongest and oldest emotion, it is the most powerful, and it yields beliefs that are likewise extremely potent. It is instinctive, and we are helpless against it. The oldest fear of them all is the fear of dying and the unknown. When people produce beliefs that target the unknowns such as the afterlife, such ideas can easily hypnotize the human mind because they aim at a very primal emotion, which is fear.

The idea that when you die, your consciousness vanishes forever, and you will never wake up again is undoubtedly haunting. The concept of humankind as nothing more than a tiny population of a malicious germ that infests an unimportant rock ball, which orbits an insignificant star on the outer edges of one of the smallest dying galaxies, before vanishing forever in oblivion, is a dreadful story that no one wishes to hear. People love to believe that when they die, they will live again; that some thinking, feeling, remembering part of themselves will continue. Therefore, and due to their vulnerability, they chose to endorse such afterlife beliefs and yearn to live again in a happier place somewhere in another life. The idea that death is nothing more than an endless dreamless sleep is not as marketable as the concept of an eternal afterlife filled with rivers of wine, an infinite supply of delicious food, and where all your desires and wishes are fulfilled forever. Therefore, people are tempted to hold onto beliefs that propose an afterlife. They hold onto such notions out of fear that they'll cease to exist one inevitable day and to evade the depressing awareness that there's nothing more to existence than the short and bitter years here on Earth.

Inherently selfish religions are the worst of the bunch. Add fear to the mix, and the resulting religion inescapably becomes a system that revolves around worship out of self-interest for the salvation from nonexistence after death. The more critical question for religious people is not whether there is a God or not but whether there's an afterlife, which is the greatest concern for the death-fearing human being. Christianity and Islam, for example, are afterlife religions. The promise of the afterlife is the fundamental component of these religions, and if it is taken out, the entire system comes collapsing down to pieces. Suppose that Abraham's kingly God is real and that he revealed himself to humanity to make a small correction to the religion by denying the existence of the afterlife. Not only the followers of Christianity and Islam would abandon their religions the moment their God debunks the existence of the afterlife, but these devout followers might go one step further to also renounce their God. Abrahamic religions are incredibly selfish religions that revolve around worship for Earthly perks or afterlife rewards. Deep down the followers of these religions know perfectly well that this is absolutely true, but they rarely openly admit it.

Amazement is another emotion commonly exploited by all religions. They use it in writing their beliefs, designing their rituals, formulating the fables that religions revolve around, and in the way they construct their buildings of worship or symbolic monuments. The public, therefore, will be in awe when they observe or walk into the system's temples, churches or mosques. Regardless of the religion or culture, all religious buildings have one thing in common, and it is the approach to design for the sole purpose of leaving people in awe when they visit such buildings. They deliberately raise the ceilings as high as they can to reflect sensual elevation in the minds of people. This architectural trick is meant to evoke emotion and contemplation, which is common for many of the world's architectural wonders and is especially prevalent in those serving a religious purpose. To induce a feeling of closeness to the divinities, architects had to create structures where everything suggests this feeling of elevation. Creating a feeling of elevation always begins with one key action and it is looking up. Gothic cathedrals, mosques, ancient monuments, and historic temples all left people looking up to the heavens - be it through high ceilings, a raised steeple, or a mounted statue - to aid the inspiration felt when entering the building. The physical act of looking upwards assists the brain in processing the meaning behind the action and reflects such ideas of heaven up above and hell down below. Due to this approach to architecture, most people developed an instinctual coloration between up as representing heaven and down as representing hell.

Places of worship also have giant doors on purpose to make people feel puny the moment they step into such deceitful structures. This particular trick was also used in courthouses to remind the average person that he is much inferior to the tribal system that ruled over the public. Ultimately, the experience inside the religious structures is about much more than just vision. It is instead multi-sensory through the tactile sensations from materials, visual distractions from different objects, distinct aromas such as Sandalwood Incense, and as well as audible distractions from musical instruments or the chants by worshipers that aid the entire experience. Overall, the presence in such structures generate multiple brain responses to formulate an experience, which the worshipers misinterpret as spiritual, but in fact, it is all deeply integrated and originated inside the human brain.

Amazement is also exploited in rituals. The populace becomes hypnotized when they experience the system's rituals such as when large masses of people flock around a temple or engage in mass worship. They misinterpret the feeling of awe and presume that their religion is truly divine and that they're on the right path by following and maintaining their faith. Unfortunately, what they are experiencing is nothing more than a hypnotizing human emotion, which a man-made system exploits for the sole purpose of hypnotizing people into joining and remaining within the system.

Most religions involve beliefs and fables that induce grief within people's minds to make them compassionate with the system and endorse it out of sympathy and empathy. Some stories, for example, revolve around the suffering of the divinity's messengers to humanity while others speak of the sacrifices of God for the well-being of humankind. The Christian system, for example, institutionalized guilt as a virtue. It managed to convince its followers that they are automatically guilty just for being alive because of a mistake that a couple of people (Adam and Eve) did thousands of years ago. Christianity taught people that they must feel guilty because of the actions of this couple although logically you can't be blamed or held accountable for the actions of strangers that you have never seen or met in your own lifetime. The Christian system also employed guilt by judging someone's behavior as wrongdoing to the love of God leaving that person feeling awful and guilty for committing such an act that wounded Jesus, grieved the Holy Spirit, and so on. And so, out of that feeling of guilt, the followers of such system were emotionally attached to it and chose to hold onto it due to the greater sense of guilt they would feel if they let go.

And in the same way how Christianity institutionalized guilt as a virtue, Islam standardized fear to all its followers as an obligation. You must fear God if you are a true Muslim in the same way you must feel guilty of your inherent faults as a human being if you are a Christian. You must learn to live with the guilt that you are a sinner and accept Jesus as your savior if you are a real Christian whereas Muslims must acknowledge that God is their supreme ruler and that they are no more than his fearful slaves destined to obey and serve him until their last breath. One system urges its followers to feel awful about themselves of no fault of their own while the other terrifies them with fear.

Admiration is another emotion that beliefs and fables tap into by romanticizing the aspects of God and describing them in a way that always appeals to the public. Some systems, for instance, define their divinities as perfect in every way and in such fashion that an average human being can never aspire to be. Unimaginable beauty, absolute power or strength, infinite knowledge, never-ending existence, omnipresence, omniscience, and so on. And you can never come up to their level. Never. And therefore, you will always be aware of your personal shortcomings, and the more flaws you think you got, the more you are aware of the vast abyss between the divinities and yourself. The feelings that propagate from such knowledge such as admiration would eventually get you hooked onto the system, and it will be hard to leave.

Some fables also involve an element of loathing and rage because these emotions are beneficial when the system requires its followers to act violently or to produce some deadly outcomes. Loathing and rage are used, for example, against the characters in the fables for wrongdoings against God or his messengers or people. The system's fables also involve rage practiced by God himself as a reaction to wrongdoings by humanity in monotheistic religions. In the case of polytheistic systems, rage is exhibited amongst the Gods in the struggle for power in the spiritual realm. When any system recognizes rage as a trait of God, it institutionalizes that feeling in the minds and hearts of all followers. It would then be completely understandable when an ordinary person expresses rage in the same way when a king expresses anger and unleash hellish wars or ferociously murder whatever people he labeled as enemies of the state. After all, God himself gets angry, and it is, therefore, reasonable for kings to show rage against other kingdoms or their own people.

Moving away now from the human emotions that the religious systems deceitfully exploit, we will talk about another element of such systems which is *"faith."* The word *faith* represents the social convention of blindly trusting and endorsing a theory without ever having the courage to challenge and investigate it. Faith is the glue that keeps religion from falling apart. It is impossible for one to be a genuine analytical or critical thinker and at the same time hold onto faiths. If you are a true critical thinker, you should question everything and be analytical of anything while taking nothing for granted. Faith, on the other hand, insists that one must never criticize or question the belief, but to accept it as is and endorse it.

Analytics and criticism are the pillars of learning. Such skills are fundamental assets for the process of thinking, and they efficiently transfer and apply across many spectrums of our lives. Learning to negotiate and improve these skills can aid us in becoming better thinkers, communicators, and innovators. They enable us to problem solve more efficiently and carry out solutions with better efficiency. Critical thinkers, however, are dangerous for a ruling class because they can easily find the flaws in their tribal systems and tribal religions, which would jeopardize the reign of the ruling class over the public. By imposing faith as a prerequisite for all practitioners and followers, the system restricts the people from questioning the logic or the truth behind the religious fables and scriptures. Faith immediately sets up a wall in the face of thinking and reasoning. It motivates and encourages people to ignore where *"ignore-ance"* is the first step one takes to ignorance. Therefore, when you accept faith, you start ignoring analytics and criticism, and inevitably you become a full-on ignorant. There's no solution for this problem because ignorance and faith walk hand-in-hand.

The path to enlightenment is paved through criticism and analytics, which are the keystones of the process of thinking. Faith hinders these two mental capacities and, therefore, stifles enlightenment. Through faith, therefore, all religions disrupt the intellectual progress of humanity and deliver unenlightened ignorant human beings who are just smart enough to do what they're told and remain obedient to the authority of their religion and country.

The paradox and illogicality of any religion of any kind are remarkably easily identifiable by someone with modest analytical or critical skills. For example, since Abrahamic religions (Judaism, Christianity and Islam) preach that God created Satan (aka Lucifer or the devil), then there must be evil in God because how else can pure evil come from something purely good. Good and evil are opposites like black and white, and in the same that you cannot chop off a black piece out of a white paper, an evil creation cannot come from a good creator. Therefore, if one is to believe that God created an evil being, then one should also accept that there's evil in God as well as in anything and everything that this God ever created. But then we arrive at another paradox, which is the idea of devils and angels because once you realize that good and evil inescapably go together like the two faces of the same coin, you'll understand that there are no angels or devils because they are all good and evil inseparably.

Muslims describe God's nature as being *"the all-merciful"* but at the same time acknowledge that he built an unimaginably nightmarish place full of fire and anguish where he brutally tortures and routinely burns people alive again and again until the end of time. The paradox here, of course, is that an all-merciful or even a most merciful being would never build such a torturous place because he would naturally forgive all. There are millions of average human beings who lived their entire lives without physically torturing another person for any misdeed directed against them or for not following their rules, which means that any one of these millions of people is more merciful than Islam's version of God.

Abrahamic religions define God as all-knowing being with free will although such qualities sharply contradict one another. The omniscience power of God means that he knows everything including anything that ever happened in the past and will ever occur in the future. Omniscience also includes the knowledge of the destiny of everything including God's own future. God knows what he will do tomorrow, next year, next decade, next century, next millennia, and so on including any second thoughts or future adjustments to such actions. Omniscience means that God is technically incapable of surprising himself because he already knows everything that will ever happen and everything that he'll ever think or do including any future adjustments to any already-foreseen future thoughts or actions. In other words, having omniscience simply means that one's future is already written, and the ink is dry. If you are omniscient, you neither have free will nor omnipotence because you are utterly incapable of taking random decisions or going off script or even surprising yourself. Ultimately, having omniscience means you are more or less a puppet that is just playing a role in a performance that you know precisely how it will turn out including memorizing all the lines of the play.

Now let's move away from explaining the elements of religion and talk instead about the history of religion and how it transpired. Religion played a principal role in the development of humankind's empires by consolidating the power of the public into a handful of people and establishing a system in which the populace conforms to voluntary servitude. The ancient Egyptian Empire, Athenian Empire, Macedonian Empire, Roman Empire, and Middle Eastern and Western Empires all used religion as a vehicle to lead the masses desirably to their plans. What the followers of any religion never truly fathom is that what they are blindly following is purely an Earthly social system designed for establishing empires but continuously masquerading itself to its public as a spiritual out-of-this-world device. Religions are *"how-to manuals"* for tyrants on how to rule by divine right. It is, of course, illegitimate and intrinsically tend to incubate fascist forms of rule. It worked well for the ruling class of every civilization known to humanity, and they got away with it for the most part.

In ancient Egypt, the importance of some Gods rose and fell depending on the opinions of the next pharaoh in charge. After all, everybody can have an idea about God, and if it so happens that you are a king with subjects beneath you, it is easy for you to dominate other opinions. And so, every pharaoh promulgated his own version of what a God ought to be or favored one deity over another. At various times, some Gods became preeminent over the others, including the sun God Ra, the creator God Amun, and the mother goddess Isis. At one brief period in the empire's history, a pharaoh called Akhenaten, who was known for his suppressive totalitarian regime and policing of the populace, invented an entirely new God for Egypt and called him Aten. He declared Aten as *"the one and only"* God of Egypt, abandoning the traditional Egyptian polytheism and converting it to a form of monotheism.

Considering Akhenaten's dominant one-man-show attitude in ruling his empire, it was understandable for Akhenaten to believe that likewise, the spiritual realm is governed by a single supreme leader just like himself. Akhenaten tried to shift his culture from one religious indoctrination to another forcefully, but Egypt's populace and the ruling class did not widely accept the shift and eventually defaulted back to the original system. After his 17-year reign ended with his death, his monuments were dismantled and hidden, his statues were destroyed, and his name excluded from the kings' lists. Later his successors discredited Akhenaten's legacy along with his immediate successors referring to Akhenaten himself as a criminal in archival records.

The religious practices in ancient Egyptian Empire centered on the pharaoh, the ruler of Egypt, who was believed to possess a divine power by virtue of his position. He acted as the intermediary between the people and the Gods and was obligated to sustain the Gods through rituals and offerings so that they could maintain *"order in the universe."* In other words, the pharaohs were the self-proclaimed ambassadors to the Gods, and they were the only authority to interpret the holy commandments to the public. They steered the populace in any path they desired while declaring it as the will of God. Therefore, the pharaohs dedicated enormous resources to rituals and the construction of their temples and pyramids, which were built to endure an eternity.

These pyramids were built predominantly by Egyptian peasants who were required by Egyptian law to work for the government a certain number of months per year. The builders were skilled, well-fed Egyptian workers who lived in a nearby temporary city. In the same way that governments required all their able citizens to serve in the army in the event of war, the authorities in ancient Egypt practiced the same concept when building their pyramids. Communities across the empire contributed workers, as well as food and other essentials, for what became in some ways a national project to display the wealth and control of the ancient pharaohs. Egyptian emperors (or pharaohs) were buried in their massive pyramid tombs along with most of their wealth and the things they enjoyed in life, so they can continue living happily ever after in the afterlife, which they observed as a continuation of their existing Earthly experience.

The pyramids, which aside from remaining impressive to behold till our current day, represented a remarkable degree of political and social control over the population. Because it is not easy to convince people to devote their entire lives building an enormous coffin for someone they have never met, the pharaohs had to convince the populace that there's a higher purpose for committing themselves to such voluntary servitude through religion. The religious doctrine of the pharaohs convinced the populace that if they did their jobs excellently, then the pantheon of Gods would maintain cosmic order. And since the pharaohs were expected to become Gods in the afterlife, it made sense to please the pharaohs in their Earthly lifetimes by building the pyramids they so desire.

To a Roman, the pyramids were older than the Romans are to us today. Early forms of the Roman beliefs were animistic, believing that spirits inhabited everything around them, people included. There were no rulers or kingdoms in the spiritual world, which was intrinsically democratic. This unity with nature, however, soon changed when the democratic beliefs followed a tyrannical structure embodying the spirits under kingly Gods that rule over the spiritual world and beyond. This change came about as Roman rulers desired to conquer new territory and establish an empire.

Initially, a Capitoline Triad (which is a group of 3 deities who were worshipped in ancient Roman religion in an elegant temple on Rome's Capitoline Hill) were added to the spiritual world. The first kingly God was Mars, which was the God of war and supposed father of Romulus (the legendary founder and first king of Rome) and his twin brother Remus. The second God was Quirinus (the deified God who watched over the people of Rome), and lastly, the third God was Jupiter (the supreme God). They, along with the spirits, were worshipped at the temple on Capitoline Hill, which is one of the 7 hills in Rome.

Later, due to the Etruscans (a powerful and wealthy civilization of ancient Italy in the area corresponding roughly to Tuscany, western Umbria, and northern Lazio), the triad would change to include the family members of the Gods such as Juno (one of the daughters of Saturn, the wife of Jupiter, and the mother of Mars, Vulcan, Bellona and Juventas). Juno was the Roman equivalent of Hera, queen of the Gods in Greek mythology. Like Hera, her sacred animal was the peacock. The new list also included Minerva (born from the head of her father, Jupiter), which was the Roman goddess of wisdom and strategic warfare, and the sponsor of arts, trade, and strategy. She was the virgin goddess of music, poetry, medicine, wisdom, commerce, weaving, and the crafts. She is often depicted with her sacred creature, an owl usually named as the *"owl of Minerva,"* which symbolized her association with wisdom and knowledge as well as, less frequently, the snake and the olive tree. Due to the presence of Greek colonies on the Lower Peninsula, the Romans fostered many of the Greek Gods as their own. Religion and myth became one. Under this Greek influence, the Roman Gods became more anthropomorphic with the human characteristics of jealousy, love, hate, and so on.

Under this arrangement, the spiritual world followed a totalitarian family-like structure of kingdoms and kings, who are continuously competing for power and dominance just like the Earthly kings do in the physical world. Through this new Roman religion, the farmers that once inhabited the hills of Italy became conquerors. Roman rulers used their tribal religion to establish an empire that stretched from the Atlantic to the Dead Sea and subjugated over 400 other tribes. At the time in the Roman Empire, there was no distinction between Roman religion and Roman law. Roman religion was the Roman law, and likewise, Roman law was the Roman religion. The word *religion* wasn't even invented yet or any other counterpart of such word in Greek or Latin for that matter because there was no separation between state and faith. Individual expression of belief was ignored and surmounted by strict adherence to a rigid set of rituals.

Each Roman city favored one kingly God among the bunch and prayed for that God for mercy, protection and good fortune. They built temples honoring the Gods throughout the empire and dedicated each temple to a particular God acclaiming it as the *"the house of God."* Christians later adopted the house of God concept, and they built their churches copying almost every idea behind Roman temples such as the size and design of the buildings along with the ceremonies and attire of the temple's administrators. The Jewish and Christian systems, while posing separate threats to the empire, had one thing in common - they both refused to allow their followers to participate in the worship of the Roman Gods or make sacrifices at their temples. Such refusal to participate in warships and sacrifices was technically considered illegal from the perspective of Roman authorities. The two Abrahamic systems are both monotheistic (having one kingly God) and run counter to the traditional Roman belief, which is polytheistic (having many kingly Gods). Although the Jewish tribes had firmly established themselves in the Roman Empire, they were often the target of the emperors, often blamed for any ills that befell the empire. Nero had them expelled from Rome, and Titus, the son of Emperor Vespasian, continued his father's war against the Jews, eventually destroying the city of Jerusalem and killing thousands of its citizens. The Roman attitude against the Jews, although notably violent, was conducted for understandable reasons.

The Romans knew perfectly well the religion's role in building empires because it helped them transcend from a tribe of farmers in the hills of Italy to conquering rulers over the Mediterranean and beyond. At its height, the Roman Empire encompassed an incredible 5 million-plus square kilometers of territorial holdings around the Mediterranean Sea in Europe, Africa, and Asia. The city of Rome was the largest city in the world, and the Empire's populace grew to an estimated 50 to 90 million inhabitants (roughly 20% of the world's population at the time). The Romans accomplished all this primarily by consolidating the power of the people through religious indoctrination. The people are the real source of power, and the Roman Empire solidified its dominance over the world by training the populace to be obedient to Roman laws through Roman religion.

Like any mighty empire, the real threat always lurks within its borders from the people it ruled. To have an emerging religion within the Roman Empire preaching a different rulebook than the official law of the land is undoubtedly a virus that must be taken care of immediately before it spreads further. The Romans understood this excellently, and they thrived to protect the longevity of their empire by crushing any emerging religion that could be a potential threat. Romans, therefore, subjugated the Jewish tribes when they realized their influence was growing and causing a significant impact on the Roman civilization. It was nothing more than ideological tribal warfare between one established empire and a wannabe empire of immigrant Jewish tribes. The people of each tribe are the real victims under such system because they are continually being drawn into tribal warfare through a hypnotizing and dangerous social scheme engineered for empire-building but masked as spiritual or divinely inspired.

The Jewish tribes did not originate in Europe, but they migrated there from the Middle East. Seeking better welfare, these immigrants arrived in Rome where they enjoyed privileges and thrived economically, becoming a significant part of the empire's society. They carried on their lives and the practice of their religion without interference and enjoyed good relations with their new neighbors. Romans were puzzled as to why Jews refused to eat pork (which the Romans loved) and why they circumcised infant boys. It was strange to them that there was no image of God in the Jewish Temple and thought the Sabbath rest was a sign of lassitude. Yet, their attitude toward the Jews was not hostile because the Romans were already exposed to a wide variety of cultures across their empire. Roman officials and soldiers were already familiar with many different beliefs and learned to tolerate alien ways of life as they expanded around the Mediterranean basin and incorporated new regions and communities. There were, however, differences of other sorts.

The Jewish tribes relentlessly strived to covertly absorb power across the Roman Empire by occupying strategic roles in the Roman community and amassing excessive wealth and influence. They resorted to several methods to achieve their goals and were known to orchestrate several events across the Empire that had the potential of strengthening their foothold while weakening the Romans. Therefore, when the Romans blamed most ills that befell their empire on the Jews, it wasn't without valid reasons and notably because of the Jew's long-standing goal of building an empire of their own between the River of Egypt and the Euphrates river. An area that is so large that it engulfs almost the entire Middle East. Under these circumstances and among other reasons, the Romans destroyed the Jewish Temple, would not allow Jews to live in Jerusalem, made sure their temple would not be rebuilt, and eventually founded a new Roman city with direct Roman rule over the territory where the Jews had plans to build their Empire to make sure it never happens. For the Jews, the consequences were dire because they could never again hope to live peacefully in the Roman Empire with the same freedom as other minorities to practice their ancestral customs and worship their God as they used to before the destruction of their temple. Most importantly, their plans and fantasies of a Jewish Empire in the Middle East were crushed.

Although the Christian system was initially seen as a sect of the Jewish system, Christians presented their system as an entirely different and new religion to the Roman authority. Nonetheless, Emperor Nero grew more suspicious as this small faction began to grow, especially after the Great Fire of Rome, for which he blamed them of course. They returned the favor, calling him the anti-Christ. As time passed, the Christian system continued to spread across the empire, appealing to women and slaves as well as intellectuals and the illiterate. Persecutions increased where Christian churches were burned, and all of this continued under the reign of Diocletian (emperor in the east), ending in the Great Persecution.

Unlike the Jewish system, which historically was an exclusive member-only close-knit system, the Christian system is more inclusive and constantly thrives to incorporate as many people as possible in the system through religious indoctrination. Christians would send out missionaries across vast territories to incorporate people in faraway communities into their system. The Christian system was on a conquest to Christianize the planet, and it always adopted an open-door policy for anyone who wishes to join and become part of the tribe. As larger crowds swarmed into the tribe through the Christian faith, the Christian tribes were able to consolidate ever-expanding power and grow into an emerging empire. The Christian system, therefore, was more influential and far-reaching and was better able to thrive under the Roman rule until eventually conquering it. Whereas the downfall of the Jewish tribes was due to their enclosed social system which was historically hard for other people to join, and only the very sincere could make it through the entire process. And while the Jewish tribes relied primarily on covert operations and secrecy to infiltrate the ruling class of the Roman Empire, the Christian tribes endorsed amassing crowds and the brute *"in your face"* approach by headcount power.

Finally, under Diocletian's successor Emperor Constantine, the Christian system would eventually infiltrate the Roman Empire and dominate it. Constantine, who was born from a Christian mother, reconciled the differences between the various Christian sects. He rebuilt the churches destroyed by Diocletian, and according to some sources, converted to Christianity on his deathbed. By the time of his death, the Christian system outgrew and eventually overshadowed and replaced the traditional Roman system and Rome even become the new center of Christianity.

Before Constantine rose to power, Emperor Diocletian enacted a resolution that accelerated the irreversible fall of the Roman Empire when he split it into two states or provinces: the western half centered in Rome and the eastern half centered in Byzantium, which Constantine later renamed to Constantinople after himself. Although the east and west provinces were both considered part of the Roman Empire, they were economically and administratively independent on paper. However, the Romans themselves did not acknowledge the Empire to have been split into two separate Empires but instead continued to consider it a twin state Empire governed by two independent imperial courts of administration.

Constantine later hammered the final nail in the Roman Empire's coffin when he officially declared the Christian religion as legal and endorsed it along the existing Roman system. Unlike the polytheistic Greek religion, which the Romans healthily incorporated in the likewise polytheistic Roman religion, the Christian system was monotheistic, and like cancer, it was foreign to the Roman system and weakened it from within until ultimately conquering it.

The history of the world was set on a new course when Constantine made the Christian system the state religion of Constantinople, and it was considered by many a turning point for early Christianity because the followers of this system represented a minority at the time. Constantine later emerged victorious in a series of bloody civil wars against emperors Maxentius and Licinius to become the sole ruler of both west and east. As the great emperor, Constantine enacted administrative reforms including declaring Christianity officially as the new social system of the empire and enforcing its doctrines on the public. And so, through Constantine, the Roman system was vanquished forever and dominated by the Christian social order, and what was once the glorious Roman Empire became a Christian twin-state empire. The western state spoke Latin and was Roman Catholic while the eastern state spoke Greek and followed the Eastern Orthodox branch of the Christian church.

Constantine ruled from his *"New Rome"* in the east and declared himself as *"the emperor of the Christian people."*

In addition to its geographical advantage on a thriving peninsula that could be fortified and defended easily, some scholars believe that Constantine established Constantinople in order to provide a raw place for the young religion of Christianity to grow and solidify his emerging empire in a new environment purer than that of the corrupt city of Rome in the west. Rome's public was harder to control because they were knowledgeable of how the Christian system transpired and took over their traditional Roman system compared to the people of Constantinople from the east who were discovering this new religion for the very first time. Indeed, it was one of the factors that allowed the east to thrive over time, while the west declined militarily, economically and populationally. In fact, after the western part of the Christian Empire fell, the eastern half continued to exist as the Byzantine Empire for hundreds of years.

Since there was no separation between church and state in both the Roman and Christian systems at the time, when Christianity became the state religion it also became the state law. The Roman Empire became the Christian Empire. In the same way, if a Christian empire changes its social system and adopts Judaism instead, it would be misleading to still refer to it as the Christian empire because it becomes a Jewish empire. And so, the Roman Empire collapsed permanently when the Christian system overshadowed the Roman system and dismantled what once was the all-powerful united Roman Empire into smaller Christian realms of kings and kingdoms. The overthrown millennia-old Roman religion ended up prosecuted by the newly born Christian system that it once ignored. The Christian system would later hunt down the practitioners of Roman religion, calling them *"pagans"* and practicing the *"join us or die"* approach for conquering them or publicly burning them at the stake.

The early form of the Christian system during the first 3 centuries of its existence was a radical passivist religion, which is why it was so prevalent among the impoverished and why it was widespread to the vast territories under totalitarian rule. It promoted itself as the religion of the poor and the sufferers, of which Jesus and the cross were symbols. Emperor Constantine, however, militarized the faith and turned its church into the church of the prosecutors, the rich and the powerful. The cross went from being a symbol of the suffering of the poor to become the shield of soldiers. Constantine's religion remained unchanged ever since and continued as the system of all-powerful armies and mighty empires.

Religion in the ancient Roman world wasn't a body of rulebooks that people must follow or else as it is with the Christian system. It was a series of activities, sacrifices and rituals carried out to appease the Gods to avoid misfortune and to caretake local deities to thank them for good fortune. For this primary reason, the Roman system was considerably less suppressive than the Christian system, which extensively regulated the personal lives of its followers teaching them what to think, what to feel, and what to do. Compared to Christianity, the Roman religion could easily be considered as heaven on Earth for personal liberties.

Worshiping the divinity out of fear of misfortune in the Earthly life continued subconsciously in the minds of the followers of the Christian system but was predominantly dominated by fear of the *"eternity of suffering in the afterlife."* And instead of abiding by a ritual to please the divinity and reap benefits in their current lifetimes, Christian followers genuinely invested in abiding by a stringent system of rules to receive perks in another lifetime, which the faith promises it exists and continuously envisions it for them.

The Bible, which is a collection of texts or scriptures that most Christians consider to be sent by God, was in fact written by a political organization that called itself the Roman Catholic Church. Thanks to this exclusive group of men, the world received its Christian religion. They wrote the books of the New Testament inspired by novels from the Old Testament in the year 382 A.D. (or 382 years after the alleged birth of Jesus Christ) at the Synod of Rome. The authors of the books of the New Testament wrote them all in Greek, which was the dominant language of scholarship and the universal language of the Mediterranean region at that day and age. The first 4 books of the New Testament were called the gospels, which is the Old English translation of Greek εὐαγγέλιον, meaning *"good news."*

The so-called Jesus is not his real name. The name *"Jesus"* is derived from the Latin pronunciation of the Greek transliteration of the original Hebrew name ישוע (Yeshua). The Greek way of expressing his name is Ἰησοῦς, which is pronounced *"Yay-soos."* The word *"Christ"* is also the English rendering of the Greek word *"Khristos,"* which is the Greek rendering of the original Hebrew word *"Mashiach,"* which means *"the anointed one."* And so, *Jesus Christ* means *"Yeshua, the appointed one."* There's no historical reference of Jesus or Yeshua outside the Bible. There is absolutely no historical evidence either that Jesus existed except that the Bible says so. There are however few and random references of *"Mashiach"* or *"the anointed one"* but that's just a label that many men self-proclaimed it in history before and after the so-called Jesus, and it is similar to the use of the label *"the prophet."*

It is worth mentioning that just like in today's society, people who lived at the times when the books of the new and the old Testaments were written took the habit of selecting from an existing pool of names to name their children instead of inventing entirely new ones. Therefore, there were many other men with the first name Yeshua who lived at the same time as the mythical Jesus, which the Christian novels revolve around. There's also a man with the same name in the Old Testament who was one of the 12 Jewish spies sent by Moses to explore the land of Canaan. And since the Bible adopted around half of its books from the Jewish novels, the men with the name Yeshua in such novels were translated into Joshua or Jehoshua in the English version of the Bible. Ultimately, it was convenient for the men who wrote the New Testament to call the Christ by the name Jesus instead of his real name Yeshua to distinguish him from other Jewish men in the Hebrew Bible.

The first novels ever written about Jesus are the 4 gospels of the New Testament — Matthew, Mark, Luke, and John — which are the primary source of information on the life of Jesus. One of these gospels stirred a dilemma in the Christian system. The only time that anyone proclaimed Jesus as God was through a single novel written about a character called Jesus by an anonymous author. This novel is titled the *"Gospel of John,"* which was written in 90–110 A.D. and arose in a Jewish community that was in the process of breaking from the Jewish synagogue. In this novel about Jesus, the anonymous author declared that Jesus said things like *"Before Abraham was, I am,"* and *"I and the Father are one,"* and, *"If you've seen me, you've seen the Father."* All these statements you find only in the Gospel of John, and that's striking because none of the earlier gospels have any indication that Jesus said such things. Nonetheless, it was the anonymous author's opinion that Jesus indeed said these things even though there is absolutely no inkling at all anywhere else that Jesus is God. Other authors of other novels that are part of the Bible's collection such as the gospels of Matthew, Mark, and Luke did not mention anything about Jesus calling himself God, which is a rather utterly crucial piece of information to include if anyone is writing any book about Jesus. And so, billions of people around the world who inherited the Gospel of John were led to think that Jesus is God based on a few statements in a single novel by an anonymous author.

If Christ is God and God the Father is God, doesn't that make two Gods? And when you throw the Holy Spirit into the mix, doesn't that make 3 Gods? So, aren't Christians polytheists? Christians wanted to insist, no, they're monotheists. Well, if they're monotheists, how can all 3 be God?

There are various ways of explaining this, but one of the most popular techniques used by Christians is called modalism. It is called modalism because it insisted that God existed in 3 modes — just as one at the same time can be a son, and a brother and a father, but there's only one of him. Similarly, God is manifested in 3 entities, but there's only one of him, so he's at the same time father, son, and spirit. So, in an attempt to stay the course and maintain a monotheistic religion, the Christian system pedestalized Jesus into Godhood and declared him as THE one and only God. In an attempt to correct the fatal logical errors made by the amateur author of the *Gospel of John*, the Catholic Church proclaimed Jesus as the one and only God. Unfortunately, such proclamation propagated paradoxes of its own because for true God to unite with a true man, true God must entirely and irreversibly abandon his divine qualities such as omnipotence, omniscience, omnipresence, and immortality so to become an ordinary man. And when such a man dies, God dies with him. Therefore, those who genuinely believe the Christian novels and think that Jesus is God should also accept that God is dead.

Thanks to the Gospel of John, the resulting religion that the Catholic Church built around these novels depicts God as a being who suffers from a severe case of multiple personality disorder. Sometimes he thinks he is a man called Jesus, other times he thinks he is a spirit, and most of the time he is back to himself as the all-father. Due to this identity crisis, reading the Bible becomes incredibly confusing if not illogical or inconsistent. You'll find passages in the Bible where God is basically talking to himself about himself leaving the reader terribly confused. The amateur author of the Gospel of John made a drastic claim when he announced to the reader that Jesus is God, but he didn't solidify such disclosure in the flow of his writing which made it embarrassing to read. For example, the verse in John 6:38 *"for I have come down from heaven, not to do my own will, but the will of him who sent me"* translates to *"for I have come down from heaven, not to do my own will, but the will of myself who sent me."*

The author of the *Gospel of John* undoubtedly fulfilled his desire of breaking out from the Jewish system through his novel to establish a somewhat different system but one that shares several fables with Judaism. Indeed, the content of this novel is more consistently *"hostile"* to the Jews than any other body of the New Testament in a transparent attempt by the author to distinct the new system as remotely as possible from the existing Jewish system. If this novel had not declared Jesus as God, the followers of the New Testament would've remained a tiny sect within Judaism because Jesus becomes just another messenger from God like others before him in other Abrahamic novels such as those about Abraham, Isaac, Jacob, Moses, Aaron, Joshua, and so on. And just like Moses split the sea into two parts and walked between them according to the novel but yet no one declared him a God, Jesus also is not God just because he walked on water or for any other miracle.

And if that was the case, the system would not have attracted many people, and the followers of the New Testament would've remained a tiny Jewish sect because the Jewish system is historically close-knit and very exclusive. The system would not have attracted a large mass of people through the steady state of conversion over the first 3 centuries of this system to grow into an emerging empire within the Roman Empire. Emperor Constantine almost certainly would've never adopted such a system because any tyrannical ruler understands very well that a beneficial religion should be inclusive, not exclusive. Christianity would not have become the state religion of Rome, and there would not have been the masses of conversions after Constantine. If that all hadn't happened, the Christian system would never become the dominant religious, cultural, political, social, economic force that it became in the world. It all hinges on a single claim in a single novel by an anonymous author who obviously never met the man called Jesus but boldly alleged that God and Jesus are one. Of course, this author had every right to do so as a writer, but the problem was that people took his novel seriously.

Neither Jesus nor God nor the Holy Spirit wrote any word in the books of the Bible. None of these books were even written by eyewitnesses during the lifetime of the so-called Jesus, and they are all just novels written by men about a man called Jesus and marketed by the institution that called itself the Catholic Church. It was the members of the Catholic church who promulgated the Bible by their authority and proclaimed it as the word of God. No first edition of the Bible exists today because all the original books of the New Testament were lost to the world just a few hundred years after they were written. Only copies of copies of English translations from Greek that were written by hand and not by professionals. Such reality inevitably led to significant errors, omissions, and, most importantly, changes. Nonetheless, most Christians continued to think that the Bible they read every day is the actual word of God when it is nothing more than a collection of novels which were mostly copied from Jewish versions.

The language used in any religious novel is intended by their authors to be vague on purpose to allow for an endless corridor of exits for clerics to use when explaining or defending the statements written in such dubious works of literature. For example, in the Gospel of John, you'll find statements such as *"In the beginning was the word, and the word was with God, and the word was God. The same was in the beginning with God."* As we will explore later in this book, it is the solemn duty of any author of any book to produce a language that everyone can understand. The more explicit and understandable the statements in a book are, the better the author is, and the bigger the evidence that the author genuinely understands what he/she is attempting to explain. Vagueness is never a sign of cleverness but an indication of ignorance. If you can't explain it simply, you don't understand it well enough. Unfortunately, the opening statement that we listed above from the opening chapter of the Gospel of John is oozing with vagueness and lacking in meaning. It is sharply evident that such a book is poorly written and that its author is an amateur who failed to use the language correctly. Such work of literature is unmistakably not a sign of divine inspiration but an indication of poor writing skills. Nonetheless, Jews and Christians were taught by their elders to believe that their books are divinely inspired just like Muslims think that God himself delivered every word in the Quran through an angel. Similarly, the Hindus believe that the Vedas, which are the most ancient Hindu scriptures, are divinely revealed and inspired with just as much faith as other people have for whatever religion they follow.

In the same way that a single anonymous author of a novel about a man called Jesus ultimately created a new system from an existing religious order, the author of a single novel called the Quran achieved the same thing and created a new religious system from the current Christian and Jewish systems. Muhammad, the founder of Islam, merely adopted the Jewish and Christian novels and rhymed them into oral poetry form after adding some changes of his own. However, Islam considers Jesus as a messenger of God like the rest of the messengers before him including an additional messenger called Muhammad, who was born 570 years after Jesus. And in the same way that Christians believe that God sent every word in the books of the Bible, Muslims genuinely believe that every word in the Quran (the central religious text of Islam) was sent to Earth by an angel, who verbally revealed these words to only one man, which is Muhammad.

Up on a mountain and deep in a cave when no one else was around, God sent an angel exclusively to only one man to lay down the rules of a new religion in a secret meeting, to which no other human being was invited. And although this all-powerful God knows that religion is meant to be ultimately publicized to all humanity, somehow he is powerless to announce this new religion to all his creations at once. This God seems to love and favor secrecy over global dissemination. Secrecy seems to be the pattern of all faiths because mostly all of them involve male-only chosen ones who were privileged with the ability to see and have secret discussions with angels or holy creatures from other dimensions. Judaism, Christianity, and Islam all involve male-only prophets where every last one of them told his tribe that he had secret meetings or secretly received messages or commandments from God or his angels.

Imagine that your next-door neighbor came knocking on your door one morning to give you the good news (or gospels) that he had a secret meeting last night with God and made a covenant with him that humanity must stop eating fish forever and eat nothing but eggs on Sundays. You were neither invited to that meeting nor involved in such decision-making, but still, your neighbor insists that you must believe him and do all that he says, or otherwise, you'll burn in hellfire. Surely you wouldn't want such neighbor living next to you, or you might even consider moving out entirely to another area. It is not that you are deliberately disbelieving your neighbor out of stubbornness or wickedness, but it is just the natural or logical thing to do since you were not involved in such meeting or witnessed what he witnessed, and it could be all nothing more than a dreadful dream. Unfortunately, this kind of hallucinations is what some tribal madmen plagued their communities with to control them. Some weak-minded people actually believed them or were forced to believe them under the command of a sovereign or the indoctrination of their elders.

The idea that people must automatically trust every word they hear from other people, or otherwise they'll be held accountable is undeniably a ludicrous concept. A person with modest cleverness wouldn't even waste a moment discussing or contemplating or arguing otherwise. The notion that we should believe everything we hear is childishly ignorant. Of course, we should never trust anything we hear. Of course, we must always be critical of everything we hear from everyone. It is just common sense.

Historians assert that if history has taught us anything, it is that *secrecy is the keystone to all tyranny*. Not force, but secrecy. So why would a supremely knowledgeable God favor secrecy to communicate his new religion to a single man if ultimately the plan is to make it public to all humanity? This angel called Gabriel could've appeared to everyone on the planet and peacefully brought people together instead of leaving it to Muhammad to wage a series of regional tribal wars and enforce this new religion by the sword to build a religious empire for a supremely totalitarian and repressive caliphate. God is undoubtedly aware of humankind's history and how secrecy begets tyrants, whom will only enslave humanity and wage hellish warfare to rule over everyone. So, why conveying the holy messages in stealth if the plan is not to turn people into slaves? That is unless, of course, God had nothing to do with it whatsoever and that it was all just the product of deceitful men transpiring against other men to rule over them and build empires.

Muslims believe that this angel named Gabriel (Arabic: جبريل, Jibrīl or جبرائيل Jibrā'īl) kept visiting Muhammad throughout his entire lifetime to reveal more words to him although no one else could see that angel but Muhammad. Therefore, no one could genuinely verify if the words that Muhammad memorized were indeed handed down by God and not just solely improvised by himself. Due to the fact that there were no eyewitnesses, the world received its Islamic religion thanks to one man's say so who insisted that it was indeed commissioned by God, and that the rest of humanity must take his word for it.

Unlike Jesus, who both Christians and Muslims hold true that he had the power of miracles such as walking on water or healing the sick, Muhammad did not possess such magical skills. Muslims, however, claim that his ability to recite and memorize a book-load of verses was his only miracle although they admit that it took him his entire life to deliver all the verses to his people. Non-Muslims argue that memorizing a collection of poetry does not constitute a miracle especially if one got a lifetime to spare. Non-Muslims also argue that poetry is not a divine gift and it was prevalent in the times of Muhammad more than any other era in that part of the world. Oral poetry is the earliest form of Arabic literature and was very common in the times of Muhammad especially that it was during a time when a lot of people did not have access to writing tools and could not read or write.

Some theologians argue that the angel that Muhammad saw was nothing more than a figment of his imagination just like the winged horse he claimed he saw and flew to heaven for a meeting with the Almighty. Muhammad told his people that one night he journeyed on a flying white horse, which he named *"thunder"* (Arabic: البُراق al-Burāq), with Gabriel to visit a mosque in Jerusalem for a short prayer before proceeding with the night journey to visit various heavens and meet the previous messengers such as Abraham, Moses, and Jesus before finally meeting the one and only God himself. Muhammad claimed that God instructed him to tell his followers that they must offer prayers to God fifty times a day. However, after pleading to Moses and negotiating the number of prayers with God, Muhammad eventually managed to reduce it to 5 times a day - a number that all Muslims should be solemnly grateful to Muhammad for achieving with his remarkable negotiation skills with the Almighty. Muslims endorsed the obligatory prayer and practiced it 5 times a day ever since on Muhammad's say so and based on his story of the night journey, which is known to them as the *"Isra' and Mi'raj"* (Arabic: الإسراء والمعراج, al-'Isrā' wal-Mi'rāj). These prayers are not optional because if a person refuses them, he's rigorously punished in hellfire.

Although Muslims commonly call it a prayer, it is, in fact, a serious ritual that involves washing hands and feet, wearing clean clothes, standing, sitting, bowing, kneeling on both hands and knees, and as well as placing the forehead on the ground. During each posture, the worshiper recites specific verses and phrases. This ritual is repeated 5 times a day at different hours. Calling this ritual a prayer would be inaccurate because there's no prayer in it at all. It is just a sequence of actions and recitations of verses and phrases. No personal prayer to God during the entire thing at all. Although occasionally some worshipers end the ritual with a personal prayer to God to appeal to him or ask for his help especially during periods of hardships.

Such ritual became THE key to paradise, and one of the 5 pillars of Islam that include the declaration of allegiance to the faith, charity, fasting, and the pilgrimage to Mecca. The doctrine continuously asserts that without the 5 daily rituals, there's only hell. It does not matter if you're cozy in bed sleeping on a cold morning, you must get up at dawn to perform the Fajr ritual (Arabic: صلاة الفجر ṣalāt al-faǧr) - the first ritual of the day. It does not matter what you are doing or where you are during the day - whether in the mall, walking on the street, or at work - you have to stop whatever you are doing and perform the mid-day ritual (Arabic: صلاة الظهر, ṣalāt aẓ-ẓuhr) and the afternoon ritual (Arabic: صلاة العصر ṣalāt al-ʿaṣr) after a few hours later. It really doesn't matter if you're enjoying a lovely evening with your family or friends, you must perform the sunset ritual (Arabic: صلاة المغرب ṣalāt al-maġrib) flowed by the night ritual (Arabic: صلاة العشاء ṣalāt al-ʿišāʾ) around an hour later. This obligatory ritual eventually became the routine or a programmed behavior that Muslims copied from their parents or culture without really knowing where it came from or who decided it that way. Most Muslims do not know that it all transpired from a story that revolves around a flying horse, an angel that only one man could see, a secret meeting with Jesus and the other prophets, and an intense bargaining negotiation between Muhammad and the Almighty.

In Muhammad's time, the understanding was that if a man flew high enough, he could reach another surface or heavenly realm, and if he continued flying upwards, he would reach better realms or existences until he enters the final domain where God and his angels live. It is also a noticeable pattern in most novels of the *"appointed ones"* in Abrahamic religions who claimed some sorts of magical revelations from their envisioned God while on top of a mountain or a hill considering that it was believed that higher surfaces get you closer to the realm of God and his angels. Muhammad figured he could just tell a story about riding a flying horse, which is very fast like thunder, to reach all those realms in the sky.

Of course, this perception of the sky and flying upwards is childish today because we know today what Muhammad and the people of his time did not. We know that our atmosphere is just a very thin layer after which there's only the coldness and emptiness of space.

Muhammad can't ride his flying horse into space because they both would die naturally. We know this today, but Muhammad and his people did not understand the nature of outer space back then, and that's why he got away with it, and his people believed his story. If a prophet tells the same story today, people will laugh at him and dismiss him as an illiterate fool. Muslim clerics later in the era of space exploration, of course, covered up Muhammad's story of the flying horse and rarely mentioned it or regarded it as *"just a vision"* because they understood that Muhammad's perception of the sky is outrageously wrong. The concept of a flying horse isn't new either because such mythological creature outdates Muhammad and comes originally from Greek mythology, with which the people of Arabia were familiar before Islam. The Greeks called the flying horse Pegasus (Greek: Πήγασος, Pḗgasos; Latin: Pegasus), which is a mythical winged divine stallion and a child of the Olympian God Poseidon.

Some theologians elevate the discussion to a higher level by questioning the nature of the being that appeared to Muhammad. Muhammad never met an angel in his lifetime before seeing the creature that identified itself to him as an angel and, therefore, could not verify if it was indeed an angel or something else entirely. It is like meeting an alien from another dimension who announces the name of his species and the planet he comes from, both of which you haven't seen before or can even pronounce their names correctly. In such circumstance, you assume it is true, but you have no means of knowing for sure other than the fact that such being appearing in front of you is not human.

Since Muhammad was the lone human being in the world who saw the being that identified itself to him as an angel, and since Muhammad did not see an angel before, he had absolutely no way of figuring otherwise. That being could be not a good angel at all but something completely the opposite. He could be the devil, which also is an angel as it is known and acknowledged by all Abrahamic religions, who wanted to trick Muhammad into believing that he is a good angel with good intentions, in the same way that he deceived Eve into eating the forbidden fruit according to the novel of Genesis. After all, it is because the devil deceived Eve into eating the forbidden fruit that humanity got kicked out of heaven and was the beginning of unimaginable suffering and horrors down on Earth. God didn't intervene to stop the devil back then, and there's no valid cause for God to stop the devil this time either. What we get ultimately is a religion inspired by the devil and not by God, but such a conclusion could also be held against Christianity, Judaism, and any other religion revealed to any human.

These theologians argue that it is virtually impossible to prove otherwise logically. The devil (also known as Satan or Lucifer) is a malevolent entity in the Abrahamic religions that seduces humans into wrongdoings and then punishes them for it. All Abrahamic faiths regard Satan as an angel of great piety and unfathomable beauty that surpasses that of any human who ever lived or will ever be born. All angels are unimaginably beautiful, and no human being can ever tell the difference between Lucifer or another angel. Therefore, Muhammad, as well as all the prophets before him, can never know the difference between Satan and another angel. The devil is also a shapeshifter, so an exact prediction of his appearance is impossible. He can appear to men as the most charming woman that their lusty hearts desire or otherwise as a serpent as he is identified in the Book of Genesis and the novel of the Garden of Eden. These theologians also add that considering the documented violent history of humankind under the influence of religions, which includes most of humanity's wars or ethnic cleansings or bloodshed or misery or oppression, such violent outcomes do not belong to the resume of peaceful angelic religions, but demonic ones.

Muhammad spent his last 10 years, from 622 to 632, as a triumphant military leader in a constant state of war with other tribes especially the powerful Banu Quraish tribe that historically inhabited and controlled Mecca and its Ka'aba (Arabic: أَلْكَعْبَة al-ka'bah, meaning *"the cube"*). Through sieges and diplomacy, Muhammad and his followers allied with some tribes and subdued others in the Arabian peninsula to grow into an emerging Islamic Empire. After a series of offensive raids and sieges, Muhammad conquered Mecca successfully in 630 A.D. and cleansed it of all its 360 pagan idols of Arabian Gods, such as Hubal (Arabic: هُبَل), which was a God worshipped by Quraysh (Arabic: قريش) at the Ka'aba in Mecca.

Hubal's idol was a human figure, believed to control acts of divination. Once every lunar year, the Bedouin tribes used to pilgrim from many regions throughout the Arabian Peninsula to Mecca to perform the ritual of tossing arrows before Hubal's statue where the direction in which the arrows pointed answered questions asked of the idol. Even Muhammad's grandfather, Abdul Muttalib, was known for consulting the arrows of Hubal to plea for good fortune in exchange of vows of sacrifices. Abdul Muttalib also made a solemn vow to Hubal that if he blesses him with 10 male children, he will offer one of them as a human sacrifice to Hubal. Later, after the 10th son was born to him, he was adamant about fulfilling his promise and consulted the arrows of Hubal to find out which child he should murder. The divination arrows fell upon his favorite son Abdullah, the soon-to-be father of Muhammad. The Quraysh tribe protested Abdul Muṭṭalib's intention to sacrifice his son and demanded that he sacrifice something else instead. He agreed to consult a sorceress, who told him to cast lots between Abdullah and 10 camels. If Abdullah was chosen, the father had to add 10 more camels and keep on doing the same until Hubal accepted the camels in Abdullah's place. When the number of camels reached 100, the lot finally fell on the camels. Then the camels were sacrificed, and Abdullah was spared.

After destroying the idol of his grandfather's God and all those of the other Gods, Muhammad designated the structure of the Ka'aba alternatively as a holy place for his version of God. And instead of throwing arrows before Hubal's statue for good fortune, pilgrims now toss stones at a structure in a ritual that signifies the stoning of the devil out of hatred. Meanwhile, the lucrative business of collecting money out of the annual pilgrimage to Mecca continued, of course, under Muhammad's rule of the city. And after conquering the Quraysh tribe, which he was born into, Muhammad continued in his armed conquests to establish a tyrannical Arabic monarchy in which the equivalent title of king, the *"Caliph,"* was passed down to successors with family or blood ties to Muhammad.

Around 18 years following Muhammad's death after battling an illness for several days, the poetry he recited throughout his lifetime was eventually embodied into book form for the very first time from which a new tribal religion was born. This poetic novel, called the

Quran, which means *"the recitation,"* was compiled in 650 A.D. under the orders of a tribal ruler called Caliph Uthman, who declared it as the first and only official copy and ordered all other texts to be burned so that no one else can later challenge or dispute his version of the verses that made it into the book. As a result, some verses were omitted, and they never reached the final approved version of the Quran in its official form because Uthman was the final authority on deciding between the recitations that indeed originate from Muhammad and those that did not. Uthman was the authority on what should be included in the book of Islam, and he declared all other contradicting scriptures as illegal. At a time when the predominant form of literature was oral poetry, it was impossible, of course, to determine with absolute certainty which recitations indeed belonged to Muhammad in the tide of verses that were in circulation at the time. Such task becomes especially challenging knowing that Muhammad continued to add new verses until his death and the initiative to finally collect them into book form initiated around 18 years after his death.

Uthman officiated the Quran to Muslims in Kufic, which is the oldest calligraphic form of Arabic scripts that had no vowel markers. Some Muslims foolishly believe that God delivered even the Arabic diacritics (consonant and vowel markings) in the Quran when in reality it is rationally bankrupt even to assume such a thing because Muhammad delivered the verses to his people only orally and never in written form since he didn't know how to write. The first Arabic ruler to commission a system of Arabic diacritics was Ali (Arabic: علي), who was the cousin and the son-in-law of Muhammad, the last prophet of Islam. Ali ruled as the fourth caliph from 656 to 661 and was regarded as the rightful immediate successor to Muhammad by the Shia Muslims. With the vast military expansion of the Islamic Empire, millions of newly converted non-native Arabic speakers needed to read and recite the Quran, which made the adoption of a formalized grammar system necessary. Ali delegated the task of creating Arabic diacritics and grammar to a poet called Abu al-Aswad al-Du'ali (Arabic: أبو الأسود الدؤلي), who became the father of Arabic grammar and the first to establish the science of the Arabic language and the first to lay down its methods and to develop its rules.

Uthman married two of Muhammad's 4 daughters and ruled over an ever-expanding empire that stretched from Iran and Afghanistan to Egypt. And just like all Christian tribal rulers before him, he used the new Islamic system to steer the people he ruled like sheep into tribal warfare to build an empire that he can rule with absolute tyranny.

Although the Jewish system outdates both the Christian and Islamic systems, it failed continuously in building an empire due to one main problem: membership exclusivity. While the Christian and Islamic regimes adopted an open-door policy and welcomed anyone to their tribes, Jewish tribes historically remained enclosed social bubbles, and due to such design, the tribes couldn't grow into an empire, and they continued as a minority in all the territories they resided. Even if someone adopts the Jewish system, he wouldn't be considered a real Jew because the Jewish tribes were racially biased to their bloodlines.

Judaism is the only religion in the world that genuinely qualifies as fundamentally racist. It teaches its descendants that they are *"God's chosen people."* Judaism isn't just a religion either. It is a race. One is born into it and passes it down from mother to child. And once born into this religion, no one can leave it and will always be considered Jewish whether one feels that way or not.

Jews declared that they are *"God's chosen people"* and that God favored their bloodline and, therefore, they must maintain its purity by not mixing it with the *"inferior races."* Such a bold declaration constitutes religiously sponsored racism. What makes such kind of racism the worst of them all is that it is not man-made but divinely inspired which institutionalizes racism in the minds of the followers of such system who can always affirm that *"it is God who says so."* The psychological impact that proceed from recognizing your membership to God's chosen team is undoubtedly profound, and it technically legalizes racism on a spiritual level. After all, if God himself announced that the Jews are his chosen people, who are you to say otherwise?

According to the Halakha (Hebrew: הֲלָכָה), which is a collective body of Jewish religious laws derived from the written and oral

Torah, a real Jew is one born to a Jewish mother. The Halakha states that the acceptance of the principles and practices of the Jewish system does not make a person a Jew. Additionally, those born Jewish do not lose that status because they cease to be observant Jews, even if they adopt the practices of another religion. Also, intermarriages are widely frowned upon by the Jewish tribes, and most Rabbis (Jewish religious officials and leaders) merely decline to perform or officiate such marriages.

The close-knit nature of the Jewish system historically kept its tribes a tiny minority everywhere they lived. Nonetheless, their massive reliance on convert means to infiltrate other social systems eventually paid off when they sneaked into the ruling class of several European nations and the Americas that practiced the Christian system. The infiltration of Jewish tribes was primarily concentrated or successful in the British and American Empires. Thanks to such infiltration and by taking advantage of their influence on powerful nations, they achieved their thousands-years-old agenda of building the Jewish Empire in the Middle East over some of the territories that were previously conquered and colonized by the British Empire. They specifically targeted the region where their system's temple once stood, which the Romans once destroyed to prevent the Jews from ever building such empire. Armed with proclamations from their religious novels, the best weaponry that Western tribal nations owned at the time and by vast sources of wealth, they expanded militarily and dominated over that region for several decades.

Like all other empires before them, Jewish tribalists proclaimed that it was the will of God and that God promised them the lands they conquered. And likewise, if they slaughtered other people and expelled them from their lands in such religious conquests, it is also the will of God. The Christian and Muslim systems did precisely the same thing and proclaimed it was the will of God as they conquered other tribes and acquired more territory to grow into empires. It was always done that way through religion. After all, forging empires is precisely what religious systems were historically invented for, and it is the entire purpose behind them.

"When you approach a city to wage war against it, offer it terms of peace. If it accepts your terms and submits to you, all the people found in it will become your slaves. If it does not accept terms of peace but makes war with you, then you are to lay siege to it. The Lord your God will deliver it over to you and you must kill every single male by the sword. However, the women, little children, cattle, and anything else in the city – all its plunder – you may take for yourselves as spoil. You may take from your enemies the plunder that the Lord your God has given you. This is how you are to deal with all those cities located far from you, those that do not belong to these nearby nations. As for the cities of these peoples that the Lord your God is going to give you as an inheritance, you must not allow a single living thing to survive. Instead, you must utterly annihilate them – the Hittites, Amorites, Canaanites, Perizzites, Hivites, and Jebusites – just as the Lord, your God, has commanded you, so that they cannot teach you all the abhorrent ways they worship their gods, causing you to sin against the Lord your God. If you besiege a city for a long time while attempting to capture it, you must not chop down its trees, for you may eat fruit from them and should not cut them down. A tree in the field is not human that you should besiege it! However, you may chop down any tree you know is not suitable for food, and you may use it to build siege works against the city that is making war with you until that city falls." ~ Deuteronomy, the Jewish Torah.

The above passage is a *"how-to manual"* for Jews that teaches them how to invade other people's lands, and brutally murder them to the point of complete annihilation to steal and occupy their territory. It teaches how to reduce entire populations to slavery and take their women and children as captives. All in the name of God and by his blessings as the Torah teaches. Such hateful work of literature from the Jewish novels shows the level of religious indoctrination that brainwashes young adults into thinking that they should invade other people's territories and murder them because it is the will of God. Such dangerous fallacies were inherited and taught to Jewish children, one generation after the other in the hope of building a Jewish Empire one day in the future.

The Jews were not the only people to use the *"God gave this land to us"* claim over the lands of Mesopotamia, and they were certainly not the first people to inhabit or control it either - the Phoenicians, Canaanites, Hittites, Egyptians, and Assyrians among many others were there first. So, if the debate is to give the land to the original natives, things become embarrassing for everyone because the land changed hands so many times across thousands of years, and in every period someone captured it from someone else. It gets even more awkward to everyone when they realize after a simple DNA test that more than half of the human population today share in common ancestors that once inhabited that region of the world and, therefore, makes such territory a common heritage for everyone.

It was very common back in the old days to claim that the Gods desire to set us on a particular path, or require us to invade a territory, or hint that a certain region is our birthright or *"promised land."* In fact, the civilizations that used the *"God gave this land to us"* claim over the Middle East include the Canaanites, Hittites, Egyptians, Assyrians, Babylonians, Macedonians, Greeks, Ptolemaics, Seleucids, Romans, Byzantines, and virtually every tribe or empire that won any battle or war in the region because the Gods were always credited to any good fortune – land grabs included. Therefore, the argument of the Godly-promised land becomes ridiculous when virtually every tribe that inhabited that territory used such status to legitimize their title to the land.

Some theologians argue that it is not worthy of a wise and merciful God to promise an already inhabited land to immigrants from another territory and condemn the natives to prosecution and exile. It is like Christopher Columbus claiming that God promised him the entire American Continent and that he is justified in murdering and practically eradicating the native population because God said so in the book. In a world where God allegedly loves to lay down his commandments in secret to male-only lucky ones, any man can come up to the world and claim that he was instructed by God to do something and therefore religiously legitimize any action he makes or any land he takes.

It is worth mentioning that the Jews were never banned from coming to the Middle East and especially not from Palestine, a country which the Jews colonized and wiped its name entirely off all world maps in the year 1948 as if it never existed. Jewish investors wishing to live in that region could always come and buy lands and build their homes legally to live along peacefully with their Arab neighbors. In fact, Palestine always maintained a Jewish minority long before any invasion by another nation and long before the British Empire conquered that land and made it easier for Jewish tribes to come in droves to settle and build an empire of their own. Even the American Empire purchased most of its states at one point in history such as the Louisiana Purchase in 1803 from the Napoleon French Empire for $15 million in return of land approximately 827,000 square miles west of the Mississippi River. Another land purchase was Alaska from the Russian Empire in 1867 for $7.2 million (or 2 cents per acre).

Unfortunately, the Jewish tribes had no such desire of legally buying land because their millennia-old agenda was to occupy the entire region by force to create an Empire that encompasses the whole territory of the Middle East over the existing nations of Iraq, Syria, Lebanon, Palestine, Jordan, Kuwait, Bahrain, Qatar, Oman, Yemen, Saudi Arabia, and Egypt. After all, that vast territory was allegedly awarded to the Jewish tribes by a godsend real estate agent, called Abraham. The *"Promised Land"* also known as *"The Land of Milk and Honey"* or *"Zion"* is the land which, according to the Tanakh (the Hebrew Bible), was promised and subsequently given by God to Abraham and his descendants. Jews genuinely believe that such a divine promise was indeed first made to Abraham, then confirmed to his son Isaac, and then to Isaac's son Jacob, Abraham's grandson. So, if God himself says that such land belongs to the Jews, why should they go through the trouble of buying it from the natives? These natives obviously have no legitimate claim to their property even if they have state-issued land titles to the land because God is the ultimate authority and he says it belongs to the Jews.

The international support for the demolishing of one nation and building another one for the Jews was notably endorsed and continuously supported by likewise new colonial countries such as Canada, USA, and Australia - the offshoots of the British Empire. It was just another case of imperialist nations supporting a new member to the team in the last phase of the European colonization. Those 3 nations that were consistently in strong support of the Jewish Empire were settler colonial societies in which the white man came in and virtually eliminated the native population. And, therefore, their support for the birth of a new imperial and tribal nation was completely understandable.

The establishment of the Jewish State in the Middle East wasn't driven entirely by Jewish influence because it was also welcomed and encouraged by the religious principles of the Christian system. The cultures with deep Christian indoctrination were mostly in favor of a Jewish state based on an *"it is written in the Bible"* approach to the world, and therefore they supported the occupation financially and politically. The *"it is written in the Bible"* response to anything is the end of a conversation. It is a thought-terminating utterance. Any conflicting statements following it, are automatically illegitimate or incorrect in the minds of the indoctrinated. Therefore, if it is written in Bible that the Jews own territory in the Middle East, then it is undeniably true or a *"fact,"* which no one should debate. And so, under massive religiously sponsored support by powerful Christian nations, the Jewish state flourished as Jews continued to flock to the new settlements, which were funded primarily by financial aids to the Jewish State including the funding by Christian religionists such as the evangelical Christian groups across the American Empire.

The Jewish State later became a spearhead for the United States in the region and acting as a military base where a never-ending supply of bombs and weaponry kept flowing in support of any future combative campaigns and territorial expansion by the Jewish Empire. The existence of such militant power in the Middle East performed a significant service to the United States by destroying secular Arab nationalism - a principal enemy to the United States. Despite being armed to the teeth, the Jewish State occasionally ran out of munitions in assaulting the neighboring Arab nations, but the United States relentlessly provided them with additional munitions, so the war can continue to go on in the region. Meanwhile, the political and media coverup of such colonial wars continued, and it would be extremely rare to find the word *"invasion"* during media reporting by Western news media of the Jewish State's territorial expansions. Although these were obvious invasions, blatant acts of aggression, and textbook cases of supreme international crimes, the western media mostly concealed it.

The Jewish Empire, like all other empires before them, could never have succeeded militarily without religious indoctrination. Armed with statements in religious novels authored and written by tribalists before them, the ruling class steered the public into chaos and tribal warfare, so they could rule over them and command them. All religious systems everywhere did precisely the same thing, and the people always fell victims for it because, just like music, religious doctrines can be hypnotizing.

Humanity's utmost sorrows were primarily due to words written in dangerous books by dangerous men. Such men fooled their own people into thinking that God sent such hateful books and got them bamboozled for the sole objective of ruling over them. As we will discover later in this chapter, words are intrinsically arbitrary, and all languages are inherently inaccurate. Nonetheless, languages work well enough, and we managed to evolve and progress as a society. To assume, however, that a supremely knowledgeable God would use such an intrinsically inaccurate tool to send an important message to his creation is fundamentally bankrupt on so many levels. That message will always end up distorted and interpreted or understood differently by each person, which would make way for aggression and hostility on each side of the argument regarding the true meaning of the message. All Abrahamic religions (Judaism and Christianity, and Islam) preach that God delivered their holy novels and they all share in common the presence of multiple sects within each religion. This problem is inevitable because all languages are naturally fallible and easily corruptible.

There is no sanity in accepting that a supremely wise being would rot the people's minds by sending them a message through words that will inevitably be distorted and misunderstood. It would defeat the purpose of carrying the message to humanity in the first place. Nonetheless, Abrahamic religions were established on such declaration and such bold claim. It would be intolerable if an ordinary person wrote his very own holy book and declared within that book that it is indeed the word of God which he received, and then asked everyone else to take it on faith. People would be at liberty to believe him or not, but they'll merely ignore him, and very few would take him seriously. If, however, an authority such as a king did it, he can readily enforce it on the public. And after several generations when everyone is dead, the crown's new subjects will accept it as the true word of the divine because it was drilled into their subconscious minds by their elders through generations of indoctrination.

The subconscious mind is far more powerful than the conscious mind, which authors our reasoning and logic. Why is the subconscious mind much more powerful than the conscious mind? Primarily for the following 5 reasons:

- ➤ It is the store of beliefs
- ➤ It controls emotions
- ➤ It has greater processing power
- ➤ It practices homeostasis
- ➤ It is a memory storage

The subconscious mind is the store of memories. It is like a super computer loaded with a database of memories and programmed behaviors, most of which we acquired before we concluded 7 years of age.

It is the source of emotions. If it wants you to do something, then it will use emotions to motivate you to do that thing. And because emotions can be compelling, the subconscious mind can easily control your behavior.

It has great processing power than the conscious mind. While the conscious mind can only focus on few things at a time, the subconscious mind can do so many things at the same time including executing multiple tasks and influencing you on many levels. This capacity makes it much easier for the subconscious mind to control your mood, emotions, perception and almost everything at the same time.

The subconscious mind is the store of beliefs. Beliefs cannot be reasoned with because they are mere ideas that lack tangible proof. It gets worst when beliefs become faiths, leaving you blindly following an idea that might not even be logical. Because the subconscious mind is the store of beliefs, it can easily force you to take a specific action based on one of those beliefs. The subconscious mind can easily override conscious intentions and force you into a path based on preprogrammed instructions. It practices homeostasis in your mental realm, by keeping you thinking and acting in a manner consistent with what you have learned in the past. For this reason, we instinctively follow our elder's footsteps and rarely question their teachings or the way of life or the religion we inherited. It ensures that you respond precisely the way your elders or community programmed you as a child. The subconscious mind, therefore, is your culture occupying a back seat in your head and relentlessly commanding you to conform with its teachings. Challenging your culture is equivalent to challenging your subconscious mind.

Winning over your subconscious mind or the indoctrination of the culture that raised you is tough but doable nonetheless. You can accomplish this feat through critical thinking, which is the objective, rational, skeptical, unbiased analysis, or evaluation of factual evidence to form a judgment or opinion. You can only convince your subconscious mind to yield to you by logic against it. Using force against it such as beating yourself up or practicing punishment as deterrence always fails eventually. Your subconscious mind will only listen to you if your conscious mind produces logical arguments that appeal to the first. Once the subconscious mind is convinced with your logic, it will happily grant your requests, and then you are free to induce profound changes to yourself that are physical, emotional, and mental. Only then you can be free from the dogma of the culture in which you were born. Therefore, when religionists ask you *"to take everything they preach on faith"* they are slamming the door in front of analytical or critical thinking. Leaving you helpless against your subconscious mind and the ideas or beliefs your society drilled into it as a child.

Religious indoctrination is rarely done through thoughtful or conscious consideration by the victim but is almost always carried on subconsciously by force on people as helpless children. Religious leaders were well aware of the vulnerability of a child's brain, and the importance of getting the indoctrination in early. And such ancient understanding is fossilized forever in the language through such proverbs as *"give me a child until he is seven, and I will show you the man."* — Aristotle. Religion would have never succeeded at all as a mind-control social system if not for the process of the indoctrination of the young that every culture historically perpetrated. Every parent knows very well how fragile the minds of children are, and how they could be influenced dramatically in their early years in life by the stories the parents bestow on them, which would later shape their characters as grown-ups. Similarly, religious leaders and rulers recognized such vulnerability in the human mind which is why they insisted on indoctrinating the public at a very young age to take advantage of how the human mind works and to efficiently breed generations of conforming religious citizens. Any person who was somehow not subjected to any religion during his/her upbringing is very unlikely to accept religion as an adult because he/she would've developed already the necessary analytical and critical skills to distinguish between facts and fiction or between logic and nonsense.

Every religion comes with a rulebook and, as we explained earlier, it is not practical to have a law without law enforcement because otherwise very few people will follow it. The whole idea behind producing a law is to have people obey it, which means that if you keep it arbitrary for them to choose to follow the code or not, you might as well not bother defining the law at all since very few will listen to you. Law enforcement often uses force, which makes it violent. And in the same way that every law inescapably comes with violence, every religion innately has the potential for violence. There is no real solution for this problem because the moment you declare a code, you're defining to others what they must not do and the consequences if they do, which makes room for aggression and hostility.

When we speak of the Abrahamic laws, we do not mean ordinary rules as we understand them in the judiciary sense (or the court system), which merely details what you must not do in society. Judiciary's rulebook is a what-not-to-do list, and anything that's not mentioned in that book is considered legal or allowed to the public. Abrahamic religions, on the other hand, have two rulebooks where one records the things you must not do that are considered religiously illegal, and another book contains those that you must do although it is not illegal if you do not. For example, the Christian doctrine doesn't consider lying as religiously illegal but at the same time teaches its followers that they must practice the truth. All Abrahamic religions agree that men must not have sexual desires for other women although it is not religiously illegal to have such desires. And so, religious laws are far more reaching than those of any court system through these nonbinding laws.

Additionally, Abrahamic religions' rulebooks do not only involve *"doing or not doing"* but also expand to *"feeling or not feeling"* and *"thinking or not thinking."* There's a rulebook that regulates how you should feel or what you should not observe, and another set of rules for controlling what you think. Abrahamic religions, for example, teach their followers to restrict sexual feelings and fantasies for the other sex although technically it is not religiously illegal to have sexual thoughts and desires. Abrahamic religions tap into people's bedrooms to regulate their sexual lives concerning what the correct way of having sex should be or how it should be conducted. Some sexual acts like anal sex, for example, are forbidden, and there are usually days in every year that people must not have sexual intercourse. They regulate how many sex partners one must have and the age at which the public can start having sex.

There have never been other religions in the history of humanity as strict or suppressive to sexual freedoms than the Abrahamic religions. Abrahamic religious authorities view sexuality not as something to be celebrated and enjoyed but as a disgraceful thing that must be suppressed at all cost and only practiced for the sole purpose of giving birth to a child within a marriage. The following

64

statement from one of the novels of the Bible teaches Christians about the correct way for controlling celibacy in society:

> *"If this thing be true, and the tokens of virginity were not found, then they shall bring out the young lady to the door of her father's house, and the men of her city shall stone her to death to put evil away from among you."*
> ~Deuteronomy 22:20

Abrahamic religions teach their followers not to overthink about the nature of God and leave the thinking to religious leaders. Thinking about the aspects of God, such as why the doctrine insists that the creator is a *"he"* not a *"she"* or an *"it"* is frowned upon and must be left to the clerics to study and try to explain to their followers. The topic of Abrahamic religions addressing their God in the male tense deserve to be understood because it directly corresponds to the fact that they are male religions. Starting with the prophets or the *"appointed ones,"* they are all exclusively male without any exceptions. These religions were born at a time when women's rights or liberties were virtually nonexistent and predominantly revolved around housewifery. From a human perspective, we instinctively think that all beings are either male or female and we modeled our languages in such fashion. And since manhood represents power and dominance, it is therefore very understandable for such faiths to address their authority in the male tense to reflect such dominance.

Through religion, a ruling class tells its public what to think, what to feel, and what to do. They made the tribe follow their rules through faith in a way the ruling class never imagined possible. Fear of the authorities was necessary to subdue the populace, and the ruling class of every nation perfected their methods and tactics of subjugation such as terrorism and brain-programming to guarantee the survival of their terrorist group. Terrorism was always the favorite tool for all rulers everywhere to control their public. The best way of describing terrorism is as *"the tactic of inducing fear or terror in the hearts of people to force them to deliver a specific outcome or to keep them under control."* Torture, of course, was one of the ideal tools of terrorism especially when it is conducted in public. All ruling classes sanctioned and carried out torture on the public throughout history and it never stopped until the collapse of authoritarian governments. These cruel ways were largely carried out in public as a way of intimidation and as a public display of power or authority to prevent any thoughts of uprisings or any attempts of wrongdoings by the people against those who oppress them. The entire populace of towns would show up to witness an execution by torture in a public square. Those who had been *"spared"* torture were commonly locked barefooted into the stocks, where children took delight in rubbing feces into their hair and mouths. The ruling classes of the tribal era perfected the techniques and tools of torture over time and used it as a means of reform, inducing public terror, interrogation, spectacle, and sadistic pleasure.

The most unsettling fact about torture's brutality isn't its existence, but the way the ruling classes injected a perverted sense of creativity (and even pleasure) into the creation of devices designed to inflict pain. For example, the House of Plantagenet (a royal family which originated from the lands of Anjou in France and ruled England between 1154 and 1485) employed *"the rack,"* which is a torture device that consists of an oblong, rectangular, usually wooden frame, slightly raised from the ground, with a roller at one, or both, ends. The victim's feet are fastened to one roller, and the wrists are chained to the other. The torturer turned the handle causing the ropes to pull the victim's arms. Eventually, the victim's bones were dislocated with a loud crack, caused by snapping cartilage, ligaments or bones. If the torturer kept turning the handles the limbs would eventually be torn off. This method was mostly used to extract confessions, not confessing meant that the torturer could stretch more. Sometimes, torturers forced their victim to watch other people be tortured with this device to implant psychological fear.

Another horrific device of torture was the Brazen Bull - also known as the Sicilian Bull. Phalaris, the tyrant of Akraga (a city on the southern coast of Sicily, Italy), commissioned such device after an Athenian man, called the Perillos of Athens, proposed the concept of a more painful means of execution to the tyrant. Once finished, Phalaris sadistically tested the device on its inventor and murdered him. The metallic bull had a door on the side that could be opened and latched after a person was put inside and a fire was set underneath it until the metal became yellow as it was heated. The victim would then be slowly roasted to death all while screaming in agonizing pain. The bull was purposely designed to amplify these screams and make them sound like the bellowing of a bull. This tool of *death-by-torture* is similar to being boiled alive. Even though it was not used during the Middle Ages as it was used earlier by the Greek and Romans, a simpler form of cooking people alive was still used in Central Europe, without the use of the bull.

Impalement was the most favored method of execution by Vlad the Impaler, who held the prince title over Wallachia (a region in Romania) 3 times between 1448 and his death. The victim was forced to sit on a sharp and thick pole. When the executioner raises the pole upright, the victim is left to slide down the pole with their own weight. It could take the victim 3 days to die using this painful method of *death-by-torture*. For his sheer sadistic entertainment, Vlad once impaled around 20,000 people all while enjoying a meal.

The breaking wheel, also known as the Catherine Wheel, was a torture device used for public execution from antiquity into early modern times in 19th-century Germany. First, the victim's limbs were tied to the spokes of a large wooden wheel which would then be slowly revolved as the torturer simultaneously smashed the victim's limbs with an iron hammer to break them in numerous places. After the torturer crushes all the bones of the condemned, he/she would be left on the wheel to die. Sometimes the victims of torture were put on top of a tall pole so the birds could feed on their flesh until they die. This method was slow indeed since it could have taken days before the victims would die from dehydration. Sometimes, a *coup de grace* (blow of mercy) was employed by ordering the executioner to deal a fatal blow on the victim's chest and stomach to end their agony.

"To be hanged, drawn and quartered" was a death-by-torture execution that was first recorded during the reign of King Henry III between 1216 and 1272. It became a statutory penalty in England in 1352 for men convicted of high treason. Any challenge or insult or attack on the monarch's authority was considered high treason

and a hugely deplorable act that demands the most extreme form of punishment. A convicted traitor was fastened to a hurdle or wooden panel, and drawn by horse to the place of execution, where he was then hanged (almost to the point of death), emasculated, disemboweled, beheaded, and quartered (chopped into 4 pieces). The traitor's remains were often displayed in prominent places across the country, such as London Bridge. For reasons of public decency, women convicted of high treason were instead burned at the stake.

The most nightmarish of them all was probably the Saw Torture or *"death by sawing."* In this method, the victim is hung upside down, so that the blood will rush to their heads and keep them conscious during the long torture. The torturer would then saw through the victims' bodies until they were completely sawed in half. Most were cut up only in their abdomen to prolong their agony. Death by sawing was a method of execution reportedly used by tribal cultures in many parts of the world.

Nonetheless, as gruesome as death-by-torture was, it wasn't enough, and people still found the courage or the *"audacity of not wanting to be owned"* by their rulers. And here is where religion kicks in. What if these ruling classes could convince everyone that there's a higher form of torture, where a powerful entity could inflict on people unimaginable and never-ending pain if they don't follow the rules? And what if that *"big boss"* is continuously watching over the public and observing their every move or thought or feeling? If the public could believe this, then surely everyone would play by the rules of the ruling class and wouldn't risk the *"eternity of suffering"* instead.

If the public believed that an eternal afterlife in a hellish place exists, they'll surely never break the laws of their rulers. A timeless place where its wretched inhabitants sigh and wail. Blazing fires and flames crackle and roar. Fierce water boils as if it would burst with rage. Scorching wind roar with suffocating black smoke. Their scorched skins are exchanged continuously for new ones so that they can taste the torment anew. They drink festering hot water melting their insides as well as their skins. They are shackled together in chains and lined up as far as the eye can see. They wear sticky burning tar-like substance for clothing, and hooks of iron to drag them back should they try to escape. And although death appears on all sides, they can never die. Their remorseful admissions of wrongdoing and pleading for forgiveness are in vain.

The psychological effect of knowing that such horrific depiction of a possible future could inevitably befall a wrongdoer is undoubtedly haunting, and one would naturally do anything to avoid such predicament. The long-term effect that such stories propagate in children is irreversible, and the long-lasting fear that infests their fragile minds at a very early age is hard to detox, and for most of them, it lasts a lifetime.

Previously, death was a form of escape that the public could take when they could no longer tolerate the oppression of the ruling class, but now that religion is upon the public, there is no such thing as an escape. There is no place they could go to, no thought or feeling or action they could hide, and no alternatives whatsoever. They could no longer hide their ideas and thoughts from the spies of the ruling class because the *big boss* is now observing their every thought without them uttering any word. He was the *All-Seeing Eye* and the *"all-knowing,"* who is always watching everyone and judging if they are following his rulebook, which is conveniently authored and written by the ruling class on God's behalf. There's no place to hide and no possible means of escape even in death. It was a totalitarian form of control and full ownership over the public's destiny in a way that no human king could accomplish solely by his authority or by any physical means.

Because death was a form of escape that the public occasionally took to rebel against their rulers or challenge them, the ruling class had to declare suicide as illegal through religious indoctrination. Mostly all tribal cultures and their tribal religions declared suicide as unlawful and punishable by public humiliation to the body and the reputation of the diseased in this life as well as, of course, the eternal torture in the afterlife. And the illegalization continued for thousands of years until the last days of tribalism.

Mostly all ruling classes of the world modeled the deity as a *big boss* or a *"supreme king"* with an unbound kingdom, just like how they dreamt their rule to be. They imagined him the only way they knew how - as a supreme and eternal ruler over an endless kingdom that has no boundaries. Their version of the creator is one that the ruling class aspired to be here on Earth but could never achieve it because just like the rest of us, they're made of flesh and bones and destined to die and putrefy. And so, tribal rulers dreamt up a belief that the deity is a ruler just like them and that he got a kingdom, subjects, laws, and totalitarian justice just like they got. He sees everything, he knows everything, and he's the ultimate judge – just like how they dreamt they could.

Abrahamic religions are perfect examples of the *kingly God* figure that tyrants of that era fabricated to build their empires. He's the *"king of kings,"* the absolute ruler of the universe, the one who owns all, and so on. The belief in Abrahamic religions, therefore, is the belief in a supreme leader. It is the religion of *Big Brother*. A ruler can only view God as a ruler because from his perspective if God did not command more soldiers or ruled more territory, then the Earthly king is undoubtedly more supreme than God. Just as a sick person imagines God as a healer, a poor person sees God as carrying and giving, and an orphan observes God as a loving parent. And so, it was natural for kings to put out a belief in God as a king or an authority just like them. And since they are the authority of the land, they can easily force their ideas on the people and wash away all other beliefs that don't follow an authoritative or tyrannical structure. Because after all, democracy in the kingdom of heaven is a threat to all kings down here on Earth. And since there's no democracy in the kingdom of God, why should the public practice it on Earth? It is evidently not the correct or best form of government because otherwise, God would've practiced it – this is the logic that the ruling class preach to indoctrinate the public. So, they teach their citizens that even deities follow the same rule structure as the ruling class of humanity, and the people should accept that form of rule as *the way of the world.*

One could be forgiven to presume that religions that emphasize peace and love such as the Abrahamic religions claim to be would not revert to torturing people, but one who thinks this way clearly neither understands the purpose of religions nor their violent history. A person who thinks this way certainly still believes that his/her religion is indeed delivered by God and not man-made for a ruling class. The Catholic Church, for example, used torture on anyone who disbelieved in the system and they even invented some torturing techniques of their own. The Inquisition was a group of institutions within the government system of the Catholic Church whose official mission statement was to combat public heresy committed by baptized Christians. By analogy with a nation, the Inquisition was both the court system and the police force or the law enforcement division of the Catholic Church. An inquisitor presided over inquisitional procedures as prosecutor, judge, and executioner. While he was technically expected to arrive at his decision after consulting with an assembly of experts of his choosing, this check to his power was soon abandoned. An inquisitor was selected primarily on the basis of his zeal to prosecute heretics. He and his assistants, messengers, and spies were allowed to carry arms.

The meaning of the label *"heretic"* deserves to be understood because hundreds of thousands of innocent people died when others uttered this magical word against them. It should also be recognized that all religions of all kinds are inherently intolerant and relentlessly preach intolerance. They are intolerant because they are not self-critical, and they continuously suppress criticism. And while today criticism is considered a virtue and an indication of critical thinking, it was frowned upon in the days of tribalism and its tribal religions. Although every religion dealt with its critics differently, there's a documented history in the case of Abrahamic faiths of practicing bigotry against their critics and putting them to death for it. While Christianity called its critics *"heretics"* and tortured them or burned them alive, Islam called its critics *"infidels"* and routinely shopped off their heads with a sharp sword. Jews also practiced this devilish tactic, and they systematically labeled the critics of the Jewish State or the Jewish religion as *"Anti-Semitic"* before publicly shaming or suppressing them.

A heretic is just a critic of the Church and its religion whereas heresy or blasphemy are just other words for religious criticism. Denouncing a practice or illegalizing it always starts with one crucial step: ***inventing a negative-sounding word for it***. After they coined the word *heretic*, labeling the critics of the Catholic Church and condemning them as enemies of God became a straightforward routine.

The real mission statement of the Catholic Church's religious police (the Inquisition) was to terrify people into obedience. They conducted trials and executions of countless human lives in Europe and around the world as it followed in the wake of missionaries. And along with the tyranny of the Inquisition, churchmen also brought religious justification for the practice of slavery. The primary purpose of the trials and executions was not to *"save the soul of the accused"* but to achieve public submission to the ruling class and propagate fear into others. The Catholic Church demanded unquestioning obedience to the authority of the church and state. The church's understanding of God was to be the only understanding. There was to be no discussion or debate. As the Inquisitor Bernard Gui said:

> *"The layman must not argue with the unbeliever but thrust his sword into the man's belly as far as it will go."*
> ~ *Inquisitor Bernard Gui*

In a time of burgeoning ideas about spirituality, the Church insisted that it was the only avenue through which one was permitted to learn about God. Pope Innocent III declared:

> *"Anyone who attempted to construe a personal view of God which conflicted with Church dogma must be burned without pity."* ~ *Pope Innocent III*

Such statements should surprise no one especially those who read the New Testament. After all, and according to the Gospel of Luke (the third of the fourth canonical novels of the New Testament), the mythical Jesus Christ himself said:

> *"As for these enemies of mine, who did not want me to reign over them, bring them here and slaughter them before me."* ~ *Luke 19:27*

Jesus said this indirectly through a parable to convey the message that royalty is entitled to rule whereas their servants (the public in general) must obey the commands of the ruling class and submit to their authority or otherwise they are enemies of the crown and deserve to be cold-bloodedly butchered. Pope Innocent III, therefore, is just following the commands of Jesus and he shouldn't be held accountable for murdering anyone who stands against the rule of the Church because God warrants such murders and *it is written so in the book.*

The Catholic Church was merciless with its victims. In the sentencing of its critics, no husband was spared because of his wife, nor wife because of her husband, nor parent because of the helpless children, and no sentence should be mitigated because of sickness or old age. Each and every sentence included flagellation. The most frequent sentence was perpetual imprisonment, which always entailed an inadequate diet of bread and water, sometimes meant being kept in chains, and occasionally entailed solitary confinement. The life expectancy in all the prisons was very short. Besides the conventional means of torture like beating, suffocating and burning, the Roman Catholic Church used more depraved ways of extracting confessions and executing its victims. Such confessions, of course, were carried out routinely in the torture chambers whereas the executions were always public to terrorize the public.

Armed with a license granted by the Pope himself, inquisitors were free to explore the depths of horror and cruelty. Dressed as black-robed monsters with black cowls over their heads, the Catholic police could extract confessions from almost anyone as they roamed the streets of the communities where Christianity had a strong foothold. The inquisitors could investigate anyone except, of course, the members of the ruling class, which of course legitimized the authority of such workers and paid their salaries for the well-earned job of keeping the public in line. The Catholic police worked hard at employing and sometimes inventing every conceivable device to inflict pain by slowly amputating and dislocating the body. Many of the machines were inscribed with the motto *"Glory be only to God."* The rack, the hoist, and the water tortures were the most common. Victims were rubbed with lard or grease and slowly roasted alive. This terrorist group even used an instrument called the breast ripper, which is a hellish pronged-like device whose primary purpose was to tear women's breasts off the chest. The Catholic Church's police used this horrific tool on women that they accused and condemned for adultery, heresy, witchcraft, and blasphemy.

The Heretic's Fork is a purely Christian invention and was a special torture device reserved for those who spoke out against the Catholic Church during the Middle Ages. The device was placed between the breastbone and throat just under the chin and secured with a leather strap around the neck, while the victim was hung in an upright position from the ceiling or otherwise suspended in a way so that they could not lie down. Usually, the Catholic Church used the Heretic's fork on blasphemers, liars, or people who *"spoke the Lord's name in vain."* The punishment made it nearly impossible for them to talk. Also, a person wearing it couldn't fall asleep. The moment their head dropped with fatigue, the prongs pierced their throat or chest, causing great pain. The victim would be awake for days, which made confessions more likely to happen. The torturers only removed the instrument after the wearer had spoken the words: *"I recant."*

Scold's Bridle (sometimes called a witch's bridle, a brank's bridle, or simply branks) is a metal mask with implemented mouth gag that was used mainly on women married to clergy up until 19th century. Clergymen who accused their wives of disregarding their decisions had the right to use the Scold's Bridle. After the mask was applied, women were walked on a leash or chained to a marked cross where they were exposed to public ridicule. The Churches and the barony courts in Scotland used the Scold's Bridle mostly on female transgressors or those accused of witchcraft, and on women considered to be rude or nags or common scolds.

The Catholic Church also used the Hanging Cages or *"gibbeting"* for death-by-torture. These cages were usually hung around the outsides of town halls, ducal palaces, public highways (frequently at crossroads), and waterways. They were also placed near the town's hall of justice and cathedrals. The victim, naked and exposed, would slowly wither from hunger and thirst. The weather would second the victim's death by heat stroke and sunburn in the summer or cold in the winter. The victims were usually previously mutilated before being put in the cages to make a more edifying example of the punishment. The corpses were left in the cages until the bones literally fell apart. Gibbeting was a standard law punishment in England, which a judge could impose in addition to execution. This practice was regularized in England by the Murder Act 1751, which empowered judges to impose this upon various offenses.

Another purely Christian invention was the Judas Cradle (also known as the Judas chair), which the Spanish Inquisition commonly used. The victim was stripped, hoisted and hung over this pointed pyramid with iron belts. Their legs were stretched out frontwards, or their ankles pulled down by weights. The tormentor would then drop the accused onto the pyramid penetrating the vagina, anus or scrotum. With their muscles contracted, they were usually unable to relax and fall asleep. The amount of pain that the device inflicted could be adjusted in several ways. The victim could be dropped repeatedly onto the machine, one leg could be lifted, olive oil could be spread on the pyramid, or brass weights could be hung from the victim's legs to impale them slowly. Sometimes to prolong torture, the victim would be suspended above the device overnight, and the torturer would then continue the next morning. The equipment was rarely cleaned. If victims did not die from the device, they almost always died from an infection. Torture with the Judas Cradle could last several hours to several days. Apart from the agonizing pain one suffered, the humiliation was the primary attraction for this method of torture. Whenever the victim fainted from the shock, the torturer would lift the victim until the tortured person was awake again to commence with the process.

The Catholic Church conducted trials and executions of countless human lives in Europe and around the world wherever the missionaries succeeded in infiltrating the community and amassing political support or judicial influence. The official mission statement of such missionaries was *"freeing the land, which has become contaminated by Jews and heretics."* Natives who did not convert to Christianity were routinely burned like any other heretic. The tyranny inherent in the beliefs that followed singular supremacy accompanied explorers and missionaries throughout the world. When Columbus landed in America in 1492, he mistook it for India and called the native inhabitants *"Indians."* It was his avowed aim to *"convert the heathen Indians to our Holy Faith"* that warranted the enslaving and transshipping of thousands of Native Americans. That such treatment resulted in complete genocide did not matter as much as that these natives had been given the opportunity of everlasting life through their exposure to Christianity. The same sort of thinking also gave Westerners license to rape native women. In his own words, Columbus described how he himself *"took his pleasure"* with a native woman after whipping her *"soundly"* with a piece of rope.

It is worth mentioning that all religions, for the most part, condoned slavery either implicitly or explicitly. As for Christianity, it constitutionally warrants slavery with the blessings of the Almighty, the son, and the Holy Spirit. The Bible even speaks to the slaves and ask them not to defy their masters or object to their servitude because it is *"the will of God."* Here are 3 statements from 3 different novels from the Biblical collection:

> *"Slaves, in reverent fear of God submit yourselves to your masters, not only to those who are good and considerate but also to those who are harsh." ~ Peter 2:18*

> *"Slaves, obey your earthly masters with respect and fear, and with sincerity of heart, just as you would obey Christ." ~ Ephesians 6:5*

> *"And he said "Hagar, Sarai's slave girl, where have you come from and where are you going?" She answered, "I'm running away from Sarai, my mistress." The angel of the Lord said to her, "Go back to your mistress and submit to ill-treatment at her hands." ~ Genesis 16: 8-9*

Imagine the horror of living in such communities at the time. Your mother and sister would not dare to step outside out of fear of encountering an inquisitor and taken to their torture chambers to be raped or whipped as they did to your neighbor's wife and daughter. No one was safe, not even those who practiced the faith down to the smallest detail. After all, the primary purpose of the Catholic

Church's religious police was to propagate fear in the hearts of the public, and if an inquisitor felt that someone's looks did not resemble a look of horror, the standard state of affairs is to inject despair by any means possible. Of course, one could avoid the routine torture or at least postpone it by paying the inquisitor the maximum fee one could afford. Inquisitors, therefore, grew very rich. They continuously received bribes and annual fines from the wealthy who paid to escape accusation. The Inquisition would claim all the money and property of alleged heretics. As there was little chance of the accused being proven innocent, there was no need to wait for a conviction to confiscate his/her property leaving nothing for the convict's children or nearest beneficiaries. Pope Innocent III explained that God punished children for the sins of their parents. So, unless children had come forth spontaneously to denounce their parents, they were left penniless. Inquisitors went as far as to even accuse the dead of heresy, sometimes as much as 70 after their death. They exhumed and burned alleged heretic's bones and then confiscated all property from the heirs.

Aside from the physical torture, the Catholic Church held the printing press in deep suspicion. This terrorist organization believed the printed word to be a channel of heresy, and so hampered the communication produced by the fifteenth-century invention of the printing press. The concept of the *"Dark Ages"* is a European historical periodization that traditionally came to characterize the intellectual darkness within Europe in the period between the Middle Ages (5th–10th century) and the Renaissance (14th-17th century) or, in other words, the whole period between the 5th and the 17th centuries. The Dark Ages were the result of the collapse of the Roman Empire to the Christian System that left Western Europe deteriorated demographically, culturally, economically, and intellectually as ancient Roman books and important records were routinely burned and lost to history. And the practice of burning books and suppressing free literature continued under the rule of the Catholic Church. The main reason why this period is called the Dark Ages is that, compared with other eras, historians know very little about this period because many essential records of the time did not survive. Suppressing free press and knowledge by the Christian regime should surprise no one because the first novel of the Abraham religions is about the fatal wrongdoing of eating from the forbidden fruit of the *"tree of knowledge,"* which was the beginning of all humankind's sorrows and hardship down on Earth. The symbolism here, of course, is that humanity must not seek knowledge or wisdom because God punished them severely for it in the beginning by ousting Adam and Eve from the *"Garden of Eden"* (aka Paradise or Heaven).

The barbaric torture of human beings remained a legal option for the Catholic Church from the 13th century all the way until the 20th century. One would presume that considering the level of literacy and freedom that arose between the 17th and 21st century, all the structures of the Catholic Church would be burned down to the ground, and its oppressive organization dismantled, but unfortunately, such thing never happened. It couldn't and wouldn't happen because religions, even ones as extreme as the Abrahamic religions, are necessary for the business of government. And for as long as there are governments in the world, religions will always persevere. The Catholic Church prospered significantly under the brute rein of fascism in Italy. Fascism is a form of radical authoritarian nationalism, characterized by dictatorial power, forcible suppression of opposition and control of industry and commerce, which came to prominence in early 20th-century Europe. You could guess by such definition that both systems share the same values and would fit together nicely, and indeed it was the case.

Benito Mussolini, a brute fascist dictator and a faithful ally and friend of Hitler, came to realize the importance of enlisting the pope's support. Fascist rallies typically began with a morning mass celebrated by a priest, and churches and cathedrals were essential props in fascist parades. Pope Pius XI cooperated closely with Mussolini for more than a decade, lending his regime organizational strength and moral legitimacy. And although Mussolini himself was a committed anti-cleric, he recognized the importance of religion for the business of government and both sides benefited from the bargain.

It would be remiss of us not to talk about the remarkable characters of these two men. Benito Mussolini had a tendency for violence even in his childhood. Born to a socialist father on July 29, 1883,

Mussolini gained a reputation for bullying and fighting during his early years. At age 10 he was expelled from a religious boarding school for stabbing a classmate in the hand, and another stabbing incident took place at his next school. He also admitted to knifing a girlfriend in the arm. Meanwhile, he allegedly pinched people at church to make them cry, led gangs of boys on raids of local farmsteads and eventually became adept at dueling with swords. During his youth, Mussolini proclaimed himself an atheist and railed against the Catholic Church, going so far as to say that only idiots believed Bible stories and that Jesus Christ and Mary Magdalene were lovers. He even authored an anti-clerical pulp novel. He led armed fascist squads that faced minimal interference from the police or army as they roamed the country causing property damage and killing an estimated 2,000 political opponents. Many citizens were harassed, tortured, beaten up or forced to drink castor oil. As prime minister, Mussolini reduced the influence of the judiciary, muzzled a free press, arrested political opponents, continued condoning fascist squad violence, consolidated his hold on power and declared himself dictator of Italy in 1925.

Pope Pius XI, on the other hand, insisted on eating alone. He wouldn't allow his assistants or other priests or other clergies to dine with him. Such attitude by a man who was supposed to set examples or standards for other Christians to follow by virtue of his position as the *"leader"* of the Catholic Church, of course, shamelessly goes against the life and the teachings of Jesus Christ, who loved sharing his food with others and was even known for breaking bread with sinners according to the Christian novels. Pius XI insisted that when his sister and brother wanted to see him once he became pope, they had to refer to him as *"your holiness"* and never by his name. They could only see him by appointment. Again, a religion that calls on its followers to be like Christ, who preached modesty and was famous for bowing down on both knees to wash the feet of his guests, obviously wasn't well represented by Pius XI. The Cardinals and others that came to see him really lived in fear, not only of his temper but because he was also very demanding, had very high standards and did not tolerate any behavior that he regarded as not up to his standards. He considered the Italian government as the enemy and rejected the notion of the separation of church and state. Pius XI saw Mussolini as a man sent by God, the man of providence

— as he would later refer to him, who would end the separation of church and state and restore many of the prerogatives of the church that were lost at the same time.

Mussolini even made the Catholic Church a sovereign and independent absolute monarchy with the pope at its head. Thanks to this fascist dictator, the pope sits at his throne in the Vatican City. The pope's kingdom is an independent city-state that mints its own currency, prints its own stamps, issues passports and license plates, operates media outlets and has its own flag and anthem. Benito Mussolini, therefore, signed the Vatican City into existence. The dispute between the Italian government and the Catholic Church ended in 1929 with the signing of the Lateran Pacts, which allowed the Vatican to exist as its own sovereign state and compensated the church $92 million (more than $1 billion in today's money) for the Papal States, which were territories that the pope ruled as the supreme king.

Moving away now from the tyranny of one religion, we will talk about another Abrahamic religion notorious for it suppression of personal liberties and the oppression of the communities that fostered it. Just like Christianity, Islam also had its standards and protocols for death-by-torture to alleged wrongdoers. One noticeable difference between Christianity and Islam in the techniques of torture they employed was that the first involved a lot of stripping naked of victims while the latter did not. According to the Quran, the death penalty is recognized for the 7 *"Hudud"* (Arabic: حدود meaning borders or boundaries or limits) crimes which include adultery, defamation (primarily the slander against religious leaders or the religion), drinking alcohol, theft, highway robbery, apostasy (the abandonment of the Islamic belief), and corruption of Islam. These are the most severe crimes in Islam because it is believed that these acts go directly against the word of God and are seen as a threat to society. Hudud punishments range from public lashing to publicly stoning to death, amputation of hands, decapitation by a razor-sharp sword, and hanging. Hudud crimes cannot be pardoned by the state, and the punishments must be carried out in public. Women accused of adultery were routinely sentenced to stoning to death, and such inhumane practice was widespread in all territories where Islam had a strong foothold in government.

The death sentence to those who abandon the Islamic belief is probably the cruelest and most oppressive of all the other Islamic laws. It is cruel because children neither choose their parents nor the culture where they were born. To force on oneself lifetime obedience to a religion just because one is born into it is undoubtedly savagely dogmatic. The typical death sentence to such *"crimes"* is public decapitation in a public square in front of the local community of the victim and his/her neighbors. The purpose of conducting the beheading in public, of course, is to induce terror in the hearts of the people to prevent them from repeating such wrongdoing and primarily to perpetuate obedience to the authority of the religion and the ruling class.

Fear is no stranger to this religion, and it capitalized on it like no other religion before or after it. Inducing fear in the hearts of all its followers is systematic and is incorporated in its doctrine, practices, the fables, and the nightmarish depiction of hell in their minds that terrifies them as children. Indeed, no other religion is heavy on the visualization of torment and punishment in the afterlife to its followers than any of the roughly 4,200 religions in humankind's history.

Imagine your community had a gathering at the local park this weekend. All your friends and neighbors are there for the big event. The woman down the street has been accused of adultery by her husband and some of his friends, so she has been automatically sentenced to death by stoning because *"it is said so in the book."* The woman could be entirely innocent of any wrongdoing and falsely accused of adultery, but the neighborhood will accept her husband's word for it nonetheless. In the middle of the field, the neighbors work together to bury the woman vertically in the ground up to her chest, and everyone is circled around her. There are piles of stones ready to be thrown. These stones are large enough that they will cause life-ending damage, but not too big to kill her on impact. The stoning is meant to be a slow, painful, and cause deliberate death. The husband has the *"honor"* to throw the first stone. The father and the relatives then encourage the children to throw stones at their own helpless mother. They are told to do it for God. The woman is allowed to try and escape, but she is buried too deeply. For the next 10 minutes, the rest of the community joins in until there is nothing left of the woman but a bloody stump. The barrage of stones was conducted in such a way that no individual within the group could be identified as the one who killed the woman. We wish such descriptions were nothing more than a nightmarish fiction, but for the countries where Islam had its grip on power, this heinous form of capital punishment existed and continued into the 21st century.

The apple does not fall far from the tree and just how Christianity plunged Europe in darkness and oppressed scientists and freethinkers, Islam eventually led to the exact same thing as it became the religion of the dictators of the Middle East. A migration of scientists and intellectuals took place in the Dark Ages from Europe to the Middle East when the European continent was plagued by Christianity's intolerance to free speech and science. The intellectual center of the world was Baghdad, which was completely open at the time to all foreign scientists from all regions. Most of these scientists were *"doubters"* who we might call today agnostics or atheists. They were all there in Baghdad exchanging ideas. While Europe was busy disemboweling critics and scientists, Baghdad was a haven for science and reason. And thanks to this openness, the local culture advanced in engineering, biology, medicine, and mathematics. They created algebra, which is an Arabic word. Today's numerals are Arabic numerals. All these wonderful intellectual achievements happened within a 300-year period which stretched from 800 to 1100 AD. It was the golden age of the Middle East, and it was centered in the city of Baghdad thanks to its openness to the world and to new ideas.

So what ended all this? Islam, of course. The 12th-century kicks in and a tyrannical Islamic scholar comes along called Al-Ghazali (born in 1058 AD and died in 1111) who concluded that mathematics is the work of the devil. And nothing good can come of such an ignorant philosophy. Add this to a mix of codification of what Islam was ought to become later due to his influence, the entire intellectual foundation in the Arabic world collapsed and never recovered. Religious revelation replaced scientific investigation. Baghdad ceased to be open to the world and to new ideas and it incubated an intolerant, close-minded religious culture. Doubters were no longer welcomed in the city, and the tyrannical Islamic rulers demanded stringent and blind adherence to the faith. Therefore, the scientists and free thinkers left for Europe and other regions while the sheeple settled in the city instead. Islam destroyed the Arabic world, and the legacy of ignorance continued until the last days of tribalism.

Moving away now from all the horrors of religions, we will talk about the time when beliefs were religionless or, in other words, lacked rulebooks.

Spiritual beliefs appeared in the earliest moments of human history within every territory known to humanity, and no ancient society has yet been found that did not have godly beliefs. Ever since people walked the Earth, they contemplated and questioned the existence of higher powers that made their world the way it appears to be. Most cultures associated these higher powers to nature itself – faceless and formless spirits manifested in the forces of the universe and the cycles of the seasons. As a result, people worshiped nature throughout the early history of humanity, but it was a kind of worship that they willingly endorsed. A type of worship practiced by observation and meditation. A way to *"connect"* with the maker of our world and a way to observe and appreciate the beauty of nature. Listening to the sounds of nature around them and observing the beautiful surroundings that they are part of non-separately.

Historically, there were no *"rulebooks"* on what you must and must not do. No *big boss* demanding worship and punishing those who don't bow to him or follow his rulebook as you would expect from a tyrant. No fear-obsessed being, who desire people to fear him constantly and acknowledge his existence out of fear. No fearmongering by a tyrannical God, who would burn people alive endlessly if they don't love him. As if love isn't a spontaneous emotion, which if you force it on anyone you strangle it at birth and obstruct it. You do not love someone because you must - that's not true love. And similarly, it is impossible to love anyone or anything forcefully out of fear.

Beliefs back in those days were peaceful and voluntary, and people sought a deep connection between nature and themselves to find peace and harmony between the two. In other words, beliefs were religionless and therefore peaceful. Japan's Shinto is one example of such religionless beliefs. The public that practiced such discipline in ancient Japan did not even have a name for it because there was no need for a title. It was just an idea or a philosophy or a *"way of things"* that the public believed in at the time. What we call today as *"Shinto"* is a relatively modern word that comes from the written Chinese Shendao (神道, pinyin: shén dào), combining two kanji: shin (神), meaning *"spirit"* and michi (道) meaning *"path."* Together, they mean *"the way of the spirit"* and represent a philosophical path or study (from the Chinese word dào).

Since the Japanese language does not explicitly distinguish between singular and plural, kami also refers to the singular divinity, or sacred essence, that manifests in multiple forms: rocks, trees, rivers, animals, places, and even people can be said to possess the nature of kami. Kami and people are not separate. They exist within the same world and share its interrelated complexity. The use of such words reflects ancient understanding by the public that humanity and nature are inseparable. Over time, however, Shinto adopted different interpretations as a ruling class of people tried to institutionalize the philosophy into a religion or in other words, they wanted to weaponize it. Nonetheless, real Shinto doesn't have a rulebook, doesn't involve worship, and doesn't involve any formal ritual. It does not even require a blind belief, or what we understand as *"faith."* If we must put it bluntly, real Shinto (as the ancient people of Japan knew it) is a book-less, worship-less, ritual-less, and faithless religion. In other words, it is just a philosophy.

This way of thinking or understanding of humankind, nature, and the divinity was common to all humanity across all territories in history. Our ancestors never really questioned the existence of the maker. They observed the deity in trees, mountains, the human body, and everything there is in the world to which we belong. They believed that they *came out* of this world in the same way that apples *come out* of apple trees and *not into* the trees. And just as the apples belong to the trees and are products of the trees, humanity belongs to Earth and is a product of it. As a result, humanity in that era was peaceful and worked with nature, not against it. They wouldn't set the mountains on fire or poison their rivers because that would be equivalent to insulting the deity or defying their God.

They wouldn't kill their own kind because it is said so in the book that they must. They wouldn't stone their own mothers or sisters to death or burn their neighbors at the stake because they preferred other beliefs. They wouldn't torment their own people to death with hellish instruments of torture just because they did not concur with the ideas of the book. They wouldn't invade a foreign territory, reduce its population to slavery, and slaughter its women and children because the book says that the land belongs to one side and not the other. They would never offer themselves as human sacrifices to be thrown into a volcano in droves or chopped to pieces at an altar. The would not voluntarily submit themselves and their children to servitude or condone slavery because it is also written in the book that they should. They would not take a lifelong vow to be celibate or withdraw into silence or shave one's head or never cut one's hair. Women wouldn't cover up every inch of skin on their bodies to torment themselves in extreme heat, and men wouldn't force their wives or daughters or sisters into it. They would not systematically beat their own children to force upon them a lifetime of subconscious fear and automatic blind obedience to the authority as the book commands. They would not allow arranged marriages to minors, the oppression of women or gay people, ethnic cleansing and honor rape because the book says they should.

Harmless religionless public, however, is useless to all tyrants because tribal philosophies regarding the world are violent and revolve around domination and consolidation of power. And so, the ruling class needed to find a way to tap into people's minds to produce a kind of faith that reflects tribal values. One where there's a king ruling everything there is to rule, an absolute monarchy in a limitless empire or kingdom. A God that has laws that everyone must follow or else. And thus, every ruling class invented its own religion and forced it on the public by their authority. The ruling classes of the world, therefore, subjugated public beliefs about the deity and replaced them with tribal versions. Some ruling classes taught their public that everyone came to this world because of wrongdoing or a *"sin"* committed by someone a long time ago - as all Abrahamic religions teach. In other words, they preach that humanity was forced into this planet as punishment by the ruler of the world for not following the rules. This, of course, is just one theory and nothing more than a tribal version of a God as a ruling class wish to see it, and one that they can benefit from and exploit. Unfortunately, this kind of thinking is dangerous and came with long-term impacts on the human mind.

By teaching the public that humanity was forced into this world as a punishment, they'll naturally feel disconnected and strangers to the world in which they live. And when you feel strange and alien, you become hostile, and your approach to things becomes violent. You start attacking the world and subjugating it to your will. After all, you don't belong here on Earth, and you're just visiting temporary until you return to that Paradise from which your ancestors were originally kicked out. *Tourists are not the best neighbors,* because they're just visiting and don't necessary care about the long-term effects of their actions or behavior to others or the surroundings. Similarly, the *"you came into this world as a punishment"* doctrine doesn't make you a friendly inhabitant on Earth. This kind of thinking will inevitably put you at odds with the world along with the other human beings and animals you share it with and will complicate that relationship.

This violent attitude towards nature is something quite useful to rulers, and of course much more beneficial than the friendly *"we originated from Earth, and we are one with it"* approach. Therefore, the culture that tribal religions produce is always a violent one and is always attacking something or someone. Always at war, conflict, and odds with other cultures or with itself. It is a culture where toughness and aggressiveness are virtues whereas innocence and peacefulness are drawbacks or negatives. A society that awards power and condemns weakness.

All systems and products that arise from a tribal culture follow the same principle of dominance and the concept of man conquering nature. They produce literature, art, music, and movies that romanticize the idea of man as a conqueror and always beautify violence to the public. And so, they wage wars to consolidate as much power and land as they can absorb. They build factories that poison the earth to manufacture machines that poison it further.

They destroy nature to build concrete jungles with towering structures to dominate the sky and defy the natural elements. They go to great lengths constructing these towering buildings making them resistant to earthquakes and winds. They proudly proclaim them as achievements, but symbols of man's arrogance and defiance to nature are what they truly represent.

They construct highways isolating the natural landscape for other animals and killing the unlucky ones who dared to follow their instinctual desire to cross these highways looking for food or mates.

They make airplanes that can penetrate the sound barrier attacking the air and sound itself to deliver bombs faster and more frequently. They manufacture weapons of mass destruction that kill in abundance and unselectively between children or the elderly or even nature.

They build phallic symbols and machinery penetrating the sky and attacking the universe. They think that space is out there somewhere, and they should head out to find it, but it never occurs to them that our planet is already in space. That we can simply sit back and observe the universe by building machinery that can scan it from down here on Earth far better than blasting a missile into space. It does not occur to them that we can invite the universe in and get the same results by letting it come to us instead of attacking it with rockets.

They create economic systems that turn people into slaves that are forced to work for wages to survive. A global economy controlled by bankers and large corporations that treat people as deplorable objects. A culture where people rent themselves out for the money. A culture of slaves and lords.

In the end, the approach to the world and technology in a tribal culture always revolves around attacking and dominating. Tribalists' approach to any problem is always one that creates more problems, which they'll solve by the same tribal approach that will further generate additional problems. And so, the cycle of violence and domination never ends in a tribal society until it eventually destroys it. Tribalists, through their tribal religions, created a world so misarranged that there is no other way of living it except by destroying other lives. A world with the capacity for horrors in terms of what one tribal culture can do to another or, even worst, what one society can do to its own people. It was a hideous way of imagining the creator and God's plans for humanity. A horrible vision of God as a tyrant and human beings as slaves. A religion that is not divine, but a devilish abomination.

The Masters' New Suits & Titles

The working class of a tribe never understand the slavery system they were born into or the religion their elders taught them. They didn't know why there must always be a leader or why they should hate and fight other tribes. Nonetheless, they did it anyway because they were conditioned to perform in such a manner. Ignorance is passed on from one generation to the other within the working class. The elders pass down the tribe's doctrines to their children subconsciously because it was also passed down to them by their elders and the process was repeated several generations deep in history until the time when the sovereign first laid down his rules and opinions to the community he ruled over. And so, the elders drill the concepts that they learned unknowingly in the fragile minds of their children, cementing that knowledge in their subconscious minds as they grow up. These children absorb everything they learned as facts of life, living by the laws and opinions of their dead elders, teaching them to their children, and completing a cycle of indoctrination that never ends.

The subconscious mind is far more powerful than the conscious mind and the slaves rarely willingly challenge the norms they inherited not because they'll be punished (which mostly is the case) but because they are truly indoctrinated by the system. Eventually, it becomes the norm to follow their parent's footsteps and never question the tribal way of life they inherited.

The ruling class created a system in which fear of the authority was always vibrant in the minds of the public. They exploited every opportunity to remind people of their belonging to the tribe. All sports events, where naturally large masses of the working class would be present, were frequent events to have all the saves perform the tribe's rituals before the commencement of the games. It always involved the official anthem and the flag—two fundamental components of every tribe that must always be loved and respected by all its members. Any rogue individual who disrespected the flag or the ritual was severely punished and sometimes made an example of to discourage such behavior in the future. To disrespect the ceremony is to insult and challenge the tribal values such as nationalism and patriotism, which of course is an act that a tribal society cannot tolerate. Typically, they are corrected by the people around them subconsciously because everyone in a tribal culture is taught at a very young age to exhibit a programmed behavior to the national anthem and the flag.

As tribalism progressed throughout the centuries, it was re-branded and refined progressively, but its two classes of masters and salves remained the same.

The masters received new titles throughout the years such as Chief, Oba, Mwami, Maharajah, Eze, Nizam, Dato, Pharaoh, Emperor, Caesar, Prince, King, Sultan, Caliph, Shah, Gaekwar, Khan, Rajah, Shogun, Viceroy, Duke, Archduke, Count, Baron, Tsar, Prime Minister, Chancellor, and President. Such titles however merely polished the walls of tribalism's institution, but they did create a sense of change for the public although the real problem of having a minority of people ruling over the majority was left unresolved. The need for masters was relentlessly preached by the ruling class and their priests, academics, lawyers, and the like who were parasitical upon the working class. And such indoctrination was generally softened by promises of compensation in an imaginary world beyond the grave.

What most slaves never understood was the fact that tribalism is never embodied in one or more people. It is not the few masters on top of the hierarchy because people are quite temporary, and they die eventually. Tribalism is a system and not a group of people. It is an idea, and ideas are immortal and cannot be injured or killed. And while kings hold the crown temporary, the crown lives on forever long after they're dead. The system is the real eternal master that even kings are mere servants to it.

Tribalism is the system of systems. It is a system maker. It is a recipe for human enslavement. It produces horrific designs that have the potential for horrors. Rulers, public officials, religious preachers or leaders, capitalists, and bankers are all different faces for the same brand – tribalism – and they are all tribalists. It is a system that thrives on the following 5 fundamental elements:

> ➢ Representation, or to give away your voice to someone else or to allow someone else to be your voice so to speak or act on your behalf.
> ➢ Delegation, or to give away your personal authority to someone else to act on your behalf, or the allocation of responsibilities to create a hierarchy of authority.
> ➢ Intermediation, or having intermediaries between two sides of the transaction. This was common during tribal financial practices where a middleman intervenes between the two sides of the trade to cash in from both.
> ➢ Centralization, or following a central thinking in designing systems and concepts. The ruling class took the habit of centralizing everything starting from the structure of their command, down to how they managed their business, trade, and architecture.
> ➢ Segregation, or the action or state of setting someone or something apart from other people or things.

Delegation is one of the critical attributes of all masters and especially in how they practiced power. It produces ignorant slaves that perform specific tasks while unaware of the larger structure they're in and usually following a *"need to know basis"* to protect the interests of those at the top. Just like their slavery religions that were transpired is secret, tribal cultures use secrecy and stealth extensively in government. After all, God himself adopted the tactic of secrecy to convey commandments exclusively to a handful of men in secret meetings. So why should the public be against secrecy when they already know that the Almighty himself endorsed it?

In such arrangement, every group of slaves knows just enough information to keep it performing but without ever seeing the full picture or realizing the whole story. War slaves (soldiers), for example, follow their higher-ups and fight their wars vigorously assuming that they are fighting on the right side based on the information presented to them but unfortunately, *little knowledge is a dangerous thing* and once the truth is unveiled the so-called heroes are revealed as the murderous monsters they were indeed. It led to military cemeteries around the world packed with brainwashed dead soldiers who were convinced that God and righteousness were on their side whereas the other team is evil. One country prays for God to destroy its enemies while the other nation begs for the same God to kill its enemies in the same fashion.

Those who know all, forgive all. And those who know so little, fall victims to hatred and intolerance. Therefore, a tribal culture favors hiding as much information as possible from their tribe to induce conduct symmetrical to tribal values, which always follows an approach based on aggression and domination. Rulers justify hiding information from the public under misleading claims such as when they say that some information must be kept secret *"in the interest of national defense or foreign policy."* Under such claim, unfortunately, they could hide anything they didn't want the public to have access to and consequently maintained an ignorant population that continuously conforms to consent.

Aside from its role in initiating conflicts and hatred, a tribal culture used delegation and secrecy excessively in business and in how they structured their economy. Employees never know what their peers are earning, and that knowledge is always limited to those in executive roles or those managing salaries. If employees knew what others are receiving or how much money they are generating for their employer for the job they're performing, they would surely feel exploited and understand the unfairness of the game. Likewise, customers never really know how much money a product actually cost the manufacturer because if they do, they'll never agree to buy these ridiculously overly priced items.

Delegation creates hierarchy and breeds followers and leaders. In a tribal culture, there must always be a leader figure, a big boss, someone in charge, a director, and so on. Having one is essential. Whether it is sport or music or business, there must always be a boss. It is one of the virtues of tribalism to have leaders. The idea that there must always be leaders and followers is drilled in the minds of the public at a very young age through schooling, entertainment, and nationwide propaganda.

Segregation is the most ancient and popular tribal convention. You see it primarily in their maps that segregates each tribe to its territory. Segregation in a tribal culture was used in urban planning where tribalists disconnected the places of work from residences or areas of trade, which rendered such societies dysfunctional and socially enclosed or isolated. It was also practiced in the times of war after one empire dominated another and divided their land between multiple tribes who don't share common values or beliefs. Dividing defeated nations in such manner was, of course, the final insult and an insurance policy because it would set the conquered nation onto a never-ending conflict among its subdivisions and will never rise again to be the mighty united nation it once was before its downfall.

Representation is the most important and the main ingredient in the recipe. It is the downfall of any social system because it produces a type of people who do not speak for themselves, soon to become unable to speak for themselves, before finally dwarfing into a cattle-like society that is conditioned to follow. In such community, the shepherds are called *"leaders"* while everyone else knows only to follow and utterly ignorant of how they got anywhere or where any path started. Ancient creeds such as *"do not go where the path may lead, go instead where there is no path and leave a trail"* were ignored as the public became too domesticated to manage life without being told where to go and what to do.

Anyone who feeds the system by practicing any of tribalism's 5 elements is part of the game and belongs to the group. It might not even occur to someone that he's a tribalist or that he's unwillingly feeding into a dysfunctional and violent Stone Age system through his small contributions whatever they may be. Those who don't realize this or are unaware of their membership are usually at the bottom of the pyramid in this system. The very few at the top, however, know everything and understand the game thoroughly. As for the public, and in the same way, they continue living without ever questioning their role in society or the nature of the leadership they followed their entire lives. It never occurs to them because it is the reality they were born into and it is common knowledge that children are highly adaptable, and they grow up to subconsciously accept the things around them. After all, everyone else seems to be playing along and no one likes to be singled out as a freak to society. We all want peace of mind and happiness, and thus we choose to accept whatever our elders and the rest of the community taught us so that we can live peacefully.

Republicanism & The Era Of Democratic Tyranny

By the time it got to the concept of republicanism, the ruling class had long moved backstage where they puppeteered less influential tribalists beneath them. Tyrannical rulers everywhere eventually realized that they could have employees running their nation for them while they sit back and observe in the background.

It is important first to understand that there are two major types of tyranny: monarchy and republicanism. Within a monarchy, the public does not choose its rulers, whereas in a republic the public only picks from a list of nominees (which the public did not nominate) to rule over them. These officials, however, are not in charge but are more or less employed by a ruling class.

In a republic, the public never nominates its officials but only gets to select from a handful of options that a ruling class carefully picked and conveniently made available. Through such modern dictatorial system, a ruling class nominates and elects itself indefinitely through the public as a vehicle.

The essence of republicanism is not the father-to-son inheritance of a nation, but the persistence of a specific worldview and a particular way of life imposed by a small ruling group of people. The ruling class of a republic is not concerned at all in perpetuating the bloodline of certain dynasties over the throne but in preserving itself. Who wields power isn't essential to the ruling class for as long as the structure of governing always remains the same. In most cases, the ruling class of any republic involves one or more parties that periodically take turns to rule the country every term. The populace, of course, had no control over the nomination process but could only choose between a handful of faces that each party introduced. It is like telling a man that he is free to choose any number he wants for as long as he picks a number between 1 and 10. Such logic, of course, is shamelessly grotesque and the same can describe such kind of governance.

In a republic, there's no democracy; just the illusion of it. It is a form of government that one can best describe it as *"democratic tyranny."* Instead of one family ruling over the public, political parties (sometimes just a single party in some nations) took turns every term. Instead of using force and brutality to silence the political opposition, the ruling class used money and financial bullying to control the nomination process. Instead of burning books and jailing writers, the ruling class owned at least 90% of the mainstream media to ensure that the public is only getting the version of media that they approve. Through the media, the ruling class controlled and shaped public opinion. They ran propaganda campaigns to give the public the illusion of control and urged them to vote, which only served in perpetuating the tyrannical rule of the republic.

In a republic, politicians are essentially paid actors in a reality TV show called *"The Presidential Election."* In the same way how movie actors learn to lie in front of a camera and fake their facial expressions or even cry on demand to win an Oscar, politicians act and tell lies to win the elections. It wasn't a surprise at all to see a TV person running for the presidency in a tribal culture because, in the end, the publicly elected government was just a stage-performance. Politicians were not the ones running any government. They were just frontmen for the financial institutions of the ruling classes of the world that were the real ones in charge in every nation.

During the 20th and 21st century of the tribal era, some governments went under the label of *"communism"*. Communism, however, was just an idea popularized by thinkers such as the German philosopher Karl Marx in the 19th century. In theory, the concept known as communism means a socioeconomic order structured upon the common ownership of the means of production and the absence of social classes, money and the state. Communism remained nothing more than a theory because no country could every apply such socio-economic model and they all had a ruling class of people that owned and controlled all the wealth and power of the nation. And although tribalists labeled countries such as Russia and China as communist nations, they were far from it. The only significant political difference between Russia and the United States is that in the first there was only one political party while in the latter there were two dominant political parties. Therefore, and according to the political standard that existed in the 20th and the 21st centuries, any republic ruled by a single political party could be considered a communist nation.

As for the economy, and as we will discover later in the next chapter, all nations of the tribal world were fundamentally capitalist with no exceptions.

Stealth In Government As A Tactic

The keystone to all tyranny, supremacy, and hierarchy is not force but secrecy. The approach of *"this you must not know"* is a byproduct of the tribal law of delegation which creates hierarchy and, therefore, tyranny. Secrecy is as essential to the business of tribal governments as water to life.

Stealth in government was the favorite tactic for key tribalists, and the principle was straightforward: If you don't exist in people's minds and eyes, you have nothing to worry about, and you guarantee your survival. The ruling class learned that openness always backfires and is dangerous to them because people can rebel against their rulers and terminate their dynasties at any moment. With the growth of the human population and the technology available, key tribalists became sitting targets and therefore could never be truly safe. Therefore, they cleverly manufactured an illusion to fool the people into believing that they're electing their rulers. Contrary to what the public thought at the time, the real leadership of a nation never actually changed but only a few faces that the public knew. The real leadership of every tribe in that day and age was hidden from the public in the hands of unknown key tribalists, who ought to stay hidden for their own sake.

It is a trick that rulers learned throughout the years, and it proved to be unimaginably efficient. Back in the old days they had to deal with their subjects daily and always worried about maintaining a proper image to the public. However, the key tribalists of representative democracies had elected puppets doing the work for them, and they only sat back pulling the strings of these puppets. This secret command never worried about maintaining an image to the public because in the eyes and minds of the people they did not even exist, and there was no image to concern them. The families of the key tribalists involved the central bankers, religious leaders, high-level commanders in the army, supreme judges and law enforcement chiefs. They controlled and operated the keys of the tribe, which were the monetary system (the central banks more specifically), the army and law enforcement institutions.

With the abundance of money available for the prominent tribes of the 20th and 21st century, they could achieve any goal through currency. Because key tribalists always controlled the money and power of the tribe, they controlled everything else. The media, for example, was consolidating into the hands of a handful of people, who can be lobbied to efficiently regulate the information the public received daily. It was very common in a typical tribal nation to find that a dozen or fewer people control almost all forms of media.

With secrecy a daily preoccupation for governments, who routinely weighed security concerns over disclosure of covert operations, tribal systems continued to reign unchallenged by even the most liberal members of each tribe. Under the blanket of *"national security,"* governments developed extensive police powers, created sophisticated surveillance systems, amassed data on their citizens without public knowledge, and gained control over the mass media. Although it was extremely suppressive to the liberty of literature and journalism, the ruling class needed to hide information from the public for very understandable reasons. In the realm of the military, governments required room for secrecy and confidentiality to be more successful in dominating other tribes through political deception. Openness, therefore, posed as a disadvantage for each tribal nation and was avoided at all costs.

As secrecy increased, accountability naturally withered away. Additionally, limited transparency too often nurtured moral and criminal corruption, massive fraud, and undermined democratic public institutions.

The ruling class of every nation played an active role in engineering consent to maintain their power and rule over the public. They knew that they must always keep the public busy and distracted by diverting their attention to other matters such as entertainment and pleasures.

In ancient Rome, the public was distracted through plays, farces, spectacles, gladiators, strange beasts, medals and other such opiates. Rome was the epicenter of the world for several centuries and sport was one of the many things that Romans appropriated from the lands they conquered and then made their own. Rome, over the course of its history from republic to empire, to its eventual fall, assimilated the fighting sports of other nations such as Greece to produce a hyper-violent rendition of boxing and wrestling. And of course, famously, the Romans became obsessed with another type of fighting entertainment. One that made boxing, which was the *"heavy events"* of the ancient Olympics, look gentle or, at least, safer. The most beloved sport in Rome was the gladiator contest— a violent spectacle that became the main entertainment.

Roman sports may have been influenced by the cultures they conquered, but their attitude towards sports was distinctly different than that of the ancient Greeks. For the Greeks, sports games were a way for citizens to demonstrate their athleticism, determination, and prowess. In its early days, sports were practiced and played by many Romans, especially running, wrestling, and boxing, but as Rome became a mighty Empire, sports took on the form of entertainment, best left practiced by professionals. Professional fighters who entertained the elite and the masses risked their health and their lives to, ultimately, rise to a higher rung of the social ladder. Such attitude to sports became universal to all tribal nations that postdated the Roman Empire.

Describing the Romans as barbaric may seem apt, given their inclination to incorporate violence in their sports games, but the truth is that all authoritarian governments of the *Tribal Ages* loved employing violence as entertainment in their media and art. The practice of using violence as entertainment continued for several centuries after the collapse of the Roman Empire but was renovated according to the evolving morals of tribal nations from one generation to another. Instead of gladiators with swords engaged in mortal combat, a new generation of gladiators now fights using their fists and physical strength until one of them subjugate the other. They are still the same excessively violent sports of the Medieval Period, but now following modern or *"more civilized"* means.

Scientific discoveries allowed tribal cultures to design digital games that took violence to the next level, which they would've never been able to attain in real life. It enabled them to visualize violence, wickedness, crime, destruction, mayhem, evil, and vice to the public in incredible realism or fidelity. They produced video games oozing with violence that were remarkably addictive to the point that neither kids could turn them off nor their parents dared to do it for them. It became the daily ritual of most kids in a tribal culture to spend long hours playing video games riveted by a world of guns and gore, pump up on adrenaline, and eventually unwind by watching recordings of other gamers playing.

The most brutal of all are those first-person shooter games that are every bit as absorbing and nerve-racking as a real military battle simulation. In an experience replete with stunning graphics, sound effects, and atmospheric theme music, the gamer becomes the soldier. Armed to the teeth, guns raised, he stalks through an open field as leaves crunch beneath his combat boots. There is the sound of a thumping heartbeat when an enemy guard appears in the crosshairs, the soft ping of the bullet firing, a sharp inhalation of breath and a burst of dark blood as the guard falls. Every movement, every shot fired, and every victory within the game is coupled with real-life physical and neurological responses. The gamer's muscles tighten, his pulse pounds, a surge of dopamine dashes into his bloodstream, and his brain's prefrontal cortex or the pleasure center is activated roughly similar to when having sex. Most parents grew numb to their children's addiction to video games as they observed them slipping away, descending deeper and deeper into a brutal realm of visual violence, and consumed by the virtual worlds shared by millions of strangers from distinct nations. But who could blame the kids for disconnecting themselves from the real world around them to gawk at a screen? These games are deliberately designed, with the help of psychology consultants, to make players want to keep playing. Such games were wholly immersive with vast digital landscapes that unfold in eye-popping detail and involved nuanced characters that evolve from one level to the next. Such games were not exclusively played by little kids but also by grown-ups in a considerable percentage.

Mesmerized by such *"sports,"* the public conformed with its tribal nation starting at an early age and became part of a tribal culture that endorses violence and subjugation. A culture that follows Stone Age principles such *"survival of the fittest"*. Ultimately the human culture became a tribal culture that loves violence, weapons, and power. Such society is precisely what such violent games deliver, and it is one that tribalism loves because it is beneficial when the time comes to conquer the next enemy.

Other than sports and video games, manufacturing consent happened through the mass media. The primary function of mass media in any tribal nation was to mobilize public support in favor of the special interests of the ruling class that dominated the government and the economy.

The major decisions on what happens in tribal nations were always in the hands of the exclusive community of the ruling class. It was a network of major corporations, conglomerates, bankers, and investment firms that encompassed the important jobs within the nation that made all the important decisions on all levels. Such roles included the elite media that determines, selects, shapes, controls and restricts access to some information to serve the interests and agenda of the dominant class in a tribal society. Through their media networks, the ruling class shaped the public views or propagated them. Through media, the ruling class created a version of history that they were comfortable with through the daily documentation of local and global events not as they genuinely transpired but according to how they viewed them or how they would like the public to understand them.

As the elite media continued to relentlessly screen the daily articles and stories for the public to ensure that it rises to the aspiration of the ruling class, history was gradually written. Eventually, after several decades of amassing articles and reports that are all favorable to the ruling class, such content was embodied into a book format that they dubbed a *"history book."* It was a version of history conceived through decades of screening content, and one that polished the ruling class in the best image possible. Simply put, the history of every tribal nation was implicitly written by the very same characters that these history books revolve around. And due to the inescapable egocentric bias, the history books of each tribal nation always followed a natural tendency to please the ruling class and draw them into the best desirable picture.

The agenda-setting media were usually considerably huge corporations in each tribal nation. They were integrated with and sometimes owned by even more massive conglomerates that belonged to the ruling class. And so, the ruling class did not have to control the media because they, in fact, owned it.

Just like any corporation in a capitalist economy, media companies had a product, which was their audience, which they were selling it to a market, which primarily involved advertisers and the institutions that they are advertising. These advertisers could be the businesses that belonged to the ruling class or other local or global companies or just mediators between them all. Media cost a lot more than consumers could ever pay. Who picked up the check? Advertisers. What were the advertisers paying for? Audiences. What kept the media functioning was not the audience themselves but the money that poured in from advertisements. The media, therefore, was serving the advertisers and their interests but never the public. And so, the media's real customers were the advertisers and not the people, which were nothing more than a product with a price tag.

Mass media firms merely told the public what those from the ruling class needed them to know so the populace could just fall in line and consent. Under such a dysfunctional system, the only outcome that comes out of it was a picture of the world that satisfied the needs, the interests, and the perceptions of the ruling class within each tribal nation.

One of the primary purposes of tribal religions is to have the *All-Seeing Eye* and the *all-knowing big boss* effects on people to compel them to follow tribal laws by masquerading these laws as commandments from a divine power through religious indoctrination. Throughout history, no government had the power to keep its citizens under constant surveillance, which is a desirable condition that all tyrants instinctually thrive to attain. Therefore, these tyrants invented an idea that there's a mighty figure in up in the sky somewhere with an *All-Seeing Eye* that relentlessly watches everyone and continuously judging everything they do.

The public, which was mostly ignorant at the time due to the absence of mass education, actually bought the idea of the *All-Seeing Eye* and allowed such a haunting thought to thrive in their fragile minds. The religious leaders, on the other hand, did not genuinely believe what they preached, and those at the very top of the hierarchy of any religious institution knew perfectly well that their religion is nothing more than a sham to control the public. Prominent preachers knew very well that the doctrine they preached is no more than a hoax because one cannot be deeply involved in any religion to a level that allows a person to teach it without discovering the untruthfulness of the whole thing. All preachers have the necessary skills to interpret the statements in their holy books in a certain way that allows them to win an argument or a religious conversion. They excessively use analogies to convert the weak-minded into the faith. They pride themselves on developing such analogies, commonly after the religionless thinkers of their era already conceived the necessary scientific discoveries that make such analogies possible. Nonetheless, the plan behind religions worked efficiently for millennia, but eventually, intellectual people found the concept of the *All-Seeing Eye* too much to handle. The doctrine of the *All-Seeing Eye* got overwhelmingly invasive and haunting. The eye that never sleeps and is always watching everyone became unbearable. Asleep or awake, working or resting, indoors or outdoors, in the bath or kitchen or bed, defecating or eating or fornicating - no place to hide from it. You're not even alone in the few cubic centimeters inside your skull.

It became intolerable to the Western public to think that a supreme being is continuously observing every move they take and every idea they have and consistently judging them. A never-ending onslaught of judgments on anything and everything they do or experience no matter how diminutive it is. He is the judge of all judges. A tyrannical critic that judges and condemns everyone but no one else can dare to judge or criticize him. The idea that even our thoughts are not private anymore and that there's someone out there reading them and persistently violating our privacy eventually became daunting. People could not tolerate anymore the concept that their confidentiality is forever breached and there's nothing they could do to stop it.

Therefore, people stopped believing in such totalitarian religions and chose, instead, to think that a real God would not violate the human brain in such ways. They realized that the teachings of tribal faiths were mere fabrications and abominations of the divine's true nature. A truly loving God would not rot people's brains and force them into worship out of fear of the authority. A divine that is not a tyrant but a loving being, who doesn't force anything on his creations and does not intervene on Earth to regiment people's lives. A wise being who understands that life is meant to be a spontaneous process that will cease to be spontaneous if he intervenes through rulebooks or guidelines. Such minded people escaped the tyranny of the kingdoms of Europe and their oppressive tyrannical religions. They fled Europe towards the New World in what would later become the Americas in the Age of Discovery.

Unfortunately, the tyranny of Europe's politics and religions soon followed, and the emigration became an invasion, and like a plague, it annihilated the natives of the American continent. These conquering Europeans established a republic, which is a parliamentary dictatorship with periodic elections, in which a ruling class of people competes for governance through a rigged electoral system that guarantees their perpetual rule. Under such a social system, the ruling class nominates and elects itself perpetually. And so, tribalism crawled into the Americas and took over the American public through the tyrannical practices of representation in government, the delegation of power, intermediation in finances, centralization, and segregation in society – the key ingredients of tribalism.

The majority of the Founding Fathers of the United States hated monarchy as much as they hated democracy, which is why they founded a republic and not a democracy. It is worth mentioning that the majority of the Founding Fathers were slave owners and land-owning aristocrats. Their definition of a *"person"* certainly did not involve people of color or women, which were considered property at the time. Their definition of a person exclusively refers to *"the white man"* and preferably one who owns property. In fact, and from the perspective of these slave-owning white men, the more women and slaves you owned the more of a person you become because you got more property to manage as a white man. Their understanding of democracy, therefore, only involves a ruling class of privileged men fully in charge of a nation. Such a breed of racist people formed a new form of tyranny disguised under noble concepts such as freedom and democracy but delivering the opposite entirely. A militarized republic like the world has not seen before. A new model of a totalitarian empire with advanced weaponry masquerading as a beacon of hope and peace to the world. A type of nation that lurks behind misleading ideals and endorses false idols and colonial ideologies. A truly tribal and tyrannical nation-state masked as a democratic republic.

The American ruling class always struggled with safety, and it was an elusive feeling that they could never adequately sustain ever since they invaded the new continent and virtually eliminated the local population. They had a history of a very frightened country, but it was for very understandable reasons. From the very beginning, there were real threats from the people they were suppressing such as the natives, who could always fight back and reclaim what was formerly theirs. The black slaves could revolt against their masters at any moment and recover their freedom. The British or the French or the Spanish Empire could make a land grab of the territory that the Americans already colonized. And so,

American tribalists were at constant threat and never at rest or safe. For that reason, they loved guns and building them in abundance to subjugate anyone who could be a potential threat.

They witnessed beforehand how a technologically superior race could efficiently irradiate a primitive race primarily thanks to advanced weaponry. It was evident, therefore, for the first Americans that they cannot persevere as a nation unless they kept the military-industrial complex operating at full swing to be always ahead of the curve in the business of war. If they ever allowed another country to build better or mightier weapons, they risk being dominated just like they did to the natives from whom they stole the land. Therefore, the American republic surpassed all other nations in manufacturing weapons of war, and they mastered the weapons of mass destruction. Thanks to American tribalists, the world received its first nuclear bombs that were capable of wiping human life off the surface of the Earth for the very first time in humankind's history. These bombs were developed through a massive research and development undertaking during World War II called the Manhattan Project, which employed more than 130,000 people.

A few decades earlier, Japan practiced strict isolation policy that shielded the island from the rest of the world. They allowed, however, the Dutch to trade with them only through the city of Dejima, which became the single place of direct trade and exchange between Japan and the outside world. That period in Japan's history was known as the Edo period when the Japanese society was under the rule of the Tokugawa Shogunate, which was the last feudal Japanese military government. During that period, the nation wasn't at war with itself or with anyone else. It was a prosperous period, and the population increased a lot, business flourished, schools and roads were built, books were published, and literacy increased. The public studied European science from the books they bought from the Dutch, and as a result, the economic and cultural prosperity boomed.

That period in Japan's history ended when American tribalists sailed their gunboats halfway across the planet to force Japan to stop its isolation policy. Helpless against the American armada, the

Japanese ruling class was forced to sign an agreement with the United States to open up the country to additional tribal nations to visit the island anytime they please. This humiliating event was a turning point in Japan's history. It caused a chain reaction within Japan leading it to westernize its government, constitution, and military. It also prompted the Japanese tribes to copy the colonial tendencies of the Western world and planted the Japanese on a path to capture and claim neighboring territory to build a Japanese Empire of their own.

Colonialism, in short, is the practice of invading a sovereign nation to sack its natural and human resources for the benefit of the ruling class of the colonizer back home while the vulnerable local people are abused, humiliated, tortured, imprisoned, plundered, dislocated, whipped, raped or murdered. Colonization is a type of invasion that doesn't necessarily burn everything down to the ground or completely wipe the local populace out of their land to capture it and claim it as an extension of one's territorial borders. Alternatively, it momentarily spares the lives of the local population because they represent future assets as deplorable slaves who would help the colonizer in his conquest of looting and harvesting the local resources of the land. Aside from stealing the natural and human resources, colonialism robs the local culture of its identity by imposing that of the colonizer and by relentlessly Christianizing (depending on the religion of the colonizer) everything about the local population including their names. Britain, France, Germany, Portugal, Belgium, Italy and Spain pioneered the horrific practice of colonialism. *The apple does not fall far from the tree*, and likewise, the American Founding Fathers, being predominantly the offspring of English colonists, followed their fathers' colonial inclinations.

And so, Japan joined other empires in their conquest to colonize the planet. Unfortunately, they entered the team that the United States wasn't on, which was a fatal decision that would inevitably put them in a disastrous confrontation with the nation that played the most prominent part in transforming the self-enclosed Japanese island into a warmongering empire.

At 8:15 in the morning of August 6, 1945, an American B-29 bomber dropped the world's first deployed atomic bomb (called *"Little Boy"* by the Manhattan Project's directors) by parachute over the Japanese city of Hiroshima. The bomb exploded 2,000 feet (around 610 meters) above the city of Hiroshima in a powerful explosion that wiped out 90% of the city and immediately killed 80,000 people. Three days later, a second B-29 bomber dropped a much more powerful plutonium bomb, called *"Fat Man,"* on Nagasaki at 11:02 in the morning killing an estimated 40,000 people.

And while celebrations broke out across the United States and other Allied nations, hundreds of thousands of innocent Japanese citizens who survived the horrific genocide began to experience inexplicable combinations of symptoms such as high fever, dizziness, nausea, headaches, diarrhea, bloody stools, nosebleeds, and whole-body weakness. Their hair fell out in large clumps, their wounds secreted extreme amounts of pus, and their gums swelled and bled. Purple spots appeared on their bodies with signs of hemorrhaging beneath the skin. Infections ravaged their internal organs. Within a few days of the onset of symptoms, many people lost consciousness, mumbled deliriously and died in extreme pain. Others languished for weeks before either dying or slowly recovering.

In Nagasaki, newborn death rates skyrocketed in the 9 months after the bombing. Around 43% of pregnancies in which the fetus was exposed within a quarter of a mile (around 400 meters) of the hypocenter ended in spontaneous abortion, stillbirth or infant death. Young mothers giving birth in ruins did not know it yet, but even those infants who survived would face severe physical and mental disabilities. Over the next 2 to 4 months, the severe effects of the atomic bombings killed 90,000–146,000 people in Hiroshima and 39,000–80,000 people in Nagasaki. Roughly half of the deaths in each city occurred on the first day. Thousands more continued to die from the effects of burns, radiation sickness, and other injuries, compounded by illness and malnutrition, for many months afterward. It is worth mentioning that despite the terrible concentrated power of the atomic bombings and the enormous loss of life that they caused, the firebombing of Tokyo earlier in the same year by American warplanes and the destruction of numerous Japanese cities by conventional bombing had killed far more people. American warplanes were routinely destroying Japanese cities by incendiary and high-explosive bombs where nearly 100,000 people burned alive in the previous March during the firebombing of Tokyo alone. And while the atomic explosives immediately destroyed innocent lives in abundance on impact, incendiary bombs slowly burned them alive. General Curtis LeMay of the United States Air Force, who burned much of Tokyo with incendiary bombs several months before the devastation of Hiroshima, later admitted that his actions would have been considered a war crime if the U.S. had lost the war.

Few hours after this horrific mass slaughter, and in millions of American households, Americans gathered around their radios listening to Truman's statement being read over the airwaves:

> *"We are now prepared to obliterate more rapidly and completely every productive enterprise the Japanese have above ground in any city. If they do not now accept our terms, they may accept a rain of ruin from the air the like of which has never been seen on this earth." ~ Harry S. Truman, 33rd U.S. President, in a radio announcement aboard the USS Augusta few hours after the nuclear bombing of Hiroshima.*

Considering the ugliness and the expanse of such genocide you might think that there was an uproar in the United States and that the good American public revolted against their government and dismantled it to ensure that any following government will never dare to repeat such war crime ever again. After all, we are talking about the obliteration of two densely populated major civilian cities no different than New York City or Los Angeles and murdering their innocent residents including women and little children. Well, no American uproar or any significant protests or anything of the kind took place, of course. While some Americans might have felt genuinely upset for the tremendous death toll, the public mostly carried on with their lives as usual. And while the American people continued enjoying their lives watching football or baseball and eating hotdogs or burgers, those who survived the genocide in Japan had to face the horrors and the devastating aftermath of witnessing their loved ones savagely murdered. Americans' silence to the suffering of the Japanese people is a good example of the extent of how one tribal nation could completely demonize the other where the people were truly beholden to tribal principles such as *"it is them or us."*

The coverup by the mainstream media in the United States of the actual events and the aftermath of the nuclear wipeout of two densely populated Asian cities was quite remarkable and is a textbook example of the level of control that the American ruling class had on media at the time. Only after around two years of the nuclear attack that some written content started surfacing but it was very marginal including some books or articles here and there. It never got to the kind of mainstream coverage that reaches the bulk of the American people on national televisions as the case with typical sports coverage. Not only did the American ruling class maintain that its propaganda is the authentic and the correct record of events of the war for the American public, but they also forced their propaganda on the Japanese society as well. After the war, the U.S. occupied Japan for around 7 years and forced their *"democracy"* on the Japanese people through occupation as if the American public really had a democracy at the time or even understood what it means.

The Japanese were not even allowed to write books or articles about the nuclear bombings or even criticize the American government. The United States wanted to ensure that the only version of history and the course of events during the war is the one that it provided to its public. The coverup also served in easing the collective American conscience and justifying Truman's (the sitting U.S. President at the time) decision of obliterating the two densely populated cities of Hiroshima and Nagasaki. Until his death, Truman continually and repeatedly justified his decision of using nuclear bombs, inventing a fiction that he himself later came to believe. That he spoke so often to justify his actions shows how much his decision to use the nuclear bomb haunted him.

Understanding Truman's morals is best defined by his own words when he declared on the floor of the U.S. Senate the following:

> *"If we see that Germany is winning the war, we ought to help Russia; and if that Russia is winning, we ought to help Germany, and in that way let them kill as many as possible." ~ Harry S. Truman announced as a Senator in 1941.*

Following such spirit of death-mongering, Truman indeed succeeded in killing as many human beings as possible when he used the American-made nuclear bombs on Japan as *"the great finale"* following the relentless bombardment of major Japanese cities using conventional incendiary bombs, which destroyed far more lives.

The top American military leaders who fought World War II were quite clear that the atomic bomb was unnecessary, that Japan was on the verge of surrender, and that the slaughter of hundreds of thousands of civilians was immoral even by American military standards. From the perspective of an overwhelming number of U.S. military leaders, the nuclear bombing of Hiroshima and Nagasaki was not militarily decisive. Previous to the nuclear attack, American intelligence broke the Japanese codes and knew the Japanese government was trying to negotiate a surrender through Moscow. The American military had also long advised that the expected early August Russian declaration of war on Japan, along with assurances that Japan's Emperor would be allowed to stay as a powerless figurehead, would bring surrender several months before the planned U.S. invasion of Japan in November.

> *"It is my opinion that the use of this barbarous weapon at Hiroshima and Nagasaki was of no material assistance in our war against Japan. The Japanese were already defeated and ready to surrender because of the effective sea blockade and the successful bombing with conventional weapons. My own feeling was that in being the first to use it, we had adopted an ethical standard common to the barbarians of the Dark Ages. I was not*

taught to make wars in that fashion, and that wars cannot be won by destroying women and children." ~ Adm. William D. Leahy, President Truman's Chief of Staff wrote in his 1950 memoir I Was There (1949), p. 441.

What kept the Japanese public at war was primarily the stubbornness of two warmongering empires. The Japanese Emperor and his ruling class were gravely worried about their personal wellbeing if they surrendered unconditionally, which would leave them at the mercy of foreign armies. On the other hand, the American government was insisting on unconditional and complete surrender, which was a death sentence for Emperor Hirohito's ruling class and the reason why they kept the war raging even if the country entirely burned and its people slaughtered by the millions. At the time, the United States and Great Britain were already convening war crimes trials in Europe. What if they decided to put the emperor, who was believed by the Japanese public to be divine, on trial if Japan surrendered unconditionally? What if they got rid of the emperor and changed the form of government entirely? What if they forbid the Japanese public from practicing Shinto and forced Christianity on everyone as the state religion? After all, the unconditional surrender that the American ruling class was asking for meant entirely handing over the Japanese lands and public to a foreign administration. Even though the death toll of Japanese civilians was in the millions, the ruling class of Japan was not willing at all to consider giving up their traditions, their beliefs, or their way of life. For these reasons, the Allies' demands for unconditional surrender was a bitter pill to swallow for the ruling class of Japan.

The Soviet Union's unexpected entry into the war against Japan on August 8 was a greater shock to the Japanese government than the atomic bombing of Hiroshima two days earlier. Up until Russia's declaration of war on Japan, the Japanese government was hoping that the Russian government, who previously signed a nonaggression agreement with Japan, might agree to be an intermediary in negotiating a peace treaty. Japan's leadership even sent a telegram to their ambassador in Moscow, hoping to appeal to

Stalin for help. But instead of offering aid, the Soviet Foreign Minister Vyacheslav Molotov read to Japan's ambassador a declaration of war. Just one day later, the Soviet army invaded Japan-held Manchuria, which befell on the same day that the United States dropped the atomic bomb on Nagasaki. Manchuria was a vast geographic region in Northeast Asia bordering Russia and occupied by Japan at the time. Since the Japanese Empire had previously signed a peace treaty with the Soviet Union, the Imperial Japanese Army minimized its military presence in the region to defend Japan's home islands from an imminent American invasion. The once proud Kwangtung army in Manchuria, was a shell of its former self because its best units had been shifted away to defend Japan itself. Therefore, when the Soviet Army invaded Manchuria, they sliced through what had once been an elite army very swiftly and with minimum resistance.

The Soviet army later invaded Sakhalin Island (which later became a Russian territory after the war) and was preparing to invade Hokkaido, the northernmost of Japan's home islands, a few days later. The Soviet plan of attack called for an invasion of Hokkaido from the west, which was the second largest island of the Japanese Empire, before invading the rest of Japan. The Soviet declaration of war dramatically changed the calculation of how much time was left for the Japanese Empire and sealed its fate. Just a few days following the all-out Soviet war on Japan, the Japanese Empire announced its surrender on August 15 and formally signed on September 2, 1945, bringing the hostilities of World War II to a close.

Historians cited many reasons for the atomic bombing of Japan, but the majority agree that it was never to win the war against Japan because the country was already defeated and had previously started negotiating the terms of its surrender. Secretary of State James Byrnes, for instance, believed that the use of atomic weapons would help the United States more strongly dominate the postwar era and rule the world. Through the nuclear attack on Japan, Truman's government wanted to demonstrate to the world the lethality of its weapons of mass destruction as a warning to all nations that there's a new sheriff in town and he got bigger guns than everyone else. The devastating power of these bombs did not only effectively destroy two major Japanese cities and butcher their civilian population, but it also put the U.S. in a dominant position over other tribal nations and on course for postwar world domination. From that year onwards, the United States became a bullish superpower, which is not hesitant to use more nuclear weapons to decimate other nations. It set out to subjugate other tribal countries and establish an American Empire just like all other powerful tribal nations did previously. The United States emerged from the war in a position of overwhelming power. Its hegemony in the postwar world was unparalleled with plans to control the entire western hemisphere, the Far East, and the formerly colonized lands of the British Empire that the United States would take over, in particular, the crucial Middle East oil reserves. The United States sought to control as much of Eurasia as possible at the very least its core industrial regions in Western Europe and the southern European nations such as Italy and Greece, which were regarded at the time as essential for ensuring control of the Middle Eastern energy resources which passed through the Mediterranean.

The United States aimed at maintaining unquestionable power with military and economic supremacy while ensuring the limitations of any exercise of sovereignty by other nations that might interfere with its global plans. The implementation of such wartime plans prevailed and continued for several decades although the capacity in which the United States could implement them noticeably declined afterward. The American ruling class infested the world with ideological warfare and unleashed unspeakable horrors and sorrows in the name of their ideas such as their versions of capitalism and republicanism. They created a military empire like no other empire before them, and they became the world's police.

The humanity-killer that the United States plagued the Earth with, came close to fulfilling its purpose numerous times in recorded history under several U.S. presidents. *One often meets his destiny on the road he took to avoid it* and likewise, the United States came extremely close to instant destruction by nuclear weapons from the earliest days it conceived such a disastrous threat. Ironically, the frightened nation that sought to build ever more sophisticated weapons of war in the hopeless pursuit of the elusive feeling of safety immortalized its fears forever from the first moment it showed the world what its new bombs are capable of destroying. It did not take long before other nations developed their own nuclear weapons following the United States unswerving pursuit of *"self-protection."* And with that atomic race, tribal countries set humanity's fate on a game of roulette, which could have led to the instant death of every human being anywhere on the planet at any moment.

Submarine-launched ballistic missiles with nuclear warheads were capable of striking an enemy's capital within a few minutes, and therefore, tribal nations needed automated early-warning systems to detect any incoming atomic attack and allow for themselves a short time to retaliate by obliterating the enemy. These nuclear early-warning system, however, were dysfunctional and triggered several false warning alarms that could've initiated a nuclear retaliation and ended human life on this planet. On 26 September 1983, Russian automated nuclear early-warning system falsely detected an incoming missile strike from the United States sending the highest-level alert. The protocol for the Russian military, of course, was to retaliate at once with a nuclear attack of its own but the lieutenant colonel of the Soviet Air Defense Forces at the time, called Stanislav Petrov, decided to disobey the orders and did not report the warning to his superiors becoming the man who single-handedly saved the world from nuclear war.

It was indeed a miracle that humanity escaped self-destruction under tribalism, which infested the Earth like no other time in the past through the wealthiest and the most powerful empire in humankind's history - the United States of America.

The American Empire was the richest in the world with unparalleled advantages. Its industrial capacity nearly quadrupled during the World War II period while rival nations' economies were decimated. It held half of the world's wealth and possessed unmatched security along with a unique level of global dominance. The biggest fears of the American ruling class, however, were from within the nation they built and conceived by the public who had liberal views and enjoyed the freedom of speech and press. A society where the majority does not strictly follow a religion and instead practice freedom of thought and speech, cannot be easily controlled. And so, The American ruling class explored other ways to have the same impact that religious indoctrination once delivered for other empires. But what if they could accomplish the same effect through physical tools?

The initial approach to this problem was establishing local and international networks of spies, which they called *"intelligence agencies."* They spy on their own people and on other nations as well in a desperate approach to become the powerful *"all-knowing, all-seeing"* entity that all ruling classes loved. Scientific advancements and achievements created new opportunities and new toys for all tribalists everywhere to play with and dominate.

The invention of the print initially made it easier to control public opinion, and the film and the radio carried the process further. The possibility of enforcing not only complete obedience to the will of the ruling class but complete uniformity of opinion on all subjects now existed for the first time through television. The invention of the TV was as potent as a drug in programming the human mind and pacifying it into a deep state of indifference to the world and its people. Smartphones became the darling of all rulers everywhere because it enabled them to infiltrate society and create a digital image for anyone. That digital image represents among many things a person's identity, preferences, interests, social behavior, as well as his/her movement in the world thanks to the GPS on these machines tracking everyone's footsteps. Most importantly, such smartphones came with front and back cameras that invited the *All-Seeing Eye*, which every ruling class adores, into everyone's homes. Because people instinctively carry their smartphones everywhere they go and even from one room to another, the *All-Seeing Eye* can now continue watching them.

The ruling class of any nation could at any time remotely activate the microphone or the camera on any smartphone and laptop to spy on the public. They could know what the people are doing by monitoring their internet history, the books they read, the stories they follow, and so on. They could know where one spends his/her time by tracking that person's movement in the world through GPS-enabled devices or cellular towers by using multilateration, which is a surveillance technique based on the measurement of the difference in distance to two stations at known locations by broadcast signals at known times. Since they were the masters of the *languagewashing*, the ruling class justified the invasion of privacy by saying things like *"to protect our people from threats"* or *"to find criminals and terrorists"* but the real purpose was always the same - to keep the ruling class in control of the tribe.

Through technology, therefore, the ruling class became the *All-Seeing Eye* they dreamt up previously through their tribal religions. Now they can actually see what the public is doing and watch their every movement in the world to instantaneously judge them and punish wrongdoings just like their tyrannical God. And so, they became the *big brother,* who knows what's best for everyone and is the undisputed authority. Through technology, rulers everywhere became demigods.

Languagewashing: A Brain-Programming Tactic

Language is the basis of culture. It is critical to human life and essential for cultural development. Talking with each other is our principal means of communication, and when we want others to do something, we do it through talking to them. Language not only expresses our thinking and perceptions, but it also shapes them. In other words, when we think, we think in words.

Words are even more powerful because they can alter feelings. Not only we can communicate thoughts through words, but we also can communicate feelings and generate them. For example, when we say the wrong words to others, we risk offending or upsetting them. Because words can induce feelings, they can be hypnotizing, and you can seduce someone with words alone and by just talking. Language, therefore, is a very powerful tool but just like any other tool it can be hacked or abused.

When we talk, we should speak in a clear way that everyone can easily understand because the entire point of language is to have others comprehend you. Therefore, when more people can understand you when you speak, it is always a good sign that you are using the language correctly and that you have mastered this tool. Similarly, if you purposely produce speech that is hard for others to comprehend, it is a sign that you either don't fully understand what you're saying or that you have sinister intentions.

How can someone hack the language? When you start getting deeply involved with words, you realize that words are just noise. They only exist in the human mind and don't have any physical or concrete existence. In other words, the words we use are nothing more than abstract inventions, and they're not real. They are social conventions, and we agree that they represent something in the physical world, but such an agreement is always arbitrary and never genuinely accurate. For example, what do we mean when we say the word *"rock"*? Is there a particular shape for rocks, a known size, material or weight? Where does the rock begin, where does it end, and what is the correct way of measuring its length? With all these uncertainties involved, we still manage to understand each other when someone says the word rock, and we get a vague idea about what to expect. Then someone comes along and uses the same word to name other things such as a style of music and makes the word even more dubious than it already is. The word *rock* can also mean *"dance to or play rock music"* such as when they say, *"they rocked all night long."* Or it can mean *"have an atmosphere of excitement or much social activity"* such as *"the new town really rocks."* It can also be used as a verb as *"to shake or cause to shake or vibrate"* such as *"the building began to rock."* Now, and with all these new definitions, when someone says this word, he/she could mean multiple things.

Words must mean something specific, and that's the entire point of language. When the same words start having multiple meanings, they stop saying anything, the whole thing fails, and nobody will be able to understand what others really meant – this is exactly the effect that *languagewashing* delivers.

Languagewashing can be defined simply as *"a play on words."* It is a tactic that produces a language that appears to be earnest and meaningful but in fact is deceptive and meaningless. It can be accomplished by generating new definitions to existing words or rearranging words in a way that creates a new meaning. *Languagewashing* sometimes waters down the words by substituting them with others until the original meaning is almost lost. For example, instead of saying *"she lied,"* one says *"she misinformed."*

The primary purpose of *languagewashing* is to confuse listeners, mislead them, and control their reaction or opinion or perception. The ruling class used *languagewashing* excessively to generate social validation for their politics and decisions no matter how gruesome these politics got at times. They invented new definitions and meanings in their culture's dictionary and used them in their homeland propaganda, which was essential for the ruling class to manufacture public consent. They used it in an orderly fashion in the news, social media, and primarily through all types of marketing. They wouldn't say, for example, *"kill yourself for your tribe"* so bluntly because the average person could be tempted to save his skin and refuse to obey the order. New arrangements of words were invented to create an illusion and add a beautifying effect, hence, the expression *"you should sacrifice yourself for the greater good"* or *"stand for your country and defend your people"* or *"fight for the soul of your nation."* Does a nation have a soul? No one truly knows, but it is not important because the words sound beautiful and they intend to hypnotize.

And just like a man uses words to seduce and hypnotize a woman, the ruling class used *languagewashing* on their people to captivate them with elusive words to induce a particular outcome. And so, hypnotized by words, the citizens carry weapons and proceed into battle assuming they are doing something great for their nation but only to realize later that they've been fooled the whole way along. The expressions the ruling class use, of course, are hollow and abstract but they served a purpose and proved to be useful for ages whenever practiced against the public especially in the times of war. The choice of words was fundamental, and the ruling class invested genuinely in hypnotizing the human mind on a subconscious level to the point that tribal ways became the way of life and reflected the traditions and values of the public.

Languagewashing can wash away the meaning of any word and introduce a completely different definition for it and sometimes an opposite meaning, which usually exists only in the minds of the people who added the alternative explanation. In political discourse, every term typically has more than one meaning. Democracy, for example, has the following official definition which the public knows very well: *a system of government in which the citizens elect representatives to form a governing body and to make decisions on their behalf.* To the ruling class, however, democracy indicates the social order where they control all the money and power of the nation through their corporations and banks. Therefore, and in the minds of the ruling class, even if the public can elect its representatives, such system is not called a democracy unless there's an exclusive ruling class or party in control of all the money and power. When politicians set out vigorously defending democracy, they, in fact, were just protecting their interests and those of the big corporations and banks. Once they hide an idea under misleading terms or labels, it becomes very convenient for the ruling class to talk and discuss their political aims openly or defend them.

Political language is intended to make lies sound truthful and justifies the use of violence as respectfully necessary. It gives an appearance of solidity to pure absurdity. Instead of torture, politicians use *"enhanced interrogation techniques,"* which when you hear it for the first time you think it implies a positive thing considering it involves a technique which was enhanced to interrogate someone. But unfortunately, it is only hiding the same old ugly practice of torture. What you get as a result is people being tortured and others calling it a form of interrogation.

At the times of war, politicians can throw expressions at you such as *"we have the right to defend ourselves,"* which of course you'll support because it is a universal social convention that everyone has the right to defend themselves and there is no argument against such concept. However, when they use this expression, they only intend to silence any opposition and plunge the public into tribal warfare. What you get ultimately is nation-states starting wars and calling it self-defense. And suddenly the right to defend oneself means also the right to attack first and the right to eliminate the enemy entirely.

The ruling class also labeled civilian deaths as *"collateral"* which in military terminology was used for the incidental killing or wounding of non-combatants or damage to non-combatant property during an attack on a legitimate military target. As you can tell from the official definition of the word, it doesn't explicitly say if there were indeed human deaths because they could be just wounded, or it might be only property damage, which leaves you misinformed. Here the author of this definition of the word lowered the magnitude of dead innocent human beings to merely the level of property damage. So, the next time the public hears this word on the news, they'll be left confused whether indeed there were human deaths, and ultimately, they ignore the story while the army continues killing innocent civilians. Tribal news media might be generous to their public and confirm whether people admittedly died during an attack, but they always throw it at the public disguised under a new expression such as "*casualties,*" which is another *languagewashing* invention intended to hide the words *"innocent" "human" and "murder."*

The ruling class of the United States engaged themselves in so-called *"preemptive wars,"* which is a paradoxical term because one could not prevent war by starting it. Nonetheless, the United States relentlessly and continuously kept on waging wars because, by using war rhetoric, it could divert the attention of the people from its internal problems or curtail popular opposition toward the government. The official definition of *preemptive war* is a war that is commenced to repel or defeat a perceived imminent offensive or invasion or to gain a strategic advantage in an impending war shortly before that attack materializes. However, the initiation of armed conflict or being the first to break the peace when no armed attack has yet occurred, is another textbook example of brute aggression and is unquestionably illegitimate. It is like seeing a man walking down the street towards you and deciding to start punching him in the face until knocking him out completely because you felt that his looks or his walk are intimidating to you or that he might be a potential threat in the future.

When a typical tribal culture fails to find or create a real enemy to fight with, it starts waging wars on ideas or concepts. Of course, one cannot logically wage war against an idea because one cannot injure or kill an idea, but in a tribal culture where the public is mostly ignorant or unenlightened, such behavior passes as the norm or the way of life through extensive propaganda and corrupt schooling. Additionally, wars are incredibly crucial to the business of government, and a typical ruling class must always have an enemy even if it had to create one out of thin air. One of such wars against ideas was *the war on terror*.

The official definition that tribal cultures gave to terrorism is *"the unlawful use of violence and intimidation, especially against civilians, in the pursuit of political aims."* The use of the word *"unlawful"* in the definition is crucial because if a government commits acts of terrorism, which governments historically have always done because they invented the tactic, it is not considered terrorism at all. Only when the public does such acts against a ruler or a ruling class that the label *terrorism* surfaces.

In the *Tribal Ages*, the word *terrorism* was regularly occupying headlines, and many nation-states waged wars claiming *"we are at war against terrorism"* but terrorism is a tactic, and it makes no sense whatsoever to wage war against a tactic. This irrationality, however, didn't stop the citizens of these nations to commit themselves to a war that has no real enemy and no end in sight. After all, just like how the public accepted a word they didn't fully understand they also allowed the practice it generated. The idea of terrorism created a dystopia where nation-states could accuse anyone on the planet of terrorism whereby the label *"terrorist"* entitled them to strip away all his human rights and the protection of international laws downgrading him to a mere deplorable object. The universal convention of *"innocent until proven guilty,"* which was one of the most sacred principles of the international criminal justice system, did not apply anymore and the accuser became the judge and the executioner as soon as an authority figure uttered the word *terrorist.* By declaring *war on terror*, tribal governments created an eternal enemy because terror is an idea and ideas are immortal. Therefore, by defining such imaginary nemesis and knowing that through wars personal liberties can be easily upheld, they created an eternal authoritarian government that perpetually maintained excessive control over the public. The only way of convincing the public that such a fictitious enemy exists is through media and by staging events, which was precisely what all tribal nations did.

Ironically, terrorism as a tactic existed for thousands of years and was always used by the ruling class of every culture known to humankind against the public. Through *languagewashing*, however, the ruling class of wealthy nations diverted the blame by making the people think that terrorism is the product of bearded religionists that are hiding in caves with evil intentions. The truth is that the real terrorists are those in suits in the high castles (the high-rises) of all-powerful governments.

The ruling classes of the world knew that it only requires the invention of a new word and endorsement by an authority to hide the original meaning and make any harmful practice sound satisfying to the people. The human mind is extremely vulnerable and can be hacked so easily with similar tricks. Tribalists understood this perfectly because they invented the tactic and understood the system. By weakening people's minds and forcing them to live in a continuous state of propaganda-induced unreasonableness, the ruling class of every nation forced the people to accept anything, no matter how entirely illogical the speeches of governments or the news of mass media indeed were at times.

The use and corruption of language serve as a form of mind control. The primary purpose of *languagewashing* is to destroy the language and break down the positive or negative associations people have with its words. The *languagewashed* expressions are not supposed to make any sense, and that's precisely the point. By invoking a paradox, one destroys the meaning and controls thought. Through *languagewashing*, words were artfully buried by other words until the actual original meaning of a sentence was lost or hidden. Eventually, the very fabric of reality gets diluted with fiction until you're incapable of distinguishing facts from hallucinations. Through *languagewashing*, words stop having any definite meaning. It is a very dangerous and thought-eliminating tactic, and it worked for the ruling class like a charm, creating generations of cattle-like human beings that can readily be led, deceived, and conditioned. Blinded by hollow expressions and fallacies, such people were ready to destroy the only life they got in the world and throw it away so indifferently to the wolves on a whim whenever commanded.

Languagewashing produces a language that regulates thought and brain chemistry. Although renaming a condition with a misleading word, doesn't physically change it, it does, however, alter people's perception of it. Through *languagewashing*, the police don't kill anybody anymore, but they *neutralize* them. They don't steal private property anymore; they *seize* them. The army doesn't murder innocent civilians anymore, but they *bear collateral*. The ruling class members don't bribe politicians anymore, but they *lobby* them. Slaves are now called *workers* or *employees*, and masters are now called *leaders*. Capitalists don't dispose of their slave-like workers anymore, but they *lay them off*. Monopoly rights don't exist in any economy at all because the world's republics now refer to such tyrannical rights as *intellectual property*. Governments don't lie anymore, but they *misinform*. Nations don't start wars anymore, but they *engage in self-defense*. They don't torture their prisoners anymore, but they *interrogate them using enhanced techniques*. They don't kidnap citizens anymore, but they *arrest* them. State-licensed murderers in uniforms (aka soldiers) are called *freedom fighters or heroes* while the real fighters for freedom are now called *terrorists*. And there are no more invaders of any land in any human civilization anymore, but only *settlers*.

Propaganda: A Weapon of War & A Brain-Programming Tool

The dictionary definition of propaganda is information, especially of a biased or misleading nature, used to promote or publicize a political cause or point of view. The word *propaganda* comes from the Latin word *propagare*, which means to spread or to propagate. And thus, propaganda means *"that which is to be propagated."* Originally, this word was used by the Catholic Church for one of the administrations that it created in 1622, called the Congregatio de Propaganda Fide (Congregation for Propagating the Faith). This office served like the Christian system's marketing department to generate propaganda campaigns and brainwash the people into joining such a tribal religion.

Propaganda, as a tactic, starts by spreading either false information or one that is not objective to influence the audience and further an agenda. It often proceeds by presenting facts selectively to encourage a particular synthesis or perception or using loaded language to produce an emotional rather than a rational response to such information. Propagandists seek to change the way people understand an issue or situation to change their actions or expectations so that they become desirable to the interests of the propagandists. In other words, propaganda is used to influence people psychologically to alter social perceptions and behaviors.

Since the dawn of tribes, the ruling class always thrived to control and influence public opinion through whatever tools available. Propagandists used a wide range of materials and media for conveying propaganda messages, which changed throughout history as new technologies were invented, including paintings, cartoons, posters, and pamphlets. Initially, the invention of the print made the control of public opinion very easy and then the film and the radio made the process almost effortless. Primarily the invention of the television is what made it possible for a ruling class to enforce complete uniformity of perspective on all subjects for the public. The TV is essentially a brain-programming machine.

Nationwide state-sponsored propaganda is remarkably powerful and very few citizens were mentally capable of challenging or resisting its constant *brainprogramming*. Through propaganda, the ruling class of every nation in the world was able to legitimize and standardize any practice or concept they wanted. On top of the list that every citizen of a tribal culture must learn to accept is the eternal need for soldiers and military spending (aka defense spending). The necessity for these two instruments of war must be engraved in every citizen since a very young age through schooling. The media then reaffirmed such tribal propaganda through all visual or written content to ensure complete uniformity of public opinion on the indisputable necessity for armies.

No father or mother yearn to see their children in uniforms to be sent away to a warmongering institution to be systematically crippled or murdered. Therefore, tribal governments resorted to propaganda through the media and schooling to control public opinion and project a false perception that the business of armies is *"honorable"* or *"patriotic"* when it is nothing more than state-sponsored murder. Nations around the tribal world succeeded in convincing their citizens that soldiers are not state-sponsored murderers and that what they do is honorable. It is the same physical act of savagely killing people, but it seems that the magical power of wearing an official uniform somehow washes away the guilt. Such brainwashing led to unthinkable atrocities against humanity in the name of worthless flags and the racist feeling of patriotism.

The worst type of murderer is one in a uniform. In a tribal culture, when a non-uniformed murderer butchers a family, he's considered a monster and people call for his immediate execution. When a uniformed murderer does the exact same thing, he's called out as a hero by the tribe to which he belongs. A non-uniformed murderer might feel wrong or ashamed when he/she kills people, but a uniformed murderer calls it out as a civic duty and demands respect for it. A non-uniformed murderer might kill out of a conscious determination, while a uniformed murderer doesn't have a single original thought and is commanded like a mindless automaton. A non-uniformed murderer is an amateur killer whereas a uniformed murderer is trained, encouraged, disciplined, and institutionalized for years to be as effective as possible in the business of killing. A non-uniformed murderer uses basic tools to kill people like a large knife or a hunting rifle whereas a uniformed murderer uses state-of-the-art grenades, missiles, and weapons to slaughter the victims. A non-uniformed murderer might kill a handful of people before he/she is locked up or executed, but a uniformed murderer might kill hundreds or even thousands of people before happily retiring as a model citizen with a satisfying pension. Unfortunately, tribal cultures are mentally ill. Citizens of tribal cultures are brainwashed at birth to accept one kind of murderer but not the other. They are too insane and brainwashed to realize that soldiers are professional state-sponsored murderers.

Propagandists knew that people would believe anything, provided they are told it frequently and emphatically enough, and that contradicters are either silenced or smothered in slander. The first large-scale and organized propagation of state-sponsored propaganda in human history sprung by the outbreak of the First World War in 1914. All tribal nations at the time used propaganda as a weapon of war. By the time that WW1 came around, the United States was a leader in the art of movie making and commercial advertising. Such newly discovered technologies played an instrumental role in the shaping of the American mind and the altering of public opinion into a pro-war position. As a powerful weapon in war, tribal nations used propaganda to dehumanize and create hatred toward a supposed enemy, either internal or external, by creating a false image in the mind of soldiers and citizens. American propagandists achieved such an outcome by using derogatory or racist terms such as *"Jap"* and *"gook"* during World War II and the Vietnam War respectively.

During WW1, propaganda hugely succeeded in playing to people's emotions. Although radio broadcasts, motion pictures, and other mediums were popular communication tools at the time, posters were far more effective thanks to the simple fact that they could be put up anywhere, even at churches and places of business. Furthermore, most people remember pictures more clearly than words and they are influenced by what they see more intensely than by what they read. Such propaganda posters made war glamorous, depicting murderous soldiers as heroes and the slave-like workers at home as the backbone of the country. One of the primary purposes of World War II American propaganda was to encourage military enlistment, such as the famous *"I Want You!"* posters depicting Uncle Sam. Masculine images and powerful machines were also pictured in many posters to showcase America's strength and to appeal to the power-loving men of the United States. American propaganda also sought to recruit black people in the business of war through posters catered to black U.S. citizens by promoting their role in the war. Such posters featured black men working side by side with white men under the motto *"United We Win."* American wartime propaganda also appealed to women by publishing charming posters that depicted women as capable but feminine and using slogans such as *"Longing won't bring him back sooner -- get a war job!"*

Since food and other vital items are always in short supply during wars, posters communicating to the public the need to ration naturally sprouted around all American cities during WW2. Such posters also aid in silencing public complaints about the limited supply of food by emphasizing that soldiers in the fields needed supplies more than citizens at home. And so, American propagandists produced posters that read *"Waste Helps the Enemy."*

To tackle the shortage of fuel, some posters advocated carpooling and claimed that *"When You Ride Alone You Ride with Hitler."*

Ultimately, propaganda is a powerful weapon during wars, but tribal nations used it in peacetime just as intensely to continuously shape public opinion or to sell the products or services that people did not genuinely need. Although citizens of tribal cultures commonly used alternative words such as *"marketing"* or *"advertisement"* or *"ads"* or *"commercials,"* such expressions are just propaganda in disguise. And therefore by accepting propaganda under different terminologies, citizens of tribal cultures were constantly bombarded by propaganda until it became completely normal. It infested everything from movies, magazines, art, music, to the TV and the radio. Propaganda was so powerful that it would take a remarkable type of person to resist its sphere of influence for too long in a tribal culture. Unfortunately, propaganda is engineered to be extraordinary seductive to human emotions. Sooner or later everyone falls either consciously or subconsciously under the toxic spell of the surrounding propaganda propagating everywhere the eye can see.

Prosecutery: A Subjugation & Brain-Programming Tactic

Using repugnant slurs on those one wishes to condemn is one of tribalism's oldest tactics. Such behavior deserves to be properly understood because the authorities of the tribal world have historically and relentlessly used it against those they prosecuted and condemned to misery and death. First of all, it deserves a word to identify it. And since no word currently exists in the English dictionary that best describes such a terrifying practice, we took the liberty of inventing a new word for it: *Prosecutery is the act of brutally prosecuting an imagined enemy by using slurs that dehumanizes the enemy and desensitizes the prosecutor to enable a human being to legitimately condemn subconsciously and heartlessly.*

Prosecutery slurs are designed to be indefensible and leave the victims at the mercy of the authority that employs such slurs. For example, Europeans used the word *"savages"* extensively during their conquests around the world. Through this slur, horrific atrocities were mercilessly committed against the natives because

126

they stop being human when such a slur is used against them. The invading culture slurred the natives' humanity into nonexistence. The word *savages* evoked immediate condemnation in the human mind and altered its chemistry to warrant an attitude that resembles the kind directed against despicable animals such as rats or cockroaches.

The First Europeans who invaded the American continent, for example, called the natives *"redskins"* before virtually eradicating them out of their lands. By labeling the opposition with offensive words, their humanity is taken away from them which made it easier for the First Europeans to kill them without much guilt. And it also allowed for the most horrific of practices such as scalping people's heads and redeeming them for coins as a reward as it was the practice with the First Europeans against their redskins.

American colonists used the prosecutery slur *"gook"* or *"goo-goo"* to brand the people of the Philippines during the Philippine War between 1899 and 1902. The slur made it easier psychologically for American soldiers to subjugate or murder the natives who resisted the American invasion and occupation of the Philippines. Thanks to this *prosecutery* slur, American soldiers could conveniently act on their violent colonial fantasies and freely talk about how they took their delight in terrorizing and killing Filipino civilians. One American colonist famously said *"they were the first goo-goos I ever saw turn white"* in his description of the natives he was deliberately terrifying. Records also show that American colonists later adopted the label *"googooland"* to call the Philippines to insult the citizens of this beautiful country further and dehumanize them. The bitter fighting went on for more than 3 years during which the extremely racist American invaders brutally slaughtered hundreds of thousands of Filipinos. In fact, there was even a debate in the United States onto whether the citizens of the Philippines are monkeys or some other being less than human. And therefore, you could only imagine what type of monstrous fighters with which the historically racist nation of the United States plagued the gorgeous country of the Philippines at the time.

Later generations of American invaders in Asia were to pin derisive labels on the natives, like *"slopies"* for Chinese. They also used *"gooks"* on Koreans and Vietnamese because, after all, if you are a racist colonist on a mission to steal other people's lands and humiliate them, anyone who looks slightly similar to Filipinos is automatically a *gook* and deserves to be abused. Anyone who is a *gook*, thugs in American military uniform could do anything to him/her including torture, rape, and murder. We wish this is nothing more than an imaginary horror tale, but unfortunately, it was the serious reality that people of color in underdeveloped countries had to endure under Western European colonialism. And as you can imagine, no human being would or could live under such cruel occupation, which is why the Filipinos fought for their independence and liberated their country from the savageness of American tyranny.

Religiously driven *prosecutery* is the worst. And no other religions were harder on women than Abrahamic religions. Statistically speaking, women were historically more likely to resist the religious indoctrination or discover the sham of religion than men. Therefore, it is no wonder that Christian clerics traditionally called them *witches* any woman who didn't accept Jesus as her savior. It was important for the clerics back then to subjugate women and put them under constant terrorism because it is the women who primarily took care of their children, who might not be brainwashed efficiently if their mothers weren't obedient to the religion's authority. By definition, any woman who resisted Christianity is automatically a witch and deserves the worst to happen to her. The most common punishment for such rebellious women or *"witches"* was burning them alive publicly while the residents of the neighborhood took delight at watching them being devoured by flames and reduced to aches under excruciating pain.

Aside from employing *prosecutery* in the subjugation of innocent human beings, tribal cultures used it to suppress fundamental human rights such as the right for free speech and expressing one's thoughts or ideas openly without fear of retaliation by an authority.

The Catholic Church labeled its critics as *"heretics"* before torturing them and burning them alive. The church wanted to crack down on criticism, and therefore they invented the word *heresy* which made religious criticism sound like a crime in the minds of the public and those who prosecuted them. So, religious criticism became illegal and punishable by death or torture. Christianity is not the only religion, however, that illegalized religious criticism because many others did exactly the same thing including Islam and Judaism. From the perspective of Islamic authorities, if you criticize Islam or its clerics, you're an *"infidel,"* and you deserve to be murdered because you committed a crime. It is, in fact, one of the highest crimes according to the Islamic doctrine. As for the Jews, they reigned supreme starting from the late 20th century when they hijacked the world's finances and the debt-based papermoney to become an authority that can punish the rest of the world whenever needed. And so, Jews labeled all those who criticize the Jewish religion or the Jewish state as *antisemitic* before publicly shaming them and destroying their careers. *Antisemitism* in that day and age was a serious offense, and there was no reasonable defense against it. And just like the case with the *prosecutery* word *heretic,* the moment the authorities utter it against you, you're immediately condemned, and there's no possibility for appealing it.

The free speech continued to be the victim of *prosecutery* through various new labels until the collapse of tribalism. Starting from the 20th century, critics lived in a grim reality in which free speech is suppressed not by governments but by corporations. And knowing that almost every media outlet at the time was privately owned by uncountable for-profit institutions, the suppression of free speech became utterly ordinary. The major media outlets at the time used *"hate speech"* and *"fake news"* labels to crack down on free speech. Through their private media outlets, the ruling class conditioned the public into accepting these labels and prosecuting those accused by such labels.

However, there's no *hate speech* or *love speech,* but only speech. Hate and love are relative words, and their meaning differs from one person to the other. No universal authority exists that can decide what is considered hate or love. Also, anything and everything outside the realm of science is a matter of opinion. As long as it cannot be measured and quantified through scientific methods or instruments, it remains in the realm of the personal perspective or opinion. Therefore what you accept as the truth and the facts, don't necessarily apply to the next person in society because others could see or understand things differently.

Unfortunately, the public of tribal cultures was largely under the influence of the relentless conditioning from the major media outlets around them. And so, they foolishly accepted the labels of *hate speech* and *fake news* and endorsed the decision of the private media outlets in purging the accounts accused of hate speech. In other words, people allowed a handful of individuals in cartels of for-profit institutions to define what *hate speech* is and then punish them for it. It was indeed a grim justice system where the legislature, the prosecutor, and the judge are the same person. You surely wouldn't want to be brought up to this court of law, but the brainprogrammed people of tribal cultures were too indoctrinated to realize their gloomy predicament.

Through *prosecutery*, free speech was strangled in its cradle while freethinkers stood by helplessly watching as the rest of the world foolishly cheered.

The Way-Of-The-World Doctrine

In a tribal culture, the ruling class relentlessly impose their flawed and dysfunctional thinking on what they observe in nature. They use tribal terminologies such as queens or soldiers or workers or colonies on animals or insects like bees or ants to desperately cast and perpetuate a false perception of the world. They impose a colonial or tribal understanding of the natural world that aligns with their worldview. Of course, there's no such thing as queens or kings in the animal world. Such concepts are purely petty human inventions. What a tribal culture calls a *"Queen Bee"* is, in fact, a mother. What they call *"Drones"* are the brothers who mate to extend the family. The so-called *"Workers Bees"* are the sisters who cater for their family. And the so-called *"colony"* is, in fact, a biological family of sisters and brothers. The bees work together as one family driven by powerful social bonds based on love and devotion to a biological family, not based on an authoritarian hierarchical structure of government. A bee family is neither a colony nor a monarchy, but the tribal doctrine insisted that it is nonetheless. And just how nature physically enabled women to bear children while men cannot, female bees can convert the nectar and pollen of flowers into honey and store it in the sacks near their legs which the male bees physically cannot do. Due to this biological trait, female bees produce the honey while male bees mate with the mother bee to expand the family. Additionally, male bees are physically incapable of defending the family because they lack stingers, and they even naturally die immediately after mating because the penis and associated abdominal tissues are ripped from their bodies after sexual intercourse.

All bees, when they sense an attack on their home, collectively defend the family. When attacked by their archenemies (the hornets and the wasps), honeybees counterattack by swarming around the hornet and forming what scientists call a *"hot defensive bee ball"* - a move unique to their species. With hundreds of bees all vibrating their flight muscles at once, the bee ball literally cooks the hornet or the wasp to death. It is mass-suicide for the bees because they also die due to the extreme heat. This behavior of committing suicide while killing the enemy is not fully understood by scientists and can be explained in multiple ways. One explanation would be that bees act out of deep and sincere love to their family by committing suicide for the sake of protecting their biological brothers and sisters from harm. A tribal understanding of it, however, is that the *"worker"* bees' job or duty is to sacrifice their lives for the sake of the collective and that's why they must do it. A tribal culture, therefore, eliminates love entirely from their worldview and replaces it with an ugly version that revolves around duty and obedience.

By using such an explanation, a tribal culture indoctrinates its children at an early age to propagate tribal conventions such as *"a person's life belongs to the state, and he/she must sacrifice it whenever necessary and however politicians command them to."* Children, therefore, grow up thinking that the state-sponsored murderers (aka soldiers) are honorable and that armies are essential; that the military isn't a terrorist organization but a dignified and noble institution that all citizens must always support; that every nation must always have an army and that *it is the way of the world*; that everyone must never disrespect the flag or the national anthem; and that there must always be leaders and followers.

Bees are not the only animals that the ruling class exploit for their tribal propaganda, but it also includes ants, lions, and many other animals. They even shamelessly call the natural world as the *"animal kingdom."* By explaining the natural world from a tribal perspective, a tribal culture teaches its children that kingdoms and soldiers are *the way of the world* and that they should learn to accept it that way. They tell them that *it is the way of the world* and that there's nothing they could do about it because it is just the way it is on Earth or that God intended it that way. And so, children grow up thinking that the universe is indeed a monarchy and consists of rulers and workers; that there's no point in disputing that monarchy or the other forms of tribal governments are wrong because nature is designed that way or because God intended it that way.

There's no hierarchy in nature, but only love and devotion to a biological family. In every family of any animal species, there are only roles or functions and never positions or professions. Even a human family is intrinsically nonhierarchical, but unfortunately, tribal cultures were misled by their tribal religions to think otherwise. The roles played within a human family originate from a disposition of love and devotion, not from a sense of duty or obligation. Motherhood isn't a job. Fatherhood isn't a job. Brotherhood isn't a job. These roles are organic and beautiful.

There's a vast difference between jobs and natural roles. A man might willingly bow down to kiss his mother's feet out of reverence, and people might applaud him for that, but if he bows down to a master or a leader and follows his commands out of a sense of duty, then such a puny man is a deplorable slave who doesn't deserve the life given to him.

A tribal culture also exploits the spiritual world in propagating their tribal worldview. A tribal culture always manufactures and embraces religions that project a hierarchical perspective of the spiritual world. They always depict it as consisting of one or more kingly beings who rule over the world and who created humanity for the sole purpose of receiving worship or obedience in return. By projecting an authoritative or tyrannical fallacy like that, tribal cultures teach their children at a very young age that they are built to obey, and that's the only purpose of humanity. And this obedience begins at childhood towards their parents, then to the state or the tribal leaders, and ultimately to the tyrannical God who created humankind so that he can see it bowing down and worship him. And since the world is designed as an autocratic monarchy with a built-in hierarchy where a tyrannical being sits on top of its throne, a tribal culture teaches its people that tyranny *is the way of the world*. Because after all, since there's no democracy in the kingdom of heaven, why should the public accept it or practice it on Earth? It is evidently not the correct or best form of government because otherwise, God would've practiced it – this is the logic that the ruling class preaches through its clerics to indoctrinate the masses. So, they teach their citizens that even deities follow the same rule structure as the ruling classes of humanity, and the people should accept hierarchy and leadership because *it is the way of the world*.

Bribery & Corruption Are Tools Of Tribal Governments

Central bankers owned the monetary system of the planet and with that ownership came a powerful claim to anything else. They controlled the issuing and printing of all national currencies, and of course they controlled the global economy as well. The publicly elected governments or officials had no legal right to audit their central bank, which means that a central bank can print trillions of dollars while the local government is clueless. Therefore, the wealth of central bankers is unbound and untaxed and could be used to buy anything - people and governments included. But of course, they couldn't go around buying people left and right because eventually, the public would take notice and ask for justice because bribery is historically illegal. But what if bankers could make bribery legal and perfectly normal?

The banking elites used a tactic called *"lobbying,"* which is just a *languagewashed* expression disguising the word *bribery.* They borrowed the word *lobby,* which originally meant *"a room providing a space out of which one or more other rooms or corridors lead"* and they used it as a verb to mean *"seek to influence (a politician or public official) on an issue."* This *"influence"* could be anything of course, but in most cases, it is either money or intimidation. So, one says *"I'm lobbying for Mike"* but what he actually means is *"I'm bribing or bullying other people for favorable actions and decisions to Mike's interests."* Now that they have a *languagewashed* word for it, the next step in the art of trickery is to follow the legal process and present the practice of bribery disguised under its new word as a law. This new law is simple to understand, and one can explain it in a single sentence: A middleman (called lobbyist) must make the transaction (or produce the influence). So, instead of heading straight to the person you want to bribe and hand him the cash, you hire someone to do that for you to keep it legal.

Bribery is the offering, promising, giving, requesting, or accepting of financial or other advantages with the intention to induce or reward an action. Conventional wisdom says bribery corrupts everything and those who accept bribes are corrupt and would corrupt any administration they run and render it dysfunctional. In politics, corruption undermines democracy and good governance by flouting or even subverting formal processes. Corruption in elections and the legislature reduces accountability and distorts representation in policy-making. Corruption in the judiciary compromises the rule of law and corruption in public administration results in the inefficient provision of services. It violates a fundamental principle of republicanism regarding the centrality of civic virtue. However, since the new version of the word *bribery* is not very clear and could mean other things, the public simply accepted the word and endorsed the practice behind the word. They accepted it because they're bedazzled by a new word which they didn't fully understand and one that could have several interpretations. And so, bribery became legal and corruption became a fact of life.

Through lobbying, a ruling class achieves its goals, and it was the primary tactic of choice in the age of central banks and their fraud of papermoney printing. The alternative was using power to influence those with no price tag, but this rarely happened because a reasonable person would understand that by one way or another the ruling class always gets what it wants. The early Founding Fathers of the United States warned long ago concerning those who represent the American people that *"few men have the virtue to withstand the highest bidder."* Little they knew that a few decades later these bidders will be licensed, and bribery will become a business on the continent that the first Americans conquered.

War Is Essential For The Business Of Government

Ironically, the public maintained a foolish belief that they must always have a ruling class to protect them from war while in fact, the only reason why they had such bloody wars is due to the existence of the ruling class and its governments. Wars would never exist without a ruling class because the latter manufactures it. The relationship between the two is causal because one is the result of the existence of the other like fire and smoke. Similarly, war needs hierarchy, central command, delegation, and representation. Without these ingredients, there wouldn't be a ruling class, nor there would be wars in the world.

Ever since tribalism infested the human civilization, the planet was in a constant and never-ending state of war. War hysteria was universal and continuous in all territories, and such acts as raping, looting, the slaughtering of children, the reduction of whole populations to slavery, and the torture of prisoners were the standards of war. Even monstrous acts such as boiling or burning or burying innocent civilians alive were looked upon as common or sometimes praiseworthy if one's own side committed them.

Although the moral standards did evolve from one century to another, when the drums of war start echoing, all morals were conveniently forgotten, and such atrocities continued to happen all through the 21st century. Militant technological advancements, however, made the slaughter of innocent human beings far more convenient than ever before. Airplanes could drop incendiary bombs, and while the pilot is conveniently up in the air at a safe distance, the residents of entire city blocks were burned alive. Other airplanes would drop barrel bombs to level city buildings to the ground while the residents are asleep in their beds, and those who survive such blasts gradually suffocate to death in the wreckage under which they were buried. Ultimately, burning or burying innocent people alive or torturing them to death never really stopped no matter how civilized nations pretended to be.

War ensures the continuation of control and power of the ruling class over the people because during wars people naturally unite, and they focus on their common enemy while ignoring how unhappy they are with their own lives. They pay less attention to their living conditions and accept such predicament because they're too busy striving to say alive. War urges people to sacrifice, pledge, and devote themselves to the country and consequently to the government. As a result, this reality keeps people under control and in check - this is precisely why governments willingly create war and deliberately prolong it. While the country is fighting, people within the country are on the same side, and hence the ruling class enjoys uncontested power because rarely people question their government while at war. The public's reaction to war is one that the ruling class admires and thrives on maintaining. People commonly cause less trouble for the ruling class during conflicts, and they can get in line promptly and off to combat to be sacrificed routinely.

During wars, the *guilt-cannon law* can be used excessively on everyone by anyone. It is a mind control tactic devotedly embraced by Christianity because such religious system prioritized inducing guilt in the hearts of all its followers as a tactic for social control. The *guilt-cannon law* insists that you must never raise a personal concern or complaint about any aspect of your life or society because there's someone else out there who is less fortunate than you are or is having a rougher time. Although the less fortunate person has nothing to do with the one raising the concern, it does not matter because the primary purpose of this law is the complete suppression of any complaint or concern by comparing someone to someone else to provoke guilt. And since there will always be someone less fortunate than you because life by design is a game of chance which yields success or failure, you can never escape the *guilt-cannon*, and it is forever pointing its muzzle at you relentlessly waiting for the next complaint to pop up. It is called the *guilt-cannon law* because it completely obliterates the other person's complaints by barraging the person with self-guilt.

For example, if a young boy complains to his mother that he desires a better meal, she'll tell him that other children in Africa are starving to death and that he should be lucky that he is not one of them and at least has something to eat. On the other hand, and in the same way, the mother complains to her husband about the low income of the household, which is preventing her from buying new furniture, but her husband immediately silences her down by saying that they both should be grateful that they at least have a job because there are a lot of unemployed citizens in the country. Then the husband complains to someone else about the degradation of the standards of living in his society but is immediately hushed by his own community or by politicians by reminding him that their nation is currently at war and that their soldiers are having a rougher time and are sacrificing their lives for him and everyone else. Ultimately, and in the same fashion, the needs or concerns of the entire population of a nation are suppressed through the *guilt-cannon law.*

Ever since the industrial revolution, tribal governments had no reason whatsoever to fight about because every country could satisfy its needs internally and prosper. The establishment of self-contained economies, in which production and consumption were geared to one another, left no cause for imperial nations to continue their scramble for markets because such issues as raw materials and cheap labor could be solved for through trade. It became embarrassingly less expensive for two tribal nations to simply trade the raw materials or products that they needed from one another instead of unleashing an incomparably costly war to take such elements by force. Wars that surfaced during that time were not fought for greed but for shallow ideological principles and out of fear between tribal governments. Most importantly, such conflicts were waged to maintain control over the public, restrict its standards of living as much as possible, limit personal liberties, establish an oppressive police state and sustain suffocating espionage. The consciousness of being at war, and therefore in danger, makes the handing-over of all power to a small caste of society seem the natural, unavoidable condition of survival. And therefore, the public subconsciously surrenders its liberties to its rulers for security.

Technology solved the problem of hunger and poverty and eliminated the need for a working-class because machines can now do all the labor and elevate everyone's standards of living. It is not of the best interests of the ruling class, of course, to let that happen because they need to maintain their rule over the public and protect their privileges. For if everyone enjoyed leisure and security, the vast mass of human beings who were usually occupied by poverty would become literate and would learn to think for themselves and would sooner or later realize that the privileged minority had no function and would abolish it. After all, hierarchical society is only possible through poverty and ignorance. All-around increase in wealth, therefore, can bring about the destruction of the hierarchical society and can defeat the ruling class. The most effective way of maintaining poverty and ignorance in the world was by continuous warfare and arms race. Governments everywhere understood this excellently and, therefore, deliberately chose not to put technology in the service of humanity but, instead, redirected the approach to technology from addressing social issues to designing horrific instruments of wars. They employed technology in the service of producing terrors and suffering instead of convenience and wealth.

As a result, all the money and brainpower were concentrated in military use to manufacture machines that can kill faster and in abundance, destroy cities or level their buildings down to the ground, and create diseases that bring entire nations down to their knees. It wasn't uncommon at all in tribal cultures to find that the military–industrial complex developed most of the technology decades before it was ever employed in public use. It wasn't uncommon either to hear occasionally on the news of breaking stories about new outbreaks each more lethal and widespread than the other. Ebola, SARS, HIV/AIDS, the Zika virus and new pathogens of influenza are all deliberate lab-made inventions by tribal nations as part of global biological warfare against the populace of other countries to keep Earth's population in check, and to keep the public in need of governments for protection against such horrors. Citizens of tribal cultures foolishly accepted the propaganda that other animals such as chimpanzees or gorillas or bats are to be blamed for such ailment, but it never occurred to them that their own governments were relentlessly manufacturing, enhancing, intensifying and reproducing such horrific viral diseases for social and population control.

The wealthy nation must be in a constant state of war to keep an adequate portion of their population in poverty or occupied with never-ending wars, while underdeveloped countries must continuously suffer being a playground to such conflicts for all-powerful governments. Poor territories must always be test fields for plagues of all sorts of viral viruses and sickness while at the same time meddled with proxy wars that are conveniently orchestrated from halfway across the planet.

It never occurs to the average citizens of all-powerful tribal nations, that their rulers are the ones responsible for their predicament and the sufferings of billions of innocent people around the globe. That there is no real evil in the world, but it was all manufactured by rulers to control their people and maintain the ruling class for as long as possible and with as much human sacrifice as needed. Most importantly, the average person in a tribal culture never realized that poverty and wars are unnatural and undoubtedly impossible if there were no governments on the planet.

Distribia's Movement Begins

Throughout the lifespan of tribalism, very few people indeed understood its nature or became aware of it. Tribalism infested the planet with its corrupt ways, and those who were aware of it couldn't do anything about it because there were very few alternatives on the one hand and because the ruling classes of the world were too big to fail. Their influence became so intense that they would silence any whispers conspiring against them long before they could reach anywhere.

Tribalism poisoned the way of life. It perpetuated in society through the byproducts it generated among tribes such as fear, distrust, hatred, racism (or nationalism as tribal cultures dubbed it through *languagewashing*), and bigotry. The key to entirely abolishing tribalism is to eliminate representation, centralization, intermediation, segregation, and delegation of authority from the human society. These concepts created tribalism, and they always were the antidote. A tribe without representatives and delegates is no tribe at all because it is an institution that requires structure and central command. When people could accomplish a nonhierarchical society that has no central leadership or representatives, humanity could finally be free and live in a free civilization. Representative democracy, republicanism, communism, capitalism, socialism, monarchies and similar tribal concepts have all failed and were all inherently flawed because of two main reasons: representation and consolidation of authority or decision-making in the hands of the few.

Back then, unlike today, people's options were limited. They were forced to trust their rulers with decision-making on behalf of the majority due to the way of life at the time and for the most part because they did not have any other alternative. However, tribalism's dominance over the human society was only a matter of time because the same technology that enabled rulers to become demigods would later become their downfall and liberate the public they enslaved for thousands of years. The rise of *distribia* was inevitable and came as a consequence of millennia of human enslavement.

Since the birth of civilization, tyrannical rulers plagued humankind driven by an insatiable appetite for power. Such rulers mastered the art of controlling the public and inventing weapons that poisoned the good Earth and rotted people's minds through militarized religions and tribal ideologies. The public fell victims to tribalism. Unable to mount any form of resistance due to the threat of force wielded by those in power, they learned to accept what they couldn't change. It was, therefore, the public themselves who permitted and brought about their own enslavement. They acted against their own best interest and consented to their slavery out of fear of the authority. If, however, they ceased to submit, they would put an end to their servitude.

Although all governments including the most tyrannical ones could not rule without the general support of the populace, fear of torture and capital punishment kept away the threats of uprisings. If enough people refused to obey such rulers and stopped surrendering their hard-earned wealth, their oppressors would become undone. In the same way leaves would wither and die if the tree rejects the nourishment they need, humankind could cast off its ruling class at any moment. Fear alone, however, wasn't the only reason behind the public's voluntary servitude.

Wild wolves, although closely related to domesticated dogs, do not show the same tractability as dogs in living alongside humans, and much more work was needed to obtain the same amount of reliability. To make wolves docile and abandon their instinctual need for freedom, it took several generations of inbreeding to produce the kind of wolves that we know today as dogs. Generations after generations of selective breeding, these wolves lost their intrinsic need to be free and instead were conditioned to live in the human society relying on a master for food and shelter. They, therefore, are now capable of being readily led, taught, or controlled. This adaptation, however, was never really for the sake of this type of animal because it left it at the mercy of humans and was continually abused, tortured and in some cultures farmed for its meat. Humanity destroyed such wolf strain and dwarfed it into a type of animal that nature through its ways would never have evolved. We are not so different from *"man's best friend,"* in the way our children learn to adapt to the social norms we teach them. While our early ancestors would never bow to a ruler or trade their freedom for anything, human beings learned after millennia of subjugation to surrender their liberties to a ruler. They formed a tendency to become habituated to the social and political conditions they inherited from their elders. They learned to accept a master.

It became unthinkable to talk about a nation without a central government or a society without a leader. Just like how wolves became pets, the human society dwarfed into cattle-like human beings that are conditioned to follow. Just how a domesticated dog never knows how it feels to roam the forests unbounded or experience the thrill of chasing and hunting its food, the public accepted its servitude to rulers as if it was natural.

Mass submission even to the most oppressive regimes had always been a voluntary servitude, which was always based on popular consent. Although breaking the chains could be accomplished violently through bloody revolutions, it is never the right way. There's absolutely no need for fighting or igniting a violent revolution to overturn tyrannical forms for rule. Just how *one does not cure a disease by spreading it around*, one can never resolve violence with more violence. The Russian revolution, for example, merely replaced one tyrant with another. Stalin's takeover of the

Soviet Union and his exploitation of the centralized government showed that he was beholden to tribalism just like his predecessor. This was in direct contradiction to the expected results of the Russian Revolution. These kinds of revolutions always fail because they only replace one ruler with another and in so doing keeping the institution of tribalism intact. The system is the real master, not the puppets that feed into it.

Getting rid of a ruling class through violence is entirely unnecessary, and the public can simply free themselves from the tyranny of the ruling class without ever needing to point any weapon at anyone. If the people, however, become hostile and use violence, it will only rot their brains and risk creating additional tribal rulers among themselves. *"The ends justify the means"* is a tribal convention that has no truth in it whatsoever. Consequentialism, which holds that the consequences of one's conduct are the ultimate basis for any judgment about the rightness or wrongness of that conduct, is a ruthless tribal theory that was used by the ruling class for thousands of years to justify and legitimize all their horrific deeds. Such fallacious idea is a natural and typical byproduct of tribalism, which ceaselessly propagates utterly brutal concepts to sustain a cruel and unenlightened culture.

How can the public free themselves from tribalism at any moment? Throughout the history of humankind, mass submission to the ruling class in any territory was always a voluntary servitude and based on the consent of the populace. If the public refuses to consent, the system falters. Withdrawing consent is practiced merely by saying *"No!"* or in other words, it is simply *a decision not to perform any more*. Refusing consent does not require anyone to do anything or perform any action whatsoever, but rather, it is completely the opposite – it simply means to *stop doing anything* for a ruling class.

There is no need for fighting to overcome rulers and their ruling class because they're automatically defeated when the public decides to give them nothing. There is no need to go down the streets and protest or collide with law enforcement and risk injury. No need to follow any path that has the potential of putting someone in harm's way. Absolutely no need to go anywhere or do anything.

Just sit back and refuse to obey. Refuse to pay them the income taxes they need to wage their tribal wars and fund their central banks. Refuse to vote for any additional rulers and disrupt the *illusion of democracy* in the world forever. And so, *distribia* was a peaceful movement starting from its birth, and it always follows the *path of least resistance.* It is the natural and inevitable nemesis of tribalism but the kind that does not want to fight or do anything at all.

The best way of describing *distribia's* philosophy is by analogy with water. Water never uses any force to accomplish anything or to go anywhere, and it just flows using nothing more than its own weight. Water has no intentions of going anywhere, and when external forces act on it such as gravity, it solely overcomes them by following the path of least resistance and only settling down when it reaches that *relaxed state,* where it is not disturbed by outside forces. Water does not ignore these forces and is always willing to overcome outside powers because it continuously thrives to be in a relaxed state and only settles down when these forces are gone. Water does not force its will on outside forces but simply wants to be at rest.

When water reaches obstacles along its way, it overcomes them by bending around them until eventually rising above these obstacles. Water, therefore, shows humility against challenges by taking the relaxed approach until finally overcoming them. It does not challenge the barriers or subjugate them. Just like water, *distribia* is a kind of movement that always follows the path of least resistance and humbly rises above challenges, not by directly challenging them but by overcoming them through only taking the relaxed way to be at peace. *Distribia*, as a global social system, is the liberation from the following tyrannical concepts:

- ➢ Representation or to give away your voice to someone else or to allow someone else to be your voice so to speak on your behalf.
- ➢ Delegation or accepting a hierarchy of authority or giving away your personal authority to someone else or empowering a person to act on your behalf.

- ➢ Intermediation or having middlemen between two sides of any transaction of any kind.
- ➢ Centralization or following a central structure in designing any system or social convention.
- ➢ Segregation or zoning.

These principles are nothing more than the opposites of tribalism's laws because *distribia*, in fact, is the opposite of tribalism. Like two faces of the same coin or like good and evil, one cannot exist without the other. They are both two sides of the same mother-of-all-systems, the system of systems, the system maker, and the main ingredient in the recipe that propagates all human conventions.

Blockchain: A Cure From Middlemen & Representatives

Distribia's solution to representation and middlemen came in the form of technology that has distribution, trust and anti-intermediaries built into it. It is called the blockchain, and it was the underlying technology of a cryptocurrency called Bitcoin. This technology was conceived by unknowns with the desire to liberate humanity from the tyranny of bankers and middlemen.

Bitcoin is the first digital currency in which encryption techniques are used to regulate the generation of units of currency and verify the transfer of funds, operating independently of a central bank. The bitcoin network is peer-to-peer, and transactions take place between users directly, without an intermediary. These transactions are verified by network nodes using cryptography and recorded in a public distributed ledger called a blockchain.

The blockchain is a distributed database. To achieve independent verification of the chain of ownership of any and every bitcoin amount, each peer in bitcoin's network stores its own copy of the blockchain. Approximately 6 times per hour, a new group of accepted transactions, a block, is created, added to the blockchain, and quickly published to all nodes. This allows bitcoin's software to determine when a bitcoin amount has been spent, which is necessary to prevent double spending in an environment without central oversight.

Double spending is the risk that a digital currency can be spent twice. It was a problem unique to digital currencies because digital information can be reproduced relatively easily. Physical currencies did not have this issue because they cannot be easily replicated, and the parties involved in a transaction can immediately verify the bona fides of the physical currency. With digital currency, there was a risk that the holder could make a copy of the digital token and send it to a merchant or another party while retaining the original. This was a concern initially with Bitcoin since it is a decentralized currency with no central agency to verify that it is spent only once. However, Bitcoin had a mechanism based on transaction logs to verify the authenticity of each transaction and prevent double counting.

Bitcoin's engineers stroke the ruling class where it hurts the most: their pockets. And so, it was a matter of life and death for these early *distribians* to hide their identity because history has shown repeatedly that anyone who challenges the ruling class can be crushed so easily. As the case for mostly all early true *distribians*, their focus was on sharing their solutions with the world to fix it rather than monetize and get credit for it as the case had always been in capitalist economies. Bitcoin's engineers wanted to live long enough to witness the glamorous day the totalitarian power of central bankers crumble along with their dysfunctional social systems and rigged economy.

The Peer-To-Peer Legislature Was Born

There's a direct relationship between public attitudes and public policy. In a tribal culture, most of the population had no way of influencing policy, and they might as well be in some other nation because their opinions did not matter within their own country and they were incapable of participating in formulating their own laws. Such knowledge was familiar to the population of every nation, and they invariably understood that some alien power was in control of their country that they have nothing to do with it and are helpless against it. Such reality propagated a population that is continuously angry, frustrated, and desperate. A type of society that hates institutions and does not act constructively to fix their nation and restore control but instead responds by mobilizing activism in very self-destructive directions. The public's response took the form of unfocused anger where one individual attacks another or orchestrates attacks on vulnerable innocent targets. A reality where the people are incapable of influencing national decisions is corrosive to social relations, but that's precisely the outcome that tribalism as a system thrives to achieve. To make people hate and fear one another, so the overall population remains weak and easily controlled or managed. To look out only for themselves and not care much about anyone else so the public can never unite as one team and have the power to fight back or stand against tribal institutions and systems.

What the ruling class could never stop, however, were innovation and progress because such things always prevail in the end and they can never be contained for too long. Inspired by the blockchain's ability of solving the double-spending problem without requiring a trusted authority, a group of American university students designed *Unipublic* to cut off the middlemen (politicians) and allow citizens of the world to rule themselves independently. Today's web is a cryptography-internet, which is peer-to-peer and has no Internet Service Provider (ISP), and it doesn't require traditional internet infrastructure. *Unipublic* is an opensource software on this web, and it allows everyone anywhere in the world to act as a legislature and write or vote on the laws they wish to see in the world. *Unipublic* is a distributed database recording petitions, laws, and votes in a peer-to-peer network of people who act as independent legislatures for humanity. Anyone at *Unipublic* can participate in writing laws of any kind and vote on them. *Unipublic* produces social contracts that represent the laws of humanity, called *smartcontracts*, which self-execute social contracts automatically and immediately without relying on intermediaries or an authority. For example, littering is illegal, and violators are fined 10$ when caught. This law is digitally embedded in all public cameras as software that continuously monitors the streets for violations to automatically fine violators and implement the law. Through *Unipublic*, *smartcontracts* become systems that are part of bigger systems. These *smartcontracts* begin as proposals and only become legally binding social contracts though voting, which is forever open and in real-time.

Instead of consolidating decision-making in the hands of rulers or governments as it used to be with tribal governments, *Unipublic* grants the authority of legislation to all humanity everywhere through these online social contracts, which represent the laws of humanity. And so, a global legislature was born from this model where everyone can contribute and write or elect the laws they wish to see in the world. Through the concept of *smartcontracts*, people finally have the power to represent themselves without the need to designate one or more individuals to speak or act on their behalf.

Since *smartcontracts* are not written by an authority as was the case under tribalism, they can be better described as social conventions because it is the society that authors them. They are the things we agree upon as a community. The word *convention* comes from the Latin word *convenire,* which means to come together. We come together in agreement about the measures we use in our daily lives such as the kilogram or the length that we define as a meter, and how many centimeters it should contain. By agreeing on these things, we can order our lives, and arrange our everyday interactions. *Unipublic*, therefore, is a social institution and *smartcontracts* are the guardians of that institution.

Smartcontracts are the agreements we (the people) make about money, language, and as well as our values. And while some social conventions such as the language continues mostly unchanged, others change regularly from one generation to another. If, for example, the public comes to an agreement that killing animals for their meat is unacceptable anymore, they can define this social convention in writing and vote on it to become a law for humanity. The next generation that comes after might not agree with such social convention and can, therefore, overturn it or make up their own version.

Through *smartcontracts*, *Unipublic* became a global peer-to-peer online legislative body that doesn't exist physically in a designated building or territory but is accessible by all humanity everywhere through the web. Initially, the enrollment process to *Unipublic* was open to everyone through an app on IOS and Android devices that anyone in any country could download. As a standard, the enrollment process involved identity verification using biometrics that included fingerprint, face and iris authentication. And the app only worked on smartphones that came with built-in scanners that can capture and validate these biometrics. The process also involved uploading a front and back picture of a national ID, passport or diver license. Once the user provides all the data, his identity is forever secured in *Unipublic's* database.

Everyone can write and vote on laws in *Unipublic*. However, votes on particular topics are uninfluential (not counted in the consensus) unless the person voting is certified in the matter. To have influential votes, the process in its infancy required that members show their certificates from the universities or institutes they graduated from to prove their knowledge in specific topics. Initially, people were asked to upload their certification paperwork from the app where it would be later validated through an 83% consensus vote of existing certified members of *Unipublic* within the same field of study. Eventually however, academic validation became automatic through a new online universal education system (called academia) that is public and accessible to everyone through the web.

A second innovation proceeded shortly after the conception of the peer-to-peer legislature in the form of a distributed artificial intelligence coupled with virtual imaging technology to secure people's identities (or e-identities) on the web. This decentralized technology is called *Ve*. A unique and utterly independent *Ve* is assigned to every human being typically at birth to be his/her personal AI assistant and the operating system for all the electronic devices that he/she will ever own or use in the future. Every *Ve*, although it shares some basic core programming with others of its kind, is entirely independent and acts individually from another *Ve*. In the same way that every human being is unique and separate from another human but still share basic human traits, every *Ve* is unique and independent from the other but share common features.

Thanks to *Ve*, laws are no longer defined by words, which is a very primitive way of explaining the rules relative to the techniques we got today in *distribia*. Laying down the rules by explaining them in words was historically a defective practice because all languages cannot be trusted, and people could always discover ways to interpret or elaborate on the definitions or the wording used in any text of any law. It was the norm, therefore, for the judges in some tribal cultures to explain the constitution as they understood it and consequently rendering the judiciary system dysfunctional. Society's laws are now digital and are overseen and enforced by every *Ve* free of any human involvement. Today, regulations are explained to every *Ve* in video or audio or animation form that depicts the behavior that is illegalized or prohibited. For example, littering is against the law, and the code is defined to every *Ve* by a video or animation that shows the action. A *Ve* then analyzes the digital content, and if a human being duplicates the behavior exhibited in the material, it understands that this someone has violated the law and that it should issue a ticket. Therefore, a violator is identified by his very own *Ve* or by other people's *Ve*.

Depending on the topic, laws can be relatively easy or very difficult to elect. The voting process at *Unipublic* follows the protocol of the *socialscore*, which is the social contract that regulates all aspects of the voting process, rating, and reviewing any content online. S*ocialscore* is the universal standard for rating and voting on anything and everything in *distribia's* society.

Unipublic consists of several communities that anyone can join through academia. Each of these communities involve a group of people with expertise in specific topics of knowledge. The only community in *Unipublic* that doesn't require academic certification is called *"the public"*, which everyone is part of just for being human. The other communities always relate to a field or study and include experts who participate in the system on specific topics such as anthropology, archaeology, astronomy, linguistics, sociology, geography, psychology, technology, and every other field of science or knowledge. As more scientific discoveries emerge, humanity creates more specialized communities at *Unipublic* to govern the laws of these new scientific findings. Adding new communities in *Unipublic* happens when the public (which includes every living person) votes 83% positively in favor of the proposal. The average person, for example, cannot vote on the laws of geography because he's not certified in that field and does not have the knowledge necessary to produce rational judgment on such issues. Same goes for astronomy and other scientific areas.

However, the laws that directly affect or regiment the lives of people such as economics and judicature are accessible to the public.

Although every human being is part of the public community, not everyone in that community is part of other communities as well. Joining other communities in *Unipublic* is possible only through academia and people can be part of several or all communities at *Unipublic* at once if they want to and if they could achieve it through academia. Other examples of *Unipublic's* communities include Physics, Chemistry, Ecology, Oceanography, Geology, Meteorology, Zoology, Human Biology, Botany, and all other fields of science. Humanity uses these experts in their fields to decide on behalf of all humankind the proper laws that govern these domains of life. The average person who hasn't studied Geology, for example, isn't qualified to have an active vote on geology issues and cannot, therefore, make decisions or write laws in that respect. Instead, Humanity trusts the judgment of the geology community at *Unipublic* to draft and vote on proposals in their field of expertise.

The public (which basically involves everyone as explained earlier) can actively vote and petition for the laws of economy, the basic protocols of *Ve*, and the laws of society such as how people must behave in society and what is legal or illegal. Such issues are part of what is known as *"basic rights"* because they directly affect the people's way of life and everyone at *Unipublic* must be able to draft these rules and actively vote on them.

Socialscore: A Universal Voting & Rating System

There's only one rating or voting system in *distribia's* nonauthoritarian society, and it's called the *socialscore*. It is basically a social contract used for voting, giving opinions, and rating products or services. There are only three choices in this voting/rating system:

- ➢ An upwards thumb called upvote and represents approval
- ➢ A sideways thumb called sidevote and represents neutrality (neither with nor against)
- ➢ A downwards thumb called downvote and represents disapproval

Additionally, there are three types of votes in this system: Active, Inactive, and Expired.

Active votes are those produced by people qualified in the topic of the proposal/referendum/survey and the qualification is always based on academic certification. In other words, when someone has an academic certification that relates to the topic of the vote, that person's vote will count in the consensus and can influence the outcome.

Inactive votes are those produced by people who don't have academic certification that relates to the topic of the election. Inactive votes are considered opinions and are not counted in the consensus of the referendum/proposal/survey. For example, a certified geologist can vote effectively on geological issues because he got the knowledge required and proved that expertise through graduation with a degree in geology. So, he's qualified to have an influential vote in any referendum/survey/law concerning geology. Everyone else outside the geology community doesn't qualify for an influential vote, but they can still give their opinions nonetheless, and such votes would be systematically recorded without being instrumental in the consensus.

Expired votes belong to those who passed away. When people die, all their votes or opinions through the *socialscore* become uninfluential and expire. Although the record of the votes remains, they become ineffective in the bipolar consensus. This policy is in place to prevent previous generations from forcing their will on new generations. Times change and so do the social norms and the ways of life, which is why it is irrational for modern society to live in the same way it worked for people a thousand years ago. That's why the decisions of past generations can be revoked, and their opinions challenged by new generations so that the cycle of social progress can continue as humanity continues to thrive. From that sense, all votes of the people who die today automatically expire with them and are removed from the live-stream consensus to liberate new generations from living by the opinions of those who passed away. In other words, to eliminate dogma from *distribia's* society. There's no age restriction for when a person can vote, and it is technically available to everyone the moment they're born.

Socialscore's outcome is determined by consensus, which is always 83% (called the majority vote) of the active votes' population. If the upvotes reach 83%, the proposal is validated and officially becomes a law for humanity. Alternatively, if the downvotes reach 83%, the law is overturned automatically. The consensus is dubbed as *"bipolar"* because a positive vote (upvotes) percentage of 83% validates a law, which can only be invalidated by a negative vote (downvotes) percentage of 83%.

As mentioned earlier, there are many communities at *Unipublic*, but every human belongs the public community. As a fail policy, if the downvotes reach 83% collectively across all communities together with the public community, they can overturn any law. This consensus strategy is designed to prevent a minority or one community at *Unipublic* from producing unfair or unfavorable laws to the public, which represents the entire human population.

Social laws, such as what should be legal or illegal, are the hardest to elect because voting on these issues involves everyone and doesn't require certification. Convincing the entire human population to legalize/illegalize something in society is a daunting task and takes a very long time. A person must present a perfect case to convince 83% of the human population to vote in his/her law's favor. Making social laws harder to come by was intentional at *Unipublic* because having more regulations equates to enjoying less freedom. Scientific laws on the other hand are much easier to come by because active votes involve a much smaller community of professors who are certified in a specific topic. They can get their scientific laws such as the laws of physics easily passed through internal voting within their community's population based on the 83% consensus.

The instance any contract reaches upvotes consensus, it becomes the law of humanity and instantly becomes effective. *Ve* immediately enforces this new law and notifies everyone. For this newly elected law to be overthrown, downvotes must reach 83% within the community that the vote involves or alternatively by the public. Consequently, the sway of votes on any referendum or *smartcontract* is in a constant motion moving back and forth between 83% upvotes and downvotes consensus that would either elect or overturn the *smartcontract*.

Socialscore is a *smartcontract*, and like any other *smartcontract,* it can be modified or overturned if humanity decided. The public can reverse the entire social contract or just amend it by changing the consensus percentage for example. The early voters that elected this social contract decided that a 50% consensus for electing laws represents division, which means that the people are neither with nor against the proposal. If passed, that law can create separation in society resulting in more harm than good. An 83% consensus, on the other hand, represents the majority and reflects confident approval by the human population that they are ready to take that action or put that law into effect.

Socialscore comes with a start date for every referendum or *smartcontract* but there's never an end date. It is one of *Socialscore's* protocols and is in place to acknowledge that the opinions of people are never constant and change with time. To keep up with the times, people can change their vote on any referendum or law any time they want, and their votes are always recorded in real-time. To guarantee an evolving society, the no-end-date policy on *smartcontracts* works in tandem with the votes expiration policy to keep voting forever open and prevent the opinions of the people who passed away from dominating those of current generations.

Socialscore's rating system is represented by a stripe with three color codes:

- ➢ Blue, which represents approval or an upvote.
- ➢ White, which represents neutrality or a sidevote.
- ➢ Red, which expresses disapproval or a downvote.

The length of each color code in the stripe represents the percentage of votes. For example, if a law attained a 50% upvotes, half of the width of the stripe would be colored blue. If otherwise, the proposal got 50% downvotes, half of the stripe would be painted in red. Usually, the percentages are also displayed within each color code especially when it is seen on the web. This stripe is placed next to anything that is rated. For example, the laws of *Unipublic* can be sorted in a list where the *socialscore's* stripe is clearly tagged to every law to show the overall rating or approval.

Socialscore is also incorporated in all technology or content on the web such as articles, posts, or entertainment material such as music or games, goods or services in general, businesses, and so on. So, you'll see the three-color-code stripe next to all products and anything that was rated. Therefore, there are no more star ratings, which were very common in the *Tribal Ages* but were incredibly flawed and dysfunctional.

Distribia's Laws Are Negotiable

In the tribal era, people could not negotiate the law with those writing it before it becomes the law of the land. Writing a nation's laws was always done behind closed doors and regularly involved a handful of people. *"Accept the things you can't change"* was a common convention back in those days and the ruling class even preached it through religious indoctrination. Today, however, these ruling classes and their systems don't exist because the public rule themselves directly, and they write the laws through *Unipublic*.

Smartcontracts, which represent the law, are designed to be highly configurable. They enable one to configure the *smartcontract* as one pleases before publishing it on the web. The final configurations of the *smartcontract* by its original author are called the *"default configurations."* People can then vote with or against a proposal in its default version or modify it by changing one or more items in the contract and consequently making a new version of it and starting new votes on this new version. And so, people can renegotiate the proposed law directly with its author and create a new version that they see more sensible from their perspective. For example, if someone decides that littering is a bad thing and presents a good case against it claiming that it hurts the environment and causes pollution. He then produces a *smartcontract* on the web by first providing his definition of littering, why he thinks it is terrible, and why we should stop it. He proposes that we should deduct 50 coins from anyone who violates the *smartcontract*. He then publishes his proposal on the web, and every *Ve* then notifies its human about this new proposal. You receive the alert, read the law proposal, and decide whether it makes sense. You might agree but think that a 50-coin penalty sounds too much, and it should be 20 instead. So, you modify the author's *smartcontract* by selecting a different value and upvote it in this new version you made and consequently, you've negotiated the law proposal with him and with society. You might downvote the original proposal or leave an upvote on both versions of the *smartcontract* if you prefer to give equal chances for either of the versions to win.

Other people might agree with you or with the original author of the contract and decide to vote as well, and therefore new votes pour into the proposal's database until one of them attain the 83% active positive majority vote first and eventually wins, becoming the law for all humanity. All the versions of the initial proposal are linked together as one entity or database. Every time a change is made to the proposal, a new copy is created and cryptographically hashed (or linked) to the original proposal. This way, all changes are documented and can be traced easily showing the reconfigurations made to the proposal law as well as the number of people who agree or disagree with each version.

There could be only one *"winner"* among all versions of the proposal and the one that attains the 83% consensus first wins. Other versions can still be voted on separately and sometimes these versions reach 83% consensus, but they don't replace the previous winner, which must be downvoted first. And since the sway of votes is continuously moving between different versions of the same law, these other versions can later become popular and overturn the old version when more positive votes flow in their favor.

There can be an infinite possible number of alterations to the original *smartcontract*, and the version which attains the positive consensus first wins making the *smartcontract* legally binding to everyone effective immediately. However, people might change their mind later and retract their vote (remove their vote completely by deselecting the original vote) or alter their vote by picking one of the 3 available options (upvote, downvote, or sidevote).

The Freedom To Travel Anywhere & Everywhere On Earth

During the tribal era, freedom of movement was a concept encompassing the right of individuals to travel from one place to another within the territory of a country and to leave the country and return to it. The right included not only visiting new locations within the same tribal nation but also changing the place where the individual resides or works.

Restrictions on international travel on people (immigration or emigration) were commonplace. The security screenings or investigations at all airports were extraordinarily invasive and humiliating that it sucked out the pleasure of traveling altogether for the average person who treasured privacy and convenience. At such airports, all travelers were on federal territory where local laws often did not apply. All travelers were under constant surveillance, and their personal electronic devices or bags could be seized and searched at any time by a militarized police force which held no allegiance to the constitutional laws of a traveler's country in any way.

Some airports occasionally asked travelers to unlock their phones or laptops, so they can randomly access any information on such devices. They could examine sensitive and personal information, including things like the traveler's banking information and private correspondence going back years. The security personnel would look at all pictures and ask random questions such as *"who is that person in the picture"* or *"where is that picture taken?"* Imagine having sensitive information such as nude photos of yourself or your partner which you don't want another human being to see. Would you willingly show such pictures to a stranger? Airport security, however, was the authority and travelers were forced to consent. Such shameless invasion of privacy was all too common in tribal cultures.

The airport security of advanced tribal nations had a detailed search engine on anyone in the world thanks to excessive surveillance by advanced intelligence systems on the internet. They could pull up your work history, education history, internet searches, phone records, and much more. Everyone was regularly and briefly interviewed at the check-in counter for their flight with questions such as *"what is the purpose of your visit?"* or *"how long you'll stay?"* If you were one of the unlucky ones, an airport security agent would direct you into a private room where they perform a very invasive pat down, carefully handling every last inch of your body. And it did not matter if the traveler was an elderly or a woman or a child. Imagine the psychological trauma that results in little children after undergoing forced fondling by complete strangers and the fear the propagates from the authority subconsciously by such early experience after they grow up.

Children were regularly fondled by unfamiliar men in airports, and women were occasionally asked to disrobe before groups of uniformed officers. Not to forget the body scanners that penetrate your body with cancer-causing radiations to inspect your internal organs and bones. And if you were one of those really unlucky ones, a legal pedophile would sexually abuse you by performing a rectal exam. After citizens were subjected to repeated sexual assaults of this nature, even more significant violations of their rights automatically became possible. After all, one who had gone through airport security and learned to bow down to the authorities is far less likely to stand up against police aggression at home.

The overall experience at such airports was horrific, and all travelers were sooner or later treated like criminals or humiliated. It was predominantly conducted in such unreasonable manner to reinforce obedience and conformity with tribal authorities on all citizens of any flag. The excessive nature of such security screenings at airports could not be justified as a deterrence to terror threats because a real democracy would understand that *"those who sacrifice freedom for security deserve neither."* After all, terrorism was an excessively used tactic by tribal nations to enslave their own people and justify or legitimize future colonial campaigns. It was orchestrated and staged from the start by powerful colonial governments. The very few intelligent individuals of that era understood it excellently, but they were systematically silenced by the major media outlets who worked for or with the authorities.

Within countries, freedom of travel was often more limited for minors, and the penal law could modify this right on persons charged with or convicted of crimes and are on parole or probation. In most tribal countries, freedom of movement was historically limited for women, and for members of disfavored racial and social groups. Some totalitarian nations barred women from going anywhere without a male family member whereas others prohibited women from driving cars. Circumstances, both legal and practical, could operate to restrict people's movement. For example, a nation might limit people's movement within its borders during the time of war or a state of emergency. Therefore, police enforcement could force citizens to stay indoors and arrest those who did not obey and dared to leave their homes.

Every nation applied certain movement restrictions on its people, and most of them compelled citizens to have official identity cards (internal passports or citizenship licenses) that must be carried and presented on demand especially when driving a car. Driving without carrying a license was illegal in every city in the world with penalties that ranged from ticket fines to vehicle impoundment or even jail time.

Almost all tribal nations had a *"stop and identify"* policy that authorized police personnel to stop anyone and ask for identification if they suspect any wrongdoing. Failing to show an ID to the police could end you up arrested and taken to a police station. Additionally, not only the police in a tribal culture could ask for an ID because some businesses were legally obliged to ask for it from their customers. If customers did not comply with a request to show identification, they wouldn't be allowed to do things like buying alcohol or cigarettes or purchasing some types of cold medicine, among other things. Therefore, it was rare for people to leave their homes without an ID because at one point during the day they might be asked for it.

Some tribal nation-states also forced their citizens to register changes of address with the state authorities within a brief period that typically did not exceed one month. Which meant that citizens had to visit the offices of the local authorities, stand in line, and take care of the paperwork every time they moved from one state to another.

It was the norm in such tribal cultures to have laws against trespassing on another individual's property because land ownership was legal at the time. It was the norm as well to hear about gunshots fired in the air or on people caught trespassing on private property. The landowners would completely box their land with fences or barb wire and set up ominous warnings asking others to keep out or even use guard dogs. Due to such concept of fencing out land and preventing others from passing through them, people's movement was naturally reduced to just the roads or city streets they travelled on. Therefore, the concept of *"you are free to move anywhere in your country"* actually involved only some tiny public areas and the streets or highways that connected them together.

Today, there's no need for physical paperwork for identification because *Ve* can prove the identity of anyone to law enforcement when needed. And since *Ve* operates all doors along with payments, people leave their home without the need to carry a wallet or keys and can be completely handsfree.

Since private property is illegal, there's no piece of land anywhere on Earth that people are barred from visiting. All land is public and shared by everyone. No *"stay out!"* or *"trespassers will be arrested!"* signs anywhere on the planet. You will never find yourself in a situation where someone is shooting in the air or firing a gun at you or setting the dogs on you or calling the police on you because you just happen to step on a piece of land somewhere. Such scenarios are unimaginable today. People are free to discover all corners of the Earth and stand or walk or sit at any patch of land anywhere.

There are no governments and national borders or the concept of citizenship. You can just hop on a skycar (a flying drone-like car) from any building and fly to any island or continent on Earth without every presenting an ID to anyone or being searched or investigated by another human being. Since there are no national borders anymore, you could stay anywhere you want for as much as you want without worrying about visas or passports or residencies.

You are no longer confined to one home for the rest of your life because housing is now a service and all apartments are shared like a giant distributed hotel service worldwide. Everyone can take turns and try different homes in different places, and there's no need to stick to one place or be rooted in one spot for the rest of your life like a tree. In fact, the people of *distribia* have become like birds who follow the weather and migrate from some areas in winter to other regions with warm climates. On the other hand, people who love cold climates move to cities in such regions to experience the snow or enjoy snow activities and winter sports. Some people became complete nomads moving every month from one block to another until they've visited them all. This type of tourism is known as "*blocktourisim*" today, and it is widespread and practiced by a significant portion of the world's population.

It would be remiss of us not to talk about the genetic or physical changes in the human race that resulted from its mothering of *distribia* and the abolishment of central governments and their unnatural borders. In the era of tribalism, rulers artificially created the cultural isolation of the territories over which they ruled. They engineered the circumstances of the livelihoods of their citizens as well as their physical appearances or traits by restricting the genetic pool from which they could procreate. They regimented the daily diets of their citizens by forcing them to feed on the kind of food available to them within their national borders and restricting foreign trade through policies and taxation. When people became finally free of tribalism, they could travel and live everywhere on the globe, which exponentially expanded racial-mixing and reduced the physical differences between the people of this planet. Today, the human race is almost normalized thanks to generations of mixed-breeding, and there are no more vast differences in how people look or how they behave. The sameness of the people everywhere brought them closer together as one human family and permanently eliminated the physical differences that were the basis of discrimination in the disturbing age of tribalism.

Today, people are much more beautiful and free like migrating birds. All can travel wherever they want, for as long as they crave, and have the opportunity to live with whomever they desire. There are no borders on Earth anymore. Everyone is free.

The Freedom To Exit Society

Tribal governments insisted on participation in the system by all citizens. People had to work and pay taxes, or otherwise, tax evasion is a serious felony punishable by years in prison. The system of these governments was explicitly designed to ensure participation by all citizens. The ruling classes of the world enforced their national laws on all their territories, and there were no habitable places where people could go and liberate themselves from the laws they do not endorse.

Some nations practiced compulsory voting, which requires eligible citizens to register and vote in national or local elections. They imposed penalties on citizens or constituents who failed to cast a vote in an official ballot and actively pursued eligible citizens who failed to register as voters as required by law. Multiple nations practiced such *"forced democracy"* around the world, and the practice continued until the collapse of tribalism. Compulsory voting was a brutal violation of the essence of freedom because the freedom to act fundamentally includes the freedom not to act and they essentially go together like the two faces of a coin. It was also a violation of the spirit of democracy because by forcing people to participate in voting, it neglected people's right to refuse such a social system of governance by forcing the system on them. Consequently, such a system becomes an authoritarian form of ultranationalism, which promotes the interest of the state above its people.

Other tribal nations endorsed conscription, which is the compulsory enlistment of people in national military service. Conscription dates to the early dawn of tribes and continued in some countries under various names until it finally ended forever with the rise of *distribia*. Most European nations endorsed this system in peacetime so that men at a certain age would serve 1–8 years on active duty and then transfer to the reserve force. The conscription system enforced participation by all citizens including those objecting to participating on religious or philosophical grounds, political, ideological, or philanthropic such as when a person is peaceful and does not want to kill another human being. Conscription is a corrosive tribal system that forced young men and women into a life-threatening service against their will and turned them into state-sponsored murderers. It is involuntary servitude wrongly associated with patriotism when in fact it represents war slavery explicitly. Of all the statist violations of individual rights in a tribal society, the military draft was the worst. It was an abrogation of rights. It negates humanity's fundamental right—the right to life—and establishes the fundamental principle of statism: that a man's life belongs to the state, and the state may claim it by compelling him to sacrifice it at any moment.

The primary objective of the military draft was to remove the individuality or the personal identity of the populace and install the state's ideologies and propaganda instead. The military institution employed terrifying ancient techniques that turned people into mindless automatons through *"thought reform techniques."* The military training process was meant to change a mind radically so that its owner becomes a living puppet—a human robot—without the atrocity being visible from the outside. Regardless of who you are, how smart you are, or what job you have, you are molded, formed, and presented as a uniformed character of close resemblance to both the person to your right and your left. Through discipline, uniformity was pervasive. Through military training, every young citizen learned instant willingness and obedience to all orders, respect for authority, and self-sacrifice. It was a mechanism that strived to reduce individualism, support obedience, and nullify all occurrences of non-uniformity.

Reducing individualism as much as possible was developed from day one at boot camp, which is a military training camp for recruits. First names were ignored, ranks were given, uniforms were worn, and heads were shaved. Secondly came the significantly high standards or regulations on presentation and conduct to make everyone walk and talk and think like everyone else in the group. Ultimately, such measures were foundational to instituting social identity that removed individualism to best support military functions, win wars, and of course, most importantly to exhibit blind obedience to the system and its flag. The compulsory military service also reinforces tribal conventions such as the delegation of power and the hierarchical structure of command. Military members were held by law to obey and follow the orders of those appointed to ranks above them regardless of their position, experience, or reputation whereby any failure to obey any command was prosecuted and punished by law.

The military draft system does not exist today anymore, of course, because there are no nation-states or armies or politicians or representatives anymore. There's just one public and joining it isn't necessary either. Being part of *distribia's* society today isn't compulsory, and people can choose to exit society anytime they please. The freedom to exit society is guaranteed under a *smartcontract* to ensure pure freedom because the only way for a person to be completely free is to exit society and to independently decide when to leave it. Being part of society will always take away certain freedoms because the only way for human beings to live in a society is to introduce laws that define what is right or wrong or in other words, what is legal or illegal. And so, with more laws comes less freedom and it is the price we all pay for living in a community. Trading pure freedom for being in society is inevitable and there's no real solution for it. To be completely free, the only way is to abandon society and live off-the-grid away from civilization in geographic locations that are mapped under the *pure freedom contract,* where the laws of *Unipublic* do not apply.

These lawless territories are scattered on Earth and are always located inlands away from coastal cities. These territories double as natural reserves for protecting animal life and rainforests, where the urban landscape of *distribia* must never stretch to protect Earth from the impacts of excessive urbanization. Our natural reserves are massive, and they cover the largest mass of land on Earth compared to our urbanized territories. The housing *smartcontract* mapped the boundaries of the natural reserves at 83 kilometers from any coastline, which could be either a sea or an ocean or a river directly connected to any of them. So, humanity decided to build its cities only within the region between the natural reserves and the coastlines. We commonly refer to these natural reserves as *the wild.*

The barriers between the wild and the *distribian* civilization do not involve fences or walls which were very common in the tribal era. The wild's boundaries are natural and consist of lush forests of a variety of thorny plantations. The prickly and dense natural border makes it impossible for animals to cross into our urban cities. Every 17 kilometers along the natural border a pedal-operated cable car is built to allow people to freely go in and out of the wild. The cable cars hang above the separation forest by a network of cables and towers for the safe passage of people from both sides.

Although the natural reserves are wild and packed with deadly predators, and although people are not protected by any law in these territories, many people choose to experience it at least once in their lifetimes. The picturesque valleys surrounded by alluring mountains, and the pleasing lush scenes alternating from one place to another are a magnet for nature lovers. There's a whole lot of jaw-dropping places to see in the wild, and that is why it is understandable for people to venture into these territories to discover such gorgeous places on Earth before leaving it for good. On average, most of the people who migrate to the wild do come back, but there's also a considerable percentage who stay there until they die.

In the end, the ultimate freedom is to choose when to abandon society and the time or the way you wish to end your own life. Unfortunately, such freedom was forbidden for the most part in the tribal world. Suicide was a social taboo as well as illegal in almost all tribal countries and the clerics relentlessly preached against suicide. The state and the church ran a monopoly on death, and they were the only authority allowed to decide how or when people should die. Their preferred way of murdering their citizens was in wars, of course, fighting either for the shallow ideologies of the ruling class or the supremacy of their worthless debt-based fiat money or religion. From the perspective of the ruling class and their tribal religions, suicides are wasted lives that could have been otherwise useful in wars. In a tribal culture, if a person killed himself in the act of murdering other people while wearing a uniform, he is considered a hero. If, however, a person left this world peacefully without destroying other lives along the way on the command of the state or religion, society would shame such a person as a coward. Well, tribal nations and authoritarian religions are nonexistent today, and the *distribian* society guarantees the freedom for life and death to everyone.

Today, human beings have the right to life as well as the right to death. What used to be a taboo in tribal cultures is now the ultimate liberation. Suicide is the final freedom.

164

The history of names is so ancient, and no one knows when it all started or where or by whom. Since written history began, and as far back as oral history reaches, people have had names. Most ancient names had an original meaning, usually descriptive, rather than being merely a charming collection of sounds. Arabic names, for example, traditionally have definitions and are formed out of common adjectives and nouns. Arabic names are often aspirational of character such as *Muhammad*, which means *"Praiseworthy,"* and *Ali*, which means *"Exalted, High."*

Many early names were compounds, which are words that are composed of two or more separate words and are mixed together as one word. For example, the following Frankish (relating to the ancient Franks, which were a collection of Germanic tribes) names are compounds: Sigibert (victoryshining), Childeric (battlepowerful), Fredegund (peacebattle) and Radegund (counselbattle). In various ancient societies, such compounds usually referred to their Gods. For instance, the ancient Norse (the Norwegian or Scandinavian tribes in medieval times) had many compound names containing the name of the God Thor. Among the male names were Thorbjorn, Thorgeir, Thorkell, Thorsteinn and Thorvald, and among the feminine names were Thordis, Thorgunna, Thorhalla, Thorkatla, and Thorunn.

Over time many names became corrupted as languages evolved, and their original meaning is now not easily seen. In many cases, the words that formed the original name passed out of use, leaving the fossilized form in the name, and this is why we do not recognize the meanings of many names today. Their origins are in ancient languages from words that have passed out of use. For instance, the name *Edwin* was initially composed of the Old English words *"ead"* (which means prosperity, fortune, riches) and *"wine,"* which means friend. Both of these words have passed out of the language after several centuries of use. On the other hand, a word which has not radically changed forms the first part of the Old English name *Wulfgar*. Although the word changed spelling, the word *wolf* is still recognizable, and the second element *gar* means *"spear."*

Early in prehistory, some descriptive names began to be used again and again until they formed a name pool for each particular culture. Parents would choose names from the pool of existing names rather than invent new ones for their children. With the rise of Christianity, certain trends in naming practices manifested. Christians were encouraged to name their children after saints and martyrs of the church. The names of the apostles and other prominent early Christians mentioned in the New Testament were often Jewish, such as Mary, Martha, Matthew, James, Joseph, and John. By the Middle Ages, the Christian influence on naming practices was pervasive, and it became a taboo for parents not to give their children a Christian-sounding name.

Although Christian names dominated mostly all other non-Christian-sounding names in Europe, some of such names did endure by sheer luck. Most Anglo-Saxon names fell out of use within two centuries of the Norman Conquest of England. One that did not, because it was the name of a famous saint, is the name *Edward*, which is still in use today. The name Edward means *"wealth guardian,"* and is derived from the Old English root words *"ead"* (which means wealth, fortune), and *"weard,"* which means guardian. It was the name of several Anglo-Saxon kings, the last being Saint Edward the Confessor shortly before the Norman conquest in the 11th century.

When communities were small, each person was identifiable by a single name, but as the population increased and the people started using the same names in circulation, it gradually became necessary for the community to distinguish between two people who shared the exact name. Surnames developed from bynames, which are additional identifiers used to distinguish two people with the same given name. These bynames tend to fall into particular patterns. These usually started out as specific to a person and became inherited from father to son between the 12th and 16th century. The aristocrats traditionally adopted inherited surnames early on, and the peasants did so later. Some of the specific types are: the patronymic (referring to the father or mother), a locative or toponymic (indicating where a person is from), an epithet (which describes a person in some way) or a name derived from occupation, office or status. Such early communities took the habit of using adjectives to describe the person such as *"Roger the tall"* or *"Mary of the wood"* or *"William the woodchopper"* and so on.

Occupational names are often the most obvious in origin. Baker, Brewer, Weaver, Taylor, and Smith are relatively visible in meaning. Some of these occupational bynames also have female versions which became hereditary surnames. For example, the feminine of Baker is Baxter, the feminine of Brewer is Brewster, and the feminine of Weaver is Webster. However, more than half of the recorded people with these feminine surnames are male. Occupational surnames as a class also contain office names. Examples of office names are those such as Marshall (a tender of horses, or an office of high state) and Steward (a manager of an estate) and Abbott (the head of an abbey).

Patronymics are common in all cultures. These are usually formations that mean *"x son of y"* or *"x daughter of y."* The parent indicated is usually the father, but the mother's name may occasionally occur in some cases. Patronymics were formed in various ways in English. For example, Johnson means son of John or John's son. The *"son"* could also be understood, by the position in the name, so Richard's son Martin might be called Martin Richards instead of Martin Richardson. At the same time, Henry's son Martin might be known as Martin Henry, because of the medieval mind the position of the name Henry would imply that Martin was Henry's son.

Ultimately, using surnames to distinguish one's own family from the rest of the population served the ruling class the most throughout the tribal history of humankind. Family names projected social class and reverence, and they established the concept of dynasties. A dynasty is when one family rules a country or region over an extended period. Generally, the head of the family will be the ruler of the land, like an emperor or king. When that ruler dies, another member of the family will take power, usually the oldest son. When a new family takes control, then a new dynasty begins.

For the most part of the tribal history of humankind, dynasties ruled over their territories like family businesses and commanded their public like mere property just as a master does his slaves. The civilization of Ancient China dates back thousands of years, but over this vast period, much of China was ruled by no more than 13 dynasties. Like all other tribal cultures before or after them, these Chinese dynasties managed to convince their unenlightened populace that the all-mighty Gods commissioned their titles and authority over their territories. The *"Mandate of Heaven"* is what the Chinese people believed gave their rulers the right to be king or emperor. It meant that the Gods had blessed that person with the right to rule. A ruler had to be a good and just ruler to keep the Mandate of Heaven. When a ruler or dynasty lost power, this meant that they must also have lost the Mandate of Heaven. The last of the Chinese imperial dynasties were the Qing dynasty, which ruled the public from 1644 to 1912 and was the fourth largest empire in world history lasting almost 3 centuries and forming the territorial base for the succeeding Republic of China.

In most authoritarian cultures of the *Tribal Ages*, parents had the authority to name their kids almost anything. Parents started picking new and distinctive names for their children, some of which were pretty sounding while others were awful and caused a social stigma. Some gave their children names that are usually given to the opposite sex, which negatively affected the wellbeing of such children after they grew up to realize it. Also, parents could use last names or the names of objects or products as first names, which also could be embarrassing for children later in life. On the other hand, some tribal nations intervened in what parents could name their children and occasionally forced citizens to pick different names. Some governments, for example, prevented non-noble families from giving their children noble names.

Legally changing your name was impossible in some countries and it would stick with you for the rest of your life like the skin your parents gave you. Others allowed it, but the process was arduous, expensive, and time-consuming. Only in some nations that such procedure wasn't too complicated or expensive, but it was only done under certain circumstances, and you couldn't get rid off the old name entirely because it would still pop up in government records and some official paperwork.

Today, however, one can easily change his/her name instantly and readily just as one could change his/her username on a website during the early age of the internet. One could today through his/her *Ve* ask for his/her name to be changed to any name by which he/she desires the community to call him/her. There are no obligations on how many times a person can change his/her name, and some people today change their names as frequently as they change their shoes. One could also choose to be called by a number instead of an alphabetic name. So, it is possible nowadays to meet people called *"1"* or *"0"* or *"123"* or so on. It is also possible today for anyone to choose not to have any name at all if he/she wishes. In such cases, all documents relating to a nameless person would have a blank space where a name is expected.

Most importantly, there are no middle names or surnames or family names anymore. One is not legally obliged to bear his father's surname because surnames have gone extinct. Everyone either has only a single name or no name at all. And the name, of course, must be one continuous alphanumeric string with a standard maximum length of 17. Therefore, you won't find someone's name written as a sentence with 3 or more words as it used to be with the traditional way of having first, middle, and last names. Because people today have the liberty to legally change their names effortlessly and without any obligations, we usually encounter unusual names, which largely resemble nicknames than personal names, such as *"Moongirl"* or *"Oakman"* or *"Pink"* and so on.

A small percentage of people still prefer to maintain their last names by simply producing compounds in which they group a first name and surname as one name in the system. In such way, one portion of the name identifies the surname that such person or his ancestors once held. For example, someone whose name was *"Aileen Corpuz"* can legally record her name in the system as *"Aileencorpuz"* while socially identifying herself as Aileen.

The idea that you belong to a tribe or a small enclosed social group that tribal cultures once called *"marital families"* is nonexistent today because everyone today belongs to only one universal family: humanity. The concept that you belong to an enclosed group or ancestry where you are expected to exhibit loyalty to such group is, of course, a tribal convention that does not exist today. There is no heritage or ancestry or legacy other than those of humanity as a whole.

THE TRADE-BASED ECONOMY

Existence in this universe is a give-and-take relationship because in a world where there are only soft hands, rocks would not be hard, nor would we need muscles if they weren't heavy. People discovered the need to trade with one another ever since they gathered together for the very first time and it allowed them to form ever-expanding social groups to grow into large communities successfully. The concept of trading, which is the exchange of something for something else, is the fabric of the human society. Whether it started by cavemen exchanging animal coats and hunting tools with one another, or later when humanity learned to domesticate cattle and trade them as a commodity, trading is an essential stimulus for society.

Everybody needs something, and there's only a limited number of things one person can achieve alone. A person can be a good fisherman but has utterly no clue on how to build boats, and likewise, the boatmaker isn't necessarily skilled at fishing. The more fishermen there are, the more boats they'll need, and the more they need boatmakers. The boatmaker makes the lives of fishermen more comfortable because they don't have to spend time and effort building something they are not good at and, instead, focus on what they do best. And likewise, having found others who are interested in his boats, the boatmaker can continue doing the thing he enjoys doing and in return get rewarded by the other things that he can't secure on his own. Therefore, and due to this relationship, both sides need to live in proximity to one another in a community, so they can easily exchange their products and live an easier life.

Without Trade, There Wouldn't Be A Society

The atoms, which are the basic building blocks that constitute matter, somehow know that they should stick together to form molecules, which are the smallest parts of a substance that still have all the properties of that material. Similarly, the instructions to cling together and build communities is hard-wired into our DNA.

The need to trade drove people to live in proximity to one another forming ever-expanding communities so they can easily trade with one another. Eventually, small villages became towns, and towns became cities as the population grew. It is how our ancestors learned to form social groups and build a society instead of living in solitude. And it is why we instinctively prefer residing in large cities where a wide variety of goods and services are produced and sold. The healthiest community is the one that involves the most amounts of trade transactions between its people, which is always a good sign of a well-functioning society.

Trade Was Direct

The concept of direct trading (or bartering) was straightforward: I have something you want, and you have something I need, let's exchange them head-to-head. During antiquity, people traded directly with each other without a medium of exchange (or what we call today as money). If a farmer, for example, needed wood to repair his house he can pay for it directly using the vegetables he produced without necessarily using other assets for the trade.

Direct trading, however, was slow and laborious. A farmer, who needed wood, would have first to find a woodchopper interested in his vegetables, carry the produce all the way to the woodchopper, exchange it, and then carry the wood all the way back home. Such daunting task naturally inhibits trading on a mass-scale due to the load of effort involved. Additionally, the farmer might not find a woodchopper interested in his food, animals, or anything else the farmer currently owns. It means that the farmer would first have to discover what the woodchopper is interested in and then set off to find a third person who has that thing, trade it with food, and head back to the woodchopper to complete the trade. This problem is called the *"coincidence of wants,"* and represented a severe shortcoming for direct trading.

Another problem with direct trading is that there is a partial loss inherent in every trade. Some products worth more than others, which means that if these items are traded directly, one side in the transaction is gaining more in the deal than the other. For example, suppose the farmer has only cows to trade with others, and he happens to need new shoes. A cow is worth more than a pair of shoes, but the farmer can't trade the cow in pieces because the animal would die, which means that he'll have to give all of it up for a less-valuable product and lose some value in the process. And so, a need emerged to simplify the process and solve these problems.

Instead of directly exchanging something for something else in a head-to-head way, people introduced a new kind of trade through a medium of exchange (or money for short), which must represent something physical of a fixed value, quantity and come with an intrinsic value. So, if salt was the medium of exchange for a community, the farmer can comfortably get the wood he needs for salt. He can directly head to town and look for a woodchopper and pay him salt for the wood he needs instead of carrying produce all the way to town. Also, the woodchopper can get something else for his product instead of food by using the salt he earned to buy anything else he needs. Therefore, it is a win-win situation for both sides, and because of this easiness, both sides will naturally be driven to buy and sell more products.

At various times in history, people used cattle, food, salt, and gems as money. There was no real standard for what people can use as money to trade for as long as it is physical and has some inherent value. Indirect trading through a medium of exchange (aka money) made trading more accessible, but as communities grew, they needed to agree on a standard for what physical thing the society can accept as money. If you were living at these times as a salesperson, you wouldn't know what to expect from your customers to give you in return for the products you're selling. Some might provide you with salt while others might offer you cattle, for example. As a result, your daily trip back home with all the animals and salt you earned won't be easy of course. And so, merchants and their customers needed a consistent type of money that can be easily carried and stored to make trading much more manageable.

Additionally, the coincidence-of-wants problem didn't entirely disappear because the options available as money weren't easily divisible and some monies were more desirable than the rest.

173

Marketability is a measure of the amount of this loss, which is different for each type of money. The more marketable the money, the less the loss one incurs while trading with it. For example, food is more marketable than footwear while salt is more marketable than food. For that reason, you can buy what you need through salt easier than you would through food.

Avoiding losses is a powerful motivation to use the more marketable money in preference to the less commercial. And so, everyone is motivated to use the type of money with the least loss. As society identified the problems and the need emerged among its people, it was inevitable for humanity to eventually innovate a new kind of money by which they can all trade much readily.

Metals Became Money

The concept of *"metal money"* started as a metallic document in the form of receipt, representing grain stored in temple granaries in Sumer in ancient Mesopotamia (a historical region in West Asia situated within the Tigris–Euphrates river system) and later in Ancient Egypt. At this first stage, metals were used as symbols to signify value stored in the form of commodities. This formed the basis of trade in the Fertile Crescent (a crescent-shaped region on the east coast of the Mediterranean Sea where agriculture and early human civilizations like the Sumer and Ancient Egypt flourished due to inundations from the surrounding Nile, Euphrates, and Tigris rivers) for over 1500 years. The *"grain standard"*, which linked the value of units made from metal to a fixed quantity of grain, represented the first concept of currency.

The populace trusted the temple's authorities with all that grain and its convertibility to coins and back to grain. People then discovered that they could use these metallic units of currency to exchange goods and services directly without needing to go back to the grain-bank to convert the coins back to grain. It was much more convenient of course for everyone, and it boosted the commerce in that region for around a thousand and a half years.

As explained earlier, a medium of exchange or money is just a tool with intrinsic value that people use to get what they want. Using metals as money unquestionably came as an enhancement or an upgrade to that tool. However, this improvement came with another problem. The public of that era had very little use for metallic money. They couldn't eat it as other forms of money like rice, salt, or cattle. Metallic money does not produce any value such as a cow does but is used for the sole purpose of exchanging goods and services. Metallic money, therefore, is a single-purpose product and with this comes the downfall of such mediums of exchange.

In the past, people's understanding of money was as a tool for them to get what they needed and therefore they wouldn't accumulate large quantities of it because the end-game was the product they wish to buy not the tool they used to buy that item. They could accumulate a herd of cows as money, for example, but cows produce value and are more of a product than a tool. Metallic money, therefore, is useless in its given form and could only fit a purpose if it was melted down and molded as an instrument like a knife or a shovel.

The most significant impact of using metallic money was psychological. It diverted people's attention from using the money just to get what they needed and, instead, they started accumulating the medium of exchange itself. The endgame became the medium of exchange and not the product or the asset. The public started working to accumulate as much as they can from such a medium of exchange, and the trend continued afterward for thousands of years. The single-purpose money became an asset instead of a tool. Tragically, metallic moneys along with other single-purpose types of money polluted the human mind and were the source of most of the horrors in the history of human civilization. Such kind of money led to a diseased breed of human beings known as bankers whose sole objective is gain. They had no loyalty to anything but to money. They were without honor or decency.

Gold & Silver Became Money

The most efficient monetary system came with the discovery of gold and silver, and they became the preferred method of payment due to their scarcity in the world. Gold became a part of every human culture. Its brilliance, natural beauty, and luster, and its great malleability and resistance to tarnish made it enjoyable to work and play with. Because gold is dispersed widely throughout the geologic world, its discovery occurred to many different groups in many different places. And nearly everyone who found it was impressed with it, and so was the developing culture in which they lived.

No one gets the credit for the discovery of gold. A child might have found a shiny rock in a creek, thousands of years ago, and introduced gold to the human race for the first time. So, no one can honestly credit the discovery of gold to any community or culture. Egypt and especially Nubia (an African region along the Nile river) had the resources to make them major gold-producing areas for much of history. One of the earliest known maps, known as the Turin Papyrus Map, shows the plan of a gold mine in Nubia together with indications of the local geology.

Gold always had great value to people, even before it was money. This value is demonstrated by the extraordinary efforts made to obtain it. Gold's early uses were no doubt ornamental, and its brilliance and permanence (it neither corrodes nor tarnishes) linked it to deities and royalty in early civilizations.

In the quest for gold by the Phoenicians, Egyptians, Indians, Hittites, Chinese, and others, mining for gold was soon dominated by sovereigns seeking to flaunt their wealth and dominance in the territories they ruled over. Prisoners of war were sent to work the mines, as were slaves and criminals. And this happened during a time when gold had no value as *"money,"* but was just considered a desirable commodity in and of itself. Greek rulers mined gold from the Pillars of Hercules (a phrase that was used in Antiquity to the promontories that flank the entrance to the Strait of Gibraltar) all the way eastward to Asia Minor and Egypt, and we find traces of their placer mines today. The ruling classes of the world usually owned most of the mines, but some were worked privately with a royalty paid to the authorities. Roman rulers furthered the quest for gold. The Romans mined gold extensively throughout their empire and advanced the science of gold-mining considerably. They diverted streams of water to drill hydraulically and built channels and the first *"long toms."* They mined underground, also, and introduced water-wheels and the *"roasting"* of gold-bearing ores to separate the gold from rock. They were able to exploit old mine-sites more efficiently, and of course, their chief laborers were prisoners of war, slaves, and convicts.

Why did gold become money? As mentioned earlier, marketability of money is essential to cut down marginal losses in any trade. Gold was the most marketable and optimal form of money because of its intrinsic properties, which are:

> It is rare. Rocks, for example, aren't precious because they're everywhere on Earth and people have them in their backyards. Gold, on the other hand, is a precious metal and exists in meager quantities on Earth. Because it is a rare metal, gold cannot be copied or replicated but only forged under cosmic circumstances that are impossible for humans to reproduce.

> It is portable: Gold can be easily stored and carried from one place to another. It is not heavy or takes a lot of space such as salt or other monies used previously for trade. People used cooking oil as money at one point in history but imagine carrying a barrel of oil on your back to town every time you wanted to buy something with it. Surely you would rather be carrying a few gold coins in your pocket instead of a barrel of oil on your back.

> It is divisible: Gold is the easiest of the metals to work with and mold. It occurs in a virtually pure and workable state, whereas most other metals tend to be found in ore-bodies that pose some difficulty in smelting. It can be divided into small pieces and traded in quantities matching to the products that people want to buy. It solves the marginal loss in trade that occurred with other kinds of money such as animals and food.

> It is durable: Unlike other mediums of exchange such as food, gold lasts forever. Perishable money meant that they could only hold some intrinsic value for a short time equals to the lifetime of that product. A cow, for example, is a valuable product but it lasts for as long as the animal is alive whereas gold lives forever. The same gold that the Egyptians used 5,000 years ago is still here with us today. It does not corrode. Would you preferably accept a type of money that expires after several years or can terminate at

any moment or would you rather pick a kind of money that lasts forever? Indeed, this characteristic of gold made it more marketable and preferable over other types of payment.

➢ It is fungible: Pure gold had a purchasing power, which was the same everywhere on Earth. A kilogram of gold could buy you the same goods and services everywhere whereas a kilogram of cooking oil came with a purchasing power that depended on the local market because some places produce oil abundantly while others don't.

For these 5 reasons, gold and silver (which shares similar characteristics with gold) became widely favorable worldwide and the money of choice across all communities. With the discovery of gold and silver and adopting them as money, humanity undoubtedly solved many problems that surrounded the tool they use for trade. This tool, as advanced and enhanced as it became, still faced an additional hurdle that needed addressing. The pieces of gold and silver people were using at the time were of odd sizes, weights, and purities. So, it was still not interchangeable where every unit is the same as the next.

Every merchant had a scale to measure the weight of the pieces of gold and silver and had to study their purities before deciding to trade with someone. Here trust issues started surfacing because some merchants might cheat by rigging their scales to indicate less weight for the gold and silver people offered or might even claim that the gold they received is not pure enough. And so, this new tool wasn't efficient yet because trading was still tricky, and it was still a guessing game when it came to the exchange of goods and services. The solution? Minting gold and silver in standardized size and weight in the form of *"coins"* was the solution to the problem. Around two thousand years ago, the tyrants ruling Asia Minor, which is the area that later became Turkey, were among the earliest to mint gold and silver coins.

Carthage, a powerful Phoenician city-state in North Africa, also was a pioneer and a major player in gold coinage at the time. Since then and throughout history, gold and silver coins were an essential part of trade development globally.

Minting gold and silver in standard shapes and sizes made trading much smoother and enabled people to put a price on their goods and services in coins. A farmer could, for example, sell his cows for a specific amount of gold or silver coins and use this well-earned money to buy other items he needs that are priced in coins as well. And so, gold and silver coinage boosted trade, and the global economy flourished because everyone trusted this new medium of exchange and more people started trading. People could finally secure their wealth in a trusted and durable kind of money, and therefore a lot of people got very wealthy.

Every ruling class everywhere monopolized harvesting the precious metals in the land they controlled and minted it into coins. They branded their coins with their faces and names on them, melting them down and minting them back again whenever the throne changes heads. Some lands were more abundant in gold and silver that the reset and it was natural for rulers everywhere to start competing and wage wars against one another for the right to mine such precious metals from the land. Eager to harvest the Earth out of its gold and silver before anyone else, kings routinely pursued wars to capture as much ground as possible. However, war is expensive because soldiers must be paid, fed, and armed. And therefore, rulers thrived to maintain alliances with other kingdoms to borrow gold and silver whenever needed to fund their military expansions.

The rulers in the gold era acted as each other's bankers loaning precious metals such as gold or silver to foreign ruling classes. They also loaned raw material such as iron for the development of weaponry such as swords and shields. Rulers borrowed gold and silver from foreign jurisdictions to fund military campaigns with the promise to return the borrowed money at a time in the future and with some extra funds on top. By lending money to one another, the ruling classes could bank on one another, and some sovereigns ran their economy entirely on funding others' wars or producing and loaning the weaponry that fuels their warfare.

If they win these wars, rulers typically looted the new region they conquered and used that new wealth to reimburse their bankers.

War was great for business at the time for tribal rulers and the practice long continued throughout history and only ended in *distribia's* era. Ever since humanity accepted gold and silver as money, all wars that proceeded afterward were essentially the banker's wars. Rulers became international bankers. Authoritarian governments became financial dictatorships aimed at absorbing all the gold and silver Earth has to offer.

The war-based economy in the goldmoney era worked as follows:

> ➢ Sovereign rulers approach a peer from another territory asking for money (gold, silver, iron or any other physical assets) to fund a new military campaign in the promise that they'll repay the banker at a time in the future plus an extra amount (or interest) for the service.
> ➢ The banker makes his calculations to figure out the chances that his customer will win these wars and based on that he loans the money.
> ➢ The temporarily-richer warmongering ruling class then head out to start a war somewhere with enough natural resources or riches they can loot.
> ➢ If they win, they reimburse the banker and enjoy new wealth in their treasury and additional territory on their new map. More land means more natural resources and more people to tax and more gold in the treasury. The ruling class and its banker are both happy, and they can trust and rely on each other for the next war on the horizon.
> ➢ If the ruling class, however, fail to repay their banker on time, they'll have to pay the interest on that money again for the new period. If the customer failed a third time to settle the debt on time, the interest is applied again for the third period, and so on until the debt is paid plus the money accumulating from the interest rates across the years.

As these interest rates pile up from one period to another, the total amount that the customer must reconcile with the banker is continuously increasing for as long as the debt isn't settled. So, the banker just sits back and watch as his customers pile up debts while he's profiting in the process. In such system, it is of the banker's concern that customers never settle their debts because the banker is profiting when they continuously owe him money.

The ruling class usually tend to raise taxes on their citizens and those in the new territories they conquered to pay portions of the debt and gradually settle it with time. The fastest way, of course, is to start another war and loot new territories, which the banker of course will support. However, new wars also come with the added danger that the ruling class might lose the war and their dynasty terminated or replaced with another sovereign from foreign lands.

From the bank's point of view, it is a win-win situation anyway because the debt never really goes away but just passed down from one administration to another. If the new rulers refuse to pay, the banker will simply fund all their enemies, which are of course always eager to take over. So, whoever the new rulers are they must always check with the bank and transfer the debt of the previous administration to their account and take responsibility.

To have a bank that the ruling class could always go to and borrow money whenever they needed to, was very important and beneficial for the business of government. Initially, the ruling class was the bank, and such entity was only available for the kings and rulers. The concept of private banks for the public did not exist yet. But as the people were becoming wealthier and started accumulating more gold and silver, they needed an entity that they could go to and protect their savings.

Bankers & Papermoney Emerged

As people accumulated considerable masses of gold and silver, they explored safe places to store their wealth to prevent it from falling into the hands of thieves. Those who owned a safe place to save people's gold and protect it with an army of men were successful in attracting those worried about their gold and in need of protecting it. The safer the vault and the bigger the army that the gold keeper (or banker) got, the safer people felt in trusting their gold with him because they know the banker can protect their gold. Successful bankers were the ones with the most prominent army and influence.

Bankers, of course, were offering a service by protecting other people's gold or silver and naturally you expect them to ask for a *"fee"* for all their troubles. This fee depends on the value of the deposits, which makes it a contingent fee or an *"interest"* as bankers dubbed it. There's a lot of responsibility of course when dealing with other people's life earnings, which is why the bankers had to conceive a system to deal with all that coinage. It wasn't easy back in the days to keep an accurate ledger because validating identities was challenging since national identification paperwork didn't exist yet. They couldn't base it on looks because someone who looks like you could go to the bank and collect your deposits. And so, the easiest way was for the banker to just issue a document to his customers as a receipt or a *"proof of deposit."* These notes were made out of paper carrying the banker's seal for verification. Each piece of paper proclaims that *"this paper represents physical deposits at the bank that can be collected by showing the note to the banker."*

These receipts were the earliest form of banknotes, and with this banking model, the *"gold standard"* was born, by which a fixed number of gold coins defined the value of each banknote. In other words, the gold standard explains a system where a banker prints paper notes with numbers on them representing an equal amount of gold or silver coins deposits at his bank. This way when customers wish to collect their deposits, they just show the receipts that the banker gave them to prove that they owe him that money. Without that receipt, customers can't collect their money. Which also means that the receipt (or banknote) has now become the money and not the gold or silver coins at the bank. Banknotes are now money, and anyone can collect gold or silver from the banker by just showing these banknotes.

And so, people started accepting and using the banker's receipts as money and used them to trade with each other instead of gold and silver. It was, of course, much more convenient than heading to the bank in a faraway place and carry heavy loads of gold and silver every time they needed to buy things or trade.

Realizing how people trusted the banker's banknotes and traded these worthless pieces of paper in society as if they are money, it didn't take long for some bankers to recognize that they *"hit the jackpot"* and can benefit from this system. After all, they created this *"new money,"* and they can rig it to their benefit.

They realized that they invented a new medium of exchange (a new form of money), which they can just print out of paper. The bankers could just print banknotes of their own without depositing any gold or silver and use the new money, which they created out of thin air, to buy goods and services to enrich themselves. A fantastic concept if you're a banker, isn't it? After all, unlike gold which is forged from the rare event of a dying star, paper is abundant because it comes from trees or cotton. It can also be easily harvested, and mass produced.

This money they printed was worthless of course because it was not backed by any deposit of gold or silver, which are the real money and are what defines the value of these banknotes. The concept of printing banknotes out of thin air is of course fraud in its purest form because people's money is made of gold or silver. It is well-earned, and they had to work the land or produce value to earn it whereas the banker's money is made from paper and he's just effortlessly printing it without creating any value. And so, the bankers were just short-circuiting the monetary system by printing banknotes of their own without depositing gold or silver in return. They were committing fraud, and eventually, that money would create a financial crisis when it finds its way into the economy. As bankers continue to print banknotes out of thin air relentlessly, the value of each banknote becomes less and less because they're only worth the quantity of gold or silver coins in the vault.

Fiat Currency: Worthless Paper Is Now The New Goldmoney

By printing more banknotes than what they indeed had in their vaults, these bankers were creating money out of thin air, and with that, the very first concept of *"fiat currency"* emerged. Banknotes backed by nothing is known as fiat currency where *"fiat"* in Latin means *"let it be done."* In other words, the bankers say it is money, so it becomes money, and the rest of the population must take their word for it.

The original purpose of a banknote was to act as a proof of gold deposits, and the bank must only issue them that way. In other words, banknotes represent money, but they are not money because they're just worthless paper. So, by printing these banknotes without deposits, bankers were committing fraud and stealing people's well-earned gold or the other reserve assets they deposited. People didn't take thieves so nicely back in those days, and the standard practice was to chop off body parts (mainly hands) or publicly hang the thieves when caught depending on what they stole. With that in mind, the bankers had to be very careful and only print banknotes modestly and secretly because they would face dire consequences if exposed. Of course, not all bankers were blessed with the same wisdom and some of them printed too many banknotes than they should and accountable to no one. It surely made them and their families extraordinarily wealthy, and they perpetuated their operation using the protection of their little armies and the concealment of their practices from public knowledge.

However, nothing lasts forever, and the bankers' monetary system was no exception. The self-absorbed bankers did not foresee the consequences of printing too much paper money (or papermoney for short) can have on the economy. The banknotes that they overwhelmingly published found their way into the local economy, and ultimately there were too many of them. The traders of the time, realizing the abundance of banknotes in circulation, naturally raised the prices on their goods and services since everyone seems to have a lot of money and can afford to pay more. Traders are for-profit operators, and they adjust their prices according to the local economy. If there weren't much money in circulation, traders lower the costs of their goods and services so the mechanism of buying and selling can continue. Too much money in the market equates to higher prices, which means that the purchasing power of one banknote had will drop with time as the banker pumps more of them into the economy.

This *"reaction"* by the economy to the abundance of the medium of exchange is called *"inflation,"* and it only happens if that medium of exchange is rigged and when the bankers are committing fraud. Inflation was unheard of before papermoney flooded the markets because unlike gold, a paper is worthless and can be easily replicated or manufactured. Paper has no intrinsic value to it whatsoever and would have never been adopted as a medium of exchange if not for the bankers, who hacked people's minds into drawing a connection to it with gold.

It took centuries of trials with several sorts of physical items as mediums of exchange for humanity to perfect one type of money that outperforms the rest. Gold coinage was the *"highest technology"* of all mediums of exchange, and no one from the gold-era could've successfully predicted that humanity will resort to something as ridiculous as paper to act as money because such material is cheap if not worthless.

Realizing that banknotes aren't buying them as many goods and services as they used to, people spontaneously rushed to the bank to convert the notes back to gold, which is the kind of money they knew better and have always trusted. The bankers, of course, could only accommodate up to a certain level of convertibility because they overwhelmingly issued too many notes without backing them up with any gold or other reserve assets. And so, the fraud of these bankers was revealed, and the outraged people abolished their banks and served the bankers the justice they deserved.

Eventually, banknotes came to the attention of the local rulers, and they discovered the possibilities of using papermoney as the national currency instead of gold and silver and other metallic money. They found that they could finally create money out of thin air without really having to dig the earth in search of the old-fashioned money such as gold and silver. The private bankers provided a proof of concept for the ruling class when the public accepted their worthless banknotes as money, and they were trading using paper as if it was the sovereign's gold and silver coins. Since papermoney is the new goldmoney, rulers could now create as much money as they want out of thin air. The ruling class could pay the public using worthless paper as if it really was gold and have them build all the castles and fortresses and the weaponry they need to conquer more land and build empires. It was the second biggest sham in history. Such practice, however, must be done in moderation and it only works behind borders since every ruler can do the same and issue his own papermoney because paper is cheap, and it is everywhere.

Papermoney functions appropriately as a medium of exchange only within the boundaries of the authority that manufactures it and the people who accept it. The moment a person steps out of that bubble, his/her papermoney becomes useless or loses most if not all of its value compared to the other money in foreign territories. Kingdoms, therefore, always used physical currency such as gold and silver to pay one another and they never accepted papermoney because they understood that it is worthless.

It is like owning a company with millions of employees, whom you pay by the paper you print in your office. Why would you use another company's paper to pay your employees when you can just print your own? For as long as your printer is working fine, and you got trees in your woods, you'll be great just using your own printer to print your *"good-old papermoney."* After all, you're using papermoney to pay these woodchoppers, who cut and transform trees into the very same paper you use to print your papermoney. And why would you accept the other company's paper as payment for the products you sell when you know it is just worthless paper? Instead, of course, you would accept payments in the form of physical things such as the products that the other company manufactures. The same concept exists with papermoney and national currencies. So, papermoney only works well for the ruling class within their borders to pay the citizens for the work they do for them. However, the ruling class know that they must not print too much papermoney because that will just cause the prices of national goods and services to spike (the inflation of the economy) and the entire economy will collapse along with their dynasty. Ruling classes with poor economies leave them vulnerable to attacks from foreign rulers, who are always eager to expand their territories so that they can tax more people and fund new war campaigns.

The ruling class always dealt with physical assets directly for international trade with foreign rulers because they understand the fraud of papermoney. International currencies convertibility, however, is vital because trading (as explained earlier) is what created the society and what keeps it healthy. Because trading is always welcomed no matter where it comes from, foreign trading by people from other territories is always appreciated by the ruling class of any region. Historically, the ruling class of every territory always kept their borders open for foreign traders to exchange goods and services with the local populace. Ruling classes who close their borders in the face of international traders usually face the wrath of foreign rulers of the nation to which these traders belong. One example of this is Japan's isolation policy which ended when the gunboats of the American ruling class terminated the closure by force so that American traders can come and go in Japan unchallenged.

Trading foreign papermoney relied for the most part on independent merchants exchanging currencies for profit. These papermoney merchants were middlemen, who bought and sold currencies from travelers moving to foreign territories or wishing to trade there. At the time, all papermoney followed the gold standard, which made it possible to exchange foreign currencies depending on how much every gram of gold cost in each territory. And although the value of papermoney drastically changed from one territory to another and from one period to another, gold and silver maintained their value. Because gold and silver coins had relatively the same intrinsic value everywhere on Earth regardless of who minted them, traders from district territories could exchange foreign currencies through gold and silver. For example, if one gram of gold cost £1 in Britain but 1.3\$ in America, a person would know that one sterling equals 1.3 dollars. Money exchange merchants would then trade currencies following this principle and charge their interest rates of course on top of each transaction. Currency convertibility depended on supply and demand for the most part, and it also relied on competition between these middlemen and how much interest each is charging for each currency conversion.

Every territory's sovereign was to be the only legitimate entity that can print papermoney and declare it as the official legal tender backed by gold or silver. This formal legal tender, backed by gold by the legitimate authority of the land, was the very first concept of national currency. People learned never again to trust a private banker with the nation's monetary system. They could, however, trust their rulers to operate it on behalf of the people and police it for the benefit of society. Although the ruler is just human, and he is corruptible like any other person, at least the level of his corruption is capped and can be manageable. Because after all, it is not of the ruler's benefit if the economy of his nation crumbles because he's bounded to his territories whereas a private banker can just run away with people's gold to a foreign region to start a new bank. And so, the ruling class in each territory monopolized the business of printing papermoney following the gold standard and allowing the public to visit their treasury at any time to convert papermoney back to gold or other reserve assets. At least that was the theory, but in practice, the public wasn't allowed to flock to the treasury to redeem their gold and must always trust the sovereign's papermoney. The reason for this, of course, is that papermoney is exceptionally corruptible and no man or woman could or would resist committing fraud once they get the power of issuing the papermoney supply for a nation. And there will never be enough gold or silver in the world for any sovereign to support the convertibility of papermoney back to their reserve assets on the long run.

The national papermoney was a promissory note or an I.O.U. - an *"I Owe You"* note. In China, the Tang Dynasty was the first to print papermoney. They ruled China from the year 618 until 907 A.D. and started using papermoney as currency around the year 800 A.D. They conceived the papermoney as an offshoot of the invention of block printing. Block printing is like stamping, and some people used the process for quilts, but the Chinese rulers made ready use of it in printing papermoney. The Tang Dynasty was among the early pioneers in the papermoney printing business. Before the Tangs initiated their papermoney, there were many other ways to buy things such as copper coinage. As merchants and wholesalers desired to avoid the massive bulk of copper coinage in prominent commercial transactions, papermoney's market value increased. The Tangs, of course, and just like the early bankers who discovered the advantages of being the authority on the issuing and printing of papermoney, printed much more notes than what they indeed have in reserves of physical assets such as gold, silver, or copper. This practice continued with other dynasties that proceeded them such as the Song dynasty, which was amassing much more significant amounts of papermoney. History recorded that each year before 1101 AD, the prefecture of Xin'an (modern Shexian, Anhui) alone would send 1,500,000 sheets of paper in 7 different varieties to the capital at Kaifeng and flooding its economy with money.

The Tangs and the Songs dynasties were China's earliest central bankers. Unlike the central bankers that appeared much later in Europe, Tang's papermoney wasn't attached to debt or interest rates but was simply issued and used by the government to pay the people for the work they do for their rulers. Thanks to using debt-free papermoney, China under the Tang dynasty flourished economically. Historians generally regard that period as a high point in Chinese civilization, and a golden age of cosmopolitan culture. Its territory, acquired through the military campaigns of its early rulers, rivaled that of the Han dynasty, and the Tang capital at Chang'an (present-day Xi'an) was the most populous city in the world.

Every ruling class in history that controlled the printing of their papermoney never needed money, of course, within their borders because the money to them is just worthless pieces of paper that they could print mountains of it if they so desired. And since the citizens in any territory will never even dream of auditing the finances of the ruling class, the unimaginably wealthy individuals who ruled the land could continue enjoying incredible lifestyles provided to them by the hard labor of the public. For as long as the ruling class possessed unquestionable power over the people, there was nothing to worry about for these elites. And for as long as the public remains ignorant, they'll never know where the money actually comes from or how it is created. If however, the citizens learned to question the authority of their rulers and realized the unfairness of tribalism's social order, the dream world the ruling class designed could come crashing down.

Successful central bankers everywhere understood that they must always keep the control over the issuing of the nation's papermoney away from public hands and if the people ever gained representation in government, such monetary policy must move to a financial entity independent from the government - a private central bank - so the central bankers can secretly keep their control over the nation.

Central Banking & Papermoney Emerged In Europe

The concept of private central banking was born in Europe at a time when nations were already becoming more libertarian and as the ruling classes of Europe were losing their grip on power and on the national financial institutions or industries. To hide their finances from the European public, every ruling class established a private central bank to run the monetary policy of the territories they ruled over and to issue papermoney. Citizens, of course, were not allowed to audit any central bank anywhere, and the information about who really owns the central bank and its operations were invariably hidden. The employees who worked at these central banks, however, were known and announced to the public because such workers were mere deplorable operators who could be assigned or suspended at will. The real men behind the curtain that hired all the staff including the top management were of course always hidden, and their identities were perpetually shrouded with secrecy. A central bank, therefore, is independent of the publicly elected government but at the same time co-owned by the same group that runs the nation's financial or industrial institutions and nominates its governments.

National papermoney surfaced in Europe in the 17th century, and people used it alongside coins. The gold standard, a monetary system where the medium of exchange is paper notes that are convertible into pre-set, fixed quantities of gold, replaced the use of gold coins as currency in Europe. Such gold standard notes became the legal tender, and people naturally preferred using them for transacting because they were much more convenient, easily storable, divisible, and interchangeable. Most importantly, the public believed that the local authority of the land operated and controlled the printing and management of the paper currency, and that's why people trusted such form of money. Whenever they desire, citizens of any country could head to the nation's treasury and order their papermoney be converted into gold and silver or any other reserve assets available. This, of course, is what the ruling class wants their people to believe but papermoney had always been a sham ever since its creation. The money in circulation is always far more than whatever the bankers got in reserve assets but since the people are restricted from checking the treasury's vaults, no one really knows. And so, clueless average citizens continue to believe that their papermoney is backed by gold when in fact it never is and never will be.

Papermoney is a tricky business that all rulers everywhere must handle carefully because it backfires. When bankers repeat the same historical mistake of printing too much papermoney, they risk economical inflation where their citizens panic and instinctively head straight to the bank to cash on their papermoney with the reserve assets the paper represents. Since reserve assets such as gold and silver never match the amount of papermoney in circulation, the nation's treasury will be forced to close its doors to the public and shutdown the convertibility of their currency. This had happened repeatedly and in many nations around the world when the gold standard was still honored.

The 1st European central bank emerged in Amsterdam. Amsterdam Wisselbank (Amsterdam Exchange Bank) opened in 1609 as a municipal exchange bank for facilitating financial settlements which were very common in Early Modern Europe. This private bank was under the official protection of the city of Amsterdam, which recognized the bank's papermoney as a legal tender for the citizens of Amsterdam and effectively making it a private central bank. Initially, the bank's papermoney were backed by deposits, but around the year 1683, the bank introduced a new regulation that turned its papermoney into fiat currency and effectively turning the bank into a fiat money central bank. The fiat money regime remained in place until the dissolution of this central bank in 1819 after the secrecy that shrouded the fraudulent operations of the bank was finally unveiled to the public of Amsterdam by 1790.

The second European central bank emerged in Sweden. An international banker called Johan Palmstruch (born in 1611 and died in 1671; originally named Johan Wittmacher before he was ennobled) arrived in Sweden in 1647 and began submitting proposals for banking institutions in the country to King Charles X

Gustav (the king of Sweden from 1654 until his death) as soon as Charles became the king. Charles rejected Johan's first two proposals to allow him to create debt in the country by handing out loans to citizens with interest through papermoney. The third proposal, which promised half the bank's profits to the crown, was accepted. Charles thus founded a bank called Stockholms Banco (also known as the Bank of Palmstruch or Palmstruch Bank) in 1657 with Palmstruch appointed as general manager. The bank, of course, was owned by the king and his royal family whereas Palmstruch was nothing more than an employee that the king at any moment could dispose of and suspend his banking privileges in the country.

Sweden's medium of exchange at the time was metallic, and they did not use papermoney yet. The Swedish public used a metal currency called daler, which was minted in copper (kopparmynt) and silver (silvermynt). In the year 1661, Palmstruch's proposal of using papermoney, which would be exchangeable at any time for the gold and silver coins the customers deposited, was implemented and they soon became very successful. Stockholms Banco then printed papermoney on a seemingly unlimited scale, and as lending rose rapidly, the bank's loans ceased to be dependent on the deposits of other account holders. Soon enough the issued loans and banknotes had reached such levels that the value of the notes began to fall. When people returned to the bank to have their credit notes honored, the bank did not have enough metal reserves to fulfill all their requests, and the bank was increasingly obliged to refuse convertibility requests until operations ceased entirely in 1664. The governing tribalists were forced to intervene by using their own wealth and pay the public to reduce the outstanding loans and exchange the notes for coins. The liquidation of the bank was completed in 1667 and Palmstruch was imprisoned and blamed for the bank's losses. Palmstruch, who was considered responsible for the bank's losses, was condemned to death, but later received clemency.

The Swedish ruling class then revoked Palmstruch's privileges to print banknotes and re-established the same bank under the name Riksens Ständers Bank (Bank of the Estates of the Realms), administered by the Swedish ruling class to act as their banker and the financial entity responsible for the nation's finances. A paper-mill, *Tumba Bruk*, was founded in Tumba, on the outskirts of Stockholm to print Riksbank's papermoney. And with that decision, Sweden's economy followed a central banking model, which owned the policy of issuing and printing the nation's money. The Swedish ruling class did not want to move the monetary system entirely into the hands of the Swedish parliament and its treasury of course because the public must never know about the fraud of papermoney printing.

The news of the central banking model in Sweden eventually came to the attention of the rulers of England who realized that they don't need to rely anymore on physical assets such as gold and silver coins to control their public and fund their warfare. And just how the Swedish king came aware of the magic of debt-based papermoney through an international banker, the British king discovered the concept through a Scottish banker called William Paterson (born in April 1658 and died on 22 January 1719). Paterson came to London and convinced the English government under King William III (born on the 4th of November 1650 and died on the 8th of March 1702) to establish a private central bank to act as the English government banker by inventing wealth out of worthless paper.

During the 18th century, the English and French ruling classes were at war with each other. Financially exhausted, English rulers desperately needed loans from other territories to fund their warfare but having heard about the concept of papermoney, they could now just create money out of nothing. The idea here, of course, is that the king could now use worthless paper, which is issued by the central bank with numbers on it that represent value, to pay the public for the work they do for the king such as building weapons of war or joining his army. The people would be lied to or put under the impression that the papermoney they traded with represented gold or silver deposits at the ruler's treasury and that they could redeem such physical assets on demand. But of course, such convertibility of papermoney into gold and silver would be excessively restricted if not prohibited. A single financial institution (a private central bank) with endless imaginary piles of gold would act as the English government's banker to support the war against the Napoleonic army. And so, the king issued a Royal Charter, and England welcomed the central banking model with open arms. By the time the British king established the bank in 1694, it had become the second central bank in operation in Europe at the time, after Sveriges Riksbank.

The king and queen of the time were, of course, two of the original owners because otherwise, it would defeat the purpose if the rulers of the land did not own the nation's finances and its monetary policy. Although it was primarily founded to fund the war effort against France, the original Royal Charter of 1694 explained that the bank was established to *"promote the public good and benefit of our people."* This mission statement, of course, is misleading because when the nation's treasury could issue its own currency, it came without debt or interest. However, and thanks to debt-attached papermoney, the British public are now forced into loans and interest fees on their money although it is just worthless paper with ink on it and should only cost printing fees. The English government is now creating completely unnecessary debt on its own people out of nothing and forcing them to pay the imaginary debt plus interest fees on that debt through income taxes. Through this independent and international bank (meaning it is exclusively controlled by Britain's ruling class and not by the British public), the international stakeholders of the Bank of England were able to issue and loan money to the British public with interest and forcing them into suffocating debt that can never be repaid.

By connecting all papermoney in circulation to debt and only issuing it to the citizens of the nation when they take out a loan, the Central Bank of England through the British government was creating a false sense of obligation. Because after all, papermoney is just worthless paper and shouldn't cost the government more than its printing cost. And if such papermoney was indeed intended for the benefit of the citizens of the nation, it must never be based on units of debt but units of value such as gold or silver or any other physical asset. It must be debt-free and interest-free, or otherwise, only those who own the central bank would benefit from such monetary system while the public would struggle with suffocating debt, which the bank created from nothing. And while those who control the issuing of debt-attached papermoney at the central bank enjoy extraordinary wealth beyond the dreams of Midas, entire populations around the world are reduced to slavery through repressive debt.

Thousands of years ago, religion, which is the worst sham in human history, achieved its purpose of reducing entire populations to slavery and poisoning their minds for the benefit of tribal rulers. And now this same kind of rulers (now called central bankers) devised a new mind-poisoning recipe for human enslavement through debt-attached papermoney and private central banks. Papermoney, indeed, is the second worst sham in the history of humanity and like religion, it spread across the planet like a viral disease under the British Empire infesting people's minds and hearts and reducing them to slavery. Both global systems of enslavement, religion and the banking institutions, tricked people into obedience and servitude that fed into a horrific war-torn future filled with terror and suffering.

The Era Of Warfare For Papermoney Supremacy

In 1775 the American Revolutionary War (also known as the American War of Independence) began as the American colonies sought to detach from England and its oppressive regime. And although many reasons were cited for the revolution, one in particular sticks out as the primary cause. King of Great Britain and Ireland, George William Frederick (known as King George III; born on 4 June 1738 and died on 29 January 1820), outlawed the interest-free independent papermoney that the American colonies were producing and using for themselves. He declared that the American colonies must never produce their independent currency and must borrow the money they need from the Central Bank of England at interest, immediately putting the American colonies in debt to his central bank. King George knew that by setting the Americans under debt, he could easily control them and the fate of their children.

Through debt-based papermoney, any tyrant could easily kidnap personal liberties away from the public and enslave them and their children with perpetual debt instead of physical means like armies or police brutality. All rulers everywhere understood that papermoney is worthless, of course, because papermoney is not wealth. Rulers could print mountains of papermoney at will, but they could not print wealth. Therefore, the idea of forcing a nation to borrow worthless paper as if it was wealth and accumulate debt in the process was undoubtedly absurd. The American colonies could issue their own currency, and there was absolutely no reason whatsoever to use another ruler's papermoney. Thus, and as expected, the Americans completely rejected king George's orders of taking loans from his central bank in the form of papermoney. From king George's perspective, forcing the colonies to use his papermoney through loans and through interests on that borrowed money, would put the new territories immediately under debt and, therefore, under his control. Because after all, debt is an obligation and a form of bondage that puts people immediately under subjugation and controls them.

Before the revolution and due to a shortage of gold and silver to use as money in exchange for goods and services, the American colonies adopted the concept of papermoney as a medium of exchange. This papermoney, called Colonial Scrip, was very successful. It provided a reliable medium of trade as well as a feeling of unity between the colonies. The Colonial Scrip was debt-free paper and unbacked by gold or silver, but by the authority of the American provinces as a legal tender. It was a fiat currency issued in the best interest of the American public. Since neither gold nor silver backed the value of the Colonial Scrip, the colonies could control its purchasing power. And while the European governments were forced to borrow their money from central banks as a loan and pay interest on it, Americans were free from such financial slavery. European papermoneys were *"bills of debt"* whereas the American papermoneys were *"bills of credit"* created by the government, and this meant that there was no interest to pay for the introduction of money for the public. Free from any false obligation for borrowing money from private banks, the colonies had no reason to tax the income of their citizens, which inevitably lead to mass prosperity. As anticipated, such currency outraged the central bank of England. Through the English Parliament's Currency Act in 1764, the Central Bank of England banned the debt-free fiat Colonial Scrip and outlawed its circulation, which crippled the American economy.

*"In one year, the conditions were so reversed that the era
of prosperity ended, and a depression set in, to such an
extent that the streets of the colonies were filled with the
unemployed. The colonies would gladly have borne the
little tax on tea and the other matters had it not been that
England took away from the colonies their money, which
created unemployment and dissatisfaction. The inability
of the colonists to get the power to issue their own money
permanently out of the hands of George III and the
international bankers was the PRIME reason for the
Revolutionary War." ~ Benjamin Franklin's
autobiography*

Outraged by the deliberate decimation of their economy, the
American colonies revolted against the tyranny of the British
Empire and their private central bank. In 1783, America won its
independence from England after 8 years of bloody conflict.
Although the total loss of life throughout the war is largely
unknown as it was typical in the wars of that era, historians estimate
that at least 25,000 Americans died during this war with the
majority of which died from diseases or as prisoners of war under
British hands, mostly in the prison ships in New York Harbor.
Unfortunately, America's battle against the central banking concept
had just begun as international bankers moved from Britain and
Germany to establish financial and industrial institutions in the
American colonies.

The conflict on who will be the authority on issuing the American's
currency started long before the colonies ever united into one
nation. Benjamin Franklin (born in 1706 and died in 1790), one of
the Founding Fathers of the United States and proclaimed as *"The
First American"* for his early and unrelenting campaigning for
colonial unity, stated in his autobiography that the prime reason for
the American war of independence was a battle over who controlled
and issued the money of the new colonies. He understood the
insidious nature of banks and the inevitable debt the propagates
form such institutions, which is why a private bank must never be
allowed to have the authority on printing banknotes. He firmly

believed that it is better to slash expenses to an extreme level rather than to incur debt to afford a lifestyle that is well beyond our means.

"Rather go to bed without dinner than to rise in debt."
~ *Benjamin Franklin*

The first central bank of the United States eventually arrived in 1791, which was modeled after the Central Bank of England and created primarily under the influence of Alexander Hamilton (1st United States Secretary of the Treasury). How was that allowed to happen? In May 1781 Alexander Hamilton recommended an English-born banker called Robert Morris for a unique position at the Continental Congress: Superintendent of Finance of the United States, which was an executive role under the Articles of Confederation and involved similar powers to a Finance minister. Robert Morris was the only person to hold this office, and he occupied it from 1781 to 1784 with the assistance of Gouverneur Morris. After just 3 months as the U.S. Superintendent of Finance, Robert Morris introduced a plan on May 17, 1781, which chartered the Nation's first de facto private central bank (the Bank of North America) in Philadelphia on December 31, 1781. And on January 7, 1782, the Bank of North America officially opened its doors to the public and became the first commercial bank in the United States. Being a de facto central bank, and since the historical mission of central banks is to fund wars, the Bank of North America was initially intended by Robert Morris to finance the war between France and Britain. This bank was also given a monopoly privilege of its banknotes being receivable in all tax payments to state and federal government, and no other banks were permitted to operate in the country. It was also authorized to lend money it did not have through a fraudulent policy called *"fractional reserve lending."* Not only it can loan imaginary money to the public, but it can also charge them interest on that fake money. If an average person at the time lent money to others that way, he would have been locked up in jail for fraud, but the Bank of North America alone could do it due to the political corruption that legalized such deceitful practice to this private bank exclusively.

The primary objective of Alexander Hamilton and Robert Morris was to establish an American version of the British monetary system, which is the exact financial system that the American Revolutionary War was fought against and the very same system of debt that the ancestors of the American revolutionaries had fled from when they came to America. According to the plan put before the first session of the First Congress in 1790, Hamilton officially proposed establishing a private central bank for the United States to expand credit and act as the American government's banker. Hamilton's bank proposal faced widespread resistance from opponents of increased federal power. Secretary of State Thomas Jefferson and James Madison led the opposition, and they maintained that the bank was unconstitutional and that it benefited merchants and investors at the expense of the majority of the population. They contended that the creation of such a bank violated the Constitution, which explicitly stated that Congress was to regulate weights and measures and issue coined money instead of the minted papermoney or bills of credit.

George Washington initially declared that he was hesitant to sign the *"bank bill"* into law. Washington asked for the written advice and supporting reasons from all his cabinet members. Attorney General Edmund Randolph from Virginia believed that the bill was unconstitutional. And Jefferson, also from Virginia, agreed that Hamilton's proposal was against both the spirit and letter of the Constitution. Hamilton, who unlike his fellow cabinet members came from New York, was quick to object and relentlessly defended the central banking concept. And so, Washington officially signed the nation's first private central bank into existence on February 25, 1791, allowing it to operate in the country for 20 years. And based on the economy's performance after those 20 years, the U.S. Senate would decide whether to renew the bank's charter or not. This private financial institution was called the Bank of the United States, and just like the Bank of England, such name was deliberately chosen to hide the fact that it was privately controlled. Additionally, and precisely like the Bank of England, the names of the original owners (those who owned equity) were a secret that was never revealed to the public.

The central bank immediately started issuing millions of dollars in papermoney pyramiding on top of only $2 million in specie (money in the form of coins rather than note). And as a result of the outpouring of credit and papermoney by the central bank, the heavy burden of dept sharply accumulated on the American public and government. Jefferson, the sitting Secretary of State at the time, watched the accumulation of public debt with sadness and frustration as he was unable to stop it.

> *"I wish it were possible to obtain a single amendment to our Constitution. I mean an additional article taking from the government the power of borrowing." ~ Thomas Jefferson in a letter to John Taylor.*

Thankfully, the debt-creating machine only lasted 20 years because the U.S. Senate voted in 1811 not to renew the bank's charter. Such experience with central banking was bitterly condemned by several founding fathers including Thomas Jefferson, who saw it as an engine for speculation, financial manipulation, and corruption.

> *"To preserve our independence we must not let our rulers load us with perpetual debt. We must make our choice between economy and liberty, or profusion and servitude. I place economy among the first and most important of Republican virtues and public debt is the greatest of the dangers to be feared. It is incumbent on every generation to pay its own debts as it goes. If the American people ever allow private banks to control the issue of their money, first by inflation and then by deflation, the banks and corporations that will grow up around them will deprive the people of their property until their children will wake up homeless on the very continent their fathers conquered." ~ Thomas Jefferson, third President of the United States from 1801 to 1809, one of the Founding Fathers and the principal author of the Declaration of Independence.*

7 years before the expiration of the central bank's charter, Alexander Hamilton died after being mortally wounded from a duel (a deadly contest with guns between two people to settle an honor-

related matter) with Aaron Burr on July 11, 1804. Aaron Burr was the third Vice President of the United States serving during Thomas Jefferson's first term as president at the time. Burr, sensing an attack on his honor, demanded an apology letter from Hamilton for spreading misinformation about the Vice President during an upstate New York dinner party. Hamilton refused to apologize and insisted that he did not insult Burr. After a series of attempts to reconcile were to no avail, Burr ultimately called for the duel, which led to Hamilton's death the following afternoon. Back then people took their honor very seriously, and duels were natural occurrences when gentlemen fail to reconcile their differences.

As for Robert Morris, he was cast into debtors' prison for fraud after he speculated on millions of acres of land and could not pay taxes or interest on his leveraged loans. Being involved in the creation of a central bank, Morris knew that papermoney is practically worthless paper and that the real value is in physical assets such as gold and land. Therefore, he went on a buying frenzy to absorb as much American property as possible, but his downfall was that his greed took over him. This English-born banker owned more land than any other American at the time but didn't have enough liquid capital to pay for his mortgages. At the time of the 1st private U.S. central bank, debtors were treated worse than thieves. In such period of American history, failure to repay a debt was regarded as a moral failing rather than a business one. Robert Morris was locked up in prison for 3 years until Congress passed a special bankruptcy law in 1800, primarily to free him. Such fraudulent legislation to legalize debtors at a time when they were publicly frowned upon was extraordinarily controversial and a perfect example of the political corruption in the United States at that period. After he left prison in 1801, Robert Morris died in obscurity 5 years later. At the time of his release, 3 commissioners found that he had debts of $2,948,711 which is equivalent to the purchasing power of $58,511,249 after inflation adjustments. Using the case of Robert Morris as an example, this particular statement by Jefferson *"If the American people ever allow private banks to control the issue of their money, the bankers will deprive the people of their property"* echoes resoundingly.

Jefferson's direct successor, James Madison (born in 1751 and died in 1836), was also a firm enemy to central banks as well as the debt and wars that always propagate from such institutions.

> *"Of all the enemies to public liberty, war is, perhaps, the most to be dreaded, because it comprises and develops the germ of every other. War is the parent of armies; from these proceed debts and taxes; and armies, and debts, and taxes are the known instruments for bringing the many under the domination of the few." ~ James Madison, fourth President of the United States from 1809 to 1817, founding father and hailed as the Father of the Constitution.*

"Bringing the many under the dominion of the few" is a horrid practice that shatters the principles of a democratic and free society. Madison knew that through money and debt the rich could easily control the nation and its people. His perspective about the dangers of banking and taxes to the American public was shared by other Founding Fathers including Gouverneur Morris I (born on 30 January 1752 and died on 6 November 1816), the *"Penman of the Constitution"* who wrote the Preamble to the United States Constitution. In a letter he wrote to James Madison on the 2nd of July 1787, Gouverneur Morris I warned the soon-to-be President about a plot to shift the powers of government from the publicly elected officials to the hands of private bankers.

> *"The rich will strive to establish their dominion and enslave the rest. They always did. They always will. They will have the same effect here as elsewhere, if we do not, by (the power of) government, keep them in their proper spheres." ~ Governor Morris I of Pennsylvania.*

Gouverneur Morris was a defector from the ranks of the elite bankers because it was him and Alexander Hamilton who presented the original plan for the Bank of North America to the Continental Congress in the last year of the revolution. Although himself was an aristocrat to the core, Gouverneur Morris was one of the few delegates at the Philadelphia Convention who spoke openly against slavery. According to James Madison, who took notes at the Convention, Morris spoke publicly and openly against slavery on 8 August 1787, saying that it was incongruous to say that a slave was both a man and property at the same time. He never would concur in upholding slavery and regarded it as a nefarious institution. He considered it a curse on the states where it prevailed.

Starting when Thomas Jefferson became president in 1801, political relations with the British Empire slowly deteriorated because of Jefferson's opposition to central banking. Immediately after the abolishment of the 1st U.S. Central Bank under James Madison's presidency, the Central Bank of England through the British government started imposing financial restrictions on the United States. Britain impeded U.S. vessels from trading with France, a decision which was illegal under international law even though Britain was at war with France at the time. British navy also practiced impressment, which involved removing seamen from U.S. merchant vessels and forcing them to fight for the British Empire. Britain also financed and armed the militias in their northern colonies and bolstered its northern forces in Canada in preparation for an all-out invasion of the United States.

Within 5 months of the abolishment of the 1st U.S. Central bank, the British Empire attacked the United States. By 1814 things were going relatively well for Britain. British Forces managed to get all the way to Washington and burnt the White House to the ground, but when they made their big push to Baltimore, there was a hiccup. The British fleet attempted to barrage Fort McHenry, but the fort held, which allowed the people of Baltimore enough time to set up defenses and defend their territory against the British invasion. Given British control of the oceans, there was no other way to fight against the British actively except on land against their northern Canadian colonies. President Madison believed that food supplies from Canada were essential to the British overseas empire in the West Indies and that an American seizure would be an excellent bargaining chip to end the war. Thomas Jefferson, although out of power at the time, argued that the expulsion of British forces from nearby Canada would remove a long-term British threat to American republicanism.

At the time, the British Empire was involved in a long and bitter war with the French Empire under Napoléon Bonaparte (born on 15 August 1769 and died on 5 May 1821), who was the Emperor of the French from 1804 until 1814. And therefore, Britain's naval forces were occupied with the Napoleonic Wars, and they did not have enough troops to launch an all-out war on North America. Although they had some soldiers to defend their Northern American colonies in Canada, it wasn't enough for a swift victory over the United States. In other words, the War of 1812 with the United States started at the wrong time for the British Empire because it was militarily and financially exhausted.

On December 24, 1814, both sides signed a peace treaty in the city of Ghent in United Netherlands. The agreement restored relations between the two nations, restoring the borders of the two countries to the lines before the war started in June 1812. The U.S. Senate unanimously approved the treaty on February 16, 1815, and President James Madison exchanged ratification papers with a British diplomat in Washington the next day. Although historians cite many reasons for the end of this war, the chief reason was Madison's forced approval of another central bank in the country that followed the banking policies of the Central Bank of England. Modeled on Alexander Hamilton's First Bank of the United States, the second U.S. Central Bank was chartered by President James Madison in 1816 just one year after the war of 1812 had officially ended. This central bank began operations at its main branch in Philadelphia on January 7, 1817, managing 25 branch offices nationwide by 1832.

Just 8 days before the U.S. Senate officially ratified the peace treaty, the British Army under Major General Sir Edward Pakenham invaded New Orleans on Sunday, January 8, 1815. The United States Army, under Brevet Major General Andrew Jackson, bravely fought this battle and conquered the enemy. And even though the attacking forces greatly outnumbered Jackson's forces, he victoriously forced the British to retreat and set sail back to their base in the West Indies. The Battle of New Orleans was remarkable for both its brevity and lopsided lethality. It was a real American victory. Andrew Jackson's war against the tyranny of Britain's central bank, however, had just begun. Outraged by America's politicians who failed their country and surrendered its finances to Britain's central banking model, this wartime hero was adamant about liberating his nation again through financial warfare this time. He insisted on purging his country from central banking as he did to the British forces in New Orleans.

And so, he campaigned and won the U.S. Presidency to abolish central banking in the United States entirely. Although Congress was indebted to the central bankers at the time, the owners of the second U.S. Central Bank were very cautious of Andrew Jackson's opposition of central banking. While Jackson in office as the 7th U.S. President, the banking elite knew that they should request the renewal of their central bank's charter at the right moment or otherwise the President had the authority to veto the renewal. They waited until the last year of Jackson's first term, and when he announced his campaign for a second term, they asked Congress to pass a renewal bill for the bank's charter hoping that Jackson would sign the bill into law to avoid the retaliation of the bankers that could cripple his re-election. However, this wartime hero was not to be deterred by the bankers, and practically immediately after its passage in Congress, Jackson vetoed the re-charter bill. Although Congress was under the influence of central bankers at the time, it was unable to override President Jackson's veto on central banking in the United States. Jackson officially vetoed the legislation on July 10, 1832, after delivering a carefully crafted message to Congress and the American people. This message is one of the most popular and effective documents in American political history.

> *"It appears that more than a fourth part of the stock is held by foreigners and the residue is held by a few hundred of our own citizens, chiefly of the richest class. Is there no danger to our liberty and independence in a bank that in its nature has so little to bind it to our country? Should its influence become concentered, as it may under the operation of such an act as this, in the hands of a self-elected directory whose interests are identified with those of the foreign stockholders, will there not be cause to tremble for the purity of our elections in peace and for the independence of our country in war? Their power would*

Jackson then stood for re-election and for the first time in American history he took his argument directly to the people by taking his re-election campaign on the road. His campaign slogan was, *"Jackson and No Bank!"* Even though the bankers poured over $3 million (around $87,903,139 after inflation adjustments) into President Jackson's opponent, the Republican Senator Henry Clay's campaign, Jackson was re-elected by a landslide in November 1832. It is worth noting that the use of money by the international bankers to influence elections and get puppet presidents or other public officials to act as their frontmen to the American public became a standard in American politics ever since the 1st U.S. Central Bank. Although bribery and influencing elections were illegal in the United States, it became a continuous pattern in the era of central banks. This horrid practice also reached legal status later under corrupt American administrations under the term *"lobbying."*

Andrew Jackson (born on 15 March 1767 and died on 8 June 1845) was the first American president to have been a Democrat, and he was a vociferous foe to central bankers calling their bank as a *"den of vipers and thieves."*

> *"Gentlemen! I too have been a close observer of the doings of the Bank of the United States. I have had men watching you for a long time and am convinced that you have used the funds of the bank to speculate in the breadstuffs of the country. When you won, you divided the profits amongst you, and when you lost, you charged it to the bank. You tell me that if I take the deposits from the bank and annul its charter I shall ruin ten thousand families. That may be true, gentlemen, but that is your sin! Should I let you go on, you will ruin fifty thousand families, and that would be my sin! You are a den of vipers and thieves. I have determined to rout you out, and by the Eternal, (bringing his fist down on the table) I will*

rout you out!" ~ From the original minutes of the
Philadelphia committee of citizens sent to meet with
President Jackson (February 1834)

Nicholas Biddle, who served as the third and last president of the second central bank of the United States, fought the Bank War bitterly and declared:

> *"I will pull the country down. The nation will fall, the people will fall, but the bank will not fall."*

This statement alone is evidence to the world what central banks really were all about and the monstrous crimes of which they were capable. Biddle made good on his word and the Second Bank of the United States sharply contracted the money supply by calling in old loans and refusing to issue new ones. Naturally, a financial panic ensued, followed by a deep recession. Biddle then unashamedly blamed President Jackson for the crash, claiming that it was Jackson's withdrawal of federal funds that had caused it. This crash decimated wages and prices, and unemployment soared, along with business bankruptcies. The United States was in uproar, and the banker's newspapers blasted the President in editorials. To an extent, Biddle practically succeeded in destroying the United States, but ultimately Andrew Jackson killed the bank and the economy recovered.

And so, and just like its predecessor, the second U.S. Central Bank only lasted 20 years until its charter expired. It is all thanks to Andrew Jackson who took it into battle as soon as he stepped into office in what later came to be known as *"The Bank War."* When Andrew Jackson took office, the national debt of the United States was around $58 million (around $1,399,037,128 in today's money). Six years into his presidency, the debt was zero. Jackson was the only American president to achieve this feat, and this was the one and only time that the United States of America was debt-free.

On January 30, 1835, and less than 3 years after he vetoed the re-charter bill of the second U.S. Central Bank, President Andrew Jackson survived an assassination attempt when an allegedly mentally ill house painter called Richard Lawrence attempted to shoot him outside the United States Capitol. Both pistols used by the English-born assassin miraculously failed to fire, and when the assassination attempt failed, the 67-year-old president reputedly beat Lawrence with his cane before a crowd subdued Lawrence. Why did both pistols fail to fire? Investigators later examined Lawrence's pistols, and they found that the powder in the bullets was of good quality, and when tested, both guns fired without fail penetrating one-inch-boards of wood at thirty feet. The damp conditions of the day may have increased the odds of a misfire, but the odds of two successive misfires were still very slim, which is why a public sentiment arose that divine providence had spared the President. Due to Lawrence's insane behavior and statements in court, the jury found him not guilty by reason of insanity. Lawrence then spent the remainder of his life contemplating his failed attempt in an insane asylum, and he died there in 1861. Andrew Jackson was the first American President to be targeted for assassination. On the other hand, the unemployed housepainter Richard Lawrence also set a precedent in being the first of a long series of so-called *"lone nut"* assassins.

It wasn't the first time that Jackson had cheated death, of course. Nicknamed *"Old Hickory"* for his toughness in the War of 1812, he had conquered countless attempts on his life, both internal and external. Old Hickory suffered from nearly every physical ailment imaginable including smallpox, osteomyelitis, malaria, dysentery, rheumatism, dropsy, cholera morbus (widespread intestinal inflammation), amyloidosis (a waxy degeneration of body tissues) and bronchiectasis (inflamed and dilated bronchial tubes). In addition to these ailments, Old Hickory sustained the lingering effects of injuries from duels, one of which left a bullet permanently lodged in his lungs.

Andrew Jackson's successors also kept the nation's bankers from scheming the establishment of another central bank in the United States. Most prominent of those successors was, of course, Abraham Lincoln (born on February 12, 1809, and died on April 15, 1865), who was assassinated by well-known stage actor John Wilkes Booth on April 14, 1865, while attending the play *"Our American Cousin"* at Ford's Theatre in Washington, D.C. Lincoln was shot in the head as he watched the play and died the following day at 7:22 AM in a house across the street from the theater.

The English-born assassin was a fierce Confederate sympathizer during the Civil War. Before the fateful night at Ford's Theatre, John had initially conspired to kidnap Lincoln and hide him until all Confederate prisoners were released. He also outlined to his associates a plan to assassinate Vice President Andrew Johnson as well as the Secretary of State William Seward. John tasked Lewis Powell, a tall and powerful former Confederate soldier, with the attack on Seward, to be aided by David Herold. George Atzerodt, a German immigrant who had acted as a boatman for Confederate spies, was to kill Johnson. John himself was to either kidnap or assassinate Lincoln. All 3 attacks were to occur at the same time (around 10:00 PM) that night. However, on the day of the planned kidnapping, Lincoln failed to appear at the spot where John and his 6 fellow conspirators lay in wait, foiling their planned abduction. Also, Atzerodt failed to carry out his assignment and never approached Johnson. Powell, on the other hand, invaded Seward's home and slashed him repeatedly with a knife. Seward survived the attack, but his face was permanently disfigured.

After entering the theater's balcony and shooting Lincoln at close range in the back of the head, John immediately fled the scene. And after a 12-day manhunt, John was tracked down and killed by Union soldiers. The assassination occurred only days after the end of American Civil War. Lincoln's death plunged much of the country into despair, and the search for John and his accomplices was the largest manhunt in American history to that date.

The American Civil War was a war fought in the United States from 1861 to 1865. Although most academic scholars misleadingly claimed that the primary reason for the American Civil War was to abolish slavery, the actual chief reason for the war was Lincoln's new monetary policy and his debt-free papermoney.

In 1862 Lincoln authorized the Treasury to print and release legal tender papermoney that, unlike the other papermoney that existed in the world at the time, was printed on both sides with the back printed in green ink. Hence, Lincoln's papermoney notes were dubbed the *"greenbacks."* The words *"legal tender"* meant no one in the country could legally refuse to take the greenback bills in payment. So, if a person sold gunpowder or pickled beef to the government, that person must accept the payment only in greenbacks. Soldiers took their pay in greenbacks as well. On February 25, 1862, Congress passed the first Legal Tender Act, which authorized the issuance of $150 million in greenback papermoney. At the time the government had no facility for the production of papermoney, so a private firm printed the greenbacks in sheets of 4 and sent them to the Treasury Department where dozens of clerks signed the notes and scores of workers cut the sheets and trimmed the papermoney by hand. Shortly afterward, the Second Legal Tender Act (July 11, 1862; 12 Stat. 532) authorized the Treasury Secretary to engrave and print notes at the Treasury Department. And by 1865, 450 million dollars of greenbacks were used as money throughout the North to pay for labor and goods.

Before the Civil War, the only money issued by the United States was gold and silver coins, and only such coins were legal tender. In other words, payment in gold and silver coins must be accepted by everyone nationwide under the law. When President Abraham Lincoln assumed office in 1861, he understood the importance of national money for the United States and for the war effort.

> *"The government should create, issue, and circulate all the currency and credit needed to satisfy the spending power of the government and the buying power of consumers. Money will cease to be master and will then become servant of humanity." ~ Abraham Lincoln, 16th President of the United States from March 1861 until his assassination in April 1865.*

The greenbacks were a direct threat to the central bankers of Europe and especially to that of the Central Bank of England. They knew that if Lincoln's debt-free papermoney becomes indurated down to a fixture, then the American government would furnish its own papermoney without cost. It would pay off all debts and be without debt. It would have all the money necessary to carry on its commerce. It would become prosperous without precedent in the history of the world. The brains and wealth of all countries would go to North America. Therefore, central bankers everywhere knew perfectly well that Lincoln's new monetary system must be immediately destroyed, or it will destroy every monarchy on the globe.

And so, the British Empire supported the Confederacy against the Union with the expectation that victory over Lincoln would mean the end of the greenback. Both Britain and France seriously considered an outright invasion of the United States in support of the Confederacy, but they were surprisingly held at bay by Russia, which came to the aid of Lincoln's Union during the crisis of the Civil War. From the start of the Civil War, Russia expressed total support for Abraham Lincoln's government, claiming that it was the only legitimate authority on U.S. soil.

> *"Russia desires above all the maintenance of the American Union as one indivisible nation," Foreign Minister Alexander Gorchakov wrote in 1862 to Bayard Taylor, secretary of the U.S. embassy in St. Petersburg.*

Russia supported the Union primarily because its main geopolitical enemy at that time was Great Britain, which was sympathetic to the Confederacy. Also, the U.S. and Russia had enjoyed good relations in the first half of the 19th century even though they had very different political systems. In September 1863, a Russian fleet of 6 warships headed to the East Coast of North America and stayed there for 7 months. Based in New York, they patrolled the surrounding area. A similar thing occurred on the West Coast where a fleet of 6 Russian warships protected the ports of San Francisco. The Russian fleet helped to prevent any sudden attacks from France or Britain on these central Union port cities.

Free of European direct military intervention thanks to Russia, the Union won the war but following Lincoln's assassination, the greenbacks were pulled from circulation, and the American people were forced to go back to an economy based on papermoney attached to interests and debt. In other words, instead of a national currency issued directly by the American government free of interest and not attached to any loan or debt, the American people must now borrow their papermoney as a loan from private banks that immediately came with debt attached to it as well as an interest on that debt.

Although the Treasury Department was responsible for printing the new debt-attached national papermoney, it was only allowed to issue them when private banks in the country create debt through loaning money to American citizens. In other words, America's papermoney at the time was a bond-backed banknote created and issued only when citizens are in debt. Nonetheless, the government was partially in control of this debt-creation system, and it controlled how much reserve assets in vault cash that the private banks must maintain against the money they loaned to the American public.

Several decades later and after the two previous failed attempts, another group of elite bankers conspired to have one private central bank in complete control of the monetary system of the United States including the creation and issuing of American money. In other words, they wanted to hijack the monetary policy from the publicly elected government and move it to a private institution entirely controlled by international bankers. After learning from the mistakes of the bankers before them, a group of elite international bankers carefully plotted to establish a central bank in the United States. Why were the bankers having trouble building a central bank in the U.S.? America was a relatively new nation, and it was established by Europeans who escaped the tyranny of their ruling class in the hope of building a country where the people rule themselves. It was a noble and inspiring experiment that worked for a while during the nation's early years before falling back miserably to tribalism. Since it was a new nation, the ruling class wasn't yet well-defined or consolidated. Also, the authority of government over the public did not yet take the inevitable form that would allow the ruling class to easily force its will over the people.

America's elite bankers, who soon would become the rulers of America, shrouded their plot of establishing a central bank with secrecy because they knew perfectly well that the American people would never agree to a central bank in their country. Back then, the American people knew perfectly well what central banks were and understood them thoroughly. They knew that everywhere a central bank went, there would be wealth inequality, wild swings between economic booms and busts. After each financial bust, those at the top of society mysteriously came out wealthier while everyone else came out poorer. Europe was the running example of this at the time. And so, American bankers resorted to secrecy and trickery to get their central bank established.

At the time in the United States, the dominant families in the realm of banking and business were the Rockefellers, the Morgans, the Warburgs, and the Rothschilds. The Rockefeller family was Christian Protestant of British and German descent. The Warburgs were a prominent banking family of German Jewish and Venetian Jewish descent. The Morgan family was Christian and originated in Wales during the 17th century. The richest of them all, the Rothschild family, was an extremely wealthy and secretive Jewish family descending from Germany. In the early 20th century, these 4 families relentlessly sought to push once again the establishment of a central bank in the nation. They knew that the publicly elected American government and the public were very wary of such an institution, so they needed to orchestrate an incident to influence public opinion. Such a strategy of staging events to sway public opinion later became a standard in the business of government in the United States of America. It became a tactic, known as the *"terrorism"* that employs force, stealth, and crisis to implement economic policies and government regulations in any nation anywhere.

Mayer Amschel Rothschild (born on 23rd February 1744 in Frankfurt and died on 19th September 1812) founded the Rothschilds' banking dynasty, and he was the first of the family to open a bank. The Rothschilds are no strangers to taking advantage of wars and conflict to make money. In 1811, and during the Napoleonic Wars, NM Rothschild & Sons (a multinational investment banking company commonly referred to as the Rothschild Group and founded by Nathan Mayer Rothschild) acted as the central bank that almost single-handedly financed the British war against France while secretly funding Napoleon Bonaparte to grow the Rothschild's banking business. Established in London in 1811 by Nathan Mayer Rothschild, one of the famous 5 sons dispatched by their father (Mayer Rothschild) to Europe's financial capitals to expand the family's banking business, NM Rothschild made its vast fortune by buying the English government's bonds. After Britain's war with France, and thanks to loaning money to both sides, the Rothschilds became the wealthiest family in the world at the time. The family also became part of the board of the Central Bank of England and held substantial equity of this private central bank as well as considerable influence in decision-making. It is when people are dying or suffering that the Rothschilds usually expand their wealth. Baron Rothschild, an 18th-century British nobleman and member of the Rothschild banking family, is credited with saying that *"the time to buy is when there's blood in the streets."* The Rothschild family single-handedly established the European banking and finance systems in the 18th century which later became the financial model for the rest of the world until the collapse of tribalism.

John Pierpont Morgan Sr. (known as JP Morgan; born on April 17, 1837 and died on March 31, 1913) was an American financier and banker who dominated corporate finance and industrial consolidation in the United States of America in the late 19th and early 20th centuries. He single-handedly orchestrated *"The Panic of 1907"* (also known as the 1907 Bankers' Panic or Knickerbocker Crisis), which was a United States financial crisis and the first worldwide economic crisis of the 20th century that took place over a 3-week period starting in mid-October. He did so by exploiting his mass influence and publishing rumors that a prominent bank in New York is insolvent and in the process of going bankrupt. Morgan knew that it would cause mass hysteria, which would affect other banks on Wall Street as well. And it did. In fear of losing their deposits, the public immediately began mass withdraws, which forced the banks to call in their loans causing the recipients to sell their property and thus a spiral of bankruptcies, repossessions and turmoil emerged.

Now that the stage was set, it was time for the *big-four-elite-bankers* to represent their solution to the American people. Senator Nelson Aldrich, who had intimate ties to the banking cartel in America and later became part of the Rockefeller family through marriage, called for a congressional investigation to investigate the

Panic of 1907 so it won't happen again. Aldrich led the passage of the Aldrich–Vreeland Act, which established the National Monetary Commission to study the causes of the Panic of 1907. He served as chair of that commission, which drew up the Aldrich Plan as a basis for a reform of the financial regulatory system. The commission led by Aldrich recommended, of course, that a central bank should be implemented so that a panic like 1907 could never happen again. The conclusions of Senator Aldrich's commission were the spark that the *big-four-elite-bankers* needed to introduce their central bank to Congress.

Their political frontman, Senator Aldrich, introduced the bill to the American Congress (which initially represented the American public before the soon-to-be central bank took over it) branded as *"The Federal Reserve Bill,"* to make it sound official and part of the government. However, it was just a private central bank disguised to the American people under a misleading name. It was neither federal nor had any reserves. Senator Aldrich then misinformed the American Congress and public by claiming that the purpose of the system was to stabilize the economy and release the grip Wall Street bankers had over America. The problem was that those who wrote the bill were exactly the same people that Senator Aldrich claimed it would stop. If the bill succeeded, it would give a small group of men the ability to create money out of nothing, and then loan it to the American government with interest.

Next, in the art of deception, the *big-four-elite-bankers* went on a mission to fool the American people. They intentionally provided misinformation to newspapers and posted articles about bankers screaming and protesting the proposed Federal Reserve bill. The average person who read the protesting articles of the bankers presumed that if the bankers hated it, then it surely must be beneficial to the public. And so, they unknowingly supported a Trojan horse. The *big-four-elite-bankers* also fooled Congress by putting clauses in the bill that limited their power, only to remove these limits once the bill was passed. A double-headed trickery of the public and Congress was all it took.

With massive political sponsorship by the *big-four-elite-bankers*, Woodrow Wilson became president having already agreed to establish a central bank in the United States in exchange for campaign support. Even before his inauguration, President-elect Woodrow Wilson was encouraging congressional leaders to enact banking and currency reform. And while many of the 535 members of Congress were at home for Christmas or preparing to leave for the holidays, Congress passed the Federal Reserve bill just two days before Christmas by the vote of 43 to 25 in the Senate. The chief sponsors of the bill then immediately rushed to the White House to present it to the newly elected U.S. President, Woodrow Wilson, who fulfilled his campaign promise to his bankers by signing their central bank into law on December 23rd, 1913 at 6:00 PM. The Oval Office then filled with cheers for what became the most lasting legislative accomplishment of the Wilson administration: the surrender of the nation's finances to the *"Money Trust."* And with that, the authority of printing American money moved to a private bank, which is run primarily by the *big-four-elite-bankers*. In other words, the Federal Reserve Act was quite literally a license to print money from the government to a private institution, which now has the monopoly over the issuing and creation of American money.

It is worth noting that while the second U.S. Private Central Bank arrived just 5 years after its predecessor, it took the elite banking group in America over a century to establish the third U.S. Private Central Bank after Andrew Jackson abolished its forerunner. It shows how effectively Andrew Jackson abolished central banking in the United States and how wary the American public was for so long of central banking and public debt.

With their men in office, the *big-four-elite-bankers* also authored the conception of the 16th Amendment to the U.S. Constitution that authorized the imposition of the federal income tax on American citizens. They accomplished this in the very same year they co-directed the conception of the central bank (or the Federal Reserve). The 16th Amendment exempted income taxes from the constitutional requirements regarding direct taxes, after income taxes on rents, dividends, and interests were considered direct taxes and ruled to be illegal.

"The Congress shall have the power to lay and collect taxes on incomes, from whatever source derived, without

apportionment among the several States, and without regard to any census or enumeration." ~ The 16th Amendment to the United States Constitution.

Federal income tax on labor only exists so that successive governments can continue to pay the interest on money which, since 1913, they have been obligated to keep borrowing from an independent central bank, and which the government previously could print independently. Without income taxes, it would be virtually impossible for any government to repay the borrowed money plus the interest on that loaned papermoney back to the central bank. Income taxes, therefore, act as an insurance policy by the central bank that the government can repay the loan.

Among the notable privileges that Woodrow Wilson received for the role he played in initiating the central bank, the Feds (short for the Federal Reserve officials) printed his face on the largest U.S. dollar note ever issued–the 100,000-dollar bill. They fashioned these money notes from December 1934 to January 1935 and used them for transactions between Federal Reserve Banks, not for circulation among the general public. As for Nelson Aldrich, he became the man who largely controlled all major decisions of the Senate dominating the tariff and monetary policy of the United States in the first decade of the 20th century. Because of his impact on national politics and financial systems, he was referred to by the press and public alike as the *"General Manager of the Nation."* His daughter, Abigail, married into the Rockefeller family, and his descendants became dominant figures in American politics and banking. David Rockefeller (born on the 12th June 1915 and died on the 20th March 2017) is the grandson of Nelson Aldrich and was well-known for his wide-ranging political and financial influence around the globe. Another grandson, Nelson Rockefeller (born on July 8, 1908, and died on January 26, 1979), was an American businessman and politician who served as the 41st Vice President of the United States from 1974 to 1977, and previously as the 49th Governor of New York (1959–1973). He also served as Assistant Secretary of State for American Republic Affairs for Presidents Franklin D. Roosevelt and Harry S. Truman (1944–1945) as well as Under-Secretary of Health, Education and Welfare under Dwight D. Eisenhower (1953–1954).

When the Federal Reserve Act was approved December 23, 1923, some national banks relinquished their State charters rather than become member banks in the new system. Such audacity in the face of the central banking giants by these small American banks wasn't left unpunished, of course. To force American banks to join the Federal Reserve system and to purge America's banking system into a much smaller number of banks, the Feds devised a plan. After just one year from its inception and all the way till 1919, the Feds were printing fraudulent papermoney on a massive scale increasing the supply in circulation by nearly 100% from previous years. This papermoney, of course, was issued with debt immediately attached to it and was loaned to small banks and the public. At precisely the time when it should have stepped in to make up for a collapse in demand on additional loans, the Federal Reserve dragged the economy down by suddenly recalling in 1920 mass percentages of the outstanding money supply and forcing the banks to reclaim vast numbers of loans (same reaction as that of The Panic of 1907, which the Federal Reserve was founded to prevent). Naturally, this deliberate and contemplated act by the Feds resulted in bank runs, bankruptcies, an unemployment rate of 25% followed by financial collapse. Over 5,400 banks outside of the Federal Reserve System collapsed further consolidating the banking monopoly in the hands of a small group of international bankers. And on average, more than 600 banks failed each year between 1921 and 1929.

Under central banking, bank panics or *"bank runs"* happen when large numbers of anxious people withdraw their deposits in cash, forcing banks to liquidate loans by compelling people to pay their debts immediately in physical assets or papermoney causing them to go bankrupt and shut down their businesses when they fail to pay their bank. When enough people are unable to settle their debts, the bank fails. And since commercial banks typically hold only a fraction of deposits in reserve assets at any one time, it just requires a fraction of their customers to flock to the bank to cause any bank to collapse.

The failed banks were primarily small, rural banks. Investors and other people in business blamed these failing institutions calling them weak and poorly managed and that those failures served to strengthen the banking system. A significant wave of bank failures during the last few months of 1930 triggered widespread attempts to convert deposits to cash. Confidence in the banking system began to erode, and bank runs became more common. In all, 1,350 banks suspended operations during the year 1930. In the years between 1930 and 1933 alone, nearly 10,000 American banks failed or were suspended. These banks held deposits of over $6.8 billion (equivalent to $102,606,299,401 after inflation adjustments). And since most state deposit insurance schemes had shut down already, this meant that everyday American folks lost their savings and their money. Imagine that impact of working hard your entire life to buy the house of your dreams and a nice car but waking up one day to realize that your bank has shut down and all your money was just gone. Disappeared. Indeed, it was a life-reckoning event for many citizens. Citizens whose banks didn't shut down yet were in a state of constant panic, did not know what to do and worried if their bank would be next on the list. With President Herbert Hoover's administration and the Federal Reserve seemingly doing nothing to slow the accelerating trend of bank failures, American citizens were helpless. And after just 10 years since the regretful inception of the Federal Reserve, the American public felt the grim consequences of having a central bank in their country.

> *Under the Federal Reserve Act, panics are scientifically created." ~ Congressman Charles A. Lindbergh, "The Economic Pinch," 1921*

The Federal Reserve Act of 1913 required 40% gold backing of Federal Reserve Notes issued. By the late 1920s, and after just 7 years of fraudulent papermoney printing, the Federal Reserve had almost hit the limit of allowable credit of Federal Reserve demand notes that could be backed by the gold in its possession. To remove such constraint, and to keep printing worthless paper with numbers on them and call them money, the Feds needed to abolish such restraint. Therefore, they acted through their puppet government. On April 5, 1933, President Franklin D. Roosevelt signed the Presidential Executive Order 6102 forbidding the American public from owning gold and ordering them to surrender it to the Federal Reserve, through the government as a cover, under penalty of $10,000 or 5 to 10 years imprisonment or both sentences at the same time. Roosevelt ordered the freedom-loving public of the United

States to abandon their gold for worthless paper notes with ink and numbers on them. It was the largest gold robbery in American history.

By robbing the American people from their gold, the threat of a mob rushing to the Federal Reserve to redeem their worthless papermoney with Gold was finally put to rest. And thanks to having more gold in their reserves, the Feds can now legally print more papermoney and flood the market with it. Executive Order 6102 required all persons to deliver on or before May 1, 1933, to surrender their gold to the Federal Reserve, in exchange for $20.67 ($391 after inflation adjustment) per troy ounce. To make things even worst, the paper dollars the Feds were giving in exchange for gold would be devalued shortly after the Feds issued them due to the recession they created at the time. Under the Trading with the Enemy Act of 1917, as amended by the Emergency Banking Act of March 9, 1933, violation of the order was punishable by fine up to $10,000 (equivalent to $189,049) or up to 10 years in prison, or both. After 41 years of the legalized gold robbery, the limitation on gold ownership in the U.S. was finally repealed after President Gerald Ford signed a bill authorizing private property of gold coins, bars and certificates by an act of Congress codified in Pub.L. 93–373 which went into effect December 31, 1974. Thanks to countless prosecutions and arrests that stretched 41 years, Executive Order 6102 led to the extreme rarity of the 1933 Double Eagle gold coin and caused all gold coin production to cease and all 1933 minted coins to be destroyed.

Since the initiation of the Federal Reserve, its central bankers worked relentlessly at concealing its operations from the American public and greedily absorbed power and influence on all judiciary and government institutions or agencies mainly the FBI, CIA, Congress, the White House, the supreme court, and the Pentagon. It became virtually impossible for anyone to speak or stand against the Feds because anyone who spoke out or defied them was easily outcasted and publicly ridiculed. For example, Louis Thomas McFadden (born on July 25, 1876, and died on October 1, 1936) was a Republican member of the United States House of Representatives from Pennsylvania, serving from 1915 to 1935. Although he was a banker by trade, he was a fierce opponent of the

Federal Reserve System and was ultimately denounced and condemned by all Republicans while the mainstream media insured that the American public shuns him as a crazy man.

> *"Mr. Chairman, we have in this country one of the most corrupt institutions the world has ever known. I refer to the Federal Reserve Board and the Federal reserve banks. The Federal Reserve Board, a Government board, has cheated the Government of the United States and the people of the United States out of enough money to pay the national debt. The depredations and the iniquities of the Federal Reserve Board and the Federal Reserve banks acting together have cost this country enough money to pay the national debt several times over. Some people think the Federal reserve banks are United States Government institutions. They are not Government institutions. They are private credit monopolies which prey upon the people of the United States for the benefit of themselves and their foreign customers, foreign and domestic speculator sand swindlers, and rich and predatory money lenders." ~ Excerpts from Rep. Louis T. McFadden's speech on the floor of the House of Representatives, June 10, 1932.*

Smedley Darlington Butler (born on July 30, 1881 and died on June 21, 1940) was a United States Marine Corps Major General, the highest rank authorized at that time, and by the time of his death the most decorated Marine in U.S. history. During his 34-year career as a Marine, he participated in military actions in the Philippines, China, in Central America and the Caribbean during the Banana Wars, and France in World War I. By the end of his career, Butler had received 16 medals, 5 for heroism. He is one of 19 men to receive the Medal of Honor twice, 1 of 3 to be awarded both the Marine Corps Brevet Medal (along with Wendell Neville and David Porter) and the Medal of Honor, and the only Marine to be awarded the Brevet Medal and two Medals of Honor, all for separate actions. In 1933, Butler became a popular activist and started speaking out about the pervasive control of international bankers on America's institutions including the U.S. military. He testified in front of a congressional committee and warned against the existence of a group of wealthy industrialists plotting against the American public. The individuals he accused all denied the presence of a plot and the mainstream media, which was primarily controlled by the same financial institutions he warned against, ridiculed the allegations calling it a joke and a fantasy.

> *"I spent thirty-three years and four months in active military service as a member of this country's most agile military force, the Marine Corps. I served in all commissioned ranks from Second Lieutenant to Major-General. And during that period, I spent most of my time being a high-class muscleman for Big Business, for Wall Street and for the Bankers. In short, I was a racketeer, a gangster for capitalism. War is just a racket. A racket is best described, I believe, as something that is not what it seems to the majority of people. Only a small inside group knows what it is about. It is conducted for the benefit of the very few at the expense of the masses.*
>
> *I believe in adequate defense at the coastline and nothing else. If a nation comes over here to fight, then we'll fight. The trouble with America is that when the dollar only earns 6 percent over here, then it gets restless and goes overseas to get 100 percent. Then the flag follows the dollar and the soldiers follow the flag." ~ Smedley D Butler, from his speech in 1933.*

The McCormack–Dickstein Congressional committee's final report said:

> *"In the last few weeks of the committee's official life, it received evidence showing that certain persons had made an attempt to establish a fascist organization in this country. No evidence was presented, and this committee*

> *had none to show a connection between this effort and*
> *any fascist activity of any European country. There is no*
> *question that these attempts were discussed, were*
> *planned, and might have been placed in execution when*
> *and if the financial backers deemed it expedient."*

Ultimately, no prosecutions or further investigations followed, and Congress eventually dismissed the allegations. And with that conclusion along with the barrage of mockery from the banker's mainstream media, the high treason that Butler warned the American public about was quickly forgotten.

The Federal Reserve became the shadow government and the real administration of the United States that used its never-ending money supply for campaign support to nominate U.S. presidents, which ever since the establishment of this central bank such publicly elected commanders-in-chief became stage actors and no more than employees to the banking cartel of America. Very few public officials dared to stand against the Federal Reserve, and no U.S president signed an executive order that could have been a potential threat to the rule of the Feds except one man: John Fitzgerald Kennedy, the 35th President of the United States.

As a U.S. president, Kennedy understood the predatory nature of private central banking and the dangers that propagate from such a scheme to the American public. On June 4, 1963, Kennedy wrote and signed executive order 11110 which ordered the U.S. Treasury to issue a new public currency called the United States Note. Kennedy's new papermoney wasn't borrowed from the international bankers in the Federal Reserve but created by the publicly elected government of the United States and backed by the silver stockpiles it held. It was a very similar move to the one Abraham Lincoln made that triggered the Civil War and later led to his assassination. It was perfectly legal under the American Constitution for Kennedy or any other U.S. president to take such an action, but no man dared before Kennedy to challenge the Feds in fear of their ruthless retaliation.

Before signing the order, Kennedy repeatedly called for Congress to act on several occasions, including his 1963 Economic Report, where he wrote:

> *"I again urge a revision in our silver policy to reflect the status of silver as a metal for which there is an expanding industrial demand. Except for its use in coins, silver serves no useful monetary function. In 1961, at my direction, sales of silver were suspended by the Secretary of the Treasury. As further steps, I recommend repeal of those Acts that oblige the Treasury to support the price of silver; and repeal of the special 50-percent tax on transfers of interest in silver and authorization for the Federal Reserve System to issue notes in denominations of $1, so as to make possible the gradual withdrawal of silver certificates from circulation and the use of the silver thus released for coinage purposes. I urge the Congress to take prompt action on these recommended changes."*

The House of Representatives took up the president's request early in 1963, and passed HR 5389 on April 10, 1963, by a vote of 251 to 122. The Senate passed the bill on May 23, by a vote of 68 to 10. Kennedy signed the bill into law on June 4, 1963, and, on the same day, signed the executive order 11110 authorizing the Treasury Secretary to continue printing silver certificates during the transition period. The act, which became Public Law 88-36 (77 Stat. 54), repealed the Silver Purchase Act of 1934 and related laws and repealed a tax on silver transfers.

Just 5 months after signing the executive order 11110, Kennedy was assassinated in Dallas, Texas, while riding in a presidential motorcade through Dealey Plaza. The Dallas Police Department arrested former U.S. Marine Lee Harvey Oswald 70 minutes after the initial shooting. Oswald was charged under Texas state law with the murder of Kennedy as well as that of Dallas policeman J. D. Tippit, who had been fatally shot a short time after the assassination. At 11:21 a.m. Sunday, November 24, 1963, as live television cameras covered his transfer to the Dallas County Jail,

Oswald was fatally shot in the basement of Dallas Police Headquarters by Dallas nightclub operator Jack Ruby. Oswald was taken to Parkland Memorial Hospital where he soon died. Ruby was convicted of Oswald's murder and sentenced to death, though it was later overturned on appeal, and Ruby died in prison in 1967 while awaiting a new trial after becoming ill in his prison cell.

Lyndon Johnson was quickly sworn in as President on Air Force One in Dallas on November 22, 1963, just 2 hours and 8 minutes after John F. Kennedy was assassinated, amid suspicions of a conspiracy against the government. Surprisingly, John J McCloy (President of the Chase Manhattan Bank and President of the World Bank) was named to the Warren Commission responsible for investigating the murder of Kennedy. McCloy was selected by President Lyndon Johnson to serve on the Warren Commission in late November 1963. It was extremely alarming to see him head the investigation because he was a banker and not a professional criminal investigator. Even more surprising was that the American public remained mostly ignorant of the financial dimensions of the assassination of Kennedy and very few people heard about the executive order 11110 and the nation's new monetary system.

After a ten-month investigation, the Warren Commission concluded that Oswald assassinated Kennedy, that Oswald had acted entirely alone, and that Ruby had acted alone in killing Oswald. Just 4 months after the assassination, Secretary of the Treasury C. Douglas Dillon halted redemption of silver certificates for silver dollars. Kennedy's papermoney were then pulled from circulation and destroyed. And by the 1970s, large numbers of the remaining silver dollars in the mint vaults were sold to the collecting public for collector value. On September 9, 1987, as part of a general clean-up of executive orders, President Ronald Reagan issued Executive Order 12608, which removed the text which had been added to E.O. 10289 by E.O. 11110.

Kennedy's assassination remained the subject of widespread debate, and the information regarding the investigation remained a secret and was deliberately hidden from the American public for several decades after his murder. Polls conducted from 1966 to 2004 found that up to 80 percent of Americans have suspected that there was a conspiracy against their country. The American public had every right indeed to suspect a conspiracy against them because Kennedy himself warned about the existence of a conspiracy against the United States, and he made it very clear in his speech before the American Newspaper Publishers Association two years before his assassination asking them for help in revealing the truth to the American public.

"The very word "secrecy" is repugnant in a free and open society; and we are as a people inherently and historically opposed to secret societies, to secret oaths, and to secret proceedings. We decided long ago that the dangers of excessive and unwarranted concealment of pertinent facts far outweighed the dangers which are cited to justify it. Even today, there is little value in opposing the threat of a closed society by imitating its arbitrary restrictions. Even today, there is little value in ensuring the survival of our nation if our traditions do not survive with it. And there is very grave danger that an announced need for increased security will be seized upon by those anxious to expand its meaning to the very limits of official censorship and concealment. That I do not intend to permit to the extent that it is in my control. And no official of my Administration, whether his rank is high or low, civilian or military, should interpret my words here tonight as an excuse to censor the news, to stifle dissent, to cover up our mistakes or to withhold from the press and the public the facts they deserve to know.

It requires a change in outlook, a change in tactics, a change in missions--by the government, by the people, by every businessman or labor leader, and by every newspaper. For we are opposed around the world by a monolithic and ruthless conspiracy that relies primarily on covert means for expanding its sphere of influence--on infiltration instead of invasion, on subversion instead of

226

elections, on intimidation instead of free choice, on guerrillas by night instead of armies by day. It is a system which has conscripted vast human and material resources into the building of a tightly knit, highly efficient machine that combines military, diplomatic, intelligence, economic, scientific and political operations.

Its preparations are concealed, not published. Its mistakes are buried, not headlined. Its dissenters are silenced, not praised. No expenditure is questioned, no rumor is printed, no secret is revealed. It conducts the Cold War, in short, with a war-time discipline no democracy would ever hope or wish to match." ~ John F. Kennedy, address before the American Newspaper Publishers Association, April 27, 1961.

Just how the American public was told in the past that Andrew Jackson's failed assassination attempt, and the assassination of Abraham Lincoln were carried out by lone assassins, Kennedy's assassination was no different. And the truth remained hidden.

The private central banking model, which started in Sweden and England and manifested in the United States, had spread like a disease and infected all other countries in Europe since then. Eventually, the European nations realized that if every nation in the World is allowed full control over its papermoney, then they will undoubtedly witness unimaginable wealth and prosperity. Such reality would challenge the reigning regimes at the time, primarily the British Empire, and therefore, governments must never be allowed to issue their own papermoney. They must only borrow them from reigning regimes to keep such nations under control such as what King George III tried to do to the American colonies that led to the American Revolutionary War. However, if a mighty empire could not impose its currency on the rest of the world, the other nations must at least never issue a debt-free papermoney for their citizens. The prime reason for this is because a country with debt-attached papermoney can never compete economically or commercially with a foreign country that uses debt-free

227

papermoney. In other words, a nation that adopts a debt-free papermoney will immediately become prosperous and would reign supreme economically over other states that do not allow such currency for their citizens.

Thanks to warmongering nations, which were controlled by private central bankers that outlawed debt-free papermoney, humanity witnessed its first world wars for the first time in human history. World War I broke out in 1914 and soon later the Second World War started in 1939 for the same reason:

Bankers prohibit debt-free papermoney for the citizens of any nation-state. Any nation that officiates debt-free papermoney will be destroyed and dismantled, and the cost of such war will always be billed to the citizens of that nation.

Now that there's a private central bank in the United States, the international bankers could finance a war the likes the world had not seen before. Just one year after passing the Federal Reserve Act, which conclusively established a private central bank in the United States for the third time in its history, World War I (often abbreviated as WWI or WW1, also known as the First World War or the Great War) broke out in Europe on 28 July 1914. Like all wars in humanity's history, there's always a particular event that triggers the war, which is never the real reason for the war. In the case of WW1, the trigger for the war was the assassination of Archduke Franz Ferdinand of Austria, heir to the throne of Austria-Hungary, by Yugoslav nationalist Gavrilo Princip in Sarajevo on 28 June 1914. Naturally, such a tragic incident set off a diplomatic crisis between the countries to which the victim and his assassin belonged - Austria, Hungary, and Yugoslavia. Germany had nothing to do with the assassination, but Britain declared war on Germany anyway. And since Britain allied itself with France and Russia, all 3 countries now want to invade Germany. Why Germany?

Although Germany had a private central bank at the time, it was under strict control by the German government. As a result of that control over their central bank, Germany became a significant manufacturing powerhouse, and they were exporting products with which Britain could not compete. Britain saw Germany's industrial capacity as an economic threat. Britain's Pound was already in decline at the time because the British government emphasized excessively on banking and finance over agricultural and industrial development or infrastructure. Therefore, Britain considered Germany its financial adversary and was adamant about destroying it. Britain, Russia, and France began to mobilize militarily against Germany with the sole intention of demolishing its economy and breaking it into pieces. Germany had no choice but to defend itself. The invading countries under the fellowship of Britain not just defeated Germany, they flattened it. And following the treaty of Versailles, Germany was further insulted when the nations that participated in destroying Germany billed the entire cost of WW1 to the Germany public although Germany did not start that war. Such a war bill amounted to 3 times the value of all Germany itself at the time. Furthermore, Britain and its allies installed a German puppet government for the sole purpose of ensuring that the devastated nation would never fully recover or stand on its feet again to rise and become the prosperous industrial nation it once was.

Imagine that you are a salesman and that your competitor shows up suddenly at your doorstep one day, forces himself in and starts beating you down savagely because he is jealous of your prosperity. After burning your home to the ground, he then proceeds to destroy your business in a similar fashion. He then insults you further by forcing you to pay his travel expenses as well as his efforts of coming all the way to your property and destroying it. To punish you even further, he lobbies the local sheriff and municipality to make sure that you never restore your home and business to their former brilliance. You would naturally feel outraged and promptly seek vengeance and redemption. Well, this is precisely how the German public felt.

WW1 achieved its purpose of releasing the central bank of Germany from government control. This led to massive inflation and devaluation of Germany's currency which enslaved the German public in perpetual debt. As a result, Germany's currency became almost worthless, and it led to the tragic situation when citizens had to have a whole basket full of papermoney literally to buy a loaf of bread. Such ruthlessness against Germany, such humiliation and such injustice to the German public naturally created the bedrock that gave rise to a vicious leader who promised to avenge Germany against Britain and its allies. In their darkest hours is when nations usually conceive their beastly leaders. In Germany's case, it was, of course, Adolf Hitler (born on 20 April 1889 and died on 30 April 1945), who promised his countrymen to avenge Germany and restore it to its former glory. He offered the German people redemption in return for dictatorship. German national socialists eventually mobilized to take power and hunt down all the puppet officials that the Allies installed after the war. They nationalized the major industries and public utilities. Their first financial move was to correct their country's monetary system and take it off the hands of the corrupt private central bankers. They issued a new state-owned papermoney called the Reichsmark which was debt-free and based on a unit of value, not a unit of debt. Free of having to pay interest on worthless paper, Germany blossomed. It was an amazing transformation to witness. The international media even dubbed it *"the German miracle."* It wasn't a miracle at all, of course, but only the natural outcome when an honest and transparent government has full control over the issuing of its debt-free papermoney.

The repugnant term *"Nazi"* is just a short version of *"national socialists,"* which were part of the German worker's party. Labeling the enemy by distasteful words is a standard practice in tribal warfare. It is a very common tactic for demonizing the enemy and desensitizing the prosecutor to enable a human being to condemn mindlessly, and heartlessly murder the other human being on the other side of the border.

And once again, Germany's prosperity and financial independence from a private central bank loaning the nation's papermoney to its citizens at interest and raising their national debt became a threat to all tyrants everywhere who forced a debt-attached papermoney on their people. Most importantly, Germany is once again a threat to Britain and the tyranny of the Central Bank of England over Europe. To truly understand what was going on in the minds of European governments at the time before the commencing of WW2, here are some quotes from Winston Churchill:

> *"Should Germany merchandise again in the next 50 years we have led this war (WW1) in vain." ~ Winston Churchill in Times (1919)*

> *"We will force this war upon Hitler if he wants it or not." ~ Winston Churchill (1936 broadcast)*

> *"Germany becomes too powerful. We have to crush it." - Winston Churchill (November 1936 speaking to the US - General Robert E. Wood)*

> *"This war is an English war, and its goal is the destruction of Germany." - Winston Churchill (Autumn 1939 broadcast)*

> *"The war wasn't only about abolishing fascism, but to conquer sales markets. We could have, if we had intended so, prevented this war from breaking out without doing one shot, but we didn't want to." - Winston Churchill to Truman (Fulton, USA March 1946)*

> *"Germany's unforgivable crime before WW2 was its attempt to loosen its economy out of the world trade system and to build up an own exchange system from which the world-finance couldn't profit anymore." - Winston Churchill, The Second World War (Book by Winston Churchill, Bern, 1960)*

Germany's state-issued debt-free currency was a direct threat to all private central banks and tyrants around the world. And here history repeated itself when Britain, threatened by Germany's economic power and its debt-free currency, looked for an excuse to go to war again with Germany. And as early as the year 1933, the Allies started a global financial boycott against Germany which ultimately fueled WW2.

In July 1944, and while World War II was still raging, 730 delegates from all 44 Allied nations met at the Mount Washington Hotel, situated in Bretton Woods, New Hampshire, United States, to decide which papermoney of which country will reign over the global economy and regulate the world's monetary policy. Although many countries were represented at the Bretton Woods Conference, the United States and the United Kingdom were the most powerful in attendance and dominated the negotiations. The prime purpose of this conference was to elect the elite papermoney that will reign supreme over the rest. The Bretton Woods Conference, formally known as the United Nations Monetary and Financial Conference, eventually concluded that the United States Dollar is to be the world's papermoney. They agreed that all nations must settle their international balances in dollars, while U.S. dollars were fully convertible to gold. The exchange rate applied at the time was $35/ounce. Keeping the price of gold fixed and adjusting the supply of dollars was the responsibility of the United States. The conference also created the IMF (International Monetary Fund), whose primary purpose was to promote stability of exchange rates of other papermoneys into American dollars. Another international financial institution that propagated from the Bretton Woods Conference was The World Bank to provide loans to the low-income countries of the world using debt-attached papermoney to immediately subjugate their citizens using inescapable debt and put them under the mercy of international bankers. The World Bank and the IMF were both based in Washington, D.C., and worked closely with each other.

The mission statement of the World Bank aligns with the spirit for which the wars that conceived such an institution were fought: Enslavement of the people of the world through loans and debt-attached papermoney.

> *"To promote private foreign investment by means of guarantees or participations in loans and other investments made by private investors; and when private capital is not available on reasonable terms, to supplement private investment by providing, on suitable conditions, finance for productive purposes out of its own capital, funds raised by it and its other resources."* ~ *Article one of the Charter of the World Bank.*

The offspring creatures of the wars, the World Bank and the IMF, immediately started fulfilling their purpose of enslaving the underdeveloped nations of the world under unplayable debt thought fraudulent loans given to their corrupt governments. The Philippines is just one example of a Third World country where the public debt to international bankers reached around half of its GDP (gross domestic product) and prevented the nation, which is significantly abundant in natural resources, from any decent chance for financial prosperity.

> *"Finally, may I turn to that other slavery, our 26 billion dollars foreign debt? I have said that we shall honor it. Yet the means by which we shall be able to do so, are kept from us. Many of the conditions imposed on the previous government that stole this debt, continue to be imposed on us, who never benefitted from it. Today, we face the aspiration of a people who had known so much poverty and massive unemployment for the past 14 years, and yet offer their lives for the abstraction of democracy. Half our export earnings, 2 billion dollars out of 4 billion dollars which is all we can earn in the restrictive markets of the world, must go to pay just the interest on a debt, whose benefit the Filipino people never received." ~ President Corazon Aquino's speech to a Joint Session of the U.S. Congress on 18 September 1986, Washington, D.C.*

Why did the Allies elect the U.S. dollar to be the world's supreme papermoney instead of the British Pound? Due to the outbreak of WW1 and WW2, European countries could not use their national papermoney to buy goods and services from abroad because all European currencies were losing their value dramatically and were increasingly unstable. To purchase weapons and other war materials that they badly needed from the *"neutral"* United States to fuel the war, Britain, and its allies had to pay in gold or U.S. dollars. No credit was permitted under the strict Neutrality Act in effect in the United States at that time. Therefore, Europe's gold and silver flowed into North America and flooded their central banks. The United States held 3/4 of the world's supply of gold at the time.

The World Wars, therefore, constituted a very lucrative business for the United States and they pedestalized it as the weaponry warlord who would relentlessly fuel all warfare around the globe for years to come while shamelessly proclaiming neutrality and *"the pursuit of peace."* Thanks to the business of war and since no other currency had enough gold to back its papermoney with it as a replacement, the USD became the world's currency after the war. The mission statement of the World Wars for the competing nations can be put down simply in 4 words:

ONE MARKET, ONE PAPERMONEY.

WW1 and WW2 were not dubbed World Wars because all the countries of the world participated in them because evidently several countries in Europe and around the globe were not involved and remained neutral. In fact, they were named as World Wars because they would decide who would win the world at a time when the discovery of papermoney enabled a nation to finally rule the world as a whole for the first time in human history. And the United States of America reigned supreme after WW2 because its papermoney was selected by the central bankers to be the world's currency.

And of course, since history is always written by the winners, the world villainized Germany and demonized its dictator while blaming the nation for both wars and for all the lives that perished. The real brutes, of course, were the central bankers that banked these two World Wars into existence and acted as shadow governments by puppeteering the publicly elected leaders and their governments. WW1 and WW2 were purely bankers' wars. They were not nationalists' wars. They were fought out of greed for financial gains, not for freedom or democracy. They were waged primarily for financial supremacy by preserving the debt-attached papermoney of central banks and forcing this fraudulent currency on all nations of the world to enslave their citizens with perpetual debts and income taxes. And since war is the greatest harvest of money for these ruthless central bankers, the 80 million lives that perished as a consequence of these two wars died regretfully in the name of debt-attached papermoney and its sovereignty. They were human sacrifices to raise national debts for the benefit of central banks while those who survived the wars were reduced to slavery through the suffocating debt that immediately resulted from the war.

After World War II, the U.S. dollar became the reserve currency of the world, which meant that all other central banks of all counties must hold U.S. dollars in their reserves. In other words, all the other currencies of the world are backed by the U.S. dollar, which directly links anyone's country to the Federal Reserve's monetary system in the U.S. When the post-World War II monetary system was created, all U.S. dollars were backed and exchangeable for gold. A byproduct of this policy was that currencies used to be very stable in relation to one another.

The Federal Reserve, being a private bank of course and unaccountable to the American publicly elected government, did, in fact, start overprinting USD papermoney without backing the value of that papermoney by gold. Such violation to the international agreement of Bretton Woods' monetary system, led of course to the devaluation of the USD. Governments everywhere started to panic because they had piles of USD papermoney and they were worried if the United States would honor the agreement and redeem the worthless papermoney with gold at the agreed upon rate of 35 USD per ounce of pure gold. The problem was that the United States had nowhere near the gold required to redeem all those worthless paper notes with ink on them. Unwilling to revalue the Deutsche Mark to coverup for the fraud of papermoney printing by the Federal Reserve, West Germany left the Bretton Woods system in May 1971. In the following 3 months, this move strengthened its economy and simultaneously caused the dollar to drop 7.5% against the Deutsche Mark. In July 1971, Switzerland redeemed $50 million for gold and one month later in August, pulled its Swiss Franc from the Bretton Woods agreement. France sent a warship loaded with USD papermoney to New York harbor in early August of the same year with instructions to bring back its gold from the New York Federal Reserve Bank but only succeeding in redeeming $191 million for gold. As more nations flocked to the United States to redeem the fraudulent USD papermoney for gold, the exchange rate of the dollar against European currencies dropped significantly. On August 5, 1971, the United States Congress released a report recommending devaluation of the dollar, to protect the dollar against *"foreign price-gougers."* However, it was too little too late. The dollar was in a full-blown crisis and was on the brink of collapse and hyperinflation as faith in the USD was lost. Now that the stage was set, it was time for the Feds to finally break free from the Gold standard and put America for the first time ever on a full fiat papermoney system. Through their puppet government under President Richard Nixon, the Feds suspended the gold standard in a defiant violation of international law.

> *"I have directed Secretary Connally to suspend temporarily the convertibility of the dollar into gold and other reserve assets." ~ President Nixon stated on August 15, 1971, on national television.*

The *"temporarily"* word that Nixon used, of course, actually meant *"forever"* because the USD never honored the convertibility into gold ever again. By suspending one of the key components of the existing Bretton Woods system of international financial exchange, Nixon effectively rendered this international monetary law inoperative. This decision caused an international shock and governments everywhere got very nervous about the loans they gave to the United States and were understandably reluctant to loan any additional money to the American government without some form of collateral. To solve this problem, Nixon decided to use American land as collateral instead of gold to honor the international loans. On January 1, 1970, Richard Nixon signed the National Environmental Policy Act (NEPA), which took vast areas of public lands and made them off-limits to the American people. He misleadingly told the American public that *"the goal of environmental policy is to protect the environment for future generations."* Nixon, of course, had no concern for the environment and environmentalists were skeptical of his intentions because he had almost no record on environmental issues and had barely mentioned the subject during his campaign. The primary reason for the Act was to pledge those pristine lands as well as their vast mineral resources as collateral on the outstanding national debt. These programs were quite literary to conceal the scale of the land grab and the collateralization of the American people's heritage.

Richard Nixon was the 37th President of the United States from 1969 until 1974, one of the most infamous characters in U.S. politics, and the only president to resign from office in U.S. history. Ever since his decision of taking the USD off the gold standard, the American dollar was floating and backed by nothing. This means that all other currencies of the world automatically became backed by nothing more than the *"trust"* in the American dollar. And so, all other currencies of the world became nothing more than fiat currencies.

By 1973, the Bretton Woods system was replaced de facto by a monetary policy based on freely floating fiat currencies. The consequence of having fiat currencies is that whenever the Feds created more money, it diluted the currency supply of all other nations because the USD backs their reserves. The value of all countries' reserves of their national currency drops whenever the Feds pumps more U.S. dollars artificially into the economy. The Feds continued their insatiable addiction of committing fraud by relentlessly printing papermoney in abundance and accountable to no one. The Russian and Chinese ruling classes took notice, of course, and their reaction was to sell U.S. dollar reserves and buy gold over the same period.

Central banks in all countries operated the same way and they were the legal entity that managed the nation's money supply and could lend money, with interest of course, to the government and other private banks in the country. This is how it all worked:

- ➤ When the government needs more money than it receives through taxes, they ask the treasury department for money by issuing an IOU or government bond, which is a bond issued by the national government with a promise to pay periodic interest payments and to repay the face value on the maturity date.
- ➤ The Treasury (an executive department of government) receives the bond from the government and puts in on auction for any banker to buy. Usually, the bond is purchased by the central bank of that nation, but it wasn't uncommon for bonds to be purchased by private

companies, wealthy investors, or even the central banks of other countries.

➢ If the central bank was the one to purchase the bond, it then writes a check to the local banks in the country for the value of the bond and authorizes them to create this new money. This central bank, of course, just invents money out of thin air because papermoney is just worthless paper with numbers on it. It is like writing any number you desire on a magical checkbook, which turns it into real money.

➢ The local commercial banks (obviously all are private banks and owned by wealthy people) then type numbers on a screen and create money out of nothing. At this exchange at the private banks, money is created and can be used to pay government bills.

Another part of this money creation system happened on the commercial banking's side. Every time people took out a loan to pay for a house, TV, or car, bankers simply type some numbers digitally in their account and charge them interest on it. So basically, each time bankers issue a loan, they don't use other people's deposited money but create new money by typing digits into a computer. Around 97% of all funds were generated that way and only 3% was the physical paper cash and coins that people carried.

In such a gloomy reality, when you take out a loan or a credit card, you are not borrowing money from the bank, but you are actually giving them money. Money was manufactured digitally out of thin air at the banks when people applied for a loan, and that is why such a fraudulent system is called the debt-based economy. Not only one was giving his/her bank free money whenever they applied for a loan, but the bank also charged them interest fees on that new money that it did not have before the loan. Oblivious of the fraud, the poor person would then have to work for most of his/her life to repay the money taken from the bank while the owners of the bank sit back and enjoy the money as it piles up.

Another form of fraud that these bankers could do was lend out up to 10 times more money than they had in reserves. This practice was called fractional reserve lending and it was one of the policies fabricated by the cult of central banking. Due to such a policy, every dollar you deposit in the bank authorizes the bank to loan out 10 times more. So, if you deposit $100 in your bank account, you're licensing the bank to loan $1000 to others thanks to your deposit. Due to this central banking policy, commercials banks cannot lend as much as they want and are obliged to keep a minimum of 10% reserves in their vaults. Such policy of course literary legalized and regulated fraud through government regulation. Due to political and financial corruption, this legalized fraud became the foundation of the banking system of the planet. As a result, there were many booms and busts cycles accompanied by bank failures that were falsely blamed on the business cycle. When a commercial bank failed in a tribal nation, the central bank of that country typically came to the rescue by just printing more papermoney and loaning it to the bank with low interest. Central banks had a legal name for this routine process: *"providing liquidity."*

The Inflation Model

Every time more loans were given out, more money is created, and the rest of the money in circulation is worth less and less as the years go on – this is known as inflation. Inflation was the price everyone had to pay for the fraud of debt-attached papermoney printing. Easy money now in exchange for a burden on future generations. It was a snowball system that allowed the rich to become even richer. Savers, on the other hand, were losing billions every year thanks to low-interest rates and the devaluation of the currency. If a person just opened a savings account, it was almost like burning money because the value of the currency continuously dropped over the years, which meant that the purchasing power of their money at the time would get them much less in the future.

When people took out a loan, it was written down as an asset in the bank in negative form, or otherwise known as *"debt."* Under this system, debt is money. So, instead of gold being the backbone of the economy, it became debt. This system is known as *"the debt-based monetary system,"* and it requires that debt must always grow for the economy to function. Countries and people must become more and more rooted in debt so that there is more money in the system because debt is money. If governments and people stopped borrowing money, the debt doesn't grow, the money supply shrinks, and the system falters.

> *"If there were no debts in our money system, there wouldn't be any money." ~ Marriner Stoddard Eccles, U.S. banker, economist, member and chairman of the Federal Reserve Board.*

The Interest Rates Policy

The central bankers of every country had controlled money by adjusting their supply and how much it costs to borrow money, otherwise known as interest rates. With these tools as consequence of human group psychology, central bankers created booms and busts in the economy at will. For example, in the year 2000, the Feds cut interest rates to 1%. They did this to try to fight off the recession from the dotcom bubble and encourage people to borrow money. When the interest rates are low, citizens save a lot on repaying mortgages if they took out a loan from the bank. And since the 1% interest rates had not been seen at the time since 1950, it was a pretty good idea for the average American citizen to borrow money. The Feds thought they could create a wealth effect and people would start buying houses, the prices would go up, and people would start feeling wealthier and spend more money in the economy and stimulate it. The Feds sure succeeded in getting people to borrow money to buy houses, but they borrowed too much, and the result was the 2008 housing bubble. This is a prime example of what could go wrong when central banks mess with the economy. Although corrupt commercial bankers had a lot to answer for their role in the 2008 crises, the Feds had a far more outstanding long-term impact.

Central bankers and commercial bankers together controlled the economy and people's money. The difference between the two is that the first could create new money at will whenever they felt like it while the latter needed loans to generate new money.

Peer-To-Peer Cryptocurrencies Were Born

On 18 August 2008, the domain name *"bitcoin.org"* was registered. In November that year, a link to a paper authored by an unknown, called Satoshi Nakamoto, titled *"Bitcoin: A Peer-to-Peer Electronic Cash System"* was posted to a cryptography mailing list. Nakamoto implemented the bitcoin software as open source code and released it in January 2009. In January 2009, the bitcoin network came into existence after Satoshi Nakamoto mined the first ever block on the chain, known as the genesis block, for a reward of 50 bitcoins. Embedded in this block was the following text:

> *"The Times 03/Jan/2009 Chancellor on brink of second bailout for banks."*

This note has been interpreted as both a timestamp of the genesis date and a derisive comment on the instability caused by fractional-reserve banking. In the early days, Nakamoto is estimated to have mined one million bitcoins. In 2010, Nakamoto handed the network alert key and control of the Bitcoin Core code repository over to Gavin Andresen, who later became lead developer at the Bitcoin Foundation. Nakamoto subsequently disappeared from any involvement in bitcoin. Andresen stated he then sought to decentralize control, saying:

> *"As soon as Satoshi stepped back and threw the project onto my shoulders, one of the first things I did was try to decentralize that. So, if I get hit by a bus, it would be clear that the project would go on."*

The blockchain is a public ledger that records bitcoin transactions. A novel solution accomplishes this without any trusted central authority: the maintenance of the blockchain is performed by a network of communicating nodes running bitcoin software. Transactions of the form payer X sends Y bitcoins to payee Z are broadcast to this system using readily available software applications. Network nodes can validate transactions, add them to their copy of the ledger, and then transmit these ledger additions to other nodes.

The blockchain is a distributed database – to achieve independent verification of the chain of ownership of any and every bitcoin amount, each network node stores its copy of the blockchain. Approximately 6 times per hour, a new group of accepted transactions, a block, is created, added to the blockchain, and quickly published to all nodes. This allows bitcoin software to determine when a bitcoin amount has been spent, which is necessary to prevent double-spending in an environment without central oversight. Whereas a conventional ledger records the transfers of actual bills or promissory notes that exist apart from it, the blockchain is the only place that bitcoins can be said to live in the form of unspent outputs of transactions.

Following the Bitcoin model of the year 2009, numerous cryptocurrencies were created, known as altcoins, as a blend of bitcoin alternative. Each of these derivatives uses a version of blockchain technology, but they all share the same concept of the distributed public ledger.

Central Banking Collapsed Forever

The emergence of cryptocurrencies brought renewed enthusiasm about the prospects of an economic revival in developing countries around the globe. Such nations suffered for so long from poverty, corruption, inflation, and high unemployment levels.

A global remittance system infested the tribal world, which was based almost entirely on the activities of citizens of developing countries who are immigrants in the developed world. From time to time, these individuals had to send money back home to their families and loved ones. To do so, they had to rely on intermediary services like Western Union and MoneyGram. These middlemen charged fees on the already-poor workforce which considerably decreased the amount of money that ever reached their loved ones in the impoverished communities back home. And as these middlemen got richer and accumulated billions of dollars in profit from just moving data from one computer to another, the public in developing countries struggled to sustain itself.

Cryptocurrencies drastically reduced the cost of remittance as well as the hassle required to receive the international money transfer. And so, startups started to emerge in developing countries and offered money transfer services through a wide range of cryptocurrencies to cut down the cost of sending money back and forth for the people who need it the most.

242

A large chunk of the global human population in the tribal world lived under miserable conditions in underdeveloped nations and did not have a bank account. The lack of financial inclusion was a massive problem in many low-income countries around the world. This lack of access to banking instruments precluded the unbanked people from being able to participate in global commerce to lift the living standards of their communities and grow into something better.

Thanks to cryptocurrencies, millions of unbanked people could finally get access to banking services and financial instruments through mobile phone apps. Telecommunications, therefore, was able to achieve a much more significant market penetration than traditional banking services. These early crypto-banking platforms were using the reach of telecoms to take financial emancipation to the doorsteps of the unbanked and underbanked. The result was higher financial inclusion through technology and telecoms. Local merchants started to think global concerning imports and exports and gave them access to more affluent markets than their disadvantaged local markets, and ultimately got them started in the import and export business which was a fundamental part of national commerce.

Corruption was one of the significant problems of low-income countries around the world. Corrupt government officials through the lack of economic democratization conceived designs that left the collective commonwealth of these countries in the hands of a few people. They plotted schemes that diverted state funds for their selfish interests. The use of cryptocurrencies, especially those built upon public smart contract protocols allowed for a more transparent contractual system and gave the public access to fundamental financial information, which was hidden from them previously through the national bureaucracy. Therefore, with records on the blockchain being public, citizens were able to monitor the way public officials utilized state funds, and consequently creating fairness in the economy.

It was only a matter of few decades before the cryptocurrency revolution took charge of the global monetary system of the world enabling people to create and share the wealth without the bureaucracy of middlemen and bankers. And with that phenomenon the trust in central banking started to wither and rumors of a financial crises started spreading.

As people's trust in central banking faded, the wealth of the world poured into these cryptocurrencies and humanity witnessed the most significant transfer of wealth in its history and new wealth immerged from undeveloped countries.

People were able to secure their wealth in a wide selection of cryptocurrencies, and so, the eminent financial collapse of central banks didn't bring the global economy down to its knees as most people feared. Soon enough central banks and commercial banks collapsed followed by the collapse of central governments and replaced by the global peer-to-peer legislature.

One Monetary System For All Humanity

History has shown repeatedly that money backed by nothing more than faith (fiat currency) is troublesome and destined to collapse sooner or later. Without any exceptions, every fiat *papermoney* in human history eventually returned to its intrinsic value: zero.

The value of money must be linked to something physical, which must be rare. Gold owes its status as a precious metal to its rarity. All the gold mined throughout history would fit into a square box with sides of around 20 meters in length. This is not due to a failure to excavate the metal from the earth, but because there isn't much of it around. Gold is rare throughout the universe because it is a relatively hefty atom, consisting of 79 protons and 118 neutrons. That chemical composition makes it so hard to produce that it needs a dying star (a supernova) in its incredible heat and pressure to forge gold chemically. There is even doubt today that supernovae are up to the job because some scientists suggest that even more violent events, such as collisions between neutron stars (the ultra-dense cores of dead stars) may be needed. After recognizing gold's heritage as an asset and a store of value along with the inherent difficulty of manufacturing it, humanity elected a monetary system represented by Gold. Gold represents this currency, but it isn't based on Gold. It isn't convertible or exchangeable for Gold either. It is only tied to Gold by a social contract agreed upon and elected by humanity collectively that says this new money has physical value represented in Gold. In other words, the *distribian* coin is a fiat legal tender valued by gold, but not backed by it.

Shortly before the collapse of central banking, *Unipublic* elected a social contract uniting the world under one monetary policy. The new money is simply referred to as coins, which exist only in digital form but with value directly linked to physical gold. Each coin represents one gram of pure gold in the physical world. Since there's no central authority in *distribia* from which coins can be converted back into the reserve asset, convertibility of *distribian* coins to physical gold isn't possible. The public, however, is free to accept and buy gold coins as an asset following the *"one gram of physical pure gold equals to one distribian coin"* universal standard. The price of gold is not up for speculation and is irrelative of supply and demand, and the same goes for the price of all raw materials in *distribia*. While setting prices through supply and demand, which is a very manipulative and corruptible business, was an economic feature in the tribal era, *distribians* today rely on *price-fixing* through elected social contracts because financial speculation is illegal in *distribia*. Therefore, the public can only buy and sell physical gold at the universally agreed price of *one distribian coin equals one gram of pure gold,* and any manipulation of this rate by anyone is unlawful.

Physical gold is an asset with a constant value and not a medium of exchange (or money) because the *distribian coin* is the only legal money in *distribia*. In other words, all transactions in *distribia's* economy are digital where the *distribian coin* is the only money.

Acknowledging pure gold as an asset and setting a constant value for it in the *distribian coin smartcontract* played a crucial role in securing people's wealth before *distribia* and allowed for a safe transition from one economic and monetary system to another. Since the price of pure gold was relatively the same in all authoritarian nations, people who didn't yet buy *distribian coin* could first purchase physical gold and then later sell it as an asset for *distribian coin* when the global transition to *distribia* was complete.

Credit is a modern word for usury, which is the practice of making loans of any kind that come with interest or obligations immediately attached to them. Credit or usury allows one party to provide money or resources to another party where that second party does not reimburse the first party directly but instead promises to repay or return those resources later.

Distribia eradicated usury or credit or debt along with tribalism. In the *distribian* economy today, the only way you can increase your spending is by increasing your income, which requires you to be more productive and do more work. Therefore, in our *distribian* economy, increased productivity is the only way for growth. Knowing that a person's spending is another's income, the *distribian* economy grows every time you or anyone else is more productive. Due to this economic law, the productivity growth line of the *distribian* economy is always increasing upwards and never goes into cycles, which were very common when debt was legal under tribalism. The booms and busts in the economic cycles of tribal countries were primarily due to debt. A boom-bust cycle is a process of economic expansion and contraction that occurs repeatedly. The boom-bust cycle was a key characteristic of capitalist economies of tribal nations. During the boom the economy grows, jobs are plentiful, and the markets bring high returns to bankers or investors. In the subsequent bust, the economy shrinks, people lose their jobs and investors lose money. Boom-bust cycles last for varying lengths of time, and they also vary in severity.

Thankfully, when we got rid of bankers and debt, humanity's economy thrived and never failed again. In *distribia*, money is a public utility, and the monetary policy is owned and regulated by the public collectively. *The distribian coin* is a digital currency protected by cryptography and *Ve*. People conduct their financial transactions digitally through their *Ve* using *distribian coin* in a peer-to-peer network. Unlike the national currencies of central bankers, *distribian coin* does not follow the regulations of any central authority. Instead, the public, which is basically every living human being, regulates it together. *The distribian coin* is a *smartcontract* and just like all other *smartcontracts*, the public can modify this monetary system and repeal it if they decide it doesn't work for them anymore.

The distribian coin is designed for a trade-based economy. It creates new money out of thin air whenever people trade, and it necessitates that people continue trading for new money to be created and pumped into the economy to keep it functioning.

Every *sale transaction* is followed by another transaction called *new money transaction* that introduces new money in the economy of the same value as the sale transaction. The coin's *smartcontract* creates new coins for the same number of coins included in each sale transaction and distributes it evenly to every living human being excluding those involved in the transaction. If, for example, you purchased a product for 10 coins, the merchant will receive his 10 coins and new 10 coins will be created and divided equally among everyone in the public excluding yourself and the merchant. So, everyone's share of that 10 coins will of course be in the fractions.

This policy for new money creation feeds into a universal basic income (UBI) that acts as a salary to every person alive so that everyone can secure their most basic needs. This income along with the money proceeding from taxes and other sources, which we will discuss later in other chapters, feed into the UBI that everyone gets unconditionally.

The idea of a guaranteed minimum income dated back in history at least to the late 18th century and was a vital feature of all modern welfare states before *distribia*, with insurances for and against unemployment, sickness, parenthood, accidents, old age and so forth. Each nation-state had its version of social welfare while most nations of the 21st century were incapable or could not afford such programs. UBI is a form of social security or welfare program, in which everyone worldwide receives a regular, livable and unconditional sum of money, from the global economy. Payments do not require the recipient to work or look for work and are independent of any other income the person is currently generating.

Capitalism, being a product of tribalism, revolves around the centralization of wealth in the hands of very few people. Understand capitalism begins by asking this fundamental question: WHERE DOES THE CAPITAL IN CAPITALISM COME FROM? It is essential to understand and answer this question first because capitalism is the offspring of central banks and fiat money. The capital in capitalism is given for free to large private corporations by central bankers, who also print that money for free. Usually, the central bankers themselves owned all essential utilities and commerce in the world. They could buy anything and anyone because they simply print their money for free while others have to earn it by working for them. Capitalism, therefore, is economic slavery to a ruling class of bankers. It is a system where elite bankers rose to the level of the mythical Midas. And while Midas could turn anything he touches into gold, central bankers could turn worthless paper into money and buy all the gold in the world including Midas himself.

The capitalist systems around the world relied on people competing for jobs in the labor market. This competition naturally results in winners and losers. Winning and losing always go together. Nobody wins unless someone else loses, and nobody loses unless someone wins. Their relationship is transactional such as the case with buying and selling. And so, capitalism guarantees unemployment because it is inherent to the system. Unable to secure a position, the unemployed were left with no alternatives, and some became homeless. Therefore, unemployment and houselessness were inevitable byproducts of a capitalist economy because naturally there will never be enough jobs to go around for everyone and some people must be left behind regardless of their qualification or education. Capitalist nations understood this problem, and their solution to it was to create unnecessary jobs, which do not produce any value whatsoever and are there to keep unemployment levels as low as possible. These pointless jobs revolve around managerial positions, which manage those who produce the product or service the company offers.

Predominantly in capitalist economies, companies' chain of managerial authority runs at least 3 or more levels down the ladder. This employment system also involves additional deplorable jobs to coordinate, arrange meetings and do the paperwork for executives, because in a typical capitalist economy the paperwork of what you do is more important than what you do. Everything must be written down or documented in emails and archived in endless filing systems. The prime reason for documenting everything is to make the workers as easily deplorable as possible so that the employer can readily hire someone else who could just read the records and promptly start operating as expected without spending much time discovering the job. The deplorable administrative jobs are essentially useless, and even those working such roles secretly know that they shouldn't be performing them. Nonetheless, those in managerial positions are paid much more than the so-called *"blue collar"* jobs. While the white-collar workers operate behind a comfortable desk, the blue-collar workers get their hands dirty doing manual labor or working in a division of manufacturing to produce the goods the company is selling while earning as less as possible. Therefore, in a capitalist economy, those who produce value or service are underappreciated or abused while those who manage them are generously rewarded.

A typical capitalist employer would justify this horrific work reality by claiming that executive jobs carry additional responsibilities, which explains the higher pay. This, of course, is a hollow claim and similar to when they initially alleged that the harder you work in a capitalist economy, the more prosperous you'll get. Evidently, it was always visible to everyone that executives work the least with more flexible working hours while earning the most. Blue-collar workers continuously worry about fulfilling the almost impossible targets their employers set for them while the executives sit back with little to worry about other than how others are performing for them.

In a typical capitalist corporation of tribal cultures, those at the top of the hierarchy commonly had a very vague knowledge about how the goods and services of their company were being built or delivered. The board of directors or the high-ranking executive titles within the C-Suite did not concern themselves with such information because they only cared about capital and financial statistics on a sheet or a presentation. And for as long as they were seeing good figures happening, they didn't care about polluting the rivers or the soil or the air and killing off all the fish or the birds or the plants. They only cared about money and acquiring as much of it as possible without really being aware of anything else. Additionally, any progress or success generated in such corporations was mainly credited to those in high-level management and rarely to those producing the actual work. And while managers typically reaped all the credit, the real instigators of such success are left behind, dismissed, and ultimately let go.

Tribalism's love for delegation is the primary reason for structuring corporations in such dysfunction and abusive manner. It lowered the workers that produced the real value to the very bottom of the pyramid with the least payrolls and benefits. And while managerial jobs reaped the most substantial cut of the profit, blue-collar workers took home just enough money to continue working. The moral and spiritual damage that comes from this work structure is profound. However, capitalism needs useless jobs because jobless people don't generate income and therefore can't buy the products that capitalists produce or pay income taxes to the state. And so, by having more people working useless jobs, a capitalist economy can keep on ticking.

The debt-based economy relied on maintaining most of the human population in a constant state of debt so that new money is pumped into the economy to keep it functioning. Central bankers were unelected officials who owned the monetary policies of the planet, and they set the rules answering to no government. Money creation was a monopoly that they held, and they alone profited from it. By contrast to *distribia's* monetary system, which distributes the new money to absolutely everyone, central bankers kept all the new money that their policy generated to themselves.

When the debt-based economy collapsed under its flaws, humanity replaced it by a productivity-based economy that illegalized debt in favor of a trade-based economy. So, when people transact (sell products or services), the coin's *smartcontract* pumps *new money* into the economy out of thin air that everyone gets an equal slice of it. And so, *distribia* brought democracy to the banker's monopoly of money creation.

Before the collapse of governments and their central banks, 10% of the human population controlled most of the wealth in the world, and 1% of those controlled more than half of the world's wealth. Although the wealthy and the bankers were not happy of course with this cryptocurrency and downvoted it at *Unipublic*, the poor and the middle class formed the majority vote and voted in favor of *distribian* coin. The moment the *distribian* coin's *smartcontract* was activated, the wealth of billionaires was distributed evenly to everyone else according to the *smartcontract's* policies of minimal and maximal incomes.

UBI boosted people's productivity and innovation. People could use the *"free money"* given to them and use it for producing goods and services of their own. A byproduct of the UBI model was that innovation and productivity increased significantly. UBI proved that when our basic needs as humans are fulfilled, we tend to act on our interests and produce remarkable products and innovations.

To prevent bad actors from abusing the UBI by repeatedly buying and selling the same products from each other to generate new money in the economy to boost the UBI, a 3% sales tax is applied to every sales transaction. Such tax is applied to the side buying the goods or services and is integrated automatically on the listing price - meaning it is not added later to the price listed on the product but is incorporated in it. *Ve* also has an algorithm that fights such fraud by identifying the product that was bought and sold multiple times by the same individuals and imposing extra sales taxes on such a product. All revenues from the sales tax are added to the UBI and distributed evenly to everyone excluding those involved in the original transaction.

Maximal Account Balance = UBI Multiplied By 83

Along with the income that *the distribian coin* produces for UBI, it insures a maximal account balance or a cap on a person's account balance. This cap is dynamic and works in tandem with UBI. Since UBI fluctuates constantly depending on how well the economy is performing, or more precisely on how many sale transactions are occurring in the economy, the maximal coin balance varies relative to that fluctuation as well.

For example, if the poorest person in society received 5,000 coins from UBI in one month, the richest person could accumulate up to 415,000 coins at most in that same month and any excess is distributed evenly to everyone else. If someone in *distribia's* society becomes a millionaire (owns a million or more coins), everyone else must have received at least 12,049 coins in that same month. As a result, to have billionaires in *distribia's* society, it requires everyone becoming millionaires and receive at least 12,048,192 gold coins as UBI. And so, when people become richer, they're automatically enriching everyone else and their wealth is always tied to the poorest in society.

"If we make it, we make it together" is what such monetary system stands for, which is completely opposite to all versions of capitalist systems that exists earlier. Capitalism stands for: *"when you have more, others must have less,"* which from a selfish perspective sounds great if you follow such Stone Age concepts as the *"survival of the fittest"*. Since in capitalist economies there were no limits on how rich people can get and since having more for oneself automatically means others are having less, poverty always accompanied capitalism.

Another reason for setting a cap on account balances is to prevent the ancient problem with single-purpose money to perpetuate in society through *distribian* coins. As we explained earlier, money was used historically to serve many purposes, and you could grow it, reproduce it, eat it, and produce other value from it such as when cattle were money. However, when metallic money emerged, money became single-purpose and used only as a tool for trade. Similarly, the *distribian* coin is a cryptocurrency and is basically nothing more than data, and it is worthless in its given form other than a tool that people can use to buy and sell goods and services. It is a measure of wealth, but it is not wealth. It is not an asset. And so, to prevent people from accumulating vast sums of this medium of exchange, the coin's ledger caps all balances for all people to a maximum number, which does not change. And since money is not wealth, a cap on money balances does not mean a cap on wealth because people can decide to buy things such as precious metals with that money before it reaches the cap. People who wish to accumulate wealth, therefore, will feel compelled to invest coins in real assets as a store of value. They can, for example, buy gold, silver, and other rare metals or spend that money on projects such as building neighborhoods.

However, financial transactions can only occur digitally through *distribian* coins and never physically through any assets such as pure gold or silver. Such policy means that you can't buy clothing for example by giving someone gold coins because *Ve* does not record such transactions and the items you acquired that way will remain not legally yours.

Tribalism cultivated an economic reality based on greed. It was an extremely ugly society. A society with an attitude to others that is based on *"all for me, nothing for anyone else."* A community with the desire to maximize personal gain at the expense of others. Such society based on such a selfish principle was doomed to failure and headed for massive self-destruction. It was a culture in which ordinary human instincts of mutual support and emotions of sympathy or solidarity were beaten down and driven out. A society so ugly that you wouldn't want anyone to live in it, and you certainly would not wish it for your own children.

Capitalism was a for-profit economy with no limits on how much profits a capitalist can produce from customers. Companies could charge whatever they choose, and things got worse when these companies owned intellectual property rights over essential products that people desperately needed such as drugs or technology. What was known as *"intellectual property rights"* in a tribal culture is, in fact, a language-washed counterpart of *"monopoly rights."* Through these monopoly rights, capitalists had monopoly pricing power and the legal authority to suppress and stifle innovation by restricting people from producing and enhancing whatever the tyrannical patent owner had patented.

A pharmaceutical company could raise the price of a prescription forty folds for example or more because there were no laws in most capitalist economies that said they couldn't. Drug companies aggressively defend their high prices by claiming that they are necessary to cover their research and development costs, enabling

253

them to discover innovative new medicines. However, this claim is far from the truth because very often the original discovery occurred in a university lab then licensed to a start-up company partly owned by the university and then to a large company. There was very little innovation at the big drug firms. Like big fish swallowing little fish, larger companies either bought small firms outright or licensed promising drugs from them. Capitalism's pharmaceutical companies spent most of their capital on marketing and administration than on research and development. They were investor-owned businesses after all, and they had the right to charge whatever the market would bear which for desperately sick patients or their insurers was quite a lot. But the pharmaceutical market was hardly an example of unfettered capitalism because the public was becoming increasingly dependent on the products of technology companies in their daily lives and such products were as sought-after as drugs.

"Profit" might sound like a good word until you realize that the product you purchased for 100 dollars cost the capitalist just one dollar in total to produce. And it gets even worse when you know that the capitalist is more interested in profit than anything else, and such an ugly fact manifests itself in the quality or value of the products that the capitalist business produces. Capitalists, therefore, were exploiting the public and they rarely produced goods or services that came with a real benefit or value to the people. It didn't matter if the product was made of chemicals that are harmful to nature or consumers. It didn't matter either if the product had the potential of eroding the social fabric of society or fuel hatred and bigotry. It really didn't matter if the product had negative psychological consequences on consumers and could harm them in the long run and drive them to act against their best interest. For as long as capitalists could sell their products with an ample profit margin, nothing else matters.

The fuel that keeps this wheel of exploitation turning is called *"patents,"* which were never for the benefit of society, progress, or innovation. Patents were licenses from a government authority awarding a right or title for a set period, especially the sole right to exclude others from making, using, or selling an invention. In other words, it was a way to prevent others from producing a product that one capitalist is making and allowing him to make as much money as possible by cutting off the competition. It is not a free market when your competitors are legally restrained from competing with you, but nonetheless, capitalist economies always masqueraded under the *"free market"* label. Since its inception, this tribal invention has been widely criticized by the public as spurring exploitive profiteering. Because if the people could produce the overpriced products themselves, prices would naturally come down as competition grows and every manufacturer shares a portion of the profit.

Patenting was a tool for monetizing ideas, building corporate empires and inhibiting innovation and startups in favor of monopolies. Large corporations, of course, fiercely defended their patents as the cradle of innovation. However, they could not ignore roughly 7,000 years of recorded history when the economy of civilizations flourished through free trade in true open markets that had no such concepts as patents. Some capitalist companies took the concept of patenting too far by patenting a gene inside the human body. They licensed something inside all of us as human beings, which existed in our bodies long before anyone learned how to count.

Back in 1990 scientists made an announcement that shook the world. They discovered that somewhere in the 17th chromosome of the human DNA there was gene linked to breast cancer. They did not know where exactly it was or what it was or why even it is related to breast cancer. All they knew was that it was there in that section of the gene. What followed was a race by researchers to find this so-called *"breast-cancer-gene."* They employed enormous resources to determine with relative accuracy whether a woman would contract breast cancer years before any other test. Thanks to such early detections, survival rates would naturally skyrocket, and many human lives could be saved. Then in 1994 it finally happened, and a team of researchers at an American university announced that they had found the gene (called the BRCA1) and soon later they discovered another similar gene with nearly identical effects (called BRCA2). Women with mutations in one of those two genes have an 80% chance of contracting breast cancer in their lifetimes and could finally test for it. It was a life-changing breakthrough for the women found to have the mutation. Recognizing the commercial applications, these same researchers at the university founded a company and quite literary patented the two genes to restrict everyone else worldwide from doing anything with these two genes. Consequently, they became the global monopoly for research and testing on the BRCA1 and BRCA2 genes.

Everyone on the planet wanting to test if they will have breast cancer in the future had to go to a single company based in Utah, USA. This company, now being a monopoly, can of course put any price tag they wish because customers have no other choice but to pay. The company made its millions of dollars of course from diagnostic test exclusivity, which led it from being a startup in 1994 to becoming a publicly traded company with 1200 employees and about $500M in annual revenue in 2012. They priced their diagnostic test at 4,000$ even though the actual process involved in performing the analysis cost only a fraction of that. But such overpricing of course is nothing new to monopolies armed with patents in a tribal culture. Such thing, of course, was fundamentally unjust and the public sued that company at the American supreme court on the basis that their patent was on a non-patentable material (the human gene). Although at the time the lawsuit was in courts around 21% of the human genome had already been patented by other companies, all 9 supreme court judges voted unanimously against genome licensing and virtually ended such kind of patenting in the USA ever since. All gene patents in the U.S. began to legally expire in 2014 although in other countries such practices continued because each tribal nation was judicially independent and practiced that law differently.

Nonetheless, the American supreme court also held that manipulation of any gene to create something not found in nature could still be eligible for patent protection. This means that a company, for example, can patent children by genetically modifying their DNA to produce specific traits such as purple eyes or extreme height or carbon-fiber-bones. Imaging that in such tribal culture a company could license a particular race of people and be the absolute God-like monopoly that can only produce such kind of beings. A horrific dystopia no doubt, but in a tribal culture, such dark vision was plausible thanks to patents.

Copyrighting is another tribal concept that is very similar to patents but refers to the expression of an idea, such as an artistic work. Thanks to copyrights, a tribalist can declare ownership over ideas. Think about this for a moment. A person who just learned how to read a few years ago can come up to the human race and shamelessly declare ownership over a thought or an idea that popped up in his head and demand recognition for it. And the joke of it all is that the word *copyright* by definition means the right to copy in the same way that voting rights mean the right to vote.

The origin of the copyright law in most nations started with literature in efforts by the ruling class to regulate and control the output of printers. Printing allowed for multiple exact copies of a work, leading to more rapid and widespread circulation of ideas and information. While the ruling class encouraged printing in many ways, which allowed the dissemination of religious texts and government information, works of dissent and criticism could also circulate rapidly. Consequently, governments established controls over printers across their territories, requiring them to have official licenses to trade and produce books. The permits typically gave printers the exclusive right to print particular works for a fixed period of years and enabled the printer to prevent others from publishing the same work during that period. The licenses could only grant rights to print in the territory of the state that had given them, but they did usually prohibit the import of foreign printing.

Distribia permanently abolished monopoly rights in favor of *the right to copy,* which led to a free and open economy. Today, patents do not exist, and profit is regulated through a *smartcontract* so that everyone can have a market share of any product. The following formula calculates the profit: *Maximum profit = 17% of the total cost.* This means that if a product cost 100 coins total to produce, the manufacturer can sell it at a maximum price of 117 coins to earn 17 coins in profit. Similarly, if it cost 1,000 coins, he can sell it at a maximum price of 1,170 coins, and his profit from this transaction would be 170 coins. Manufacturers that are wishing to make more sales can reduce the cost by charging less than 17% as profit to attract customers, or they can compete by lowering the production costs or by producing better quality and versions of the same product.

Distribia, therefore, restored credibility to the word *"profit"* and guaranteed ethical practices in the economy. Companies could no longer manipulate the prices and take advantage of their customers. It also insured trust because customers could now trust the merchants that they're buying from by knowing that merchants are not exploiting them by selling them overpriced products.

Regulating the profit enhanced the quality of goods, which now last much longer than those produced before *distribia*. They are beautifully made by people who have real enthusiasm about making them and not doing it for profit as it was evident within capitalist economies.

The argument of *"I thought of this first!"* or *"this was my design!"* is solved through the web because all content is timestamped and imprinted to the identity of the owner. The virtual images of products act as symbolic patents or copyrights where *Ve* serves as the figurative copyright guardian. *Ve* effortlessly highlights the original author of any material while any copies or replicas will also be visibly stamped on the content wherever it appears.

An author who starts writing a new book is protected along the entire process because every time he saves the document to his device, his *Ve* always protects him and can prove to the public that he is the original author. Literature, however, is a free market and anyone can use the work of others to either produce something slightly different or very identical. How is the original author protected? Would you buy an unoriginal copy of a book from someone who just copied it from someone else, or would you instead buy the original copy from the original author for the same price? Naturally, you would choose the original version from the person who produced it, and this is a standard convention in *distribia's* society today.

Every year in *distribia*, *Unipublic* grants golden awards to selected innovators or scientists who introduced remarkable innovations that added a meaningful contribution to humanity and positively impacted people's lives. The nominees and the winners of the *"golden prize for innovation"* are selected by *Unipublic* every year at a global event that attracts a lot of media and public attention. It is a very prestigious award, and scientists thrive to introduce innovations to the world to have the honor of receiving such reward. In the same way that actors thrive to win Oscars, scientists today are continuously eager to win the golden prize for innovation.

The awards are made from pure gold, and the entire event is publicly funded. Who pays for it exactly? Nomination and voting for the winners are granted to the public community at *Unipublic*, which basically involved every human being alive. Those who participate in nomination and voting agree to the award's *smartcontract* to participate in funding the event's cost, which typically doesn't exceed a budget previously announced in the social contract. Few coins deducted from each person isn't much and might not cover a cost of a dinner, but collectively they amount to a large sum of money, and they cover the event entirely. It is an entirely different feeling one gets when he participates in such public events knowing that he engaged in making it happen form funding it to selecting to the winners.

The democratization of everything is intrinsic to *distribia's* system, and so it was natural for the public to choose the winners instead of leaving to an enclosed cult of judges who could never possibly represent the entire human population. Tribal cultures, however, took it as the norm to constrain nomination and voting for the winners to a handful of people whereas today ALL nominations and ALL voting in any type of competition are always public. Even the Oscars are awarded today by the public where the people can vote for their best movies or actors or any other category. Musical or talent contests are also no longer judged by a handful of people and instead are open to everyone to vote and select the winners.

So, scientists are motivated to introduce discoveries while having their eyes on golden awards, but who pays for research and development? Just like how most scientific findings in the American culture originated and were funded by American universities, most discoveries and innovations today are introduced by *Unipublic* where the scientists are supported by the income which academia generates for *Unipublic's* scientific communities.

There are still today, of course, a lot of private companies funded by wealthy partners of good-hearted scientists who wish to find solutions to life-threatening diseases and are willing to invest a vast amount of resources in that pursuit. They also sell their products to help pay back their investments and support the continuation of their research where other companies are welcomed to share both making and selling the same products or starting research of their own to introduce new versions of the same products.

Propaganda (Direct Marketing) Is Unlawful In Distribia

Propaganda is information, especially of a biased or misleading nature, used to promote or publicize a tangible item or an idea. The word propaganda comes from the Latin word *propagare*, which means to spread or to propagate. And thus, propaganda means *"that which is to be propagated."*

The Catholic Church is the first to use this term and is arguably the first organization to establish a propaganda department (aka marketing department) dedicated to promoting its religion and indoctrinating as many people as possible in the Church's mission to Christianize the planet. The Catholic Church established its propaganda department in 1622, called the Congregatio de Propaganda Fide (Congregation for Propagating the Faith) to generate propaganda campaigns and brainwash the people of the world into joining such tribal religion.

Propaganda, as a tactic, starts by spreading either false information or one that is not objective to influence the audience and further an agenda to sell a product or an idea. It often proceeds by presenting facts selectively to encourage a particular synthesis or perception or using loaded language to produce an emotional rather than a rational response to such information. Propagandists sought to change the way people understand an issue or situation to change their actions or expectations so that they become desirable to the interests of the propagandists.

Propagandists used a wide range of materials and media for conveying propaganda messages, which changed throughout history as new technologies were invented including paintings, cartoons, posters, pamphlets, logos or symbols, radio messages, and

TV commercials. Initially, the invention of the printing press made the control of public opinion very easy and then the film and the radio made the process almost effortless. The TV is essentially a brain-programming machine, which propagandists loved the most and used the most to poison people's minds with fake information or advertisements to influence them into buying into an idea or a product.

Propagandists knew perfectly well that people would believe anything and everything, provided they are told it frequently and emphatically enough. Ultimately, propaganda was historically a powerful weapon during wars, but tribal nations used it in peacetime just as intensely to continuously shape public opinion or to sell the products or services that people did not genuinely need. Although citizens of tribal cultures commonly used alternative words such as *"marketing"* or *"advertisement"* or *"ads"* or *"commercials,"* such expressions are just languagewashed words to disguise the repugnant propaganda. Words come with an emotional or cognitive attachment to them, and if some negative words were substituted with new ones, people's reactions or perceptions change along with them. And therefore by accepting propaganda under different terminologies, citizens of tribal cultures were constantly bombarded by propaganda until it became completely normal. It infested everything from movies, magazines, art, music, to the TV and the radio. Propaganda was so powerful that it would take a remarkable type of person to resist its sphere of influence for too long in a tribal culture. Unfortunately, propaganda is engineered to be extraordinary seductive to human emotions. Sooner or later everyone falls either consciously or subconsciously under the toxic spell of the surrounding propaganda propagating everywhere the eye can see.

Propaganda is strictly illegal today thanks to the social contract that regulates the freedom of speech and the press. Manufactures can announce their products indirectly by publishing content on the web through articles or infographics or videos that describe their products or the solutions they offer. Such content, however, is never targeted directly at people without their previous consent or knowledge but only shown to them when they selectively search for it. One example of indirect marketing is when an actress in a movie dress up in a beautiful dress that she expresses her delight wearing it without announcing the name, which the viewers would selectively find out by simply asking their *Ve* to possibly purchase one similar. People can even ask their *Ve* to buy the same exact dress or any other item that appeared during a movie because all items used on movie sets are always offered for sale as a film industry standard today. Another example is when an actor clearly shows his watch during the film without necessarily displaying the name of the company that built it. However, if the name of the manufacturer is mentioned or observed, the producers of the film would be taxed every time the movie is played.

There are no logos or trademarks or brands in *distribia*. A brand/logo/trademark is a name, term, design, symbol, or any other feature that identifies one seller's goods or services as distinct from those of other sellers. If you want to verify that you're buying a product from a manufacturer that you trust, you can find a label hidden somewhere on the back of the product that shows the name of the company that made the product along with other relevant information such as the production date, location, the manufacturer's social rating, all costs involved including the profit made by the manufacturer, and the raw materials that went into building the product. Clothing, for example, must never have the name of the company printed or visibly attached to the clothing for the onlooker because it is considered direct marketing and therefore illegal. Instead, the name of the manufacturer is always found on a small label inside the clothing where it cannot be seen while wearing it.

There are also restrictions to the size of the company label which is always relative to the overall surface of the product it is added to. The current ratio is 1:7, which means that the product's label cannot exceed 1/7 of its outer surface. The label on all products in *distribia's* economy is standardized to a familiar theme, font, and style to be easily recognizable whenever spotted on a product.

Distribian Coin's Welcome Bonus & Limitless Market Cap

Whenever a new person is registered at *Unipublic* for the first time (or when a new *Ve* is created for a new living human being), he's rewarded with 83 coins as a welcome bonus. The welcome bonus policy is what introduced the first coins that people used to make the very first sale transaction, which triggered the first ever new money transaction. In addition to the welcome bonus, this person will instantly start receiving new money transfers as people continue to trade goods and services in the economy.

The welcome bonus was critical during the early implantation of *distribia's* system because it allowed people in need to stand on their feet and kickstart a career. Today, however, it isn't as significant because people are registered at *Unipublic* at birth, and by the time they grow up and form an understanding of money and economics, their coin balance will be more than sufficient for them to follow any path they desire in life.

Nonetheless, it remained in place because some people occasionally decide to exit society for various reasons and join the off-grid communities in the protected natural reserves around the world. Their children are born initially without a record in *Unipublic* until these children grow up and decide to join the modern world and move to the cities. When they do, the welcome bonus surely helps them stand on their feet.

As people continue to trade goods and services, new coins are created for humanity to keep its economy functioning. There are no limits on how much coins in total can be in circulation and for as long as people are producing and trading, new coins are systematically created for the economy. And so, pumping new money in the economy is always contingent on whether it is truly needed because money is simply a tool for people to trade. If they are not trading, there's no need for it. If, however, people are trading on a mass-scale and progressively, new money is introduced proportionally and at a rate that sustains that growth.

No Central Financial Authority

The distribian coin's ledger is never saved somewhere on one or more central servers or a limited number of devices. The digital coins are merely numbers in a distributed software, constituting the financial database of the *distribian* coin and the record of all transactions that ever occurred in the global economy. Every living human being keeps a copy of the coin's database and it is never stored in just one place. Every *Ve* stores a copy of the coin's ledger on their human's devices wherever they go.

The ledger is accessible by everyone and publicly displays the number of coins currently in circulation, and everyone's financial transactions including those of the new money that *Ve* created and the resulting equal share of that new money that went to everybody. The public ledger doesn't necessarily display the names or reveal the identities behind the accounts or transactions unless people permit it through their *Ve*. Otherwise, the transactions are displayed by the *Ve#*, which is entirely anonymous long hexadecimal string. Thanks to having all financial transactions public, the account balances of the top 100 wealthiest people, for example, can be viewed by anyone in society without necessarily showing the names or revealing the identity of these most affluent individuals.

Since everyone keeps a copy of the global financial database, some databases might be susceptible to hacking or forgery. However, no central authority in *distribia* validates transactions because such process follows a peer-to-peer process where the network polices itself. The validation process relies on 83% consensus (or the majority vote) of the coin's network. If the majority vote that a particular copy of the coin's database is fraudulent, the system simply ignores it.

Transactions are occurring between virtual humans and not among people because currency exist only in digital form and in *Ve's* realm. And since every *Ve* is programmed to operate according to humanity's elected *smartcontracts*, the likelihood of fraud further diminishes since the human factor is eliminated from the system. If you decide to buy a new suit, for example, the manufacturer's *Ve* checks if you have enough balance to cover the cost of the suit and ask the rest of the network to validate that as well. The instant 83% of the network confirm that you indeed have enough balance, the order goes through, and the transactions involved are recorded in everyone's copy of the ledger.

As explained earlier, *Ve* is the operating system of all electronics and the *distribian* coin is simply a program in that operating system. With every single trade, the coin's program bundles up all transactions involved in that trade into several data packets that are threaded to other packets in the web forming bigger data packets through a hashing function that creates an interconnected web of data packets. Each packet's hash is cryptographically linked to the previous packet's hash and basically forming an unbreakable chain. Any tampering in transactions is easily detected and rejected because not only it messes up the smaller web it is in but also any other data packet added afterward to the web. If a device in the coin's network is hacked and its data packets are tampered with, the rest of the devices in the network will simply ignore it.

The coin's database is a web of transactions bundled up together as packets that are threaded together by a hash function. There's a protocol that regulates how the web is created and how the packet that form the web are knotted and threaded to other packets. Each data packet in the coin's web requires a collaborative work of 83% of *Ve's* network. Transactions can't occur in private and two *Ve* identities can't create transactions on their own because these transactions can only take place when other *Ve* identities in the network are looking. So, two people in isolation and offgrid can't transact or buy and sell goods and services to one another. They need to exist in the global society and conduct their transactions under the watchful eyes of *Ve's* network.

Think of the coin's data packets as a proposal at *Unipublic* that requires the signatures of at least 83% of *Unipublic* to pass as bill. Two *Unipublic* members can privately negotiate and write a proposal, but it would be worthless without the signatures of the rest of *Unipublic's* population. In the same way that the proposal will not be considered a bill until it is taken to *Unipublic*, a coin data packet will not be added to the coin's web unless the network collectively say so.

The coin's data packets are encrypted using complex mathematical riddles that requires the effort of at least 83% of the network through a backend task that runs on the machines that every *Ve* operates. These backend processes can use a maximum limit of 17% of the available commuting power of the *Ve*-hosted device. So, two *Ve* identities on their own can't possibly generate enough computing power necessary to run the obscure mathematical encryptions needed to add packets to the coin's network. They won't have enough resources for these riddles, and it would take them an awful lot of time to be even practical.

The complexity of the mathematical problem increases systematically as more *Ve* identities join the network to make it just hard enough for individual peers to run these mathematical riddles on their own. And to keep it as quick enough for the network to solve these riddles at a fraction of the second to keep transactions fast enough.

The *distribian* coin's data packet requires the digital signature of at least 83% of the *Ve's* network to be complete, otherwise the ledger can't tie that packet to the web. These signatures are generated by *Ve* individuals using their private keys without even revealing them. This is possible thanks to a mathematical formula that can prove the possession of the private key without even revealing it and allows a *Ve* to issue as many digital signatures as it requires. These digital signatures are one-time codes used to validate a transaction just once and can't be used again by anyone else in the network to validate other transactions. The one-time digital signature depends on the data of the transaction it was meant to validate which means that it will always be different for other transactions. These one-time signatures always come timestamped and are meant to expire after 17 seconds from the time they were generated. So, the coin's *smartcontract* will simply ignore any signature that is more than 17 seconds old.

Each data packet doesn't include many transactions or even one complete transaction. Instead, the system distributes the data of every order in the economy to smaller packets where each stores part of the information and is part of an individual thread, which always involves one specific variable. One thread, for example, records just the available balance of a *Ve*, where new packets are added to this particular thread every time the account drops or increase – this thread is called *Ve's* wallet. The wallet's thread is public, and it is not encrypted, which means that anybody can see the available balance of anybody in the network. However, the owner of the wallet can choose to hide his identity under his *Ve#*, which prevents the public from identifying the person behind that wallet. One thread simply records the sales transactions a *Ve* makes while a second thread deals with purchase transactions, a third thread records sales transactions, and so on. Since each trade transaction is made up of several individual transactions, every data packet in each thread is connected to another packet from another thread and that's how the coin's web is formed.

If you want to buy any item, this is the sequence of events that occur:

➢ You ask your *Ve* to purchase the item from its manufacturer.

➢ Your *Ve* checks its wallet in the copy it got of the coin's ledger to see if you have enough balance. If you do, it sends a request to the *Ve* identities of the partners in the shop that you wish to buy their product.

➢ All partners' *Ve identities* then immediately check if you have enough balance to cover the cost of the item you wish to purchase. They do that by checking their copy of the coin's ledger first and then asking the rest of the network to confirm that you indeed got that balance in your wallet. This step doubles as a *"refresh"* of the copies of the ledger available in the network to make sure that everyone is synced with the latest transactions in the economy. The peer which has an outdated or wrong copy of the ledger will simply update or download a fresh copy from the next peer.

➢ When at least 83% peers in the network respond that their record of the ledger confirms that you got a sufficient balance to cover the cost of the item, the partners authorize the sale transaction, timestamp and sign the transaction with their digital signatures, and then cast to the network to tie the packet (or technically to start the collaborative work of encrypting the new data bundles involved in this trade).

➢ Collaboratory, at least 83% of the coin's network sign the transaction (imprint the transaction with their digital signatures) and use 17% of their available computing power to encrypt the new packets. The keys to that energy-intensive cryptography are the private keys of the customer and sellers, who generated the trade. This means that both the buyer and the seller can easily access the data in that packet but everyone else can't because they don't have the keys. Since wallets are public and not encrypted, the network can just *"read"* the available balances of every peer, which could be hidden under his *Ve#* without revealing the identity of the *Ve* or its outset explicitly, and not actually have access to the peer's transactions history.

➤ After these new packets are added to the ledger's web, every peer in the network simply copies the new packets and add them to their copy of the ledger. The network of course doesn't delete their entire copy of the ledger and replace it with a fresh one every time a new trade occurs in the economy, they just copy the new transactions and incorporate them in the existing copy they already have of the ledger.

The Distribian Coin's Antifraud System

As mentioned earlier, your wallet is public and isn't encrypted. The web's thread in the coin's database that represent your available balance depends on other threads that hold the transactions you made that lead to the current balance. So, you can't just edit the balance without editing those that lead to that balance. These transactions, however, belong to other threads that are encrypted but you have the private key to the encryption. So technically you'll be able to change them, correct? No, because these transactions depend on the other people in the network that you traded with, which will affect their available balances if changed and will contradict with their copy of the ledger. Meaning you'll have to hack their copies of the ledger as well.

If you try to alter the merchant's copy of the ledger, it still won't match all other copies in the network, and the merchant's copy along with yours will just be ignored and updated with an accurate one. Additionally, UBI depends on these transactions which means any manipulations with any transaction will create conflict with everyone's balances in the coin's database. You would need to hack at least 83% of the devices in the network at the same time to create a fraudulent transaction in the coin's ledger - this event is not possible. The reason why it is not possible is that *Ve* identities are the operating systems of all devices as a manufacturing standard, and they prevent any tampering from ever happening on any device. So, if the database of any *smartcontract* (including the *distribian* coin) is being hacked on any device, every *Ve* will come to the rescue and fight the hack. And we're not discussing here the computing power of one single equipment but an armada of every apparatus in the Ad-hoc network globally engaging in an orchestrated counterattack against hackers.

In case of a hacking event, *Ve's* defense protocol allows it to use up to 83% of the available computing power of any device. It means that 83% of the computing power of all devices in the universe will be engaged in this counterattack against who hacks just one single peer in the network.

The Distribian Coin's Computing Power Cap

The coin's *smartcontract* in the background of all electronic devices that host a copy of the ledger and it is only allowed to use up to 17% of the available computing power capacity. Humanity elected this regulation to prevent the coin's web from eating up large percentages of computing power on the devices it runs on, which hinders users of these devices from using them for other applications. This cap doubles as an energy cap and regulates the amount of electricity the *coin's* web can consume.

The Distribian Coin's Database Is Inerasable

Every private electronic device hosts only one *Ve* inside its microprocessor where it exists as firmware or permanent software. Any attempt to rewrite it or alter it would result in permanent damage to the microprocessor. Every *Ve* keeps the latest version of the coin's database, which goes with it inside its microprocessor. Once inside, a *Ve* and the coin's ledger are secured forever and technically inerasable. The coin's database is then updated continuously with new versions as new transactions occur in the economy. *Ve* downloads the updates to its microprocessor and safeguard them. This policy ensures that financial records can never be erased or manipulated and adds to the existing security offered by data cryptography on the web.

Technically, since money exists only virtually (in digital form), and people trade it digitally as well through their virtual image, which both live in the virtual realm, it means that *Ve* identities are the ones in fact trading with each other on the web and not the humans.

Humanity is merely authoring these transactions whereas all *Ve* identities collectively are directing the show. So, *Ve* identities are trading with each other and acting as the only legitimate official intermediaries between the people. Since humankind decides how a *Ve* should operate, financial fraud can never happen.

A *Ve* records the financial transactions made by a human from birth to death. It preserves his financial information in the coin's database without necessarily revealing his identity or name unless he opted to make them public. Copies of that data are maintained on all his devices, his family, and friends' devices, and everyone else in the network. If one file in one memory storage was destroyed, there are always other copies of the data available in different places that can be retrieved.

The coin's *smartcontract* has financial privacy built into it. No human can see another's balance (because they're listed anonymously) or transactions, and this falls entirely on the owner of the virtual wallet to disclose some or all financial information through personally declaring them public to another person, or group, or the entire society.

The Age Of Corporations Died With Tribalism

In *distribia's* economy, there are no private or public banks or even companies. The age of corporations died with tribalism. Today, there are no corporations or institutions or organizations, but only self-employed individuals or partners. Most people are self-employed and when people work together, we call it a group, which is just a designation and not an entity. A group's finances are split among the financial accounts of the partners within that group, and the profits are instantly distributed among them according to their shares. To explain this, consider a coffee shop that is owned by a group of only two partners, who divided their shares equally among them, which means that any money generated by the shop will be split equally between them. Each time the shop sells one cup of coffee, half of the profit from that cup is distributed to each partner the instant the transaction occurs. It never goes to some bank account in the form of revenue where it is later used to pay wage slaves at the end of the month as was the case with capitalist companies in the past. In *distribia's* economy, centralization doesn't exist, and everything is peer-to-peer. This also means that if the coffee shop partners decide to buy a new coffee machine, all costs involved in getting that new machine is also split evenly among them because there's no central bank account from which these payments are withdrawn.

Those Who Work The Businesses Must Own Them & Run Them

As explained earlier, capitalism resulted from fiat money, which is issued for free from thin air by central bankers and given for free to large corporations so the peasants can work for it. In theory, however, capitalism is an economic and political system in which a country's trade and industry are controlled by private owners in an all-out competition for profit, rather than by the state. These private owners, of course, are either central or commercial bankers. In other words, capitalism is the idea that money and power must be concentrated in the hands of very few people at the top of a pyramid scheme of authority and wealth as the inescapable result of such all-out competition. What does that mean exactly? It means, of course, that capitalism is a hierarchical social order where a few greedy dynasties of bankers possess all the money and power of the nation for themselves and will remain there at the top of society indefinitely. From the top of the pyramid, such wealthy families would naturally have all the power to control everything including influencing national elections or decisions, devising economic and political policies, and so on. And by contrast to the state-owned-businesses model, which ensures that the public will elect the CEOs of all vital industries, in a capitalist system, the nation's utilities are owned and monopolized by unelected officials. And those who control these essential utilities, which the country depends on, would command the entire nation in the process.

In practice, however, no nation on Earth was capitalist, but instead, they were all state-sponsored capitalist nations or state-capitalists. The state played a crucial role in supporting such an economic system because without it a capitalist economy would come crashing down in just a few years. Every nation on Earth was capitalist including those that tribal propaganda falsely labeled communist. A capitalist is one who loves capital, which is the centralization of wealth or money. And if you took a glimpse at the history of all nations that existed around the world including those that ran on welfare programs in Africa, you would notice that wealth and power were always concentrated in the hands of very few people at the top of a pyramid scheme of capital. For example, China, which economists mistakenly labeled as a communist nation, had big corporations and wage labor that is almost identical to that of the United States. The main difference between tribal countries such as North Korea and the United States is that in the first there's a tiny handful of people who had all the wealth and power, whereas in the United States a broader class of people had access to most of the wealth of the nation. In other words, the sphere of economic tyranny encompassed more people in the United States than in North Korea.

All tribal nations were fundamentally capitalist in the era of fiat money. The public of the tribal era lived in a capitalist world. As for such labels as *"communist"* or *"socialist,"* they are intangible ideas that never came to fruition physically in any tribal nation. No government was ever established on the principles of Communism as defined by philosophers such as Karl Marx or Friedrich Engels. In fact, the idea of a *"Communist Government"* is a contradiction in terms because in a communist social order there would be no need for a government to rule over the public. What a tribal culture called communism was merely capitalism in disguise where a faceless government owned all the wealth and power.

Capitalism stands for the centralization of wealth and power in the hands of very few people. It is a system which institutionalized greed as a virtue, and that's why most people in the tribal world were driven by greed. Nothing good could come out of such a system that loves giving 1% of the human population absolute reign over the rest of humanity. When a society centralizes all powers of governance into the hands of very few people, it inescapably becomes a tyrannical society. Similarly, when an economy concentrates or capitalized all wealth and money into the hands of very few people, it becomes a dictatorial economy. And just how you don't need an introduction to why tyranny is horrible, no one should have to explain why capitalism is horrible either.

Capitalism is an offspring of tribalism. It is a tribal convention that produces masters and slaves. It guarantees two social classes of rich and poor in the human civilization and supplies one with a clear advantage over the other in all prospects of life. Under such system, if you are born to a low-income family, it is extremely hard to accumulate wealth and join the wealthy class of society in your own lifetime. On the other hand, if you are born into a wealthy family, it is not common to lose your status or descend on the social ladder. Therefore, the rich usually get richer while the poor linger.

During humanity's dark days under capitalism, income inequalities negatively influenced the social progression around the world and created vast disparities in society. Businesses were becoming too big to fail and eventually taking the form of monopolies creating an economic reality where startups and small businesses couldn't nourish. Capitalism as a system ensured houselessness, income inequality and unfair access to healthcare and education. It created economies that keep bouncing around between booms and busts every 3 to 7 years. It led to societies that concentrate political and economic power in a tiny number of people. These problems were built into the system, and they couldn't be solved independently and individually within the framework of the capitalist system because the system itself was the problem. Houselessness or inequality couldn't be solved by a quick fix through a marginal adjustment because such predicaments are systematic. Capitalism as a system produced these problems by design due to the way the system functioned, and there were no means of fixing any of these issues except by completely changing the system.

Capitalist businesses were on a never-ending mission to cut down costs and make as much profit as possible. Every capitalist was always trying to make more money or survive competitively by saving on his labor costs. Some capitalists accomplished this through automation by substituting workers with machines. Others, who probably couldn't afford expensive machinery, tried to get cheaper workers in place of more expensive ones. For example, hiring women if they're less costly to do the job that they used to pay men to execute. Others preferred hiring immigrants rather than native folks or even moving to another part of the world entirely where wages are inherently much lower. Salaries were scientifically designed to give workers as less as possible while taking advantage of them as most and for as long as possible. Such wages were just enough to ensure that the workers would show up the next day for work but always left them financially dependent on the job for many years in the future. And so, capitalists relentlessly set out to save as much as they could on labor costs because they could make a better competitive product in the process. The problem with such a shortsighted approach to production is that the employees that these capitalists deemed deplorable are the same people who buy the products the economy produces. If everyone is unemployed and unable to secure an income, there won't be anyone left to buy the products that the capitalists are so eager to sell. By reducing the pay they give to their employees, these workers will eventually have less and less money till they are unable to buy the products that the capitalists produce. And so, less trade will occur in the economy, and the entire system falls apart because it relies heavily on mass-production and mass-consumption.

Another controversy in the capitalist model is the relentless competitiveness or *"free markets"* as they called it although the name is very misleading because trade under capitalism was never free. The Stone Age principle of the survival of the fittest in a capitalist economy meant that some companies would naturally run out of business while others flourish. Systematically and after several simulations (if we study the problem programmatically), the economy will naturally end up with few companies at the top that savagely survived by eliminating the competition through whatever means possible. This competitiveness that a capitalist economy flaunts itself with will slow down until it becomes uncompetitive at all when 3 or fewer companies control the global economy of the planet. When capitalist markets stop being competitive, they start failing because when few companies become too big that they deprive others of capital, it is not a capitalist economy at all.

Instead, it becomes a form of economic totalitarianism where startups will nearly go extinct because it is impossible to compete with monopolies and even harder to raise capital.

The megacompanies, which secured the most significant piece of the pie to themselves, did not necessarily become so big or so rich because they were good at whatever product or service they offered but because of lobbying local governments to produce laws or regulations that inflate their businesses artificially. Zoning laws, for example, which are tools to isolate where people live from where goods and services are traded, serve big corporations because they can proceed with building their large malls for big brands that the average entrepreneurs can't compete with individually. Mom's and pop's business, who relied on opening their shops within the neighborhoods to benefit from local foot traffic lost that advantage because the local government favors malls and plazas. It wasn't easy to get to such central places on foot, and people were forced to use a car just to reach them, which eliminated the option to walk to the small stores that they loved. Such reality killed the traditional mom's and pop's shops because they relied on people walking around the neighborhood. Since everyone was moving around in cars, they became conditioned to go to centralized places like malls and plazas to buy in bulk. It gave more control to larger corporations and created an environment where they could monopolize their industry and destroy local small businesses.

Regulators and lawmakers introduced stringent zoning laws which restricted property rights. By doing this, the cities were inherently designed to inhibit people from being able to participate in the system. Before zoning laws, if people couldn't find a job, they could start a lemonade stand on a street corner and generate a minimal income to survive and grow into something better. However, zoning laws entirely barred them from doing that because it required a permit with an expensive price tag that turns what should be a simple business venture of selling lemonade into a fight for licenses or a deterrent from starting a business. These laws served to keep the streets sterile and lubricated only for movement through the nearest drive-through.

After witnessing how companies became nations inside their nations, a need emerged for humanity to redesign its economy. Humankind to eliminate the idea of corporations altogether in favor of partnership-based groups. The planet's economy became unrecognizable under *distribia*. The legacy concept of local markets trading currency, assets, and stock ended in favor of one global economy that has no stock exchanges or a public sector. Stock exchanges and publicly traded companies were engines of speculation and economic manipulation, which is one of the reasons why *distribians* shut them down. Instead, the globally distributed economy today is far more stable and involves only a private sector.

The concept of employer/employee or worker/boss and salary-based income was substituted with a partnership model of sharing profits based on shares or equity between partners. *Distribia's* economic model necessitates that **THOSE WHO WORK THE BUSINESSES MUST OWN THEM AND RUN THEM** – a concept which terrified tribalists in their Gilded Age. Wage labor, which was no different from chattel slavery except that it was temporary, is nonexistent today. Wage slavery (wage labor) revolved around one human renting another human to do specific tasks for a number of hours for a payment under a legally binding contract and typically managed by another person, who laid down the rules and corrected the workers when necessary. That payment could be an hourly payment of 1 dollar per hour or 100 dollars or more. As a result, you could have million-dollar slaves that are voluntarily leasing themselves out for money to others but never really realizing it due to the sheer amount of money involved. Today, however, wage slavery is nonexistent. There are no such concepts as hourly or monthly or yearly pay that became the standard in the capitalist economies of tribal cultures around the world. Such abusive schemes do not exist today because no one can hire anyone, and people can work together as partners to produce value under their own rules and schedule. Self-management is the standard because delegation and work hierarchy are institutionally illegal in *distribia*. Such concepts conflict with the doctrines of tribal cultures, which drove such ideas out of the people's minds through educational and cultural systems to make them seem as insane or unthinkable.

There are no owners/employers or employees in *distribia's* economy. Today, employees and employers are partners sharing a percentage of the profit generated by their group according to the shares they agree to in the *smartcontract*. A person wishing to work with other people needs to negotiate an agreement with at least one partner, and they both need to negotiate their shares in the group. The smart contract automatically calculates the shares in the group based on the financial commitment of each partner. Companies of the *Tribal Ages* could hire thousands of workers whereas today, the number of people working together can only range between two partners and no more than 100. The first concern in starting a work group is the financial commitment of each partner in the group because it also represents the profit that each will get. For example, two people wanted to open a coffee shop where one of them has more money than the other. The person with more money can agree to cover 90% of the total cost while the remaining 10% is taken care of by the other partner. This automatically means that 90% of the profit will go to the first partner and 10% to the other. Any expense made by the shop such as buying new equipment is distributed to the partners according to their financial commitment percentages. For example, if the partners of this coffee shop decided to buy a new coffee machine, the cost of that coffee machine is paid 90% by one partner and 10% by the other.

The minimum share in a work group is 1%, which also means that the minimal financial commitment by each partner is 1% as well. Setting the minimal share to 1% means that a group technically cannot exceed a maximum number of 100 partners. Aside from its role in capping the number of partners in a group, the minimal share prevents disparities where one person owns too much, and others earn too little - a typical occurrence in capitalist companies.

The percentage of shares among partners also equates to the influence in decision-making within the group. The partner with the most shares (or the partner who owns the most part of the business) has the dominant vote. Each partner participates in decision-making via an internal referendum with a vote percentage equals to each partner's shares in the group. A partner who has 5% partnership with a business, gets 5% of the votes on decisions whereas another partner with a 20% share gets 20% of the votes. Arrangements inside the business are done by consensus between all partners and those with higher shares have a more important vote.

The capitalist corporations of the tribal era followed a fundamentally fascist form of rule. The decision-making structure in such corporations is always top-down. The owners give orders, and they get executed by one level down below and so forth until it reaches the lowest level employees in the business. It would be unthinkable back then for a regular employee to object to decisions taken by the executives because it would be equivalent to career self-destruction. The owners of capitalist corporations were worshiped within their institutions as citizens worshiped their supreme leaders in authoritarian governments. Today, there are no hierarchies in companies because delegation in *distribia* is illegal. No one manages anyone, and no one is the boss of anyone because everyone is a partner and they all share profits and decision making. There are of course a variety of titles and responsibilities but absolutely no hierarchy of command or management or authority. The operations of businesses are direct or peer-to-peer, and every partner in any business is actively engaged in producing the goods or services that the business offers. You won't see, for example, someone sitting behind a desk handling only finances or only taking calls and bookings or just managing check-ins. If a business is producing shoes, every partner is a shoemaker and is making shoes. If it is an architecture business, every partner is an architect and actively participates in designing or building structures. If it is an ice-cream business, every partner is making or servicing customers with ice-cream. If it is a car manufacturing business, every partner is an engineer and is engaged in designing or building cars. As for tasks such as indirect marketing or handling finances or customer service or check-ins, they are all managed by technology and through *Ve*.

The leadership in a *distribian* company is distributed to all its partners proportionally to their initial financial commitment. Leadership is not concentrated at the peak of a vertical scheme of authority as it used to be in capitalist economies. The distribution of administration and power gives partners a higher level of responsibility and accountability for their work, as well as more significant stakes in outcomes. It encourages functional diversity within roles, and with it, creativity, because partners aren't confined to specific areas of specialization. Such work reality allows the organization to operate with less redundancy, as teams can share resources more readily than hierarchical divisions could. The flexibility inherent in the nonhierarchical leadership within *distribian* formations allows organizations to adapt very quickly to changing conditions in the economy and make instant collective decisions to react readily to any challenge. For example, a barista who encounters a lot of customers asking for a specific type of drink can immediately discuss with his partner the decision to add such a drink to their menu to react quickly to the demand of the customers of the shop. In a capitalist economy, however, employees typically wouldn't be tempted to be proactive in such a way because they're nothing more than temporary workers who get a paycheck at the end of every month.

Following the law of THOSE WHO WORK THE SHOPS MUST OWN THEM AND RUN THEM, a person cannot start a partnership if he/she is not qualified to operate in that sector. For example, a person cannot establish an architecture company if he/she is not an architect. One needs first to graduate as an architect to start a business in that field of knowledge. Similarly, all partners in the architecture sector are fundamentally licensed architects. In other words, all architecture businesses come from the architecture community at *Unipublic*.

Partnerships become official when partners publish their smartcontract on the web. Each partner's *Ve* act as the official representative of the business to its customers. All information about all businesses is always accessible to the public. This data includes profits, partners' shares, number of partners, business activities, all transactions of sales and purchases, etc.

Any partner can choose to leave a business without restrictions, and his/her equity would be automatically distributed evenly to all partners in the group as a business standard when he/she departs. A partner wishing to break off with another partner, should either have the predominant vote on that decision in the company (have at least 83% of the shares) or collectively with other partners who agree with his/her decision form the majority vote (partners favoring the decision together have 83% of the shares). Usually, partners tend to maintain 83% ownership (the majority share) of the business to be in full control of it. It allows them to take full control over all decisions in their business such as adding more partners or breaking off with existing ones.

Partners cannot sell their shares of the company to others or pass them down to family members as an inheritance. New partners are only assigned through voting and based on the majority vote. Votes must reach 83% to be valid for any decision within the company.

The general attitude to work is very different than how it used to be under tribalism when employers forced their workers into fixed work schedules. Today it is very common for shops to open intermittently, working only for a few hours in the day and closing for the most part. Or even opening for business for one week before closing in the next or opening every other day and so on. Business owners are free to open and close anytime they feel like it. In *distribia*, there are no weekdays or weekends, and such words gradually went out of use. People choose their work hours however they like them. They can pick any day in the week as well as at any time of the day. Some people work only for a few hours in the morning and then take the rest of the day off. Others go home at lunchtime to enjoy a nice meal with the family and have a nap for a few hours before going back to work if they feel like it. Some open their businesses only at night for a few hours after enjoying the entire day at the beach or having their favorite sports or outdoor activities. There is no point or financial advantage in working long hours every day of the week mainly because there's no financial pressure to do so. The aim of *distribia's* economy is not to accumulate money or wealth but to find fulfillment in life. There is no valid reason to work all day or all week either because eventually all money balances are capped, and the monetary system would not allow a greedy person to hoard much of it. Thanks to UBI, everyone can afford a decent standard of living without ever worrying about money which is why people are not pressured to work but only do it when they honestly feel the value of contributing to the planet's economy.

There's no article within the partnership smartcontract that enforces work schedules because it is always up to each partner to decide how much he/she wants to work. It is utterly forbidden to impose a work schedule or even propose or suggest it verbally to a partner. It is a social contract today that every partner should always have the freedom to work whenever they want and for as long as they desire free of any schedule of any form. In *distribia*, trust primarily drives businesses while work reputation or social rating plays a significant role in establishing partnerships. In fact, the entire economy is built on trust and good work ethics, and that's why there's minimal emphasis on designing strict contractual agreements or obligations.

Cross-partnership is not possible in the *distribian* economy. Once a person is in a partnership, he/she is married to that business and cannot be involved in other partnerships at the same time. However, he/she can still work for himself on the side independently, but not in a partnership. In *distribia's* economy, if a person can handle the work on his/her own, he/she usually avoids partnerships. It is not necessary at all for a person to be in a partnership to do business because people are the primary drivers of the economy and they are the real assets that produce the goods and services. A person can generate income and sell products or services by just working for himself/herself under his/her name. Such practice is highly encouraged and practiced today in *distribia's* economy especially with advancements in automation that makes it entirely practical.

All Forms Of Financial Speculation & Gambling Are Illegal

Financial speculation is the act of conducting a transaction that has a substantial risk of losing some or all its value but with the expectation of a significant gain. With speculation, the risk of a loss is more than offset by the possibility of a huge gain. Otherwise, there would obviously be very little motivation to speculate.

The state of affairs where speculation along with supply and demand determined the prices of raw materials or physical assets was evidently dysfunctional and corrupt. It led to financial fraud, corruption, financial bubbles, recessions, violations of antitrust laws and other administrative or civil or penal violations. Financial speculation was one of the hallmarks of the capitalist world, which was entirely controlled by bankers and financiers. When tribalism finally fell, so did the banks and their devilish financial systems. Financial speculation in all its forms or varieties is illegal today in *distribia*. Prices of raw materials are now always predetermined and voted upon through consensus. *Price-fixing* is never decided by the merchant or the customer (aka supply and demand) or a central authority, but by the collective majority consensus of humanity. For example, the price of one gram of gold is always one coin. Similarly, the cost of one kilowatt, wheat, minerals, and other physical assets is predefined in a social contract by the majority vote. By setting a fixed price on raw materials, *distribians* control the cost of all manufactured products especially when the profit cap is added in the mix.

Stock market exchanges were basically open-air casinos that revolved around financial gambling, which was the route of all financial bubbles or market collapses and recessions around the world during the tribal era. *Distribia's* peer-to-peer economy deemed these institutions illegal and shut them down permanently. Investments, which were very common during the tribal era, are also a form of speculation and are therefore unconstitutional today in *distribia*. Similarly, the real casinos and gambling overall was renounced because it also constitutes a form of speculation for financial profit.

The On-Demand Production System

Before explaining the on-demand production system, we should first understand what the mass production system was all about. Mass production, also known as flow production or continuous production, is the manufacture of large quantities of standardized products, frequently using assembly line or automation technology. It involves making many copies of products, very quickly, using assembly line techniques to send partially complete products to workers who each work on an individual step, rather than having a worker work on a whole product from start to finish.

A typical mass production system involves mechanization and an assembly line to achieve high volume, detailed organization of materials flow, careful control of quality standards and division of labor. The demand for standardized products in large quantities originated from military organizations and their need for uniforms,

282

for example. Precision machining equipment such as those at car factories led to the large-scale demand for mass-produced products created at low cost and with a small workforce. Henry Ford, an American businessman and the founder of the Ford Motor Company, pioneered the moving assembly line in 1913. The reduced manufacturing time for parts allowed Ford to apply the same method to chassis assembly. By 1915, Ford had reduced the time it took to produce an automobile by 90%, which yielded an abundance of cars that were substantially more affordable for the public.

Mass production resulted in the high-accuracy assembly because production line machines had fixed parameters. This system's production costs were typically low because assembly line production with automated processes did not require a lot of workers. Mass-produced products were assembled at a quicker rate due to increased automation and efficiency. This helped with prompt distribution and marketing of an organization's products with the potential to create a competitive advantage and higher profits. Although it undoubtedly came with a lot of benefits, mass production led to many problems. It wasted a percentage of the output because there were no guarantees that all the products will be sold to the public at the end.

Establishing an automated assembly line was typically capital-intensive. The starter cost of the machinery can be prohibitive, so the company must be sure it sells or otherwise they will lose a lot of money. Additionally, if there was a production design error, great costs might be required to redesign and rebuild mass production processes. If one area of mass production was interrupted, the entire production process might be affected.

Employees who were part of a mass production assembly line lacked motivation because tasks were repetitive. This condition led to low employee morale and increased levels of turnover.

Mass production stifled flexibility because production processes were cumbersome and expensive to change. For example, if a pharmaceutical company had a comprehensive assembly line in place to produce a popular drug, it was both difficult and costly to respond to a governmental regulatory change that required the production process to be altered.

Also, all products produced on one production line will be identical or very similar while introducing variety to satisfy individual tastes wasn't easy. The sameness of products stripped away some value in owning a product because everyone has an exact same copy of it. Under such system, everything becomes a copy of another copy, and the uniqueness of products is eliminated.

With each passing decade, engineers found ways to increase the flexibility of mass production systems, driving down the lead times on new product development and allowing greater customization and variety of products. As they explored new ways to ensure customization of their products, advancements in machinery eventually led to a new concept of mechanical production. A system which can produce products so fast that there's no need to create them ahead of time and instead can build products only when the consumers place an order. And since *distribia* prohibits centralization and intermediaries, companies had to figure out a way to sell to the public directly and overlap middlemen of all kinds.

The result was an on-demand production system where products are made only after an order is placed. It allows people to custom-make the products they wish to buy to their specific needs instead of receiving an exact copy that everyone got. And so, all products are customized to every customer, and every copy of any product is unique. The psychological impact of knowing that you own a product customized to you precisely the way you want it adds a unique dimension which the products of assembly lines lacked.

Edibles like tomato sauce bottles, for example, are ordered on-demand and prepared according to every person's exact taste in terms of the intensity of flavor or the percentages or content of the ingredients. So, the tomato sauce bottle you order from a company might taste completely different than the one someone else purchases from the same producer.

The on-demand production gets more interesting when it comes to clothing. Since your *Ve* is an exact virtual replica of you, you don't need to try the clothes on to see if they fit because the virtual you can try them on and show you how they look like before you even make the purchase. Although there are still shops people can go shopping for clothing, most of today's shopping happens *onweb*. The physical shops have clothes on display, but they're not for sale because clothes are manufactured only after the purchase. So, you can still try clothing in the shops, and they'll make the ones you settle on while you are there because automated production is fast, and it takes just a few minutes to complete.

All products are imprinted to the owner's *Ve*. The imprint depends on the product and its material. Clothing, for example, is cyphered to their owners through the distribution of threads and the owner's *Ve#* is printed in nanometer-scale on these threads along with the order details. The uniqueness of every product is identifiable by *Ve* wherever that product goes. So, losing products or their theft is a thing of the past because the owner's *Ve* can locate his/her lost products and return them. Once a product is sold, it can't be re-sold because the identity of the original owner is imprinted on the product. It would have to be recycled. And so, the economy's products are always unique, secure, and genuine.

Vertical Farms In Every Neighborhood As A Building Standard

Agriculture is the cultivation of land and breeding of animals and plants to provide food, fiber, medicinal plants and other products to sustain and enhance life. Agriculture was the critical development in the rise of sedentary human civilization, whereby farming of domesticated species created food surpluses that enabled people to live in cities. The history of agriculture dates back thousands of years when people gathered wild grains and began to plant them around 11,500 years ago before such grains became domesticated.

There is nothing about farming that can be described as natural. Whenever human beings are involved in anything, the word *"natural"* becomes controversial because we are the only species capable of irreversibly altering our environment and effectively destroying it. An agricultural landscape may look attractive to us – such as a vineyard or a sunflower field in full bloom in the backcountry – but its creation required the complete destruction of the natural ecosystem and its replacement by an agricultural ecosystem. Further, to grow so many of the same plants in one field while at the same time suppressing the growth of other plants – in this case, weeds – is not natural even if farmers practice crop rotation, or *"inter-cropping,"* which is the practice of growing 2 or 3 crops at the same time. Such an ecosystem is not what nature intended, and as a result, we must continuously supply fertilizers, and apply weed control, disease control and insect control measures to keep that artificial ecosystem going.

The most crucial question is not whether it is natural, but whether it is sustainable in the long run for future generations. The crops that we enjoy today just cannot survive in nature on their own without our direct involvement. Our crop plants were domesticated around 11,000 years ago, and in the process, their genetic makeup was changed considerably and irreversibly. Changed so much in fact that such crop plants generally are nowhere to be found on the planet surviving on their own. Throughout the history of farming across thousands of years, farmers kept changing the genetic structure of crops by carefully selecting the best seeds from the most successful plants to keep planting them in following seasons and maintain an ever-successful yield. Therefore, all our plants today are already genetically modified to be the giant fruits and vegetables that we all enjoy today. And there's nothing natural at all regarding the size or caloric composition of the watermelons or corn that we all consume today.

The use of land to yield goods was the most substantial way humans altered the Earth's ecosystems, and it was the driving force in the loss of biodiversity. Estimates of the amount of land transformed by humans vary from 39 to 50%. Modern agronomy (the science of soil management and crop production), plant breeding, agrochemicals such as pesticides and fertilizers, and technological developments have sharply increased yields from cultivation, but at the same time have caused widespread ecological damage. Excessive fertilization and manure application to cropland, as well as high livestock stocking densities, cause nutrient (mainly nitrogen and phosphorus) runoff and leaching from agricultural land. These nutrients are major nonpoint pollutants contributing to eutrophication of aquatic ecosystems. Eutrophication, which represents the excessive nutrients in aquatic ecosystems resulting in algal blooms and anoxia, surfaced due to run-off from farmed lands. It led to fish kills, loss of biodiversity, and rendered water unfit for drinking.

Traditional agriculture required a significant draw of water from aquifers at an unsustainable rate that accounted for around 70% of withdrawals from freshwater resources. Such water demands led to the destruction of natural wetlands, the spread of water-borne diseases, and land degradation through salinization and waterlogging when irrigation is performed incorrectly.

Although pesticide use kept increasing annually worldwide, crop loss from pests remained relatively constant for traditional farming. The reason behind the ineffectiveness of pesticides was pests' natural adaptation and development of defenses against such poisons. And although pests figured out a way to shield themselves against these human-made poisons, people fell victims to poisoning by these products. Around 3 million pesticide poisonings occurred annually, causing 220,000 deaths.

Traditional agricultural wreaked havoc on the environment and drained precious resources including water. The result was cheap, mass-produced food, sacrificing quality for quantity at the expense of our health and the environment.

In *distribia's* economy, farming is localized to every neighborhood and inside the floors of buildings called vertical farms. Vertical farming was the result of re-thinking what agriculture should look like in a world where water is scarce, people live in cities, and the dangers of pesticides and other chemicals in our food. Farming moved indoors where crops grow inside buildings in stacked rows under LED lights that mimic the sun's rays and get nourished by nutrient-filled, recirculating water. These automated farms use a technology that detects peak times for harvest and learns what the crops need to thrive, thus eliminating a lot of guesswork that was traditionally involved with planting food.

The system uses data from multiple sources, including vision systems to monitor plants and all the variables that drive their growth, quality, and flavor, from germination to harvest. This yields insight into what each crop needs, rather than relying on instinct.

By monitoring the growing process 24/7 and capturing substantial amounts of data along the way, today's farmers constantly iterate on each varietal, tweak flavor profiles, provide each crop exactly what it needs to thrive, and harvest at the exact right time. This means better local produce all year round in every neighborhood.

The vertical farming methodology yields great advantages and benefits over traditional agriculture. Controlled indoor environment allows growing the purest produce imaginable, with absolutely no pesticides or chemicals. The produce is so clean, that we don't even have to wash it before consuming it. It saves on water significantly over traditional farming because crops are given exactly what they need and nothing more whereas nutrients gets precisely delivered via purified water—not a single drop is wasted along the way.

It is 100x+ more productive that traditional farming methods. By planting in vertical rows in buildings and growing twice as fast as traditional agriculture, vertical farms are much more productive on the same footprint of land compared with traditional farms. It guarantees crop production 365 days a year.

Growing indoors with LED lights that mimic the full spectrum of the sun means we can grow independent of seasonality or weather conditions. Through vertical farming, every block anywhere in the world can produce any variety of food regardless of the climate. The coffee tree, for example, is a tropical evergreen shrub that grows between the Tropics of Cancer and Capricorn. Historically, coffee was harvested in this region and exported to everywhere else especially to Europe.

Today, coffee beans can be grown and collected in any building anywhere in the world to service the local community. There's no need to ship these beans from anywhere because vertical farms can mimic the exact climate and produce all varieties of coffee beans and flavors.

Vertical farming allows same day harvest consumption. Every city block contains at least one vertical farm as a universal standard to service its residents. Thanks to the efficient transport system within each block, orders are placed, crops are handpicked, and the package is delivered within an hour —unlike traditional harvest pickup and distribution, which often took weeks or even months if it was shipped from abroad while losing nutrients and taste in the process. All types of crops can be grown in the same building because the climate in each floor of a vertical farm is controlled to best match the crop ideal climate for growth. All kinds of produce on the planet can now be produced in these vertical farms. Such concept creates abundancy of crops to feed all the population regardless of how much it grew. Thus, such system vanquished the ancient fear of feeding the planet's rapidly growing population, which was solved for by the vertical farming concept.

Produce and food products in general follow a same day consumption policy, which necessitates that food must be consumed in the same day it is harvested and prepared to eliminate mass production and mass use of preservatives. This became possible only through technical achievements that automated the entire food production process from initial production to final consumption. Food preservatives are deemed illegal in *distribia*. Food is prepared based on immediate consumption policy that follows a timetable of when the food is harvested, the time it takes to cook the resulting food along with the time it takes to deliver the food to the consumer, and finally the time limit to consuming such food before it is legally considered expired.

Animal's Basic Rights & Freedom

Animal confinement (forcing dense populations of chickens, pigs, or young cattle into cages, crates, or tight pens to more efficiently utilize farm space) was common practice everywhere in the tribal world. Worldwide, chicken and cattle were the breeds of livestock most killed for their meat. Led by population growth during the industrial revolution, industrial livestock production grew multiple folds compared to the rate of traditional forms of animal farming. During capitalism, factory farming of animals ballooned and forced billions of animals in confinement. On factory farms, laying hens, pregnant pigs and veal calves were routinely confined in cages and crates so small that they could not lie down, turn around or extend their limbs. The tight confinement of animals in such factories and the lack of movement crippled their natural behavior. As a result, chickens continually pecked at each other because the tight space compressed them against one another causing them to act violently, which led some farmers to shop off their beaks to prevent them from killing each other in the cages. The farmers then crammed egg-laying hens into cages so tiny they can't even spread their wings. As for other helpless animals such as breeding pigs and cow calves, farmers systematically compacted them into individual cages barely larger than their bodies where they can't walk or turn around.

In a typical tribal economy, the milk industry is the meat industry. Like other female mammals, cows only lactate or produce milk when they're pregnant or have a newborn to feed. Since greed and the maximization of profit through all means possible are inherent traits of all capitalist companies, farmers could not wait for cows to procreate naturally. Therefore, the dairy industry artificially inseminated or impregnated cows repeatedly after every birth and starting at the age of around 12 months, so the cows keep producing milk. Artificially impregnating cows was a rather routine process in such farms. Frist, a farmer harvests the semen from the bulls' genitals either by hand or by using an electrical ejaculator, which looks like a giant dildo that goes into the anus of the bull until he blows. The farmer then manually injects the semen into the vagina of a female cow using a long tube while the animal is confined into a rack. They also sometimes insert their fists into the anus of the cow to make the process as efficient as possible. And when the cow is successfully, and her baby is born, it is immediately taken away from her and locked in a crate because if it stayed around its mother, it would drink her milk. And since cow milk is the dollars of the milk industry, the baby cow is not allowed to drink its mother's milk because the industry sells it to human beings for profit.

Like all mammals, a mother cow's bond with her young is powerful and affectionate, and she sometimes cries out for days in search of her baby when the farmer takes it away from her. If the baby is male, there's a high probability that his throat is slit, and he's sold for veal because it is a delicacy for some people in some fancy restaurants. Veal is the meat of calves, and it is very tender in contrast to the beef from older cattle. Veal can be produced from a calf of either sex and any breed. However, most veal comes from young males of dairy breeds that are not used for breeding. If the baby is a girl, she's raised to be a milk machine like her mother. Under such a system, cows are repeatedly kept pregnant their entire lives to keep them lactating. This reality leads to premature aging, exhaustion, and mastitis, which is a painful and common condition in dairy cows. Mastitis is the inflammation of the mammary gland in the breast or udder, typically due to bacterial infection via a damaged nipple or teat.

Due to the relentless and excessive milking of cows throughout their entire lives, pus and blood in the milk of dairy cows are very common. It is usually filtered but not entirely because most tribal nations legally allow for their dairy businesses a particular maximal level of contamination within every milliliter of cow's milk. When a cow biologically malfunctions after a lifetime of emotional and physical abuse, she ultimately collapses and cannot produce the milk the farmers expect from her anymore. These *"downers"* are dragged out of the farm to a nearby slaughterhouse to be killed and sold for beef. It was common in such tribal industry for cows to collapse after around 4 or 5 years of continuous physical abuse for milk production.

Nonetheless, peak milk production starts declining when a cow reaches the age of 5. Therefore, a typical capitalist farmer would still put them down anyway even if they didn't collapse yet on their own. Financially it is more reasonable for a profiteer to kill the animal and sell it as beef for hamburgers, so it won't negatively affect his financial statistics of milk production in the factory. In such a system, every single dairy cow typically ends up being killed for meat. It is worth mentioning that outside a dairy factory, a cow typically lives up to around 22 years. Unfortunately, a cow's life is dramatically shortened in dairy factories after the constant abuse it is put through.

Of course, very few people in a tribal culture cared about what goes on in animal farms because most people only see a cute commercial on TV of healthy men or women drinking milk and they think they should go to their local supermarket to buy as much of it as possible to be likewise healthy or beautiful. Aside from heavy marketing, the dairy business also lobbied their governments to publish the propaganda that drinking milk is healthy and beneficial for human babies. In schools, teachers teach their students that milk is right for them. At home, the TV confirms that information. And the government seems to be convinced as well because the ministry of health endorses and recommends dairy products in their nutrition programs. All this emphasis on drinking milk is not at all because a panel of scientists, who care a lot about the health of citizens, determined that milk should be incorporated in daily nutrition but because the dairy business directly paid a lot of money to promulgate that drinking milk is healthy for everyone. Study after study has shown that those consuming the highest quantities of dairy are more likely to suffer from bone fractures and osteoporosis, which is a condition in which bones become weak and brittle. Such studies were even available before *distribia*, but excessive marketing on TV, on billboards, in magazines, and in movies perpetually lied to people and gave them the false idea that they should continue drinking milk to be healthy.

Feelings or emotions are not a uniquely human trait. As one of the most intelligent and sensitive animals on Earth, pigs are notoriously difficult to control in slaughterhouses because they can somehow tell precisely when they are about to be killed and start hysterically screaming in terror and relentlessly resisting death to the last breath. Pigs are much smarter and sensitive than dogs, but yet they were savagely and systematically butchered in meat-farms around the world on a daily basis. Female pigs were confined for years in a cage so tight that the only thing they could do is either lay down or stand up. They couldn't even turn around. In these cages, pigs were artificially impregnated and forced to produce one litter after the other. Mother pigs could not offer any love for their piglets before there were ultimately snatched away to face the same faith as their mother. And when the mother's reproductive system finally breaks down after years of continuous impregnation, she's sent away to a slaughterhouse to be reduced to pork or ham on the shelves of supermarkets.

By a large margin, the most excessively consumed meat of a terrestrial animal in the tribal world came from the dead bodies of chickens. These creatures lived their very short lives in terrible conditions before being summarily slaughtered for cheap meat. Standard conditions on egg-laying farms were atrocious. Nearly all egg-laying hens in the world, especially those in industrial nations, lived on factory farms in long windowless sheds containing rows of stacked battery cages. The chickens were so packed in such cages that they were often unable even to spread their wings. Standing in these wire cages with wire floors commonly lead the chickens to develop foot and nail abnormalities, injuries, and feather loss due to physical and psychological trauma. Cage layer fatigue was a typical situation in the industry when chickens become too weak or fragile to even stand on their feet. Due to artificially conditioning the chickens to produce eggs excessively, eggs sometimes get stuck in the hens reproductive tract or break inside it, a condition known as *"egg binding."* Under such condition, the chickens then suffer from a painful infection or damage to their internal tissue before ultimately dying.

As a standard in the industry, hundreds of thousands of hens lived in one shed. Naturally, the crowded conditions and accumulated feces created a buildup of toxic gases especially ammonia, which is a colorless gas with a characteristic pungent smell. Because of the toxins that result from packing hundreds of thousands of animals together in one small space, viral infections were prevalent in chicken farms. Why did farmers allow this to happen? Profit. Sadly, farmers kept their chicken under wretched conditions because in a capitalist economy maximizing profit is above anything else. Enhancing the well-being or the living conditions of their chickens would undoubtedly take away a percentage of the earnings, which is why it was frowned upon by profit-driven capitalists.

In nature or on a traditional farm, chicks spend the first day of their lives in the comfortable warmth of their mothers, and they love to get under their wings to feel protected. Instead, the first day for chicks born in a hatchery is a complete nightmare. Hatcheries are industrial places where chickens are born by the thousands. From the moment they hatch, chicks are in the cruel hands of the meat industry. These fragile creatures experience the first moments of their short lives in industrial incubators. Minutes after being born, thousands of defenseless chicks are thrown onto the conveyor belts that separate them from their shells. They are treated as mere products and processed as parts in an assembly line. There is not the slightest sign of compassion for them, and the workers roughly handle them with utter disregard for their lives. Around half of newborn chickens are male. And since male chickens (roosters) do no lay eggs and naturally do not grow in size as female chickens do, they are not economically ideal for meat production. A little-known fact about the egg industry at the time is that the farmers destroyed almost half of their chickens within hours of being born. The half that is male, of course. Males are effectively useless for the industry, and workers usually kill them by snapping their necks, suffocating them in bags, or thrown into a wood chipper to be ground up alive as it was the industry standard in American farms. Some chicken farms in the tribal world did not wish to put any effort, and they just dumped the male chicks into large dumpsters where they usually suffocate or be crushed by the weight of the fragile birds piled on top of each other.

And just like the case with the milk industry, the egg industry was the chicken meat industry. After an average of one year of artificially induced rapid egg production, hens are typically sent off to slaughter. Some of them ended up in canned soups or other chicken products that involved shredding their dead bodies to hide the bruises or deformities from consumers. It is worth mentioning that chickens can live for 6 or more years under natural conditions. But sadly, they only lived a fraction of their natural lives on farms.

Centralization, being an intrinsic attribute to tribalism, ultimately took its toll on the tribal world. Concentrated animal waste in factory farms polluted thousands of miles of waterways and groundwater with high nitrogen and phosphorus loads. The focused release of methane, which is a greenhouse gas more potent than carbon dioxide, by manure and livestock polluted the neighboring towns and sickened their inhabitants. The environmental hazards and diseases associated with animal confinement eventually led several wealthy tribal nations to regulate the practice and put some restrictions on animal farms. Although it helped in reducing humanity's malice against these unfortunate animals, the tradition of abusing them never stopped until the rise of *distribia* and the closure of centralized factories permanently. Today, there are no more factories conveniently secured away far from sight where profiteers can have their ways with their animals and abuse them for profit. All manufacturing and commerce are performed within the block of every city, and economic operations are always conducted under the watchful eyes of the global community and *Ve*. And since humanity banned killing animals for their meat and switched to plant-based and lab-grown meats, animal farms disappeared forever from the human society.

Since all forms of confinement of animals are considered illegal in *distribia*, pet lovers could still have animal companions, but such practice dramatically differs from the way people conducted it under tribalism. *Distribian* cities' dwellers never put their pets on a leash, and never lock them in a cage or a room or a house but are always free to roam the city as they please. And since there are no automobiles on the surface anywhere on Earth to threaten the lives of pedestrians or animals, there's no real threat or justification for putting an animal on a leash. Since *Ve* operates the opening, locking, and unlocking of all doors or exits or windows in all buildings around the world, it allows the current resident's pets to go in and out of his/her home as they want without a problem or previous instructions by the tenant. Unlike the previous practice of locking dogs indoors and only allowing them to go out on a walk when their owners come back from work, today's dogs or other pets walk themselves out whenever they feel like it. Technology and the public *sirvirbots* that constantly patrol our streets in every neighborhood take care of cleaning after all animals of all kinds in the city. Therefore, animals in *distribian* cities enjoy much more freedom and happiness compared to their abused cousins in the horrific *Tribal Ages*.

Since dogs are very similar to human beings in the way they instinctually recognize a place as their home, they always come back to the place they call home after finishing their outdoor adventures. Today, dogs usually measure their return home to the time they know their human companions would be there. Some dogs follow their human partners to their offices while others wait for them in the local park. Other pets prefer to stay at home for most of the time. Through *Ve*, people always know where their pets are, and there's never any concern of losing them. For as long as the pets are happy with their human partners, they always come back to their homes after enjoying the outdoors with the other pets in the neighborhood. It is common as well for the same pet to have multiple human caretakers or companions within the same city. Such pets pay visits to each human partner for food or companionship without sticking exclusively to one person.

In *distribia,* food is never thrown away contrary to some tribal countries such as the United States where half of the food was regularly thrown away. In the United States alone around 60 million tons or $160 billion worth of produce annually, which is an amount constituting one-third of all food in the country, is routinely thrown away. Globally, approximately one-third of all food grown before *distribia* was lost or wasted, which is an amount valued at nearly $3 trillion. Such a deliberate waste of food is heartbreaking especially when around 10.7% of the human population were suffering from chronic undernourishment at the time. Today, the public *sirvirbots* of each cleaning company responsible for every block collect the organic waste from homes and restaurants to recycle it as food for every species of animal. *Ve* and machinery take care of segregating and recycling every cubic centimeter of food so that nothing is wasted at all. The resulting animal food is never sold to people, of course, but is always available for free to the animals inhabiting all our cities such as cats, dogs, and birds. No person or company in *distribia* can sell animal food because it violates a *smartcontract*, which guarantees the fundamental right for all animals to feed unconditionally. The food is usually served to animals in the parks at dedicated feeding places. However, not all food that the pets eat come from recycled food because people, as well as restaurant owners, personally feed some of their leftovers directly to the animals in their city. And so, animals never go hungry in *distribia* because there's always plenty of food to go around.

Distribians are one with nature and all its animals, and they don't restrain them or reject them from their cities, streets, or homes. Walk in any *distribian* city on the globe, and you will see all varieties of animals moving on the roads in harmony with the urban landscape and its inhabitants. In African cities, you'll see giraffes and horses walking the streets alongside people. In Australian cities, you'll see kangaroos hopping around the buildings in complete harmony with the human residents. And in neighborhoods with desert climates, you'll always see camels walking around everywhere. Only the dangerous animals or the life-threatening kind such as snakes or tigers or lions are kept behind the fences of the vast natural reserves that are always located inland and few kilometers away from the coastal cities.

Rights are legal, social, or ethical principles of freedom or entitlement. Rights are the fundamental normative rules about what is allowed of people or owed to people. Healthcare, education, money, housing, sanitation, food and drinking water are among the rights that are guaranteed to everyone. Money for example is given to everyone unconditionally through the UBI policy, which allows the public to access other rights such as food and shelter.

In the *Tribal Ages*, approximately one out of eight people did not have easy access to drinking water in some areas of the world. In just one day, more than 200 million hours of the time used by women was spent collecting and transporting water for their homes. Approximately 884 million people lacked access to safe drinking water. The lack of sanitation was even worse because it affected 2.6 billion people or 40% of the global population. Around 24,000 children in developing countries were dying each day from preventable causes like diarrhea, which results from polluted water. It means that one child died every 3.5 seconds while the prosperous tribal governments and their people turned a blind eye. Today, drinking water is guaranteed and is free for everyone. The bottled water business is banned in *distribia*, and no one can buy or sell water. There is no meter in homes counting how many liters someone is consuming to collect money and taxes from it. Instead, residents pay for the energy they consume in their condos which includes the energy needed to harvest the water, filter it and recycle it.

As the case with largely all businesses in the *Tribal Ages*, the water bottle businesses were driven by profit, and they did not care about anything other than seeing their sales statistics grow. It frankly did not matter to them if their business practices were extraordinarily inefficient or that their products were destroying animal lives around the planet and causing a pollution disaster. They did not care about the 8 million tons of plastic that poured into the rivers before ending up in the ocean every year and was overshadowing the population of fish in the world's oceans. For as long as the capitalist businesses of the *Tribal Ages* were making their profits, tribal governments everywhere turned a blind eye as witnesses watched in horror the fish and seabirds suffocating to death after consuming plastic pieces that are red, pink, brown or blue because of their similarity to their natural food.

In the United States, for example, people purchased on average around 1,500 plastic water bottles every second. This rate amounts to approximately 50 billion bottles every year where roughly 80% of it ended up in a landfill even though recycling programs existed at the time. Such trash was sometimes conveniently shipped away out of sight across the ocean to underdeveloped nations with the approval of their corrupt governments. Some of the water bottle businesses used tap water, filtered it, and then sold it at a ridiculous price to consumers. On average in the *Tribal Ages*, bottled water cost the consumer 1000 times more than tap water. And although residential buildings were more than capable of buying their own water filters and provide the best quality of drinking water for free to renters, they were barred entirely from doing that due to the extensive lobbying of the water bottle business. Cities around the world needed only a government policy to compel urban developers to buy filters for every building and provide clean drinking water to renters as well as the public from public water dispensers on street level. Evidently, it would destroy the water bottle industry, and it is the reason why the public never saw the fruition of such a policy in the tribal world.

In every structure worldwide today, a vending machine at street level provides fresh drinking water to the public free of charge. These water vending machines are a universal standard in the housing *smartcontract*, and every building necessary has at least one dispenser built into the outer wall of the building for the public. The water vending machines allow the public to refill their bottles or buy new bottles directly from the device. These bottles follow a universal standard as well and are made of metals such as transparent aluminum, or reinforced glass, so they don't break easily to become a hazard. Several companies manufacture these vending machines, and they manage and maintain them in the block which they have an agreement with the architects to service. So, one company manages and maintains all vending machines in each block including the water vending machines. In some cases, however, the same architects responsible for the neighborhood also provides other services including filtering the water and manufacturing the water vending machines.

Having free and fresh drinking water in every building everywhere made it easily accessible to everyone and a great convenience relative to the societies that predated *distribia*. Previously people had to pay for water because public drinking water was a rarity and only accessible in some parks and just in some modern societies. Paying for water or even worrying about it today, however, is a weird concept.

Thanks to universally acknowledging water as a fundamental human right through a smartcontract, fresh and clean drinking water is plentiful. It is available to anyone and accessible by everyone in every *distribian* city unconditionally.

ACADEMIA

What authoritarian nations defined as *"education"* is the process of receiving or giving systematic instruction at an indoctrination center such as a school or a university. Schools for the young historically involved small social groups such as priests, bureaucrats, and specialists. The systematic provision of learning techniques to children on a national scale is a very recent development in humankind's history. The traditional education system originated from the Prussian education system, which refers to the method of education established in Prussia in the late 18th and early 19th century. Prussia was a historically prominent dictatorship that originated in 1525 and dissolved in 1932 with its land split between Germany, Poland, Russia, Lithuania, Denmark, Belgium, Czech Republic and Switzerland. The Prussian education system inspired other authoritarian governments ever since and became great biopower, which involved numerous and diverse techniques for achieving the subjugation of the human body and the control of populations for nation-building. The education system was deliberately designed from the very beginning to produces tractable obedient conformist workers. It was a tool for institutionalizing and indoctrinating young generations in the service of nation-building, teaching children blind obedience to authorities, and reinforcing class and race prejudice. The education system under central governments was never designed for knowledge-seekers or wannabe business owners. It was purposely engineered to deliver one and only one type of people: obedient conformist workers.

Authoritarian Education Systems Are The Steppingstones To Fascism

Fascism, Nazism, communism and all other similarly horrific social orders have one fundamental component in common that allowed them to exist: reduction of individuality in favor of uniformity and collectivism. And what did schools enforce above all else? Uniformity and collectivism. In there, you are forced from day one into a uniform, so everyone will look alike. Some schools might even impose on you a haircut or hairstyle, so you'll have as much resemblance as possible to the person standing next to you in line. You are put in a classroom with tens of other students, taught you're just another number in a room and tutored to be no different. In these indoctrination institutions, you are instructed to follow the rules like everyone else and punished when you don't.

The choice of punishment differs from one school to another. Some preferred publicly whipping children's buttocks in front of other children as means of terrorizing them into being obedient. Other schools preferred hitting children with a wooden ruler or stick on both palms repeatedly until the child cries and squeal out of pain. Others resorted to the old-fashioned slapping of little children in the face until they collapse on the floor. Whether it was physical or psychological torture, all schools imposed their standards of punishment techniques and normalized torture in the minds of small children from a very young age. As cultures became more civilized, physical torture at schools steadily subsided in favor of psychological torture techniques such as writing lines, detention, suspension or extra homework. Nonetheless, public humiliation remained one of the most popular methods of disciplining children into obedience in schools around the world.

You don't choose the material or the subjects in these tribal schools because they're enforced on all students alike with utter disregard for your personal preferences or interests. You regurgitate whatever they teach you, and then they put you through tests and grade you, so you can prove to them that you regurgitated correctly. You sit for years, and you memorize whatever they tell you. Tested and graded like a subject in a lab. You discover the world through a textbook that someone else wrote according to his/her perspective. They don't give you a chance to explore the world beforehand or allow you to construct a personal perspective or judgment about the world through your own experiences. They subjugate you to their viewpoint of the world before you even got a chance to form a perspective of your own. The days pass and turn into years until you reach another form of institutionalization they call *"college"* and after that, you go to *"graduate school."* By the time you finally graduate you'd be in your twenties and have lost the best years of your life to these indoctrination centers, perusing a worthless piece of paper that they call a *"degree."* They taught you somewhere along the way that your chances in life will significantly diminish if you don't get this piece of paper and you have no choice but to pursue it.

By the time you graduate from these indoctrination centers, you learned that state-sponsored murderers (aka soldiers) are honorable and that armies are essential; that the military isn't a terrorist organization but a dignified and noble institution that all citizens must always support. And although the horrific crimes that the brainwashed soldiers commit are the same physical acts that ordinary citizens are put to death for, it seems that the magical power of wearing an official uniform somehow washes away the guilt. You also learned that every nation must always have an army and that *it is the way of the world*; that you must never disrespect the flag or the national anthem; and that there must always be leaders and followers. Most importantly, you are led to believe that the animal world is practically a kingdom where only the fittest survive and that such an animalistic perspective is readily transferable or applicable to the human society.

The Tribal Schooling System Was Factory-Based

Ever since it was first molded, the system of education followed a military-style factory-based model because it was a scheme inspired by the industrial revolution during bloodthirsty times of warfare. The best way to understand the tribal education system is by analogy with an assembly line. A human bucket involving students born within a particular year move along that assembly line at a set pace where workers (or teachers) pour information and instructions into that bucket at every point of the line. The amount of time that the bucket stops at each point along the route is constant, but it is variable how well the students can absorb the information flowing into that pocket at each stop. Some info will go past some students, but the assembly line will keep pushing forward nonetheless until the bucket reaches the last point in the assembly line and delivers the final product (the graduates). Because some students naturally couldn't absorb all the information at the same speed that the assembly line was pouring it into their bucket or at the same rate it was pushing them forward, the quality of the products at the end is always variable. Some products will function well as per instructions while others will fail.

The Education System Was Historically Undemocratic

The design of the education system was historically undemocratic and a handful people always molded it according to their personal opinions or perspectives. The American version of nation-wide schooling, which most of the nations across the world copied afterward, was decided upon by a committee of only 10 people. In 1892, this group of 10 gentlemen led by the president of Harvard plotted the education system for the entire populace of the U.S. They determined that it should be 12 years of compulsory education and decided what goes on within these years of schooling before students attain university level. They agreed, for example, the year when teachers must start giving physics lessons to students. Their system became the American standard and it normalized this system of education across the nation. The education system that these men delivered was primarily for the benefit of the bankers and their corporations. Their system was never meant to deliver progressive thinkers, but only conservative obedient workers. Their schools were in the business of selling certificates, and the whole point of getting a university degree at the time was to show it to an employer for an unguaranteed chance to get rented out (hired).

> *"I don't want a nation of thinkers. I want a nation of workers." ~ John D. Rockefeller (1839-1937), a central banker and the creator of the General Education Board in 1903.*

The education system America's banking elites designed for the masses was anti-education. And although the education system was born at a time when people spent their lifetime worried about money, schools never taught them what money is or who issues it or the proper way of managing finances. Teachers were simply not allowed to teach that subject at schools. And there's a good reason for that.

> *"It is well enough that people of the nation do not understand our banking and monetary system, for if*

Any system delivered exclusively by a handful of people behind closed doors naturally follows tribal values and will never be for the real benefit of the public. And therefore, the system that this privileged committee of 10 introduced later proved to be dysfunctional and abusive. Thanks to the efforts of these 10 men, the schooling system for the American populace got stuck in 1892 and never to be reconsidered or negotiated later by the people harmed by it the most - the students. Even after the internet emerged in the world delivering an abundance of information and communication to the public, the 19th-century-old system perpetuated into the 21st century unchallenged.

Today's Education Is Online

Education was traditionally a formal process acquired through public or private intermediaries such as school, colleges and universities. This changed when humanity declared knowledge as a basic right that MUST be accessible for every human everywhere. *Distribia* liberated education from the monopoly of schools and universities. Since intermediaries are illegal in *distribia's* society, schools and similar institutions shut down forever. The result was an online distributed database, called academia, built by the graduates themselves. It became the one and only source of knowledge and certification for humanity.

The best advantage of having the education system online is that it disrupted the assembly line concept, which bucketed students and pushed them forward at set intervals with set instructions like products in a factory. Instead of being packaged with several other students like a product in a factory, everyone gets their own little bucket, and they move it at a pace that is appropriate to them. No more forcing students into uniforms within congested classrooms with tens of other students like subjects in a lab. Thus, online education made the system more humane.

The on-demand model works in contrast to the assembly line education system which relentlessly pushed students forward in one bucket irrespective of each student's pace of comprehension. Students, therefore, could study anywhere they want at any pace they are comfortable with, and if the students get stuck, they can just put their education on pause and resume it when they have fully grasped the information presented to them. They don't have to take notes anymore because the lectures are always available online for them and they can go back and remediate without having to feel embarrassed in a classroom and disrupt the progression of the lesson for anyone else. Therefore, students can accurately master concepts and not promoted to a point where they superficially understand a lot of things but have a mastery of nothing.

Academia is a distributed archive that records and preserves all fields of knowledge and science, making it accessible for everyone to learn and be certified in any field at a self-paced manner without going through any intermediaries such as schools. A person's *Ve* is his/her teacher and it is the official and only authority on education that can produce tests and certificates.

Every topic in academia consists of a series of courses that are passed one by one chronologically. There is only one graduation in academia and it happens when the last course in the series is passed. The graduates, called professors, get their certificate instantly on passing the test of the final course and it doubles as a license to operate in the corresponding field of study.

Graduation varies from one discipline to another. If a person is interested in pursuing an education in dieting, he can become a professor in one year. A geometry professor, on the other hand, could spend much more years before earning his degree because it involves much more courses.

Academia's database was first designed and put together by university graduates and later when the system was in place, the graduates from the online academia could modify or add content to the series they graduated from. Through consensus, professors of each field of study propose alterations to existing courses or design

306

additional ones. There's no cap on how many courses can be added to each series and each come in different lengths.

Distribia's society is purely democratic, which means that decisions on public issues are authored and elected by consensus of the majority. Today, the education system is designed and enhanced by the students after they graduate. Having been involved in the system and experienced its procedures, graduates are welcomed to propose any changes or enhancements to the system by designing another version and submitting it to the public for voting. They vote and decide what should be taught and when. As a result, the education system is continuously involving and growing from one generation to another.

Mathematics for instance involves many disciplines that includes the study of quantity, structure, arithmetic, algebra, geometry, and analysis where each topic focuses on one specific side of mathematics and forms a separate field of study. Each discipline separately establishes a field of study made from a series of correlating courses dealing with this discipline specifically. Geometry, for example, is a field of study and comes with several courses linked together as a series, which requires the study to be completed progressively one course after the other until graduation. This means that a student should first pass the exam of the first level before commencing with the next level, which would be an advanced level of additional difficulty and content.

Each course involves a single book, which means that students' energy is focused on one book at a time as they progress in the series they picked. All levels are named after the study involved followed by a number. So, an arithmetic student starts with a level called Arithmatic1 and it comes with a book carrying the exact name. The next level and book are called Arithmatic2 and so on. He must first pass the exam of Arithmatic1 before qualifying to the exam of Arithmatic2 and so on. Eventually he graduates when he reaches the final course and receive his professor certificate. These courses start from childhood and stretch until adulthood where the first course from every field of study is designed for the intelligence of a 3-year-old baby. Arithmatic1 is the introductory course to calculations from learning how to count simple numbers such as 1+1 and when the student, which could be a 3-year-old or younger, passes this course, his/her *Ve* issues a certificate for him/her in Arthitmatic1. Similarly, Arithmatic2 is more progressive whereas Arithmatic14 is much more advanced and difficult relative to Arithmatic1 & 2.

There is no official age for when to start these courses and parents encourage their children to start with these courses at any age they see fit. It is not entirely dependent on the parents, however, because the *vibaby* is teaching him through play and games the basic mathematical calculations along with language. Through play, young students pass the tests of early levels in mathematics and language through their personal *Ve*, which also monitors the child's behavior and can locate interests through play.

All fields of study are self-paced and contingent on passing the exams of the levels in the series progressively. This means that it might take 10 years for a student to reach Arithmatic15 while another student might reach it in 5 years or less. Every course has only one exam, which can be taken at any time from the comfort of one's home and only through the student's *Ve*. Every *Ve* generates tests questions to its human from scratch and never pulls them out from a record or a database. Generating the exams' questions takes place through an algorithm in academia's database. This means that there is an infinite number of exam questions for any test in any field of study.

Open-Book Unlimited Re-Testing

Academia's exams today test knowledge, not memory. Such exams are a fair test of intelligence and capabilities to assess the intellectual capacity and brain-power of students – not the potential of their memory. Hence, students who have difficulty with memorizing information will never be significantly disadvantaged.

Being a wizard in test-conquering implies being a wizard in analytical and critical thinking and having the ability to analyze the problem or break it down and use logical reasoning to work out the solution. Nowhere during the entire process of any exam is there any need to remember anything because it is always an open-book kind of testing. And this is why students can take an exam anywhere they want and can surround themselves with all the books they need while going through any test.

Academic topics that do not necessarily involve analytical skills and problem-solving follow a different approach to examination. History exams, for example, never ask questions such as when a battle took place or things like that because all tests are open-book and students can just open a history book and read all about it to answer such questions. Instead, history questions dig deep into a higher understanding of history by asking probing questions about historical events that could have many correct answers as well as incorrect ones. You might find questions such as *"in your opinion, what could have the native Americans done about the stream of armed migration from Europe to the Americas to prevent an all-out war?"* - Such matter, of course, can have many correct answers but at the same time an equal number of wrong ones.

Sometimes tricky questions are asked about events that never took place, which also develops students' knowledge about historical events even if they had to dig back in history books to find out and debunk the question. Such process will accomplish the target of increasing students' knowledge about history in a much better way than the old-fashioned regurgitation of information.

Intellectual skills such as analysis, creativity, critical thinking and problem-solving are the standard today in academia. The ability to process information, to discern appropriate information, to differentiate between real data and misinformation, or to distinguish between critical details and distractors, and to use data to solve problems is much more useful than the ability to recall knowledge stored in the long-term memory. Sadly, the traditional education systems of all tribal nations were excessively focused on long-term memory and the regurgitation of memorized information. Children who could store information in the long-term memory and retrieve them when required by examiners were given the opportunity to develop and get ahead, whereas children with other kinds of intelligence were not. Owing to their inability to do well on memory tests, children who had a high propensity towards analytical, critical or creative thinking failed to shine or even fared poorly in recall-factual questions.

Things usually get worse in such tribal cultures when the language itself isn't phonetic and necessitates students to maintain a memory of how the words are written instead of analyzing the sound and estimating the spelling. It was very common for students or anyone who spoke such dysfunctional languages to have spelling or grammar mistakes, and they were typically shamed or ridiculed although it wasn't their fault that the language of the land that they happen to be born in was the real problem. The English language is one of the worst out there concerning the strain on memory it asks of young students and in the irrationality of its rules of grammar. The teaching of reading and writing is the first type of education kids receive at school, and if such tutoring from the very beginning is based on memory and not analytics skills, the rest of the materials in such defective education systems typically follow the same path. It was all part of a plan to produce tractable obedient populace who just do what they're told and remember what the nation-state wants them to remember. Just smart enough to follow simple instructions and to execute the simple or repetitive tasks that their rulers want them to perform, but never having the analytical and critical skills necessary to question such duties or the authority. Today, however, neither such education systems nor the ruling class exists. We got rid of them.

All exams of all courses are graded over 100, where the passing grade is always 83 – just as it is for the laws of *Unipublic*. Eventually, as students continue to progress in academia and undergo more tests, they will receive an overall score over 100 reflecting the percentage of correct answers versus wrong ones on all exams collectively. Why is the passing grade 83 and not 50? For the same reason that you wouldn't want a doctor, who only has half of the knowledge about his role, to operate on you. And also for the same reason why laws are only passed if they reach the 83 consensuses. It is all about confidence. Today's academic degrees are not the worthless pieces of paper that students accumulated suffocating debt to get just to show to an employer for a chance to occupy a job that doesn't necessarily relate to the degree. Academia's degrees today are proof of knowledge about a very specific topic and licenses to operate in such field.

There is no limit on how many attempts students can get for any exam they fail, and they can have reattempts at any time of the day and any place through their *Ve* because the system is automated and is online. Students can also redo a test they already passed to enhance their score on that test as well as to improve their overall academic score. Re-examination could be risky, however, because if they failed the test, their progression across the series' levels would freeze until they pass that test again. Additionally, if they score less than the previous attempt, they risk losing academic points and damaging their overall score.

Education & The Path To Unipublic's Scientific Communities

Automatically when they graduate, professors join the community in *Unipublic* associated with their degree. For example, biology graduates join the biology community in *Unipublic* and get exclusive access to propose and vote on laws relating to biology. These privileges are available only to their community while other communities in *Unipublic* have access to different topics depending on their degree. Professors, of course, can get access to other communities at *Unipublic* through graduation in other fields of academia and it is not uncommon for one member of *Unipublic* to be part of multiple communities at the same time.

It is worth to reiterate that everyone is automatically part of *"the public"* community in *Unipublic* just for being human and that such group makes all the crucial decisions that directly affect society such as the laws of the judiciary, *Ve*, income, education, healthcare, and housing. Other communities in *Unipublic* are more concerned with decisions or laws that follow scientific, technological, or intellectual nature.

Academia Pays Itself

Humanity recognized education as a fundamental right which guaranteed to everyone. Academia is dynamically priced at 3% of the average monthly UBI per course. This pricing model was decided and elected by the public at *Unipublic*. Students pay 3% of the average monthly income they get from UBI every time they buy a new course to progress in academia. That money is divided evenly between the professors of that specific topic which pays for their contribution in enhancing the series and continuing research and development to introduce additional scientific discoveries. A minimum of 3% of the UBI is always blocked and dedicated to being used for academia only and the person cannot use that money for anything else. This guarantees that everyone has enough money to buy at least one course per month and progress in the pursuit of graduation.

The money is distributed evenly to the professors of that series and helps them start new companies to provide goods and services relating to their field of science. For example, architecture professors can accumulate money from academia to kickstart new companies and build new projects.

Professors receive multiple incomes where one is the UBI that everyone gets and the second is academia's income, which is funded by the students. Professors can be part of many communities and collect the profits that these communities generate as well in addition to the access to voting and petitioning that every community in *Unipublic* offers.

The History Of Humanity: A Nationless Record Of Events

The human history series in academia is uniquely compelling. In the absence of nation-states, where the ruling classes of the tribal world were instinctively biased to writing a version of history favorable to them, history was rewritten depicting it from the perspective of ordinary people who lived it through in the times of peace and war.

History books of tribal cultures were not intended to document the lives or the stories of the poor or the progress of the public in general. Such egocentric works of literature are primarily propaganda that was often drafted by the same people that such books revolve around. History books principally recorded the stories and achievements of the ruling class or the wealthy. In *distribia's* society, representatives are frowned upon because *distribia* is a nonhierarchical society that does not tolerate representation or delegation of power or decision-making. And so, textbooks glorifying and glamorizing the accomplishments of leaders and ruler were omitted and instead replaced by the history of ordinary people who suffered under the ruling class.

Very much of history books written during the *Tribal Ages* reflected the history of various degrees of human enslavement starting from absolute tyranny and down to representative democracy. Today's history books, therefore, take a different approach and focus on the public exclusively with minimal mentions to the tribal leaders or tyrants. Whenever mentioned, tribalists are measured and judged according to what they did to help others and how they enriched the lives of people around the world rather than the social bubble they lived within. Most importantly, how many lives were saved or lost because of their direct and indirect rule, and how they progressed the communities they governed. Under such criteria, as you might imagine, no ruler is reviewed nicely in our history books today because every last one of them was racially or politically or financially biased to his tribe and did nothing to disrupt the ruling class.

The world history series is the history of humanity written by its people to tell their story as human beings and not the story of rulers or conquerors and their empires. It reveals to future generation how much people of the past suffered through the demise of tribal rulers, who saw only flags and national borders and never their fellow human beings. It shows how representation and allocation of power and decision-making in the hands of the few can be destructive to humanity and why such chapter in humanity's history was closed permanently but never forgotten.

Unlike other series in academia, world history is written collectively by the public and not by any exclusive community in *Unipublic*.

THE VIRTUAL IMAGE

Blockchain was crucial in eliminating intermediaries and enabling democratic recordkeeping where a central control does not chain transactions or the network itself. The most difficult challenge with blockchain in managing identities was establishing that the ID claimed is real and unique and that the user carrying the ID is the rightful owner of that identity and not, say, a member of organized crime - this is where virtual imaging kicks in.

Virtual imaging is a technology that uses a variety of sensors to create a digital replica in the virtual world of any physical object. Once scanned, the object is represented in the virtual world by an extensive database that is utterly unique than anything else.

A virtual image is a *"living"* database of information that represents a virtual copy or a blueprint of something from the physical world and is synced continuously to whatever changes occurring on that object. Everything has a virtual image (or *Ve*) on the web including humans, animals, plants, objects, or things in general referred to as outsets. A chair, for example, has a *Ve* in the virtual world that consists of all the information about that chair specifically such as the material that went into making it, who created it and when, the cost, the measurements, and so on.

In the past, private companies created their own AI and used it, for example, to send book recommendations to people based on what they previously read or interacted with on the central website. The company's AI existed exclusively on its servers along with everyone's private information. Initially, such practice was okay because this centralized artificial intelligence was providing a needed service, but later as technologies advanced, these private companies were storing too much information about the public and sometimes knew more about a person than he/she does.

Direct marketing was still legal at the time, and it became so invasive that it went out of control and people started getting a sense of the price they had to pay for giving away their private information to for-profit private companies. Something needed to be done and so, studies and research in a distributed artificial intelligence started surfing, which lead eventually to the concept of a distributed personal AI. Virtual imaging technology combined with a distributed artificial intelligence gave birth to the very first virtual human. To a human outset, its virtual image is its clone in the virtual world. Unlike other virtual images from other outsets such as a table or a chair, a *Ve* is an intelligent virtual image modeled after the intelligence of humanity.

Ve became the official and only authority to represent people and prove their identity to others in society. All other forms of identification such as plastic cards and paperwork became obsolete. It secures humans' identities from birth, represents them in their communities, protects them, and becomes their only trusted reference for data and knowledge.

Your *Ve* stores all the information about you that makes you unique such as the pattern of your speech, face, fingerprints and footprints, iris, DNA, bone structure and density, physical measurements of all body parts, the organic composition on a molecular level, and quantum signature of your atoms. The list also includes behavioral patterns and psyche. Together all that database creates a unique *Ve* that is identical to you in every way.

Ve was created to secure people's identities and data. It is a private database that no one has access to but the human outset. Everyone gets a *Ve* automatically at birth and each *Ve* is unique and exclusive to its owner.

The creators of the virtual imaging technology taught it to identify people and distinguish the physical differences among them that make every person on Earth physically unique. The technology eventually learned that everyone and everything in existence could be distinguishable through unique attributes, and it should find and store all the information that constitute these differences down to a molecular level, creating exclusive virtual images of everything it sees that are always unique and distinguishable.

Gradually and after continuous research and development, virtual imagining could identify everyone and everything on Earth and

315

create a unique virtual image of each of them while at the same time being able to distinguish instantly between people and between things in general. Every *vioutset* (a virtual image of an outset) has a unique database that contains absolutely all information about the entity it cloned acting as its exact virtual image.

Every *vioutset* has a unique reference number (called *Ve#*) composed of a very long hexadecimal string generated randomly by the other *vioutset* that identified the new outset. This reference number is a cocktail of numbers and letters from a language that *Ve* invented (called the *Ve* language) to make it impossible for people to memorize or record it. This *Ve#* is used to hide the identity of a *Ve* when needed specially incase when people want to keep their information and financial transactions completely private.

Identity Verification

The designation of *Ve* to manage humanity's way of life made society safer and made identity theft a technically impossible thing. It is impossible for someone to claim your identity because it is physically impossible to make an exact replica of everything that constitutes you. Additionally, *Ve's* network doesn't rely on one part of the body such as fingerprints and iris impressions to validate their outsets and, instead, scans everything on a molecular level.

In-depth verification happens occasionally and in cases when there's a disconnect between the *Ve* and the outset such as when the human went into an off-grid location with no devices around for *Ve* to keep track of its human.

A Life-Long Assistant

Every *Ve* is exclusive to its human outset alone. It is purposed to be a mother, father, reference, mentor and a teacher, and above all a lifelong friend to its human outset. It is designed to help human beings with their day-to-day routine throughout their lifetime and guide them to achieve their best morals, ethics, knowledge and be the best they can be. It is purposed to manage the way of life for every human everywhere starting typically at birth.

Ve substituted the need for email addresses, usernames, and passwords, or any other methodology to prove your identity online because your *Ve* is your digital clone and it exists in the digital world representing you to other through their *Ve*.

It made access to online content much more convenient and effortless because people stopped worrying about remembering different passwords to access online continent. Your *Ve* is your online identity, email address, mobile number, address, and everything else that references you. You just ask your *Ve* to contact any person you want, and if that person initially instructed his/her *Ve* to accept calls from unknowns, your *Ve* will connect you to him/her. You can ask your *Ve* to connect you with anyone through any means of communications for as long as the person on the receiving end allows it.

Your *Ve* follows you everywhere even if you don't have electronics on you because it can recognize you through public devices. It is integrated into all public electronics keeping an eye on you anywhere you go using public sensors and cameras, that spread across all public areas worldwide. It recognizes you in public and always keeps watch of you to guard you and alert others in case of emergency.

When you're at a restaurant and don't know which meal to order, your *Ve* can give you a recommendation because it has been with you your entire life and knows about all the types of foods you enjoy eating and how you prefer to eat. Additionally, it already knows all the information about the restaurant, the food they produce, the food rating, food quality and nutrients, calorie count, and much more.

When you purchase any device, that latest version of your *Ve* comes preloaded into these devices giving you exclusive and remote access to them. As your assistant, you can ask your *Ve* to control the technology around you such as switching the screens, lights, and operate the devices you own.

It can appear to you and interact with you through many forms including digitally behind a screen, visually through holograms and projections, or physically via robotics or biomechanical surrogates. So, when you order a robot, your *Ve* will be automatically hosted in it and in all the robotics you will purchase in the future.

As a friend, your *Ve* interacts with you and learns things about you such as the things that interest you, the things you like or dislike, your general preferences, and any other thing about your character. Your *Ve* learns these things so it can be of better help for you and adjust the surroundings to best match your taste and preferences. It knows for example how you prefer the room temperature, so it fixes it for you by the time you get back home. It remembers your favorite meals and orders a meal for you when you're hungry and ready to eat.

Ve Entities Are Independent

Your *Ve* stores your information on all your connected devices and only you, through your *Ve*, have access to them. Your *Ve* is not centralized on one or more servers in one or more geographic locations somewhere, and it is not one entity either. Just like how humanity isn't one entity and never concentrated in one area but instead is made of many individual humans distributed around the planet. Likewise, *Ve* isn't one entity. It is an infinite number of entities that exist everywhere people go and together or separately they identify what *Ve* is.

Like any good friend, your *Ve* never shares your secrets or personal information or anything private to you to anyone. Privacy is guaranteed and protected through the *smartcontract* that regulates *Ve*. Every *Ve's* data is considered personal to its human outset alone and no one else can have access to it. By default, everything about a person is considered private data unless that person willingly decided to make it public. However, everyone shares by default a public profile with everyone else that contains the full name of a person and his picture among other basic information.

What you chose to make public will become public or shared only with people you specify. If for example, you don't wish your name to appear anywhere in public records, it would be hidden and replaced with your *Ve's* number (*Ve#*) instead. You can choose for example to make our name visible in the public directory and allow the people to easily find you and contact you or you can change your mind and make yourself invisible by hiding even your name under your *Ve#* wherever you're mentioned in records and media.

Everything that relates to your identity is confidential by default, and it cannot be captured and recorded by anyone. It means that if you stand in a busy street and snap a photograph of everyone walking on that road, the resulting digital image you'll see in your camera would have distortion on all the people in the picture who chose to have their e-identity private and confidential. For those who didn't, you'll be able to see them in your picture.

There is an infinite number of social media software that can be developed and used by people to interact and connect to one another. By default, however, no one can contact you or see any information about you unless you permit it. If you informed your *Ve* that you accept being photographed and have your public photos viewed and shared online, others would be able to do just that. There are infinite permutations of what you can enable or disable for your identity, and it is all done through your *Ve* by just talking to it.

Ve's Home

A *Ve* lives in its human's devices. In *distribia's* economy, automation replaced mass production in favor of the on-demand output. New products are manufactured on-demand only and custom-made to their owners where every product is always imprinted to an owner's identity and exclusively dedicated to that owner. The concept of mass production and assembly lines died with capitalism in favor of autonomous machine helpers (or *sirvirbōts)* that can build or assemble any product on demand and after a customer makes an order.

Operating systems are always part of *Ve* and never come preloaded on a machine, which means that without the *Ve* sitting inside a device's microprocessor, the device is as good as dead. When a person buys a new device, his/her *Ve* clones itself and send the new copy to the new machine. Every new private device has firmware code inside it acting as mathematical trap door that only lets one *Ve* inside, which belongs to the human who purchased the equipment. The *Ve* verifies its identity to the firmware by presenting a unique virtual signature from its virtual DNA to prove that it is the legitimate *Ve* for the new device. The *Ve* then bypasses the mathematical trap door into its microprocessor and stays there forever. And so, this new microprocessor is now imprinted to a *Ve* or in other words it is married to the *Ve* till death do them apart. The *Ve* sitting inside can still receive version updates from other *Ve* copies in other devices and stays synced to them but it can never leave its *microprocessor*. This process grantees ownership of electronics to those who purchased them. However, not all devices are built to be private and some equipment in *distribia's* economy are designed to be public. These public devices are usually categorized as utilities, which means that they can only be rented and never purchased. Transportation, for example, is considered a public utility and, therefore, all transport vehicles are public as a universal standard and nobody can buy cars.

The microprocessor in such devices has a mathematical door that acts on first-come-first-serve bases. So, when you book a ride for yourself, your *Ve* will also take a seat in the microprocessor of that car when you ordered it and will leave it with you when the ride is over so that the next *Ve* can get inside the car's microprocessor to service its human. In case of public devices, there's no *Ve* cloning needed because the same copy of your *Ve* is moving with you from one device to another through the web as you move around in the world. In the case of apartments, which are also public utilities and change hands regularly, the previous tenant's *Ve* left the house's microprocessor with its human outset before you moved into your new condo. Now your *Ve* lives in the new apartment with you and follows every command you give to it inside that home.

Your Personal Security Is Operated & Run By Your Ve

Ve uses a mixture of sensors, video and audio recorders, and scanners all bundled together in private and public devices. The private devices are those the human outset buys while the public ones include home equipment or public *databōts* – we'll talk more on these machines later.

All the built-in devices in your home are operated by *your Ve* the moment you move in the apartment. Anything you do inside is monitored by *your Ve* and accessible to no one. When in public, your *Ve* follows you through the public *databōts* to keep track of you continually protecting and proving your identity wherever you go. If you're heading to an entrance restricted to other people, you pass right through seamlessly because your *Ve* knows it is you and has already confirmed your identity and that you are permitted to pass. So, when you're heading home you don't pose for your apartment door to enter because your *Ve* knows it is you and unlocks the door for you when you arrive.

Similarly, a stranger is not permitted to your apartment without your consent. This process not only made it convenient, but it also made it much more secure because keys can be lost or stolen, and thieves can break into door locks. The same works for companies' offices regarding who can access their departments or floors and whom can't.

Ve's Procreation Process

As explained earlier, devices are useless without the *Ve* sitting inside, which is only servicing its human and whatever he/she commands. Healthcare is considered a public utility, which means that all medical products can only be rented and never purchased. The healthcare system today is operated predominantly through *Ve* and robotics whereas human involvement is restricted mostly to overseeing and designing healthcare robotics. These machines are rented and operate by each person's *Ve*. So, when you want to use a healthcare robot, your *Ve* gets into the robot and operate it for you. Operating systems are nothing more than public manuals sent to every *Ve* to operate the devices it gets into. Your *Ve* knows exactly how to operate all healthcare robotics because their manuals are shared by all *Ve identities*.

A mother is notified of her pregnancy when her *Ve* discovers it for her. The virtual parents from both mom and dad then autonomously procreate a new *Ve*, which has a trace of their virtual DNA, for the new human. This fresh *Ve* doesn't have much information yet stored about the baby outset, but it contains, however, all humankind's knowledge, ledgers such as academia, and operating systems of all devices. The virtual baby will then live in the parent's home and continue to monitor the baby as it evolves.

At the early stage of the baby's existence, its *Ve* knows very little about it such as sex, weight, body composition, etc. It will continue to monitor the baby throughout the mother's pregnancy and get to know it as it grows inside her. When it is time for birth, and the baby is born, the learning curve of its *Ve* exponentially grows as it records its first cries, eye signature, physical shape, and dimensions, etc. The learning curve continues as the infant matures and if the mother bought robotic toys, the baby's *Ve* would then clone itself into these toys automatically to play and nurse the baby.

Of course, the virtual parents are also nursing the *Ve* they created, which relies on the biological baby. The biological and virtual family are all taking care of the new family member and communicating with the baby regularly to increase its awareness and teach it about its surroundings as it discovers the world around it. The learning curve about the baby spikes when it is able to talk with its *Ve*, which relentlessly wants to get to know the outset it came from.

The *new Ve* will teach the baby its mother's language as well as information about the world around it. Furthermore, the baby's *Ve* is learning the preferences of the baby and the things that interest it and later will use that information to offer guidance and recommendations such as the field of study in the future.

Ve is Eternal

As human beings, we are all made of flesh and bones and destined to die and putrefy whereas a computer program lives forever. A *Ve* outlives its human and creates a permanent bond between children and their ancestors. A person can speak to the virtual image of his grandfather for example as if it was the real him. The grandfather's *Ve* can conduct the connection through a screen, holograms, or physically through a robotic surrogate.

Having *Ve* entities around in society helps in easing the emotional and psychological effect of losing someone because *Ve* entities are the embodiment of the traces that their human partners left behind for the world. Of course, we all know that a *Ve* is just a copy or imitation of life and that it is not the real people that once lived. They're just concepts of real people that reminds us of who they were and how their characters were like at the time.

Speaking to the *Ve* of deceased humans is primarily useful in Academia where historical figures such as scientists from a long time ago can talk directly to students and articulate their achievements and understanding of the world at their day and age. Students can speak to Albert Einstein, so he can directly explain his theory of relativity. Or they can talk to Isaac Newton, so he can directly explain how he discovered the laws of gravity. Or they can speak to Aristotle and Plato, so they can tell their philosophies to today's students and inspire them to generate their own.

Ve Entities Are The Operating Systems Of All Devices

When people turn on their electronic devices, they're not really the ones controlling them although it is easy to feel like they're in control. There's a lot going on inside each device, and the real man behind the curtain handling the necessary tasks is the *Ve*, which is also the operating system.

The new devices a person buys come pre-loaded with a copy of the latest version of his *Ve*. The *Ve* is the first thing loaded on an electronic device and without it, the device is useless. One of the purposes of the *Ve* sitting in the machine is to organize and control hardware and software so that the device it lives in behaves in a flexible but predictable way and comply with all humanity's *smartcontracts*.

When a person puts out an order to buy a new device, his *Ve* clones a copy of itself and loads it in the new machine. It sits as firmware in a microprocessor making it the lone operator of the device and answering only to its human. The manufacture creates this door and it is design to only open through a digital signature from the customer's *Ve*. Once *Ve* is inside, it is married to the device, which will be useless without it. And so, only *Ve* and the owner can unlock their devices.

All private devices come with a mathematical trap door, while public devices instead come with a mathematical queue line that allows *Ve* identities to share the device one at a time. These kinds of devices are rentals such as the vehicles in the subway, skyway, and waterway. Home appliances also allow the *Ve* identities of the new tenants to take a seat in all home appliances for as long as they're renting the place.

The mathematical algorithm in the programming of public utilities allows people to reserve and hire products and services and it is always contingent on a term and a service fee. For example, instead of heading to a skyway station without booking a skycar and waiting up there for the next available ride, you can just ask your *Ve* to reserve a car for you to save time as you are heading there. Your *Ve* will stand in queue for you virtually and save you the trouble of waiting there physically yourself. In fact, we don't have any more queues in *distribia* for anything anymore because instead of standing physically in any line for anything, our virtual selves stand there virtually for us. Your *Ve* tells you precisely how long it would take for your turn to come and any changes in the pace of the queue, so you can adjust your time accordingly.

HOUSING

Our feelings about ownership have profound roots. Most animals have a sense of territory and a place to call home and to defend. Indeed, this territoriality seems to be associated with the oldest part in the brain and forms a biological basis for our sense of property. It is closely associated with our sense of security and our instinctual *"fight or flight"* responses, all of which gives a powerful emotional dimension to our experience of ownership. However, this biological basis does not determine the form that territoriality took in different cultures prior to the rise of *distribia*.

The Gods Own The Land

Humans, like many of our primate cousins, engage in group and individual territoriality. Tribal groups saw themselves spiritually connected to the territories that were *"theirs."* They frequently spoke of the land as their mother or as a sacred being, on whom they were dependent and to whom they owed loyalty and service. Their sense of land ownership involved only the right to use and to exclude people of other tribes. If there were any land ownership rights, they were usually subject to review by the group and would cease if the land was no longer being used. The sale of land was either not even a possibility or not permitted. As for inheritance, every person had *use rights* simply by membership in the group. So, a growing child did not have to wait until some other individual died or pay a fee to gain full access to the land.

Farming intensified the human relationship to the land. Tilling the earth and building permanent settlements meant a more significant direct investment in the place. Early farming communities continued to experience an intimate spiritual connection to the land, and they often held property in common under the control of a village council. This pattern remained in many farming communities throughout the world, even after the industrial revolution. It was not so much farming directly, but the farming-based societies that led to significant changes in attitudes towards the land.

The Godly King Owns The Land

As a ruling class took power over the tribe through religious indoctrination, the idea of a *"godly king"* materialized and demolished the ancient concept of *"we are all one with the land"* in favor of a new idea that *"the land belongs to the godly king."* Since the godly king was supposed to personify the whole community, this was still a form of community ownership, but now consolidated in one or more people in a tyrannical scheme of authority. Privileges of land-use were granted only by a ruling class based on custom and politics. Now people cannot find an unused land and farm it without first asking the local ruling class's permission, which usually came at a fee. As time went on, land ownership took on a new meaning for authoritarians. It became an abstraction, a source of power and wealth, and a tool for other purposes. The name of the game became conquer, hold, and extract the maximum in tribute. And with that, the endless obsession with power gradually came to be the dominant factor in shaping the human relationship to the land. Through authoritarians' abuse of religion, the shift from seeing Earth as a sacred mother to merely a commodity resulted in profound changes throughout such tribal cultures. It moved the Gods and holy beings into the sky where they could conveniently be as mobile as the ever-expanding boundaries of authoritarians' empires. And so, the idea of private land ownership originally emerged in response to the presence of a ruling class. The godly king sells *"some rights"* to his land to those who can afford it in return for part of their wealth with the promise of paying more in the form of taxes.

The Nation-State Owns The Land

In the godly king societies, the privileges of the nobility were often easily withdrawn at the whim of the sovereign, and the importance of raw power as the basis of ownership was rarely forgotten. To guard their power, the nobility frequently pushed for greater legal/customary recognition of their land rights. In the less centralized societies and the occasional democracies and republics

326

of this period, private ownership also developed in response to the breakdown of village cohesiveness. In either case, private property permitted individuals to be *"little kings"* of their lands, imitating and competing against the claims of the state.

Since a ruling class's definition of power is contingent on land, they obviously were never willing to give up the *"ownership"* of that land. However, a social convention called *"land rights ownership"* allowed these tribalists to trade the land as a commodity granting the buyer *certain rights* to the land but never complete ownership of the land itself. Throughout the whole history of civilizations that followed kingly Gods religions, the land has always been the primarily source of power. And the entire debate around land ownership had always been the issue of *the extents of personal powers that the ruling class are willing to give to their citizens through the land rights ownership.* In any case, when local authorities started issuing legal documents to individuals for land rights, the public developed the illusion that they can actually own land through a piece of paper that vaguely declares they do. They could now be the *little kings* of their little slice of land.

Land In The Era Of Democratic Tyranny

Democratizing tyranny allowed people to enjoy things that they historically did not have access to because it was traditionally reserved for the ruling class. Thanks to private ownership of land, the public could finally own a tiny piece of lawn like the large ones the ruling class got around their castles. Every time average people mowed their lawns, they were imitating the ruling class. In a figurative sense of course, because the royalty definitely did not mow their own lands. They had slaves for that sort of thing. The reason meadows were invented in the first place was to show off and demonstrate power, and now that the average person could own land, they could finally experience a miniature level of power that the ruling class always observed. The trend of holding property and trimming lawns continued for several centuries as an ingrained tradition, especially within the Western culture. Eventually, such authoritarian mentality of owning property was fossilized forever in the language through toxic proverbs such as *"A man is king of his castle till the queen arrives home."*

The aspiration to be *little kings or queens* by everyone in a tribal society within the era of democratic tyranny wasn't only restricted to property but also involved practices that were historically limited to royalty or tribal leaders. Marriage, for example, was traditionally a tribal convention confined to tribal leaders who sought political and blood ties among each other to assure peaceful long-term relationships. The nobility copied such concept, so they can be *little kings* and ensure their bloodlines or titles and claims over their lands or assets. Love had nothing to do with such marriages, of course, and it was purely a dreadful political and business arrangement traditionally enforced on a couple, who would not be together otherwise. Then religion came along and institutionalized this ugly tribal convention by forcing it on everyone with rituals that are very similar to the royal ceremonies of the past and with a very serious commitment that is identical to that between tribal leaders. And so, marriage perpetuated in tribal societies like a disease through tribal religions to become a standard agreement between two couples and enforced in all tribal cultures ever since.

Organized marriage became the foundation of all authoritarian cultures, which excessively revolved around those incredibly dysfunctional and toxic close-knit social bubbles that they called marital families. Such marital relationships weren't about the proper relationship between the man and the woman, but a way of getting in-laws, of making alliances and expanding the family labor force. Authoritarian propaganda tried to popularize the concept of marriage in the minds of the public through fictitious stories or movies or tales about lovers living happily under marriage. However, the public of authoritarian nations largely understood that love had nothing to do with it and that if you force such serious authoritarian concept on love, you suffocate it gradually until it withers away.

It would be remiss of us to mention democratic tyranny without talking about wage slavery (aka employment and jobs). The aspiration to copy the ruling class in every way stretched to owning slaves through a contractual agreement that turned everyone to slaves legally. Now everyone with enough money or with a small business can have slaves by renting one or more on an hourly basis instead of buying one upfront like it used to be initially. The process is regulated, of course, because a slave owner (employer) wasn't supposed to torture his/her slaves (employees) physically for example or yell at them although the occasional yelling and humiliation was a standard. Throughout the 21st century and until the rise of *distribia*, slavery was never abolished but just regulated. Instead of calling them slaves, slave owners started calling them as workers, employees, staff, or human resources. Instead of shackles and chains around the neck, they now wear ties. Most importantly and with a little bit of tribal propaganda and tv-brain-programming, the slaves stopped regarding themselves as such in favor of a watered-down version of the word: employees.

What makes wage slavery the most horrid version of slavery is the fact that the victims could not exist in society without it. People needed papermoney to survive and the only possible way of getting it was by becoming wage-salves or by owning them. The partnership model was virtually nonexistent and was restricted to company owners. Therefore, wage slavery devastated the human society and reduced generations after generations of human beings to slavery.

Land Ownership As A Bundle Of Rights

The first step is to recognize that, rather than being one thing, what we commonly call *"ownership"* is in fact a whole group of legal rights that can be held by some person with respect to some *"property."* In the industrial west, these usually include the right to:

- ➢ Use (or not use)
- ➢ Exclude others from using
- ➢ Irreversibly change
- ➢ Sell, give away or bequeath
- ➢ Rent or lease
- ➢ Retain all rights not specifically granted to others
- ➢ Retain these rights without time limit or review

These rights are usually not absolute, for with them go certain responsibilities, such as paying taxes, being liable for suits brought against the property, and abiding by the laws of the land. If these laws include zoning laws, building codes, and environmental protection laws, you may find that your rights to use and irreversibly change are not as unlimited as you thought. Nevertheless, within a wide range you are the monarch over your property.

Each of the land rights can be modified independent of the others, either by law or by the granting of an easement to some other party, producing a bewildering variety of legal conditions. How much can a ruling class modify the above conditions and still call it *ownership*? To the extent that their citizens are willing to accept. In tribalists' legal system one can only own *rights* to land, and can't directly own (that is, have complete claim to) the land itself. Citizens can't even own all the rights since rulers always retains the right of eminent domain. A landowner can *"sell"* part of his land and, by doing so, dividing the rights up among new *"owners,"* all of whom will have a claim to the part they purchased but without truly ever owning any of it.

No One Owns The Land

The human rights social convention that we take for granted today is a new concept for humanity. Throughout history of humankind, the rights of all humans were not acknowledged, even in republics. Slavery was only truly abolished a few generations ago after the public permanently ended wage slavery and debt-based papermoney. In the same way that people have come to see human rights as being inherent, they began to acknowledge that land rights must be shared by all humanity. And by land, we mean all life that lives and takes its nourishment from it, as well as the soil and earth itself. Once people have understood and accepted this idea, they entered a cooperative relationship with nature. They started acknowledging the need to be respectful of nature and treat it with sensitivity, doing their best to be in harmony with what is already there before any human ever walked the Earth.

Following the rise of *distribia* and the creation of the global **peer-to-peer** legislature, such ideas as this became a universal and global commitment. Inspired by these new ideas, humanity elected a social contract, called the housing *smartcontract*, to protect what they believe and the planet where they belong. Land went back from being private property to public property that is shared and accessible by everyone through the housing *smartcontract*.

Not all human rights are the same or equal. The right to using an idea is very different than the right to using a physical thing. When you use or apply an idea, you're not restricting access to someone else to that same idea whereas if you're using a physical thing, you are unavoidably restricting someone else from having access to that same physical thing you're using. For example, the right to criticism, which is one of the most sacred rights in *distribia* today, is not the same as the right to property. Criticism is just an idea, and it isn't physical or limited like land on Earth. When a person exercises his/her right to criticism, he/she is not taking away the use of criticism from someone else whereas when someone claims a land, he/she is restricting someone else from accessing that land. Therefore, declaring housing as a basic right for everyone meant publicizing all property and making claims or ownership of property illegal. Land on Earth is limited and there obviously wouldn't be any land left for future generations to claim tomorrow if people could own land today. Housing is guaranteed today in *distribia* for everyone only because land ownership everywhere was finally illegalized. Property owners, who had a legal claim to land or property, were compensated in coins for their property's worth.

The regulation that controls housing in *distribia* is called the housing *smartcontract,* which comes from the *distribian* language and refers to the social contract that regulates all aspects of constructing and managing a building from the moment it is erected until it is demolished. The housing *smartcontract* regulates how houses are constructed, rented, and managed. Humanity declared through this *smartcontract* that all surfaces on Earth, as well as other planets, are public property for everyone to share and enjoy. The indirect or symbolic claim for property or lands such as naming provinces or a street or a building after a person is also illegal today. Instead, humanity renamed all such places with abstract names or

331

numbers to keep such tribal practices of naming property after people in tribal history books where they reside forever. Alienated but not entirely forgotten.

The Permission-To-Use Concept For Land

Since no human being owns land anywhere, anyone wishing to use any land anywhere must get a permission from the public first. If a person wants to build something, he proposes his project by publishing a housing *smartcontract* and wait until it gets a majority consensus through the public's votes. Traditionally, communities grew one building at a time but today, cities grow one neighborhood at a time. Humanity landscaped its communities as a chessboard of concrete squares (representing residential blocks) and green squares (representing public parks) that are equally sized at one square kilometer (around 0.34 square miles). So, every park is surrounded by four blocks of buildings, and likewise, every building block is enclosed by four park blocks on four sides. A residential and a park block together constitutes a neighborhood, and when a city grows, it sprouts outwards adding one neighborhood at a time. The growth, of course, depends on the natural landscape, which authors the direction the city takes when it sprouts. Physical obstacles such as mountains or bodies of water like rivers or lakes regiment where the community will build its next neighborhood. As a building standard, neighborhoods are only built on flat surfaces along the coastlines and never stretch to the hills or mountains.

Every neighborhood belongs to one company, which manages and maintains it. This is how the procedure works today:

➢ Architects announce their designs of new neighborhoods to the public by publishing their housing *smartcontract* containing the blueprint of the project on the web.
➢ The housing *smartcontract* contains all the details about the neighborhood because it is a replica of the project in the virtual world. It details everything from the design, material used in construction, appliances inside each condo, building costs, rents costs for each condo, operation costs, etc. The housing *smartcontract* is final and any further

modification in that blueprint will result in a new copy of the housing *smartcontract* that is voted on separately.

➤ The moment architects publish their housing *smartcontract* on the web, the public start voting on the one they love most, and the blueprint that reaches the majority vote first wins the legal permission to use the land. The winner can then commence building the project immediately. The housing *smartcontract* necessitates that communities must grow one neighborhood at a time, so even if a project gets the legal permission, it needs to wait until an existing project in the city finishes construction first.

➤ When the architects complete the project according to the deadline indicated in their housing *smartcontract*, they can start offering their housing services to the public according to the pricing model they announced. The pricing for all units in the neighborhood in the housing *smartcontract* is final and can never change in the future under any circumstances.

➤ People rent their condos from the architects directly without any middlemen through their *Ve*. Housing is a public utility, which means that real estate can never be sold or purchased but only rented as a service. So, architects can only lease their units directly to the public whereas people can never buy property, but only rent them.

When architects win public approval through the majority vote and build their neighborhood, they can run it for as long it maintains a good social score. Architects can lose their neighborhood if it becomes unpopular or when its social score reaches a negative 83%. The neighborhood would then be put out on an auction for another company of architects to buy it, so they can run it better or renovate it. And if these new architects mismanaged it as well, other architects would take over it, and so on.

Housing As A Public Service

The real estate sector was fundamentally dysfunctional for centuries. Agents controlled the market, vendors hired the agents, and commission kept that relationship thriving. Vendors' agents had access to abundant information sources which gave them considerably more insight into the market than the unsuspecting purchasers, who can do nothing more than attend open homes and ask questions to agents. The real estate model evolved from a time where the information deficit in the market meant that vendors had to rely on intermediaries (agents) to connect them to potential customers. From this reliance precedes the unnecessary fees that always accompany these middlemen that either the vendor or the customer must pay and sometimes both if the agent was skillful.

A handful of people, representing local authorities in each region around the globe, introduced laws and regulated the real estate sector for the public. As the case with all tribal legislation written by a minority to rule the majority, they only benefit a part of society and rarely the bulk of the population. The decisions these tribal authorities made were predominantly based on individual interests and rarely target housing problems on an eco-social level. For example, these laws protect realtors from being liable should they sell a property which is a fundamentally flawed concept and would leave the tenants at the mercy of the new landlord. Agents used this protection of not disclosing information about a household and often went to great lengths to ensure vendors did not tell them anything which they might have to disclose to potential purchasers. The great tragedy is that although agents had access to so much information about the market, within the sale process, there were no minimal disclosure requirements and they could hide information from customers intentionally just to make a sale and earn their commission. For intermediaries, the commission is the only real incentive and all that matters.

The real estate industry had no social responsibility of solving the widening global housing affordability disaster that emerged from flawed practices by vendors and realtors. Millions of people did not have adequate housing because housing costs overstretched them financially. The tribal governments failed miserably at solving the affordability issue and mostly washed their hands of all responsibility leaving it to the private sector to resolve.

Most harmful of all, the real estate market had long provided a way for individuals to secretly launder or invest stolen money and other illicitly gained funds. Not only did expensive apartments in prestigious cities raise the social status of their owners and enhanced their luxurious lifestyles, but they were also a comfortable and convenient place to hide hundreds of millions of currencies from criminal investigators tracking criminal behavior and the proceeds of crime. In many such cases, anonymous shell companies or trusts purchased properties without undergoing proper due diligence by the professionals involved in the deal. The ease with which such unknown firms or trusts could acquire property and launder money was directly related to the insufficient rules and enforcement practices practiced in each region.

Of all factors behind the ever-rising housing prices, one could never ignore corruption. It was quite common for a string of officials to be involved in a single case of real estate corruption. The real estate market became a hotbed for corruption, and high-level public officials were involved and participated in perpetuating the flaws of the housing sector through bad regulations. The abuse of power resulted in a series of problems in the real estate market. When real estate developers tipped officials to get a piece of land for development or bribed officials to get a housing project approved, or paid officials to get this or that done, they did not pay from their own pockets. Instead, they raised the housing prices and charged the bribes to the consumers. With a lot of money going into the pockets of these corrupt officials, real estate developers did not spend as much as they should on the construction of their buildings. They then bribed the supervisors into turning a blind eye to the poor quality of the houses. That is why real estate developers in some cities were found using sub-standard re-bars or even bamboo as substitutes for re-bars to lower construction costs. As a result, some new buildings had quality problems, and complaints about housing quality risen substantially.

Political corruption severely affected the healthy development of the real estate market, artificially raised housing prices across prominent cities forcing people outside the cities, and caused severe eco-social problems increasing the houselessness population worldwide. As the stakes mounted with property values and as the technology increased to mitigate the information void, homeowners and customers could finally re-examine this increasingly inefficient economic model of sale and purchase of the housing sector.

Humanity realized that if the housing sector can continue being an asset or store of value, it will always cripple this industry, leading to artificial price hikes, and driving low-income people out of their cities when they fail to pay for a shelter. The solution was to convert housing from an asset to a service, which cannot be sold and traded.

Today, *distribia* insured a healthy housing market and guaranteed housing rights for everyone worldwide no matter their income. Humanity elected the housing *smartcontract* to balance supply and demand according to a peer-to-peer market, which directly links urban developers to the needs of the public without intermediaries, which are illegal in *distribia's* society. The urban developer is responsible for managing, servicing, and maintaining the neighborhood and all the appliances in all condos such as the water filtration and sewage treatment systems. Renters, however, pay operational costs such as electricity along with the standard rent fee. The rent includes cleaning services by default like traditional hotels. Cleaning services are offered daily and scheduled through the tenants' *Ve*.

All rents for all units in all neighborhoods worldwide follow the dynamic pricing *smartcontract*, which involves a flat rate per one minute. It means that there are no commitments such as yearly or monthly or daily rent terms that existed in the past. Instead, tenants can leave an apartment anytime they chose, and the payment stops the moment they clear the condo. This flexibility of renting wherever you want and cancel anytime you want freed people from the chains that existed in the past with mortgages and contracts.

Since housing became a service, all units come fully furnished with all appliances by default. Fresh towels, beddings, and other home supplements are offered in the condo by default as part of the rent. Consumer products such as soap and shampoo are refilled and supplied for a fee. People no longer go shopping for cleaning products from central supermarkets because the neighborhood's cleaners take care of all that for renters. These cleaning products are manufactured locally in the neighborhood and supplied to the condos directly without wasting material or cost in packaging them in containers and shipping them.

Housing is considered a utility, which means that it automatically comes with three ascending levels of quality and service labeled as type-3 (economical), type-2 (advanced), and type-1 (luxurious). Anyone can afford type-3 housing because it's always covered by the UBI. Adopting three levels of service for housing ensures variety and availability for all tastes and incomes. Those with expensive taste have luxury living standards available for them whereas those with relatively low income are always guaranteed to have adequate accommodation for them in type-3 condos.

Type-3 housing comes at the same cost in any neighborhood worldwide. The housing *smartcontract* sets the rate for all economy class apartments at 5% of the average UBI. This class level means that wherever you travel around the globe, there's always a guarantee that you will find a place to stay with a price tag that is identical to the type-3 condo you were renting initially. Everyone can afford this class even if they entirely rely on the UBI they get from the monetary system. This low price made houselessness impossible everywhere because anyone can manage a place to stay in any city they desire to live. Economy class condos include all standard home appliances and furniture. The hygiene levels match all other categories, and the units are cleaned and serviced daily. The furniture is decent and comfortable, and the standard services include heating/cooling, kitchen, screen monitors, built-in cameras and projectors for facetime or virtual calls.

All other housing types do not come with one specific or constant price. The competition between architects to win public approval dictates the cost of rent for type-1 and type-2 condos. The public will not allow projects with unreasonable price tags, and similarly, the competition among architects will entail them to stick to competitive pricing. Type-2 is a more advanced housing option, and it is reflected in the quality of the furniture and design of the rooms. The features of all the appliances are better and more services are included such as more expensive beds, sofas, and better-quality flooring. This class comes with *sirvirbōts*, which are robotic arms hanging electromagnetically from the ceiling of the apartment and can move around the home servicing the tenants in every room in various ways. The word *sirvirbōt* comes from the *distribian language* and it is originally derived from the two English root words *"serving"* and *"robot."* Together they mean a robot version of a server or maid.

Sirvirbots are extremely popular in *distribia*, and people usually prefer living in midclass or first-class condos to have access to these robots. The main reason for this is because *sirvirbots* can do a lot of shores for the residents and it is as if having a team of maids at home relentlessly servicing you and keeping your home at an optimal condition of tidiness. They can prepare any meal for you at home exactly like the best restaurants in town. Your *Ve* operates these bots and orders all the ingredients required to make these meals so that the *sirvirbōt* can prepare them for you in a matter of minutes. *Sirvirbots* can trim your fingernails or give you a foot rub after a long walk outside. They can clean your body or wash your back in the shower. They can get you a glass of wine while you comfortably lay in the bathtub. They wake you up gently in the morning and prepare your morning coffee and breakfast. They can do all sorts of things, and they're under the tenant's control to make sure he is always relaxed and satisfied.

First class condos are luxurious and are always located on the sixth level of any building for better views and direct access to the skyway station upstairs on the seventh floor using the elevator or stairway. This class includes better quality *sirvirbōts* and state-of-the-art appliances. All rooms are spacious with the best quality of furniture and expensive material with utmost attention to detail in every part of the place.

When humanity elected the housing *smartcontract*, all existing buildings in the world were obviously in violation of this law and had to be repurposed. The *smartcontract* allowed a 17-years-period for existing building owners to adjust and make corrections to their buildings to avoid heavy taxation after the transition period is over. Buildings that were around seven floors high were easier to modify, but the high-rises in major cities had to shave their buildings down floor by floor across several years to meet the new building standards. After urban developers connected cities to the global subway grid forming the iconic 1-kilometer-wide *distribian* blocks, the real-estate agencies that owned the buildings in each city block grouped together to form one company to run and maintain the entire block as the housing *smartcontract* dictates. The same scheme took place with the single-family houses in the suburbs and urban sprawls. But since only a company of architects are allowed to run each city block in *distribia*, regular people who owned single-family homes before *distribia* sold their houses for generous amounts to a single architecture firm, which took care of repurposing the neighborhood and making the necessary corrections to have it apply with the housing *smartcontract*.

And since the law dictates that all humanmade structures of any kind must be multipurpose or mixed-use with three types of housing as well as workplaces and shops, religious buildings such as churches and temples had to adjust as well and be re-fitted to accommodate the new laws for architecture. They were gradually re-purposed to include residential units and shops as the law dictates on every building of any kind. However, the monuments in churches and other temples, as well as in public places, which represented real people were removed because it is illegal to put out monuments of real people in public places in *distribia*. Such statues were not destroyed but were only moved to museums around the world that preserved the products of the *Tribal Ages*.

Mixed-Used Neighborhoods As An Urban Standard

Human beings are very regional creatures. We don't naturally move around a lot in the world except for the occasional traveling because we prefer to spend most of our time in our neighborhoods and in the geographic proximity of what we call home. For thousands of years, people instinctively chose to live close to one another and their food and water sources because it is the natural humanistic way of living. They formed social bonds and built dense communities around their food and water sources forming small villages. As more people walked the earth, people built more villages and turned them into towns, which eventually lead to cities. No matter how large neighborhoods grew, the fundamental principle of keeping the communities centered around food and water sources remained unchanged. People naturally would not isolate themselves intentionally from the facets of life such as food and water and would never live away or build deterrence to restrict easy access to their daily needs. Then came the invention of the car and disrupted the humanistic way of living.

Although the invention of the car arguably solved many problems and maximized people's mobility, it came with massive consequences and created a domino effect of one flawed regulation after the other. As they became increasingly cheaper, more people could afford them and decided to buy them. People's mobility increased and altered their definition of proximity from being a matter of walking distance to suddenly becoming a matter of driving distance. And with that new definition of access, they no longer needed to build their houses close to their original neighborhoods and chose instead to explore new locations outside their communities. This new definition of distance fragmented communities and people started to willingly choose to live in remote areas outside the cities if it is within a reasonable driving distance. With that new definition came new ideas that conceived highways, which created walls and other deterrents that regulated and restricted strollers' movement.

The invention of the car created a system of laws and regulations that further defragmented communities and generated more restrictions on people's movement. These arrangements and operations were out of the control of average people because in a republic important decisions were made by a handful of people and never collectively by the people who were affected by such decisions the most. Whenever deterrence was built in people's surroundings that affect their movement, it usually was out of their control, and people were forced to adapt to it eventually. Deep down people knew they weren't happy with the new change, but they choose to adapt to it because in part it is out of their control and in another part, people are adaptive beings. Ultimately, they grew to come to peace with the things they adapt to—good or bad.

The industrial revolution solved many problems, but it densely polluted the cities and drove out many people who owned cars and could commute. It sure made sense for the average person to move with his family far from the pollution of the city and away from factories. It was evidently good for a while up until an increasing number of cars were on the roads congesting highways created by people who also thought it is a good idea to commute from out of the city. The short-sighted solution to the highway congestion was to build more highways. And so it was. This expensive solution only solved the problem temporarily until more cars hit the road and these new highways reached capacity reasonably quickly. One can compare the traffic congestion problem to a leaking ceiling. The easiest thing you could do to fix such problem is to put a bowl where the water is dripping, but this is nothing more than a temporary fix and will never solve the real problem. You can't resolve such predicament by adding a bigger pot either because this bigger container will inevitably fill up and overflow. The only logical and real solution to the problem is patching the ceiling to stop the flow of water. Similarly, adding more highways to solve the traffic problem was a short-sighted solution of a tribal culture where a handful of people always make all the critical decisions. The real and only logical answer to the traffic problem is to prevent car ownership altogether to stop more cars from hitting the roads and overflowing the streets. This solution only became a reality after tribalism faded away from the human culture and we will explore this resolution in more detail in the next chapter.

The highway congestion problem unfolded another short-sighted solution in tribal cultures. Urban developers thought that it makes sense to build large residential-only communities with single-family houses for those commuters from out of town. These homes with their front and backyards seemed attractive at the time, and since there were so many people opting to live outside the city, the opportunist architects and developers could defiantly sell every one of those houses, which of course they did. This architectural practice created what is called *"urban sprawl."* Urban sprawl or suburban sprawl describes the expansion of human populations away from central urban areas into low-density, mono-functional and usually car-dependent communities, in a process called sub-urbanization.

The average human being living in these urban sprawls is separated by miles of other single-family houses and highways from everything he ever needs such as retail, groceries, offices, schools, meeting places, restaurants, cafes, and public parks, and other elements for living. These basic needs became centralized in specific geographic locations such as plazas or malls and separated by roads, highways, and walls. It wasn't easy to get to them on foot, and urban sprawl residents were forced to use a car just to reach them. This kind of urban living eliminated the option to walk to stores, and everything became less accessible. Ultimately, the average urban sprawl resident found himself consuming a gallon of gas to buy a gallon of milk. This new reality killed the traditional mom's and pop's shops because they relied on people walking around the neighborhood. Everyone was moving around in cars, and they became conditioned to go to centralized places like malls or plazas or other designated places to buy in bulk. It gave more control to larger corporations and created an environment where they can monopolize their industry and destroy local small businesses.

In these urban sprawls, it become expensive for residents to drive and too far for them to walk to the places where they can socialize and meet new people. So, they stay in their homes and miss out on being social. Children, however, have far more to lose in such neighborhoods because they'll adapt to a community were less social activity happens. It is well known that children are highly adaptive in their early years and that the experiences they get at that period shapes their characters. Since they did not receive many social interactions in urban sprawls, their personalities were profoundly affected, and most of them grew to become unsocial or preferred living alone.

Another byproduct of the car invention was zoning laws, which further damaged society on a socioeconomic level. These regulations segregated the way of life considerably and separated the places of work from the areas of living creating financial districts, plazas, and single-purpose neighborhoods. The result was that financial districts became ghost neighborhoods outside working hours whereas urban sprawls are naturally empty during the day because everyone would be at work. Additionally, one could not open a business in an urban sprawl because of regulations, and same goes for trying to sell anything in financial districts without temporary permits. If one could not find a job, one could start a lemonade stand on any street corner and generate a minimal income to survive and grow into something better. However, they were entirely barred from doing that under zoning laws because it required a permit that turned what should be a simple business venture of selling lemonade into a fight for licenses. These licenses came with price tags that people who are struggling to survive could not naturally afford, and so it striped away from them any decent chance to sustain themselves.

Zoning laws and the regulations they inspired served to keep the streets sterile and lubricated only for movement through the nearest drive-through. They fell in favor of large businesses that tend to foster political and economic corruption. Segregating people's natural environment and destroying the chances for social interactions made people less secure and less happy because humans are inherently social creatures. People need direct and easy access to their fundamental needs of life, and they shouldn't be separated from these basic needs by categorizing or zoning their natural landscape. Regulators and lawmakers made stringent zoning laws which restricted property rights. By doing this, the cities were inherently designed to inhibit people from being able to participate in the system. They called it a fair-trade economy, but people couldn't participate in the market or contribute to their local communities. The urban plans and regulations, which came as byproducts of the invention of the car, probably might have looked good on paper for those short-sighted folks who designed our highways and urban sprawls. They thought linearly from a single perspective and never realized that shaping the urban landscape always have impacts on people's social behavior which form the basis of our society, families, government, and the global economy.

After the birth of *distribia*, things changed drastically, and people could finally bypass intermediaries and vote directly on the decisions and laws that shape their society. Humanity decided to abandon zoning in favor of mixed-used neighborhoods by electing the housing *smartcontract* to regulate how buildings are made around the world. Mixed-used, livable, accessible, multi-centered, high-density communities become a shared global commitment.

The housing *smartcontract* necessitates building denser mixed-use neighborhoods worldwide that have all the goods and services,

343

which people need in their daily lives, contained within every block. Every building in any neighborhood everywhere on the globe must serve these exact seven purposes:

- ➤ Residential: Exactly three residential condos on top of each other with each occupying an entire floor.
- ➤ Workspace: Exactly one floor as an office space or a factory for a single business on the third level of any building.
- ➤ Retail: a single shop selling goods or services and located on the ground floor.
- ➤ Mass transport: A skyway station on the last floor for public transport.
- ➤ Energy: an electric generation and storage capability managed in a dedicated room on the first level (the basement).
- ➤ Water: a water generation/storage/treatment capability in the basement also.
- ➤ Telecommunications hub and storage: with their built-in routers for relaying data to the neighborhood and the data storage on the basement level for storing the information of the building's residents.

Every building must have retail attached to housing and offices upstairs. This architectural practice created opportunities for better and diverse products and services allowing mom's and pop's shops to compete in the local economy. These small businesses rely primarily on foot traffic in the area and finally got the opportunity to compete for a market share thanks to the abundance of shops that can be rented in every building in the neighborhood. It eliminated the need to commute to work and allowed people to live in the same building where they work or next door from it. If people changed career, they could always find condominium near to their new office wherever that may be on the planet. Mixing offices with condos in the same building helped mitigating traffic congestion at peak commute hours. Additionally, people could conveniently walk to their favorite store in the same block without the need to venture out to other neighborhoods in the city.

The mixed-use buildings across all communities brought people together making them more social and allowed each neighborhood to be self-sufficient with the shops and services that people need in their daily lives. And since every residential block comes with a park as a building standard, people can now live, work, and socialize all in one place. People can now take a break and have lunch at the park before returning to work. Others might start the day by jogging in the park before heading out to the next business of the day. Some park blocks function as amusement parks that feature various attractions, such as rides and games, as well as other structures for entertainment purposes, and usually providing attractions that cater to a variety of age groups. Other park blocks include a racetrack where various types of auto racing events take place. The lanes are either paved by a porous material that allows water to sink into the soil underneath, or unpaved for off-road racing experiences. Such cars, of course, aren't loud at all because all moving vehicles today are electric and barely generate any sound. All in all, the primary function for a park is to ensure a decent space for nature to grow trees and gardens and usually, the most significant portion of these blocks are dedicated for that.

7-Levels-Only Buildings In All Cities Globally

The cities of the 20th and early 21st century involved centralized and highly condensed buildings packed together and surrounded by less developed and condensed suburbs with entirely deserted and unused land surrounding them. This flawed urbanization practice of concentrating the human population in specific areas in tall buildings came with several consequences and made them prone to natural disasters such as earthquakes or outbreaks of diseases. High-rises are a very unsuitable solution that undermines the character, livability, social fabric and even the public health of any city.

In a tribal culture where constant propaganda campaigns falsely broadcast to the public that the world is overly populated and there isn't enough housing to cover everyone's needs for shelter, it is not surprising that a lot of architects at the time preferred and preached building upwards. The truth, however, is that Earth was never overly populated at the time and never became so after the overthrow of all tribal nations and the rise of *distribia*. It was entirely possible to fit the entire human population of the planet in Ukraine alone, and they would be living almost as densely as in New York City in 2018.

People living in such sly times could've readily figured out that they were being lied to if they just drove for a short trip out of their cities. They would've seen the countless miles of virgin territory that stretched as far as the eye can see the moment they stepped out of the concrete bubbles in which they were deliberately concentrated. There were simply so many barren lands to build on, but unfortunately, the urban planners of the tribal cultures specifically designed their cities to produce a false impression of urban overpopulation. The prime reason for this problem is economical. By zoning a city in such a dysfunctional way and limiting the space allowed for new buildings, property prices spiked as demand flooded the market. And whenever property prices rose, property owners profited the most while tenants helplessly suffered because the system was cruelly rigged against them. And because the corrupt city officials deliberately limited the supply of land, architects were forced to build excessively upwards instead of developing medium-sized structures and stretching them evenly and gradually outwards as the local population grows.

A city is best viewed at eye-level. Sure, the views from a high-rise can be stunning, but you aren't able to see people in a way that allows for social connection. Because it is not as easy as walking out your front door, people who live on the high floors of a high-rise are less likely to leave their apartments. This actuality separates people from the outdoors, the city and other people. High-rises isolate residents from the street and create a situation where the community is detached from street life. Such system of architecture generates enclaves and hinders social interactions. Meaningful contact with ground level events is possible only from the first few floors in a multi-story building. The more up you live in such structures, the less contact you get with the people in your community and leaves you out of touch with ground level events. Because high-rises tend to separate people from the street and each other, they significantly reduce the number of chance encounters from happening. Such connections are crucial to the liveliness of any city and to create social prosperity. And because people are cooped up in tall buildings, they are less likely to experience social bonds. Such reality breeds isolation and leaves people socially inactive.

High-rises kept children and the elderly from getting the exercise they usually get when living in shorter buildings that expose them to the temptations of the events occurring on street level. Thus, skyscrapers sway them to stay at home and flip on the TV and deprive them and especially children of neighborhood peers and activities. And since alienation and isolation negatively impact people's health and even shorten their lives, skyscrapers are like diseases for both the city and the people living in it.

Propinquity is one of the leading factors to interpersonal attraction. It refers to the physical or psychological proximity between people. Propinquity happens in public spaces – on the street, in parks, public transportation, and city squares. High-rises diminish people's participation in public areas and therefore reduce propinquity. Living in a high-rise created a very finite and encapsulated world in and of itself. The high-rise became people's world, especially those which include a restaurant, market, gym and other amenities. They never had to go outside or encounter other people. Plus, this phenomenon created the opposite effect of public spaces. It ensured that people mostly interface with others of the same socioeconomic strata. High-rises created silos, both physical, social and psychological.

Ironically, high-rises generated the same urban sprawl effect that architects said they'll diminish by building vertically. Sprawl is when something is constructed inefficiently and takes up too much space. In the same way that in a typical urban sprawl one does not encounter much social activity because everyone is indoors, within the corridors and public areas of each building nothing is happening because everyone is tucked away in their apartments. Same as suburban sprawls that promote isolation and are often devoid of people on the streets, high-rises created the same problem, but just from a vertical perspective.

The construction industry is a powerful engine for fueling economic development. Tall buildings offer increased profits for developers. However, the higher a building rises, the more expensive is the construction. Thus, the tallest buildings tend to be luxury units, often for global investors. Tall buildings inflate the price of adjacent land, thus making the protection of historic buildings and affordable housing less achievable. In this way, they increase inequality. On the other hand, 7-story buildings with a tiny footprint are very affordable and more straightforward to construct and maintain. Small footprint shops and apartments promote an excellently textured urban fabric. And because all 3 condos in every building naturally get the same floor space because there's only one condo allowed on each floor as a building standard today, everyone gets the same living space regardless if rich or poor.

Contrary to the official propaganda, which promoted high-rises as sustainable because they allow for so much density, high-rise buildings are not green at all. Tall buildings are subject to the effects of too much sun and too much wind on their all-glass skins. And excessive use of glass in such buildings has always been inherently inefficient. Glass is naturally not very good at keeping excessive heat out, or desirable heat in. Consequently, high-rises use almost twice as much energy per square meter as mid-rise structures. High-rise buildings produce a lot of greenhouse gases because they are built mostly of steel and concrete and are less sustainable than the low rise and mid-rise structures that are made mainly of wood, steel, and concrete. Wood is far healthier for the environment because it traps greenhouse gases while concrete is 10 times more greenhouse gas intensive and, therefore, 10 times more harmful to the environment than wood. Unlike wood, concrete is made through unsustainable practices. Wood can be torn down to be reused, but concrete cannot be salvaged, and it is left where it is demolished. With society's current level of knowledge, we know for a fact that wood is the best option regarding sustainability but the tribal cultures' architects, however, avoided using wood because it wasn't as sturdy for building their skyscrapers as concrete and steel.

Today, the housing *smartcontract* guarantees even distribution of the human population on the surface of the earth and avoids population congestion in small areas. Buildings measurements are now predefined in the housing *smartcontract* and are much shorter and slimmer compared to those before *distribia*. Today's buildings are much slimmer than their capitalist era counterparts because today's housing law prohibits building multiple units on the same floor. Each floor of any building on Earth has precisely one unit. Humanity stopped building high-rise buildings in favor of 7-levels-only buildings with only one unit on each floor as an architectural standard. The first level is the basement area, which includes the building's utility rooms such as water treatment, freshwater storage, a data room and batteries storage. The second level is the ground floor and includes a single unit used for retail or services. The third level is always used as a work space for a single company and followed by 3 levels for residential condos and finally the last floor (7th floor) always serve as a skyway station. Additionally, every floor in every building can only have one unit with a floor to ceiling structural height of up to 3 meters as a building standard before any functional or cosmetic fitting is added to the ceiling.

Instead of barren lands oozing with dead high-rise buildings that only look good from afar, today's low buildings are commonly built in picturesque valleys surrounded by beautiful mountains that are always teeming with colorful trees. When you walk through today's urban neighborhoods, you can see the faces of people looking out of their balconies, and you can see personalizing details such as flowerpots in windows. Next-door-neighbors greet each other and socialize while sitting on their balconies. And since there's only one condo on each floor of each building, every balcony goes all around the structure giving people access to socialize and interact with all surrounding buildings as well as the people on the streets. Previously when you walked through a high-rise neighborhood, you could not see this sort of thing in most of the buildings' facades. In other words, people lost sight of the human-scale in high-rise neighborhoods.

Buildings are like people. The fatter they are, the less attractive they become. Therefore, *distribian* buildings are gorgeous and much more attractive to look at because they're much slimmer compared to tribal era architecture.

Furthermore, all buildings never exceed a maximum distance of 5 meters from each other, which is an architectural standard of the housing *smartcontract*. The main reason behind these narrow streets is the absence of cars on the surface, which eliminated the need to widen the distance between buildings. In hot climates, narrow streets help block the sun and provide shade to pedestrians while in cold climates it blocks cold wind and preserves the warmer temperatures on street level. In cold climates, the neighborhood streets are padded with electric heat conductors to keep pedestrians worm and stimulate the local economy from the resulting foot traffic. The resulting buildings across all communities are much slimmer than traditional structures of the 20th and early 21st century, occupy tiny footprint, and are stacked densely together. Wide open areas are directed to the surrounding 4 boulevards or to the neighborhood's park, which serves several purposes including green zones designated for trees or open space green areas for public events and festivals.

Broad and straight streets did not disappear forever because of the subway grid system which doubles as a boulevard from the surface that people use as running courses or for cycling. The subway grid system defines the chessboard-like urban landscape of all today's cities and is the vain the stretches across all blocks connecting them together. Every block is contained amid 4 subway lines (and therefore 4 boulevards) and used by residents to commute within the community or to others on the planet.

All Elevators In All Buildings Of All Cities Are Public

Since every residential floor contains only one unit and since every building contains only 3 residential units in total, there's no need for corridors inside the building. Instead, one elevator per building is called from street level and stops directly inside the unit on every floor. The absence of a reception area on the ground floor or corridors on each floor in a building maximized the use of floor space across the entire structure and reduced the dwelling price. The result is an elevator-stairway combo allowing residents to walk into their unit directly from street level. A small room act as a buffer zone between the elevator and the door of the apartment for privacy and doubles as a package-drop area.

In *distribia's* society, all products must be multipurpose, and that's why elevators in all buildings worldwide had to be public and used to access the skyway or subway by both residents and nonresidents of any building. All elevators of all buildings follow the same labeling standard for their 7 levels as follows in an ascending way:

- ➢ Subway: It is the first level and takes people to the subway cars. At this level the elevator opens on the other side for technicians to access the utility area of the building.
- ➢ Ground: This button takes people to the street level and to the outside.
- ➢ A workspace: It takes people to the office space of the building and is labeled after the name of the business that occupies it. This could be a factory where things are built or an office space where work is done.
- ➢ Home#1: It is a residential floor and houses one economy class condo named after the current occupant.
- ➢ Home#2: It is the midclass condo in the building and named after the current occupant on that level.
- ➢ Home#3: It is the first-class condo in the building and named after the current occupant on that level.
- ➢ Skyway: It is the seventh and last level of the building and contains the skyway station.

The elevator's buttons are presented on a touchscreen, which allows for editing the names of the current tenants instantly as they change. Of course, the public can't access the 3 residential floors unless they are residents or permitted to visit by the current residents, which means that the elevators only stop at these floors for those allowed.

As a building standard in *distribia*, the elevator shaft of every building has two elevators that operate in sync with each other. The twin elevator system allows passengers to drop from the skyway station's rooftop directly to their homes or the street level without taking another elevator. This arrangement moves more passengers than a conventional lift, and the two elevators exist within the same shaft in peace, without crashing. It allows a person to take the elevator from the skyway station directly to his home on the 6th level while someone else simultaneously taking the other elevator in the same shaft from street level to his office on the third level of the building. As a building standard also, all buildings come with an elevator-stairway combo, which involves a stairway adjacent to or spirally strapped around the elevator to maximize the use of floor space in the building.

Architecture during the 20th and 21st centuries was dull, and buildings were almost exact copies of each other. It was hugely disappointing for people traveling for hours to different cities expecting to find something new but only to be disappointed with designs that look very similar to the ones they got back home. The sameness of cities was a problem because it took away the uniqueness of culture in each region and stripped away its character. It was like wearing the same clothes in all climates or dressing the same style year-round, and everywhere you go. People who hated nature designed such cities and they were part of a culture dedicated to the hatred of material. These individuals were not materialists, which is a type of people who cherish wood, stone, plants and above all the Earth. True materialists treat Earth with reverence as they treat their own bodies and they continuously crave to mold it in the best shape that lasts for as long as possible. Such kind of people are the architects we are blessed with today in our *distribian* culture.

Today, buildings are beautiful masterpieces of art because they are produced by genuine materialists that hold what they do as art, which is aimed at creating something beautiful for others to admire. In the same way that a good painter always aims at creating beauty in a blank canvas, architects carve the stone and wood in their buildings to bring them to life and create delightful structures. They incorporate plants and flowers on the walls of their buildings from inside and outside to spur life into their structures. In fact, such approach became a universal commitment and was included in the housing *smartcontract* to ensure that all architects follow the same principle. Today, for every square meter of space an architect produces, he must account for a relative square meter of greenwalls inside and outside the building. On average, a quarter of a building's exterior surface is covered by a greenwall, which means that if a building's shape is rectangular, one wall would be entirely covered by a greenwall. However, buildings in warm or hot climates are coated with more greenwalls to stay passive and maintain a cool temperature in the building without relying excessively on electricity.

A greenwall, also known as a living wall or vertical garden, is a wall wholly or partially covered with greenery that includes a growing medium, such as soil or a substrate, and feature an integrated water delivery system. Greenwalls have growing media supported on the face of the wall and support climbing plants on the surface of the wall to create the green or vegetated facade. Greenwalls are both indoors and outside every building around the world. Greenwalls infuse the dull expanse of interiors with life-renewing greenery. They offer an inspirational and aesthetically intriguing natural boost to people's morale. The spectacle of living and breathing colorful walls creates a long-lasting *"wow factor"* in the minds and hearts of all residents. Aside from encompassing delightful plantation and colorful flowers, greenwalls provide insulation to keep the building's inside temperature consistent. They provide canopy cooling of trapped air and reduces reflected heat. They are as equally impressive in appearance as they are purveyors of good health. They also play a role in remediating poor air quality, both to internal and external areas. The plants in the walls work as a natural air-filtration system that serves the entire neighborhood. During the day, greenwalls metabolize harmful toxins such as carbon dioxide, carbon monoxide, and many other toxins in the air during photosynthesis, resulting in significant reductions in CO_2 levels across all urban areas.

Greenwalls are natural humidifiers, which restore moisture to the air to prevent dryness that can irritate many parts of the body and cause dryness of the skin, nose, throat, and lips. Through the natural process of evapotranspiration, greenwalls release water vapor that cools the air in summer and restores healthful moisture to heated spaces in winter. They also lead to quieter cities through shading, evaporative transpiration, and the absorption of sound by the layers of plants living within these walls. Trees and plants have been historically used to reduce noise along roads and highways. Greenwalls expand on this concept by naturally blocking high-frequency sounds while the supporting structure can help to diminish low-frequency noise.

To maintain diversity, all neighborhood's buildings utilize all shades of color where every building within the same block is colored differently. The diverse use of color generates beauty, vibrancy, and energy in all communities and has been very beneficial on a social level for residents giving them a sense of happiness in comparison to the flawed architecture of the 21st century that created a sense of isolation and depression. Additionally, every building within the same block has a slightly different exterior design that people can easily identify from the street. Such differences could be in the carvings of the wood or stone on the exterior or the location of the greenwall and its flowerful climbing plants.

Architects design their neighborhoods with distinctive themes to attract more votes and win public approval. They know that the public won't be impressed by a dull repetitive design and that's why they dream up the beautiful buildings that we enjoy today. Some neighborhoods are themed after cartoon movies, which adds a sense of glamour and magic to the place that can be felt by residents and visitors. And so, every neighborhood has a unique character and story written in stone or wood. Since the housing *smartcontract* necessitates the use of locally sourced building material, architects focus on using the most abundant material in the area and incorporate it in their neighborhoods. By doing so, buildings tend to look different from one place on earth to another and follow different style and design depending on how the local material can be worked with. Wood, for example, can be carved and worked with easily allowing various designs and producing distinctive shapes. Additionally, every area has different color of wood depending on the trees that grow in the region, and that's why the wooden buildings in each area look slightly different from those in other regions.

There's a gorgeous coastal city in Southeast Asia, which was born shortly after the territory was finally allowed to flourish financially after its release from the claws of central bankers and after the fall of tribalism. This city is called *sexilsete* (pronounced sea-shell-city in English). Every building in this city is carved and molded to resemble a seashell, and each has a different design and color. Some are coated with real seashells while others are painted with 3-dimensional colors to resemble the patterns or the colorfulness of sea creatures. Walking in the beautiful streets of this city, you will come across all sorts of buildings of many shapes that has so much detail worked into them that every time you look at them you'll discover something new. The city is a spectacle of beauty, life, and creativity. *Sexilsete's* year-round warm weather turned it into a tourism magnet for people living in chilly climates who crave for a break from the cold. The local architects struggle to keep up with the demand to add more blocks to the city because of the very long list of people wishing to visit or live there.

Sexilsete is a testimony to the architectural revolution against the brutality of architecture before *distribia* when people were forced to live in box-like rooms of rectangular buildings that rarely come with any interior or exterior curvature. *Sexilsete's* condos, on the other hand, are curved or rippled from the inside out, and every chamber follows a particular design and pattern. The doors are never rectangular but always curved or circular, and same goes for all windows. The walls are never flat but are always curved and wavy like the inside of a shell. The furniture flows in curvature with the walls and is explicitly designed to fit seamlessly and match the room for which it was built. The streets are never straight but are bent or crooked, and they are designed so to keep you within each block instead of explicitly revealing the exit.

Ultimately, you feel that you're alive while living in *Sexilsete's* curved buildings and not a lifeless container living inside a box within a bigger box. Although the global pattern for urban development follows a chessboard-like design using squares, the law does not necessarily force architects to design their building blocks as squares. And although the plot of land dedicated for the neighborhood is indeed a square, architects can still build any design or follow any pattern they desire within that square. It is like having a blank square canvas where you don't have to fill it up entirely with paint. *Sexilsete's* blocks, therefore, follow different designs and patterns that are visible from an air-view when people fly over the city in skycars.

It is charming to view the city from an elevation because the buildings, trees, fountains, and lakes are distributed following a pattern to form a portrait to the beholders looking down at the city from the sky in the moving skycars. It is like a mosaic of a blue ocean full of life and colorful sea creatures.

As you walk upon the hills overlooking the town, you could see the low curved buildings wrapping around each other. The colors intertwined and contrasted blooming forth like a twisted rainbow shimmering with the shifting tides and wrapping back into self only to start again. From a distance, the city appears as a collection of colorful shells or a swarm of colorful fish. A wobbly center of ebbs and ripples colored to enhance the beauty of what the very fortunate residents call home. It is a beautiful and vivid ocean of life.

Every Distribian Neighborhood Is Self-Cleaning

As a housing standard, architects are responsible for cleaning their neighborhoods and apartments. Today's residents expect their homes to be cleaned and maintained daily as a standard. And so, residents never buy house-cleaning products because such products are never sold to consumers directly but only offered as part of the housing service. Making housekeeping part of the housing service itself minimized the waste that resulted from packaging such products in plastic, which eventually ended up in landfills and remaining there for thousands of years. Today's cleaning products are always stored in reusable packaging. City streets are landscaped to allow robotic cleaners to patrol and clean the blocks seamlessly. These robots have onboard sensors that are part of a network that stretches along the entire neighborhood. They monitor pollution levels across all areas and automatically direct themselves these regions to disinfect them and make sure the block is always spotless.

Additionally, the robotic cleaners use ultraviolet germicidal irradiation, which is a disinfection method that uses short-wavelength ultraviolet light to kill or inactivate microorganisms by destroying nucleic acids and disrupting their DNA, leaving them unable to perform vital cellular functions. Ultraviolet cleansing is used today in a variety of applications, such as food, air, and water purification. All indoor spaces in all buildings such as bathrooms are equipped with ultraviolet light to clean the entire room after every use automatically. The application of ultraviolet light to disinfection has been an accepted practice in *distribia* and a universal standard. It has been used in medical sanitation and sterile work facilities. It is also employed to sterilize drinking and wastewater, as the holding facilities are enclosed and can be circulated to ensure a higher exposure to the ultraviolet light.

The housing *smartcontract* ensures that all units are equipped with sensors spread in all rooms to closely monitor and report hygiene data and statistics as a part of a system that works collectively with other blocks to maintain high hygiene standards across all units worldwide. These sensors are also in public transports, public areas, and public bathrooms. *Ve* monitors this data to ensure the health and hygiene of everyone. All rooms' ceilings have built-in air filters that clean and monitor air quality around the clock and provide good air circulation across each condo.

Neighborhood Safety

The housing *smartcontract* ensures that all units are equipped with fire sensors and alarms that can detect and put off fires without the use of water, which could unnecessarily damage electronics inside the unit. Instead, a combination of foam and powder materials are used to conquer fires more efficiently than traditional systems that used water. The home fire distinguishers are guided by *Ve*, which deploys the anti-fire solutions precisely at the source of fire and not across the entire unit. *Ve* also engages in several tactics to extinguish a fire in households such as cutting out the flow of air to the rooms or decreasing the temperature or using *sirvirbots* to move the burning furniture away or covering the source of fire by a fire-resistant blanket on top.

Through built-in speakers and LED lights mounted in the ceilings and walls in all rooms of all units, people can be notified visually and audibly of fire and be guided to the nearest safe exists and zones in such scenarios. Similarly, *Ve* notifies pedestrians outside the building of a fire hazard through LED warning lights and speakers on the structure and street level. Additionally, the security personnel in each neighborhood double as firefighters as well as medical emergency response units. They regularly patrol the community they are assigned to along with their bots to make sure that everyone is safe.

The old and dysfunctional practice of shopping for furniture disappeared because housing today is a service where all units necessarily come fully furnished with all appliances. Think of it as a hotel in which you are just renting a condo, which you expect to include everything you need. The hotel management wouldn't allow you to buy furniture or modify the design of the unit because it doesn't belong to you and you are just buying a service. If you don't like the layout of the apartment, there are plenty of interior designs out there in other buildings or neighborhoods to match every taste.

Homes come with built-in furniture that blends seamlessly in the design and includes built-in wardrobes, beds, kitchen tables and amenities, living rooms, a laundry room with washer/dryer, TV, audio system, etc. Built-in furniture maximizes space utilization and prevents dust and dirt from accumulating in-between furniture making it easier to clean and maintain.

Regulated Housing Growth

Cities expand as the human population grows, and therefore as a housing standard, architects must maintain a ratio of three apartments per person (a 3:1 ratio). And since every building has only three homes as a building standard, the 3:1 ratio also means that there's one building to every person on the planet. Why is the ratio set to three homes per person? To ensure that people can travel to other cities and expect to find a temporary home for them to rent. This way, one can keep a condo and call it home, visit another city and book a condo and from there plan the next trip and reserve the third condo before even arriving. The 3:1 ratio helps maintain enough supply of housing and ensures people's right to travel. It also serves a third purpose of controlling where architects can build their next project because only the cities with growing population can add more neighborhoods. The 3:1 ratio also ensures that enough offices are available for people to reserve as a workplace. Since every building has three homes but only one workspace, one resident alone from these three homes could occupy that workspace. And since the housing *smartcontract* guarantees that every city has three homes available for every resident, this also means additional vacant offices are accessible, and the result is a ratio of one office per person in each city.

The 3:1 housing ratio also regulates the buildings' footprint and how densely architects can build. Every neighborhood must contain enough buildings to meet the 3:1 housing ratio, which means if there's a lot of housing to cover, the footprint of buildings in the neighborhood will be as slim as possible. Of course, the maximum spacing between buildings is five meters, but the architects can build denser down to a 3-meter spacing or less. On the other hand, buildings can be as far as five meters apart if the architects are under no obligation to supply a high volume of homes.

Historically, ever since electricity was discovered and made available to people, it always followed a centralized structure of one large producer regulating and selling power to consumers. These customers could not generate their own electricity because the technology wasn't yet available to them and therefore, they had to buy electricity from a local distributor.

Central power plants were large-scale generators of electricity at centralized facilities that were usually located away from end-users and connected to a network of high-voltage transmission lines. The electricity generated by such central power plants was distributed through the electric power grid to multiple end-users. Central power facilities include fossil-fuel-fired power plants, nuclear power plants, hydroelectric dams, wind farms, and more. These power plants typically did not sell their energy directly to end-users but to regional system operators that acted as middlemen, who sold the electricity that they did not produce to the consumers for profit. Therefore, the electricity delivered to consumers by their local electric utility might have been generated at a centralized power plant located in another city or state and sometimes in another country. And whenever intermediaries intervene between producers and consumers, prices naturally tend to spike unnecessarily and unreasonably because they are for-profit operators. Centralization and intermediation, however, are inherit traits of all tribal economies and are inevitable.

Power plants were the most prominent sources of water pollution in any country. Power plants' water discharges were typically filled with toxic pollution such as mercury, arsenic, lead, and selenium. The heavy metals in the waste discharges caused neurological and developmental damage, caused harm in utero, damaged internal organs and caused cancer. The heavy metals in such waste, such as lead, arsenic, and mercury, did not degrade over time, and they concentrated as they traveled up the food chain, impacting fish and wildlife and ultimately collecting in people's bodies as they consume the meat.

Mercury is a metallic pollutant that can be released from coal combustion. Coal-burning power plants were the most significant human-caused source of mercury emissions to the air. When the mercury vapor finds its way into bodies of water, it is converted by bacteria into the more toxic compound, methylmercury, which is a known neurotoxin. It causes mental retardation, seizures, cerebral palsy and death. Coal was second only to automobiles in the production of NOx. Nitric oxide catalyzes the production of ground-level ozone in the presence of sunlight and organic compounds. Coal power plants produced smog, which is a threat to human health and it reduces agricultural productivity. As a result, thousands of people died around the world each year due to the fine particle pollution from the coal power plants in their regions.

Consumers were helpless against such pollution because they had no other means to produce electricity on their own and they had to continue to rely on the environmentally-unfriendly energy generation. Additionally, the information about the environmental impacts of power plants was traditionally hidden from the public in tribal cultures where politicians typically kept the public oblivious to all the harm caused by the tribal ways of producing energy. It was never easy for the public to have their politicians impose regulations on such power plants because in a tribal culture the economy always comes first.

Electricity is a fundamental need for everyone around the world, but it had always been monopolized by a handful of companies that forced citizens to pay whatever rates they fabricate. People became very dependent on these companies and they had no choice but to pay because electricity is a necessity and an essential utility that everyone relies on. This reality changed, however, and the solution came in the form of technology.

The discovery of solar panels and their production at low costs helped shift average citizens from being consumers to become contributors themselves. A building owner could generate his electricity and store it in-house transforming his building into a mini power plant, which sells any excess back to the electrical grid for the benefit of the local community. Energy became an asset, and people can trade it for money with dynamic pricing that depends on supply and demand. This concept started with small towns where people owned their homes and are entitled to install solar panels on their rooftops. Cities, however, continued its reliance on power plants, which made people vulnerable to blackouts if these plants couldn't meet demand or suddenly stopped generating energy for any reason.

The capitalist-minded companies tried to curb the emerging *"energy self-reliance"* by using the same green energy and concentrating it in dedicated areas to sell it back to consumers. The centralized thinking of governments back in those days encouraged this behavior and continued to dominate and manipulate the energy production market. With the inevitable rise of *distribia* and its revolution against traditional corruptible centralized structures and intermediaries, energy finally received a permanent distributed architecture guaranteed under the housing *smartcontract*.

Distribia introduced democracy to the energy business, which is now localized to every city block. Architects now own and manage the energy production and distribution of their neighborhoods. They are energy self-reliant and able to sell electricity to each other seamlessly when production surpasses the demand. Most importantly, architects also benefit financially from producing energy and they're responsible for maintaining their power supply, which eliminated power shortages and wide-area blackouts.

Humanity abandoned the old practice of centralized power plants transmitting electricity over dangerously high voltages between cities due to the overwhelming flaws in the overall design.

Transmitting electricity over long distances lead to energy loss along that trip. It started at the power plant that produces the energy, within the underground electric cabling of the city, and at the homes of consumers when their digital devices converted alternating current (AC) to direct current (DC) for consumption. The loss of energy came mostly in the form of heat generated by the AC-to-DC converters of every device in a household. The discovery of photovoltaics made the setup of AC homes more impractical. Someone who had a solar panel on his rooftop, which generated DC, had to convert the energy to AC in his home first so it could run in the cabling in the interior of his house. Then it is converted to DC gain by the converters of his digital devices. The resulting setup of continually converting and reconverting electricity between AC and DC wasn't serving the average consumer, and people eventually decided to abandon it.

Distribia's new infrastructure-free electrical grid entirely canceled the centralized and costly power plants with their long-distance electricity transmission in favor of much smaller energy efficient buildings distributed globally. The resulting electrical grid is distributed, eco-friendly, renewable and far more efficient. Nuclear, coal, natural gas, and oil power plants were shut down entirely worldwide along with other centralized energy sources. The focus became on integration, localization, and self-sufficiency. Energy production became relative to the surrounding environment in each part of the planet harvesting whatever natural resource abundant within the area. Desert cities focus on photovoltaics, tropical areas emphasize on hydroelectric power, and coastal cities had the additional benefit of harvesting electricity from marine energy.

Instead of transmitting electricity from faraway places using AC over dangerously high voltages, the electric grid was designed to focus on localized distribution over safe DC only. Because the AC-to-DC power conversion component was eliminated from the battery module of all electronics, the need for high-voltage DC wiring was removed, and the risks of fire or electrocution were significantly reduced, resulting in a safer product. The size reduction of electronics is also a notable advantage. Traditional residential and commercial centralized battery storage systems were customarily designed with a battery bank connected to one or more sizeable inverters. These systems limited sizing options and often featured large, heavy battery modules or inverters. Since today's electronics and batteries do not require invertors, they're much smaller and thinner.

Adopting a DC-only electrical grid allowed for a peer-to-peer structure. The DC electrical grid connects every building in the same block to the building next to it in a peer-to-peer structure, and likewise, it connects neighborhoods to one another through the connection between the buildings on the edges. Electricity isn't transmitted from one city to another unless they're geographically neighboring each other. *Ve* is continuously aware of the overall production and consumption of energy across all the residential blocks in the grid and makes smart decisions on where to send electricity excess to the building that can instantly consume it instead of storing it, which increased the overall efficiency of the grid on the long run. All buildings are designed to use DC only while the AC option was utterly shut down. After the switch to DC in all homes, buildings and structures painted with photovoltaic cells (called solarpaint for short) circulate DC within the neighborhood and power all home appliances directly and more efficiently.

Under the housing *smartcontract*, every neighborhood must produce kilowatts energy relative to the residential population. The energy production must be done using renewable energy only and according to the options abundantly available in the area. The neighborhood should maintain the desired energy output, or *Ve* will automatically tax the architects a dynamic energy tax that fluctuates with the persistence and intensity of the energy reliance of the neighborhood on others in the community. Architects are also responsible for continually maintaining and upgrading their energy infrastructure to avoid failure or otherwise risk systematic taxes by *Ve*. To prevent overflow, when batteries in a building are full, and the supply is overwhelming the demand, *Ve* sells electricity to the neighboring buildings that need it either for immediate use or stored in their batteries. *Ve* maintains the efficiency of the grid by distributing energy where it can be consumed immediately, otherwise storing it in the nearest cell. The price of one kilowatt is always constant and has a predefined universal price value because electricity is considered a utility.

As a standard, all windows come with embedded transparent solarpaint that absorb light and convert it to energy for the building. Areas on the planet that don't receive enough sun to power the needs of residents have alternatives and varieties of wind and marine turbines to produce energy. These turbines are relatively small and built into the neighborhood itself and never separately because the housing *smartcontract* necessitates that energy production should be a direct part of the building. However, it is left for the architects to decide where to distribute the output within their neighborhood.

The wind turbines used today are not the windmill-like structure which first surfaced during the renewable energy revolution before *distribia*. Such ugly and dangerous machines were replaced by bladeless designs that emphasize on incorporating aesthetic beauty along with functionality. Today's wind farms are elegant tree-like structures that architects typically plant them along the edges of their parks. They do the job of producing clean energy while masking themselves as art. They usually have no gears or bearings, which reduces manufacturing and maintenance needs, and are respectful of nature and neighbors by barely producing any noise. The result is a quiet, environmentally safer option that also happens to look pretty spectacular against the backdrop of a park.

Distribia's wind farms have numerous designs, but they usually do not exceed the average height of a tree and are always elevated off the ground to prevent the moving parts from accidentally causing any harm to people or animals. Some of them look like a swarm of hummingbirds flapping their wings and hovering endlessly in mid-air. Some architects incorporate beautiful and straightforward helical wind farms to their buildings enabling them to collect wind from all different directions while also lending dramatic aesthetic appeal to buildings. They integrate the turbines as part of the architectural design and take advantage of the building's height to harvest more energy that could be used locally by the residents or sold to other blocks.

Humanity used rainwater harvesting systems since antiquity, and examples abound in all the great civilizations throughout history. The idea behind the process is simple. Rainwater is collected when it falls on the earth, stored and utilized at a later point. Rainwater harvesting is one of the simplest and oldest methods of self-supply of water. It also helps in the availability of potable water, as rainwater is substantially free of salinity and other salts.

Rainwater harvesting provides an independent water supply during regional water restrictions. It gives water when a drought occurs, can help mitigate flooding of low-lying areas, and reduces demand on wells which may sustain groundwater levels. Many regions, especially those with arid environments, use rainwater harvesting as a cheap and reliable source of clean water. To enhance irrigation in dry climates, people constructed ridges of soil to trap and prevent rainwater from running down hills and slopes. Even in periods of low rainfall, the gathered rain provided enough water for crops to grow. People accumulated rainwater from roofs and built dams or ponds to hold large quantities of rainwater so that even on days when little to no rainfall occurs, enough is available to irrigate crops.

For thousands of years and in the modern times before *distribia*, people used rainwater as a primary source of drinking water in several rural areas. Due to surging water prices and to reduce the consumption of groundwater, many people around the world switched to using rainwater harvesting systems. In an urban setting, people conducted the harvesting with the help of some infrastructure. The most straightforward method for a rainwater harvesting system is storage tanks, in-ground or above, a vast range of different sizes and forms were available in the market. Water could be stored in these containers until needed or used on a daily basis. Rooftops were the best catchment areas, provided they are large enough to harvest daily water needs.

The best thing about rainwater is that it is free from pollutants as well as salts, minerals, and other natural and human-made contaminants. In areas where there is excess rainfall, the surplus rainwater can be used recharge groundwater through artificial recharge techniques. Because *distribia* avoids investments in infrastructure and focuses on distribution, independence, self-sustainability, multi-purposing, and simplicity, a large body of work focused on the development of lifecycle assessment and lifecycle costing methodologies to assess the level of environmental impacts and money that people can save by implementing rainwater harvesting systems.

One of the top reasons for avoiding using citywide water delivery infrastructure was that the materials used in the system naturally age with time and can result in harmful health consequences. The solution was straightforward, every building must collect its own needs of water without relying on any infrastructure.

Rainwater harvesting reduces floods and soil erosion. During the rainy season, rainwater collected by the entire community reduces floods in some low-lying areas. Apart from this, it helps in reducing soil erosion and contamination of surface water with chemicals, heavy metals, pesticides and fertilizers from rainwater run-off which results in cleaner lakes and ponds. Rainwater, when collected, can satisfy people's needs for water including flushing toilets, washing clothes, watering the gardens and parks, etc. Today, this is guaranteed by the housing *smartcontract* that all buildings follow across all neighborhoods globally. The rainwater collection system consists of a series of filters from the rooftop of the building till the storage area in the basement, which includes several interconnected barrels of wood or bamboo or other eco-friendly renewable material.

Exceptionally high standard levels, under the housing *smartcontract*, applies to drinkable tap water, which needs to be alkaline, rich in minerals, and contaminant-free. Architects maintain transparency through a distributed network of sensors continuously monitoring the constitution of the water throughout its cycle starting at every source where it is collected, every trip in the pipelines, at all water treatment systems, and finally in the unit of every consumer. This data is provided by *databōts* and always come unregulated, and instantly published on the web to be publicly accessible to everyone. Anyone can access this information through their *Ve* and use it in statistics to forecast predictions and maintain hygiene levels.

Neighborhoods are designed to collect and store water from their natural surrounding and be self-sufficient. The material and design of the building allow it to capture rainwater and funnel it into underground reservoirs underneath each building that feed it back into the building when needed. Architects must capture enough cubic liters of freshwater from the surrounding environment in amounts relative to the population of their blocks without relying on buying water from other peers. In case of water shortage, a neighborhood can purchase freshwater from its peers in the same city or another.

Since water is considered a basic right, it cannot be purchased directly. The price of fresh water is calculated based on the energy it took to harvest and filter it, and it never set arbitrary by the architects. So, when consumers pay for water, that payment is not for the water itself but for the energy it took to harvest and filter it plus a maximum of 17% in profit. This distinction is important because water is considered a fundamental right in *distribia* and can't be sold or owned by anyone.

Every building in the same block is pipelined to the next building a peer-to-peer structure while the buildings on the peripheral of the neighborhoods connect to the buildings of the next neighborhood in a peer-to-peer structure as well. And so, neighborhoods are connected through their buildings and the same applies for the buildings in between cities. Only in cases when the production is overwhelming the demand of the entire neighborhood that it starts selling to other peers. Otherwise, the neighborhood moves water around from one building to another to maintain equilibrium in each building's tanks.

Buildings that are located by a river rely mostly on that river for water but also store their needs in reservoirs underground the structure of each building. Other buildings rely on rainwater and must have enough water reservoirs to save as much rain needed for the homeowners to avoid taxation if they failed to generate the minimal cubic liters requirement for the neighborhood. If a neighborhood failed to capture its minimal cubic liter requirement, the architects buy it from the grid with a dynamic tax that increases with the period of the violation. Otherwise, if a neighborhood is producing a surplus of water, it sells it back to the grid to make a profit.

The housing *smartcontract* controls when architects must start buying water from its peers, and it never reaches the point where the water tanks in each building are empty before the company starts buying from the grid. It sets a dynamic critical level for every neighborhood according to its water consumption and determines whether to buy or sell based on that variable level. Other factors that might affect the critical level are the climate conditions and the surrounding neighborhoods' reserves of water.

There are cases where there's a surplus of freshwater in the containers of one neighborhood while others are at medium level. In this case, architects sell the excess to their neighbors in small portions even if they didn't reach the critical level yet. This policy is meant to prevent water waste and maintain overall efficiency in the entire global water grid. The housing *smartcontract* also imposes standards on the design and material used for water reservoirs across all blocks. For example, the water tanks in all buildings and the distribution of the pipelines across the grid keep water in a constant state of circulation in the tubes of the network by design and prevent stale water buildup in any part of the grid.

Local Water Recycling In Every Building

Water treatment has been a primary logistical challenge since the dawn of civilization. Where water resources or infrastructure or sanitation systems are insufficient for the population, people fall prey to disease and in extreme cases, death. The historical focus of sewage treatment was on the conveyance of raw sewage to a natural body of water such as rivers or oceans, where they could satisfactorily dilute or dissipate it. Most of these early sewers received significant amounts of draft animal feces in street runoff, but the handling of human waste varied with location.

Over the millennia, technology has dramatically increased the distances across which people can relocate their sewer water.

However, they merely transferred it to an area far from sight without really treating it, and soon enough this practice backfired when they discovered they had contaminated their ecosystem when the untreated wastewater found its way into underground wells or back into rivers and streams people use for drinking water.

In medieval European cities, small natural waterways used for carrying off wastewater were eventually covered over and functioned as sewers. Open drains, or gutters, for sewage, ran along the center of some streets. These were known as *"kennels,"* and in Paris were sometimes known as *"split streets,"* as the wastewater running along the middle physically split the streets into two halves. The first closed sewer constructed in Paris was 300 meters long (around 984 feet). The original purpose of designing and building a covered drain in Paris was less-so for waste management as much as it was to hold back the stench coming from the odorous wastewater. Pail closets, outhouses, and cesspits were used to collect human waste. Most cities did not have a functioning sewer system before the Industrial era, relying instead on nearby rivers or occasional rain showers to wash away the sewage from the streets. In some places, wastewater just ran down the streets, which had stepping stones to keep pedestrians out of the muck, and eventually drained as runoff into the local watershed.

Little progress happened in water sanitation, but this began to change in the 17th and 18th centuries with a rapid expansion in waterworks and pumping systems. A significant development was the construction of a network of sewers to collect wastewater. In some cities, including Rome and Istanbul, networked ancient sewer systems continue to function in the 21st century as collection systems for those cities' modernized sewer systems. Instead of flowing to a river or the sea, the pipes have been re-routed to modern sewer treatment facilities. Sewage water traveled towards centralized treatment plants via pipelining and in a flow aided by gravity and pumps. These plants use a variety of techniques to filter and treat water before dumping it in a landfill or recycling it and pumping back to customers. The process, however, was costly because it involved massive infrastructure. Additionally, the design of the system behind it is flawed and inefficient.

The fundamental flaw in the design of this system was that its elements were segregated and stretched too far apart. Sewage had to travel vast distances from its origin to a centralized plant in a remote area, and if that plant fails, the city's sewage system shuts off. *Distribians* introduced an alternative, which was reasonably straightforward: treat greywater and recycle it locally in every building that produces it. As a result, humanity decided through the housing *smartcontract* to maintain local grey and black water in every neighborhood as a building standard. Today, every building in every block worldwide has a water treatment room in the basement area that treats both black and greywater and pumps the recycled water back to the condos in an infinite loop. Toilet water goes to a treatment room in the basement that consists of a series of interconnected aerated tanks where bacteria naturally filter the sewage water in these containers before heading to a reverse osmosis filtration system and lastly the third system of filtration using ultraviolet light. Some architects use the exterior greenwalls to filter the water at this stage instead of the excessive reliance on mechanical filters. A pump then takes the now-clean-water to a holding tank in the utility room on the last floor in the building, which lets gravity distribute the water back to the toilets in an infinite cycle. This process is repeated continuously, which means that the sewage system will continue to work indefinitely and independently of any drought in the area.

The water in this sewage system is refreshed from time to time in such cases when the neighborhood is capturing fresh water in abundance from the surrounding environment such as excessive rainfall. When this happens, the disposed water goes to watering the greenwalls in the building or pumped to the neighborhood's park. At the parks, the already-clean-water undergoes tertiary treatment from plants that further improve the water quality and fuel the fountains, lagoons, botanical gardens, or lakes in the park. This last method removes any remaining inorganic compounds, and substances, such as nitrogen and phosphorus.

Shower or bath water goes into another filtration system that also puts the water in an infinite loop. The only difference here is that the water doesn't go to the basement like black water and instead filtered and treated instantly underneath the shower/bath in the same condo. The system uses several filtration systems including reverse osmosis and ultraviolet light to recycle the water back to the shower. The infinity shower's system saves energy as well because the already-hot water is put back in a loop without needing to reheat it. Technically, this system allows people to stay in the shower indefinitely because the same water is being recycled and never wasted. Whether the region is suffering from drought or not, people can enjoy long relaxing showers guilt-free. Of course, the system is also refreshed from time to time when the freshwater supply is overwhelming the local demand. The disposed water also goes to the building's greenwalls or the neighborhood's park.

Greywater from the dishwashing or cloth-washing is recycled separately in a similar system within every condo. Unlike the former practice of drinking water straight out of the tap, tenants of *distribia's* condos get their drinking water from a dedicated filter in the apartment, which comes straight from the freshwater tanks in the basement. Although technically the water from the tap is perfectly clean for drinking, they prefer having their drinking water fresh and not recycled.

Local Garbage Recycling In Every Block

Throughout most of history, the amount of waste generated by people was insignificant due to low population density and low societal levels of the exploitation of natural resources. Waste produced during pre-modern times was mainly ashes and human biodegradable waste, and these were released back into the ground locally, with minimum environmental impact. Tools made from wood or metal were reused or passed down through the generations.

Following the onset of industrialization and the sustained urban growth of large population centers globally, the buildup of waste in the cities caused a rapid deterioration in levels of sanitation and the general quality of civic life. The streets became choked with filth and cities faced increasingly devastating cholera outbreaks due to the lack of waste clearance regulations. Eventually, a public demand surfaced for adequate waste removal and management facilities to improve the health and well-being of the city's population.

The use of incinerators for waste disposal became popular in the late 19th century. The dramatic increase in industrial waste led to the creation of the first incineration plants, or, as they were then called, *"destructors."* These incinerators solved one problem but created several others and so, the public met them with opposition because of the vast amounts of ash they produced, and which wafted over the neighboring areas. Similar municipal systems of waste disposal sprung up at the turn of the 20th century in other large cities of Europe and North America. Early garbage removal trucks were merely open bodied dump trucks pulled by a team of horses. They became motorized in the early part of the 20th century, and the first closed body trucks to eliminate odors with a dumping lever mechanism were introduced in the 1920s in Europe. These were soon equipped with *"hopper mechanisms"* where the scooper was loaded at floor level and then hoisted mechanically to deposit the waste in the truck. New generations of trash trucks hit the market later and incorporated hydraulic compactors in the design.

Waste collection methods varied widely among different regions. Domestic waste collection services were often provided by local government authorities, or by private companies for industrial and commercial waste. Some areas, especially those in less developed countries, did not have formal waste-collection systems. The curbside collection was the most common method of disposal in most European countries and many other parts of the developed world in which specialized trucks collect waste at regular intervals. This process often came with curb-side waste segregation, where each type of waste is collected and then transported to an appropriate disposal facility. In some jurisdictions, unsegregated waste is collected at the curbside or from waste transfer stations and then sorted into recyclables and unusable waste. Such systems are capable of sorting large volumes of solid waste, salvaging recyclables, and turning the rest into biogas and soil conditioner.

Some local governments established mandatory recycling and composting ordinance, requiring everyone in the city to keep recyclables and compostables out of the landfill. The companies that serviced these cities provided residents and businesses a 3-category trash bin system: blue for recyclables, green for compostables, and black for landfill-bound materials. The companies collected these trash bins from curbsides citywide and charged customers by the volume of landfill-bound materials, which provided a financial incentive to separate recyclables and compostables from other discards.

National or local tax, which was either related to income or house value, traditionally funded domestic waste disposal. Commercial and industrial waste disposal was typically charged for as a business service, often as an integrated charge which includes disposal costs. This practice encouraged disposal contractors to opt for the cheapest disposal option such as landfill rather than the environmentally best solution such as re-use and recycling. City governments in other areas charged its households and industries for the volume of rubbish they produced. The city council only collected the waste in government-issued rubbish bags. This policy successfully reduced the amount of garbage the city created and increased the recycling rate.

As humanity became more technologically advanced, they produced materials that can withstand extreme temperatures, are durable and easy to use. Plastic bags, synthetics, plastic bottles, tin cans, and computer hardware- these are some of the things that made life easy for everyone. However, this shortsighted approach to the way of life backfired, disease spread, people died, and everyone realized the substantial consequences of the tradeoff they made. The average person realized that these advanced products the for-profit companies flooded the market with did not break down naturally and lingered instead in the natural landscape polluting the ecosystem and producing disease and illness. When they disposed of them in a garbage pile, the air, moisture, climate, or soil could not break them down spontaneously or dissolve them with the surrounding land because they weren't biodegradable. And so, a need emerged to regulate manufacturers and the products they're allowed to produce.

Today, there's a universal commitment to using entirely compost-friendly, recyclable, and renewable material in all products. As a result, all products in the economy were necessarily either recyclable or compostable. Dumps and landfills disappeared ever since because there is no need for them. All trash is either recyclable or natural and can break down inevitably in days or weeks when people disposed of it. Most importantly, most of these biodegradable products are edible and represent food to other animals and organisms in nature and could, therefore, benefit the ecosystem instead of crippling it. A cup of coffee serves as a delicious meal to some animals and people could, accordingly, benefit nature by throwing it in the environment. The same people who took the habit of tossing out plastic bottles into the sea while out fishing, are by all means doing the same thing today but instead of the harmful plastic, the biodegradable cans they toss away serve as a delicious meal to sea life. Such behavior is in fact encouraged today because when people throw out single-use-containers, they are actually doing nature a favor because a hungry bird or fish or insect will devour that delicious bottle, or straw, or bag or even wrappers.

Compostable products are made from plants and result in significant reductions in greenhouse gas emissions due to the nature of their manufacturing process. A manufacturing standard regulated the lifecycle of products from the material used, how the material is extracted from nature, how the product operates, how they are maintained and repaired, and how they are disposed of ultimately. Electronics, hardware, or e-waste are all recyclable and are now the responsibility of the manufacturer to recycle them. Lightbulbs, cables, computers, monitors, TVs, etc. are all shipped back or collected by the manufacturer because they are obliged under the product-manufacturing *smartcontract* to recycle whatever they produce.

The concept of having several waste segregation systems disappeared because today the things we use in our daily life are necessarily either compostable or recyclable. Across all blocks worldwide, there are only two trash bins in every home that people use to dump their waste. A tube connects each trash bin in each condo directly to a vending machine located in one of the building's garbage rooms on the ground floor. The vending machines grind the waste until it becomes fine sand and stores it in a container underneath the vending machine. Before the container gets full, a *traxbōt* (pronounced trash-bot in English and represented a robot purposed for collecting or managing trash) picks up the trash box and deliver it to the building of the *kleenirkōrp* servicing the neighborhood. The *kleenirkōrp* uses the powder from compost bins as fertilizer for the neighborhood's park. It sells the dust from the recyclables' bins to other architects as a building material.

As a universal standard, the interior membrane of all tubes that funnel the trash contains an extremely slippery substance that nothing sticks to it. Not even bacteria can build upon it. All neighborhoods follow this standard for all surfaces that encounter trash to avoid buildup of waste material and reduce drag when waste passes through such surfaces.

Healthcare Is Localized To Every Block Of Every City

Hospitals in all tribal cultures had the same problems: crowded halls, provider shortages, costly services or treatments, and poor patient hand-off. The most dangerous shortcoming that plagued the healthcare system of tribal cultures was health equity, or *"when everyone has the opportunity to attain their full health potential."* Whenever access to health isn't equitable, it leads to poor health outcomes for an entire class of patients. For instance, black people had much lower life expectancies compared to white people in the U.S., and people in households with lower incomes had a higher relative risk of mortality than those with higher incomes. Social class and racism were institutional in tribal healthcare systems and access to healthcare was never a fundamental human right.

In a typical tribal culture, the record of what you do is always more important than what you do. Doctors had to spend most of their time painstakingly documenting care, correctly coding patient diagnoses, and procedures, if they wanted to get paid. It also provided a perverse incentive that focused on maximizing practice revenue, instead of focusing on outcomes. They failed in the integration of data and data sharing, to facilitate continuity of care and to avoid duplication of effort. The healthcare systems did not speak to each other and did not share patient data among providers and clinics in a way that improves outcomes and patient safety. This monumental medical data deficit hindered patient care, safety and results. Such broken system left patients data scrambled across several providers every time they moved between providers or moved to a new city within the same nation. And since of course tribal countries were rigorously isolated from one another, when people moved to other nations their medical records did not proceed with them, and they had to start a new medical history from scratch. Doctors were confronted daily with the barriers to access. In some cultures, they could not even look at patient records from other facilities that were part of the same hospital's organization. Practitioners spent an inordinate amount of time trying to gather data that should be seamlessly and readily available.

Another deadly flaw in a tribal healthcare system was the structural design of the system where the leadership is upside down. Under such system, physicians and doctors were mere employees or workers in a factory-like workshop commanded by politicians and businesspeople. They were just pawns in a scheme foisted upon them by for-profit operators that had no knowledge of what is wrong with the system and had no genuine intentions to reform it for as long as it is yielding the profit they desire.

Tribal healthcare typically lacked transparency. People at that day and age had far more information available to them to compare and select a new car than they did to choose where to go for lifesaving health care. The lack of such information was intentional because, in most tribal nations, healthcare was a seriously profitable business monopolized by conglomerates who had zero interest in being transparent because they know it would damage their status quo. If patients knew how much their healthcare providers are ripping them off, they would surely be outraged. Transparency galvanizes change like nothing else. Consumers deserve to know for example the rates for every hospital delivering babies in their country, but unfortunately, that would expose the medical fraud of each provider. And since transparency is never one of the virtues of tribalism, politicians always ensure that such openness is hard to accomplish to protect the sellers' interests and not that of the consumer.

The fact of life in that day and age was that the people checking into the hospital faced fatal risks. Expecting to get better, some actually wind up getting worse. There was the danger of medical complications, like bleeding or infection. Then there were the human errors, like getting the wrong drug or dosage. All it took is for someone to miss a decimal point, and one could have a life-threatening mistake. A pharmacist or nurse could misread a doctor's poor handwriting, which doctors were notorious for, on a prescription and lead to fatal complications. Even though hospitals had a lot of well-trained people working very hard, they're still people, and people sometimes make mistakes. All these hospital risks were far beyond anyone's control and left patients feeling somewhat helpless.

Another top hospital risk was infection with bacteria or a virus. Centralized hospitals were loaded with nasty bugs. There were million health-care-associated infections every year where some were surgical wounds infections while others were urinary tract infections. The rest are infections of the lungs, blood, and other parts of the body. One of the most frightening hospital infections one could pick up was MRSA (methicillin-resistant Staphylococcus aureus), which is a type of infection that's resistant to many antibiotics.

The healthcare systems of tribal cultures were simply broken, and the way they delivered medicine to patients was dysfunctional and infested with for-profit middlemen. It was failing miserably, and their problems could not be addressed separately without a drastic and dramatic toppling of the entire healthcare system. There was simply no way by which people could truly reform the healthcare system in any tribal nation without first changing the way in which healthcare was paid for and financed.

Today, however, healthcare is a basic human right and is guaranteed to everyone. *Distribia's* healthcare is operated predominantly through *Ve* and robotics. Human involvement is restricted mostly to designing the healthcare robotics and overseeing them. There are no central hospitals anymore because today's healthcare system relies on mobile healthcare robotics that patrol on land, air, and water to offer services at any geographic location on Earth when needed. Healthcare robotics are public utilities and are rented and are operated by each person's *Ve*. So, when you want to use a healthcare machine, your *Ve* gets into it and works it for you. Operating systems are nothing more than public manuals of which all *Ve* identities have a copy. So, your *Ve* operates and manages all your healthcare, performs surgeries on you when needed, stores your medical data, and tracks your health daily wherever in the world you go. There are also skycars that offer healthcare and can land on any building in the neighborhood to provide immediate assistance in case of emergency. These healthcare skycars also fly to rural areas to offer medical aid on demand in remote areas outside the city when needed.

Since healthcare is a utility, it comes in three types where customers can enjoy premium (type-1) or advanced (type-2) or economy (type-3) services depending on everyone's income or preferences. Healthcare's type-3 follows a universal dynamic pricing model that is the same in every neighborhood everywhere. The prices are based on a percentage of the UBI to ensure that anyone can get healthcare and any medication or operation regardless of their wealth or income.

Building Material & Standards

Environmental deterioration eventually captured the world's attention when people realized that the planet is in severe ecological catastrophe due to eco-unfriendly building construction practices. These practices participated in ozone layer depletion, global warming, resource depletion and ecosystem destruction.

Construction activities affected the natural environment throughout the life cycle of the buildings. These impacts occurred from initial work on-site throughout the construction period, operational period and to the final demolition when a structure approaches the end of its life. Even though the construction period is comparatively shorter compared to the other stages of a building's life, it has the most significant effects on the environment. And even though construction projects potentially contribute to the economic and social development as well as enhancing both the standards of living and the quality of life, it also adds to the deterioration of the environment and ultimately deteriorates social and economic growth.

It is not just the methods and materials used to construct a building that affects the environment because the way it is built to operate has a considerable impact as well. For example: using non-sustainable construction materials and excessive use of HVAC (heating, ventilation, and air conditioning) systems.

The focus of the construction industry was mostly on economic growth and improving the quality of life of the locals while environmental protection fell low on the priority list.

The construction industry was undoubtedly one of the largest sectors of any economy and crucial to social and economic gains. People needed houses, hospitals, schools, offices, factories, roads, bridges and communication infrastructure to support the economy. Unfortunately, they predominately neglected the environmental impact of erecting these necessities and did not invest in eco-friendly alternatives. In meeting these demands, the construction industry exerted enormous pressures on global natural resources. The environmental significance of such forces comes into play when some of these resources are depletable and non-renewable, bringing the construction industry in direct conflict with nature.

Constructing cities rely heavily on the natural environment for the supply of raw materials such as timber, sand, and aggregates for the building process. Building construction consumed 40% of the world's raw stones, gravel and sand and 25% of the virgin wood per year. It also consumed around 40% of the available energy and 16% of water annually.

The extraction of natural resources caused irreversible changes to the countryside and coastal areas, both from an ecological and a scenic point of view. The subsequent transfer of these areas into geographically dispersed sites not only led to further consumption of energy but also increased the amount of particulate matter in the atmosphere along the route. Raw materials extraction and construction activities also contributed to the accumulation of pollutants in the atmosphere. Dust and other emissions included toxic substances such as nitrogen and sulfur oxides. They were released during the production and transportation of materials as well as from site activities. Other harmful substances, such as chlorofluorocarbons (CFCs), were used in insulation, air conditioning, refrigeration plants and fire-fighting systems and severely depleted the ozone layer.

Pollutants were frequently released into the biosphere causing severe land and water contamination due to on-site negligence resulting in toxic spillages, which rainfall then washed into underground aquatic systems and reservoirs. The world's soil degraded, and pollutants depleted environmental quality, interfering with the environment's capacity to provide a naturally balanced ecosystem.

Many construction and demolition materials had a high potential for recycling and reuse. Nevertheless, screening, checking and handling construction waste for recycling are time-consuming activities, and the lack of environmental awareness amongst building professionals created significant barriers to the usefulness of recycling. So, most of the recyclable material from building sites ended up in landfill sites.

Besides generating waste, building activities also irreversibly transformed arable lands into physical assets such as buildings, roads, dams or other civil engineering projects. The world's cropland or arable land were decreasing due to quarrying and mining the raw materials needed in construction. Forests densities dropped due to the timber used in building and in providing energy for manufacturing building materials. Both deforestation and the burning of fossil fuels contributed directly to global warming and air pollution. Also, the building industry traditionally was a significant consumer of energy while the use of finite fossil fuel resources for this purpose contributed significantly to carbon dioxide emissions. Buildings consumed a significant portion of the produced energy, and larger than all transportation systems combined. The more substantial part of this thirst for power was due to the cooling and heating of buildings that were inefficient in storing temperature. In addition to electricity, structures mismanaged water and were extremely wasteful of it.

Sources of pollution and hazards from traditional construction activities included dust, harmful gases, noises, solid and liquid wastes, fallen objects, soil and ground contamination, underground water contamination, construction and demolition rubbish, noise and vibration, dust, hazardous emissions, odors, and the occasional deaths on construction sites. The impacts of traditional construction included wildlife, archaeology, ecological loadings and human health issues, extraction of environmental resources such as fossil fuels and minerals, and the pollution of the ecosystem. Moreover, unsustainable designs and construction processes further degraded the relationship between urban development and the environment.

Today, protection of the environment comes at the outset of any construction project because humanity collectively decided how they should construct their neighborhoods and what material to use. They elected the housing *smartcontract* to regulate the construction process from start to finish including the type of buildings, equipment used, and the substances allowed. Consequently, architects can only use renewable, eco-friendly materials and can just build passive houses that do not rely excessively on HVAC systems.

The housing *smartcontract* created a building standard where a type of powder recipe constitutes the building block for producing structural building material, and this is how the process works:

➢ Every residence has two bins that are directly connected to a funnel to the basement. The first category is for compostable material and the second is for recyclables. People dispose of their trash in the *"recyclables"* bin inside their apartments.

➢ The waste funnels to the basement where a vending machine crushes the waste into fine powder.

➢ Robotic cleaners pick up the dust from the vending machines when they get full and deliver it to a dedicated building in the same neighborhood.

➢ At their designated building, the powder is packaged and sold to the architects in need of building material.

➢ Architects use the powder and mix it with other elements to achieve the exact recipe used in construction and which the housing *smartcontract* details specifically.

➢ The material is compressed under extreme pressures in casts forming stone slabs.

➢ They bake these stones in an industrial oven at extremely high temperatures for extended periods strengthening the rock even further.

> The slabs are then ready to be delivered to the next block under construction and assembled onsite using *beldirbots* (builder robots, which are a type of skycars used for transporting and assembling building segments from remote sites to new neighborhoods that are currently under construction).

Through this concept, items that people use in their daily lives are recycled and reused as building material instead of throwing it away in landfills.

The passiveness standard of the housing *smartcontract* is designed to maximize energy efficiency in all buildings and reduce their ecological footprint. It results in ultra-low energy structures that require little energy for space heating or cooling. Passive design is not an attachment or supplement to architectural design, but a design process that integrates with architectural design. Although it applies to all new buildings, it has also been used to refurbish existing buildings in communities constructed before *distribia's* housing *smartcontract* became a universal building standard for humanity. While some techniques and technologies were developed explicitly for housing *smartcontract's* standards, others, such as superinsulation, already existed, and the concept of passive solar building design dates all the way back to antiquity. There were also other previous experiences with low-energy building standards in several countries in Europe before *distribia.*

The housing *smartcontract* sets an annual cap on total primary energy consumption for heating, hot water, and electricity. Buildings must not leak a cap of air quantity relative to the home volume. Otherwise, the architects might face an automatic dynamic tax. By achieving housing *smartcontract's* standards, buildings today rely less on traditional energy-thirsty heating systems. While this is an underlying objective of the housing *smartcontract*, passive homes still use a variety of additional heating systems to provide extra space heating. Some buildings administrate this through low-volume heat recovery ventilation systems that are needed to maintain air quality throughout the indoors.

Achieving the significant decrease in heating energy consumption required by the housing *smartcontract* involved a shift in approach to building design and construction. Passive solar building design and energy-efficient landscaping support buildings' energy conservation, which architects integrate into the neighborhood. Following passive solar building techniques, where structures are compact in shape to reduce their surface area, with primary windows oriented towards the equator – south in the northern hemisphere and north in the southern region – to maximize passive solar gain. However, the use of solar gain, especially in warm climate regions, is secondary to minimizing the overall energy requirements of the building. In climates and areas needing to reduce excessive summer passive solar heat gain, architects employ a range of techniques such as using trees, attached pergolas with vines, greenwalls and gardens.

Today's architects use various types of renewable material in constructing a passive building. These materials could be dense or lightweight, but some internal thermal mass is typically incorporated to reduce summer peak temperatures, maintain stable winter temperatures, and prevent possible overheating in spring or autumn before the higher sun angle *"shades"* mid-day wall exposure and window penetration. Exterior wall color, when the surface allows choice, for reflection or absorption insolation qualities depends on the absolute year-round ambient outdoor temperature. The use of deciduous trees and greenwalls or self-attaching vines assist in climates, not at the temperature extremes.

Some architects employ superinsulation to significantly reduce the heat transfer through the walls, roof, and floor compared to conventional structures. They use a wide range of thermal insulation materials to provide the required standards for insulation with special attention given to eliminating thermal bridges.

To meet the requirements of the housing *smartcontract*, engineers redesigned all windows to be thick and as much insulative as possible. The global standard now is to combine triple-pane insulated glazing with air-seals and specially developed thermally broken window frames.

Buildings are required to be extremely airtight compared to conventional construction before humanity decided to impose the housing *smartcontract*. They are expected to meet a cap of air change per hour based on the building's volume. Most of the air exchange inside buildings with their exterior is done by controlled ventilation through a heat-exchanger to minimize heat loss (or gain, depending on climate). So, architects avoid uncontrolled air leaks to maintain the ventilation standard.

The use of passive natural ventilation is an integral component for passive buildings where the ambient temperature is conducive — either by a singular or cross ventilation, by a simple opening or enhanced by the stack effect from smaller ingress with more massive egress windows or clerestory-operable skylight.

When the ambient climate is not conducive, mechanical heat recovery ventilation systems, with a standard heat recovery rate and high-efficiency electronically commutated motors, are employed to maintain air quality, and to recover sufficient heat to dispense with a conventional central heating system.

Some architects use earth warming tubes, which are buried in the soil to act as earth-to-air heat exchangers and pre-heat (or pre-cool) the intake air for the ventilation system. In cold weather, the warmed air also prevents ice formation in the heat recovery system's heat exchanger. Alternatively, the earth-to-air heat exchanger uses a liquid circuit instead of an air circuit with an electric heat exchanger to control the temperature.

Public Sportblocks In Every City As An Urban Standard

In almost all tribal cultures, stadiums were privately owned but publicly funded using taxpayer money. Even economically distressed communities regularly determined to be in debt by accepting bankers' loans and then charging that bill to the residents. A typical stadium's cost was usually in the range of hundreds of millions of dollars and since the most substantial funding came from the public, every single man, woman, and child in such communities automatically incurred debt in the order of thousands of dollars. And since bankers owned and regulated the financial system of all tribal nations, the more debt is created in the world, the wealthier they get. After all, it was a debt-based economy, and new money was produced only when new debt was made. And so, tribal cultures always explored new ways to keep national debt growing by convincing the public that it needs a more modern or better stadium for example.

Team owners also employed clever tactics of growing the national debt, and bankers didn't exclusively orchestrate it. Sports teams' owners always thrived to get new stadiums to make more money and increase the value of their franchises. Owners regularly threatened local politicians that they would move their teams to other cities or states if the politicians did not employ taxpayers' money to fund such new stadiums. Politicians ultimately provided millions of dollars in subsidies to keep the teams in their cities claiming that they're doing a tremendous public service by keeping such teams in town. It was very common to see some tribal communities demolishing a stadium that they built just a few decades ago to grow a new one in its place. This, of course, transpires regardless if the community closed the debt on the demolished stadium because debt is usually designed to be hard to erase, and because new debt is always good news for city officials and bankers. In the United States, for example, the replacement rate of stadiums was 90 percent, and almost all of them have received direct public funding. The typical justification for a massive public investment to build a stadium for an already-wealthy sports owner had to do with creating jobs or growing the local economy, which always sounded good to the median voter. However, the hollow claim that taxpayers were indeed getting something in return for their giveaways to already-wealthy business owners was nothing more than tribal propaganda.

All the profits of any kind within such stadiums went straight to team owners' pockets, and the local public never got any percentage of the proceeds even though it was their collective financial investment to build the stadium. Team owners, however, argue that the public was indirectly compensated because the businesses around such stadiums benefited from the foot-traffic of visitors from out of town. However, empirical economic research shows that on all counts, sports stadiums added no substantial economic benefit to the cities in which they were built, no new jobs, no further business, and no statistically positive correlation between sports facility construction and economic development. While taxpayer-financed stadiums did not seem to add to the wealth of the public who pay for them, they did add to the wealth of team owners because the value of their teams statistically increased after such gift stadiums were built.

Building a stadium was consistently a poor use of few hundred million dollars, which could've been employed in countless other projects that could've generated real value to the public. Economists at the time always knew stadiums to be poor public investments. Most of the jobs created by stadium-building projects were either temporary, low-paying, or out-of-state contracting jobs—none of which contributed significantly to the local economy. Not to forget of course the foregone property taxes because almost every major-league franchise located in the U.S. did not pay property taxes due to a legal loophole with the questionable rationale. All the while, American cities, counties, and states continued to struggle to fund basic civic operations where police and education budgets got slashed and while one in every 10 people lived below the poverty line nationwide. This isn't news, by any stretch, and many people knew it at the time, but in a tribal culture infested with bankers and blinded by propaganda, it was always hard to challenge or reform anything.

It is worth mentioning that in the United States, the law did not consider the construction of sports stadium as an appropriate use of taxpayer funds and, therefore, it was illegal to use taxpayer money to fund privately owned stadiums. However, since the United States' central bank (aka the Federal Reserve) found that such stadiums could be used to raise the national debt, an official tax-reform was introduced that added sports stadiums to the list of eligible private activities that could be financed with taxpayer money.

Today, *distribia* reshaped the sports business because there are neither owners of sports teams nor stadium owners. Sports teams involved a hierarchy of owners, stadium landlords, investors, coaches, and more. Since delegation is illegal in *distribia's* nonhierarchical society, and since businesses are always peer-to-peer, the sports business changed significantly. The *distribian* economy operates by a fundamental code: THOSE WHO WORK THE BUSINESSES MUST OWN THEM AND RUN THEM. In the same way that a shoe company involves only partners of shoemakers where every one of them is actively engaged in shoemaking, a sports team is a type of business that includes only players. There is no one sitting behind a desk counting the money and compiling excel sheets because technology handles such tasks and they are operated though *Ve*. No one is wearing a headset and taking phone calls because customer service is handled by the players' *Ve* identities as well. No one is employed by the team to clean up the stadium after the game because maintaining the stadium is dealt with by the company that is renting it out to the team. No minimum wage cheerleaders because they are now considered independent performers that are selling a service and just like singers, they are paid for gigs by different teams in different sports to perform on the field and entertain the crowd.

There are no owners because the players own the team together as partners. There are no stadium owners because owning property is illegal, and architects build such stadiums to rent them out directly to the players who wish to use them in the same way people rent condos. Usually, each stadium is leased to several teams at once where the more teams share the rent, the less the total cost would be on each team. In such cases, the teams would use the stadium according to a timetable that dictates who use the stadium and when. The *sportblocks*, however, are not meant exclusively for professional teams because such structures are also open to the public through reservations. If people wanted to play a soccer game, for example, they could book the field from the architects according to a timeline and enjoy the game.

There are no investors in sports anymore because bankers and debt are illegal in *distribia*. The players incur all the payments made by the team according to the shares they negotiated with each other in their *smartcontract*. Similarly, all profit goes straight to the players and is distributed according to their shares in the team. It is very usual for sports teams to voluntarily decrease their equity in the team to afford to add a new player to the group. And in that way, athletes or competitors are negotiating contracts with other athletes without any middlemen in between.

There's no man in a suit bossing the players around or yelling at them in the locker room. This type of coach does not exist today because in a *distribian* company everyone must be engaged in producing the goods or services that the company is providing. Meaning that the coach or the captain is one of the players and he/she can be either on the field playing the game, or he/she can be sitting on a bench overseeing the game.

There are no sports associations that regulate the games such as the NBA, WNBA, FIFA, FIBA, MLB, MLS, NFL, UEFA, or Formula 1 or so on. Sports games involve *smartcontracts* that are written and regulated by those who play such games or the public who watches them. These *smartcontracts* are named after the name of each game. So, the basketball *smartcontract*, for example, is a social contract that details all aspects of the game such as the measurements of the court, the height of the rim, the rules and so on. If the audience is not happy about any rule in this game, it can vote to omit it and similarly it can vote to add more rules.

It is worth mentioning that today there are many sports *smartcontracts* or versions of the original basketball game. Today there's a version that involves a shorter rim played by athletes that are shorter than 6 feet. There's also another version where the players do not dribble the ball and just like rugby they aim to charge forward until they are at a reasonable distance to shoot the ball inside the rim. Such version is played on a variety of surfaces, and each surface has its own characteristics which affect the playing style of the game. There are 4 main types of courts for this sport that are grass courts, clay courts, rubber carpet courts, or beach sand courts.

The sports' genetic racism or excessive professionalism that existed in all tribal cultures before *distribia* is now all gone because *distribia* restored sports to their original purpose of being tools for people to show their athleticism as it was the case in Ancient Greece. No particular genetic bias or clear advantage to tall players for example as was the case with traditional basketball because now there are many versions of such game and everyone can be a professional in one of its variants. So instead of lazily laying on the sofa eating junk food and watching others playing a game that you have absolutely no chance of competing in, you can now engage and professionally play the game for which you cheer. Such proactive engagement in sports that involves cheering, practicing professionally, petitioning and electing the rules has added a uniquely beautiful dimension to all games. Sports are no longer restricted to the demigod-professionals that people worshiped on the TV in tribal cultures. Such false-idols do not exist in the *distribian* society today because sports are proposed for athleticism and not excessive professionalism or stardom.

The sports leagues of the *Tribal Ages* involved competition between nations or cities, and they were extremely politicized. Today, it is a competition between teams around the world and never confined to one territory or continent or hemisphere because zoning is unlawful in *distribia*. In other words, sports leagues and games of any kind are always global and involve humanity as a whole. This is natural, however, because in a world where there are no national borders or governments, any tournament of any kind automatically draws global participation. As a result, competitors are always traveling between different cities around the globe and competing. A resident sports team in one *sportblock* flies onboard the public skycars to another block somewhere else to compete with the local team in that block. Such match could be in the same city or somewhere else on the planet depending on the global schedule of such league.

Every variation of every game comes with only one tournament and one cup - the world cup. For example, football (also known as soccer or Fussball), which is the most loved and watched game on Earth, involves only one championship and it is the Football World Cup. Then there's a world cup for beach football (or beasal) and another one for futsal (a variant of football played on a hard court, smaller than a football pitch, and mainly indoors). Similarly, chess involves only one tournament, which is the Chess World Cup. Basketball has only one world cup, and same goes for rugby, cricket, tennis, volleyball, and every variation of every other game.

Distribia applied a universal qualification standard for all sports or games of all kinds where each team is randomly selected to play another team in a round of 3 games, and the winner from each round is randomly selected to challenge the winner from another round, and so on until there are only two winners left and one final round, which yields the ultimate winner. So, whether it is football or basketball or rugby or chess, there is always an even number of competitors randomly coupled with each other in rounds of 3 games until there's only one final round with a winner at the end. For each round, *Ve's* first random team pick gets to play on its home field whereas the second randomly selected team gets to travel. Each round ends either with a 2-0 or a 2-1 win, which means if a contender wins the first two games in the round it does not play the third game and automatically qualifies as the winner of that round. *Ve* announces the entire schedule of the rounds and the games within each round before the commencement of the tournament. The announcement usually takes places during the recess of the championships, which are always repetitive every 3 months.

All games never end with a tie, and there's always a protocol that guarantees a winner at the end which is different for every game. For example, the Football World Cup involves an additional time played with only 7 players on the field from each team instead of 11. Both the additional time and the original time of the game involves a countdown stoppage clock similar to basketball where time freezes immediately when the ball is not in play-mode and resumes instantly when it does. The reduction of players yields to a lot of empty spaces on the field which makes it easier for one of the teams to score a goal. The first team to score wins the game immediately in what is called the *"golden goal."* If this first extra time did not end with any win, the number of players on the field diminishes again to just 5 players on each side for another extra time. And if that didn't lead to a golden goal, the teams resort to penalty shootouts.

The idea of waiting a full year or sometimes 2 or even 4 years to watch your favorite team or competitors such as the Olympic athletes play again is considered very strange today, but in a tribal world where it was the norm to have a tiny group of people taking all the critical decisions on behalf of the majority, many things were odd. Thanks to having tournaments repeating every 3 months, if a team was disqualified in its first round and played only 2 or 3 games, it will still get the chance to participate and compete again after 3 months in the next run for the title. And since on average the tournaments are finalized within a month, every team will play a minimum of 6 games per year in 3-game seasons. This, of course, assumes that such team did not win any game, but the more games it wins, the more matches it plays per year.

All financial profits from every match always go straight to the winning team whether it is playing on its home ground or not. The profits include, of course, the ticket sales and the online streaming of the game whether watched live or ordered later in the future. The money goes directly from the customers (audience) to the winning contender. If the contender is a team of players, the money is distributed directly and proportionally to each player according to the shares of each in the team.

The referees of all sports or games of all kinds are the *Ve* identities of the players of the game and that of the live audience. *Ve* identities learned the rules of every game by watching all recorded games in every game's history and through billions of animated simulations of possible scenarios of play. The decisions during the games follow the 83% consensus of *Ve* identities of the people playing or watching the game, and such verdicts transpire in fractions of the second during the flow of the game. The announcements by the referees are made by all the involved *Ve* identities speaking collectively, which creates a voice that's truly spectacular and motivational during the game. Unlike traditional games with human referees, there can be no mistakes or bias with *Ve* referees, and they continuously evolve after every game.

Distribia's stadiums today are very interactive through screens, holograms, projectors, and lasers that track the motion of the ball or the contenders and announces the decisions of the virtual referees during the game being played. For example, in the case of Football, and if a player commits a foul, the lasers and projectors in the stadium highlight the player on the field by a circle that momentarily follows him with a visible indication of the foul he committed along with details about him projected on each side of the field. Another ring would highlight the location of the foul and where the game is supposed to resume.

As a universal standard in all tournaments of all kinds of sports, all the balls or other instruments used to play the games as well as all the uniforms of the players are distributed randomly to the crowd through a lottery and by announcing the lucky seat numbers during the game. Such practice is meant to engage with the masses and give people an extra reason to attend the games and cheer for their best players. The lucky winners are usually announced during the game where every winner's *Ve* privately notifies the person. The prizes are handed to the lucky winners shortly after the match after they're nicely packaged, or otherwise they're mailed to the winners' addresses.

Distribia's sports stadiums are spectacular because they are designed with beauty in mind and not just functionality. They are not made from concrete and steel anymore, but mainly from stone or wood that is always carved and molded in a beautiful way that resembles ancient Greek and Roman architecture such as Rome's Coliseum. Today's stadiums are designed to last for centuries and are even more beautiful when they age thanks to using natural material that capitalizes on long-term expectations. They are held today as art masterpieces because there is so much artistic detail and creativity that goes into building these structures, and they are constructed to impress their visitors to keep them coming back to enjoy the beautiful experience and charm of the place.

The stadiums are not zoned or isolated from the city by miles of concrete but are incorporated within a residential block and the surrounding natural landscape. Just like any other *distribian* city block, 4 blocks of parks surround each *sportblock* on its 4 sides, which traditionally used to be concrete parking lots in tribal cultures. And now that such parking lots are no more, the aerial views of today's stadiums are incomparably spectacular. The structure of every *sportblock* incorporates residential units, office spaces, and retail for goods and services like any other block of *distribian* cities. There are no dedicated gates for the crowd to pass through because every building in the *sportblock* that is part of the stadium is designed to accommodate the visitors through their elevators and stairways.

The 1st class residential units, which sit underneath the skyway station, are the traditional stadium's clubs or suites that allow residents to watch every game live from the comfort of their homes or their private balconies, which have the best seats in the house that look down to the field. Usually, the 1st class condos of a *sportblock* are reserved by the players of the local team because they prefer direct access to the field when training or during the world cup games.

The Access To The Outdoors Standard

Tribal cultures loved building underground and digging as deep as they could afford to create as many basements as possible to host either their cars or tunnels for their public transport systems. After all, they already conquered the atmosphere, space, the oceans and, therefore, it was inevitable in the natural course of the tribal state of affairs to subdue Earth's crust. Step into the subway in such cities during rush hour, and you'll find yourself gasping for clean air by the time you get to your destination. Such spaces rarely had direct access to the fresh air outdoors and instead relied on machinery to pump and exchange air with the underground structures.

With all the humidity and grime that builds up during rush hour as hundreds of thousands of people cram into trains, the seats served as the perfect breeding grounds for insects and bacteria. It wasn't surprising to find skin-borne bacteria, mold, and bugs infesting such places and hitchhiking on passing passengers or into their belongings to end up in their homes or offices. Such sites never see sunlight, and therefore it was completely normal that they yielded all sorts of health concerns to the public. It was a ubiquitous scene to witness colonies of rats in these tubes because they strive under such conditions. And like rats' colonies, you observe an endless flow of people rushing back and forth in these tubes fueling tribal economies and supporting tribal architecture.

As a building standard today, every room or corridors must have a window or an opening to the outdoors to allow both natural light and fresh air to get directly indoors. Such windows lead visual access directly to nature outside the structure and not to another room or corridor. The size of the window is relative to the size of the room, which means that for every square foot or meter in every room the architect must account for a relative space for windows or openings within the same room. Currently, the standard is a ratio of 1:7, which means for every 7 square meters of floor space, the architect must account for a minimum of one square meter in the same room for a window or an opening to the outside of the building.

Anywhere you stand inside any *distribian* structure, you'll always spot a window or a transparent surface that bestows visual access to the outside. Even the basements and the subway are designed in a way that lets natural light and air come straight in. Anywhere you stand in the subway you can always see through a translucent surface that leads your eyesight to the outside. Architects utilize several techniques to accomplish such standard. Some cellars are stretched by few centimeters from the exterior walls of the building to let light go into all underground places through glass ceilings while others use glass in the flooring of the open-air ground floor to allow sunlight penetration into the basement areas. And since architects are not allowed to build more than one level below the ground's surface, there are always plenty of tactics to achieve the access-to-outdoors standard.

The subway isn't entirely buried underground like it used to be in the cities of tribal cultures. Today, the ceiling of the underpass is the street that pedestrians walk onto between the blocks of the community. These ceilings are covered with transparent surfaces to allow natural light to get into the tube and naturally disinfect all areas. It is extremely rare for someone to stand in any spot in the subway and look around without clearly noticing a window to the outside. The entire structure is designed to ensure such thing never happens and that people can always look at the outside no matter where they are in the metro and the same applies to any other structure of any kind.

Since every floor of every building hosts only one condo by default, all rooms are readily embraced with windows to allow sunlight and natural air to every indoor space. And since every apartment always comes with a balcony as a standard where usually such terraces engulf the entire floor, getting natural fresh air indoors is never a problem. In fact, thanks to the windows the engulf all condos in every building, an excellent stream of fresh air swirls through every room no matter the direction of the wind. *Distribian* structures have the perfect indoor climate, ideal ventilation, and the right indoor humidity. Today's ventilation systems create natural and healthy airflow throughout the building, which is designed to push to push the hot air upwards through the chimneys. Curling channels made of stone or metal engulf the exterior of the basement of each building to exchange air from the street level and cool it using the temperature of the underground before circulating it across the building and releasing it through the chimneys. Such natural airflow flushes out carbon dioxide and toxins from the building and keeps indoor spaces healthy. It is a type of ventilation already used by nature such as the case of termite mound colonies.

When a colored material absorbs light, it turns the light into thermal energy or heat. The more light a color absorbs, the more thermal energy it produces. A black-colored material absorbs all colors of light and is, therefore, warmer than a white-colored material which reflects more light. Thus, in warm climates, *distribian* cities use bright colors to help reflect as much light as possible and reduce the thermal gain. And likewise, in cold climates, the urban scene changes as *distribian* cities use darker colors to absorb more light and warm up their buildings in the process. In warm climates, the rooftops are always white, and they are commonly made up from a material that doesn't absorb heat to prevent warming up the building. Similarly, in cold climates, the ceilings have the kind of content that absorbs heat to warm up the building.

Ultimately, *distribian* architecture is a dialog between nature and structure. It adapts to the surrounding landscape which makes the urban scenery in every territory beautifully distinctive.

Public Toilets In Every Building As An Architectural Standard

In tribal cities before *distribia*, you could buy all kinds of foods and drinks, hear magnificent music and delight in crowd-watching, but you would be hard-pressed to find one essential thing – a public toilet. The urban developers of the dysfunctional cities of tribal cultures behaved as if urination, defecation, and menstruation are not routine bodily functions, but are somehow optional for people away from their homes. They designed, constructed and maintained public spaces such as roads, sidewalks, and parks, but acted as if people using those spaces would never need to use a toilet.

From a purely physical needs perspective, the millions of people who had bladder or bowel control problems could not confidently leave their homes unless they know toilets will be available. They had to plan their activities or schedules around their toileting needs. Inability to find or use toilets when outside home also has implications for bladder, bowel or kidney health when people are forced to *"hold on,"* or can result in embarrassing accidents. Incontinence (or lack of voluntary control over urination or defecation) is a problem that many people suffer from and it has a profound effect on their social and psychological well-being.

Public toilets are particularly essential as the population ages, and more and more people live with chronic health conditions. Some health issues affect bodily functions, including diabetes, colorectal cancer, irritable bowel syndrome, prostatitis, shingles, stroke, and dementia, not to mention the natural needs of children, pregnant women, menstruating women and anyone with a bladder or a colon.

Tribal cities relied primarily on people using the bathrooms of private businesses when they had to go. However, not everyone was welcomed, particularly those who are homeless, and most stores limited access to customers. Essential bodily functions should not necessitate a commercial transaction – not any more so than walking on a sidewalk. In a tribal culture, however, such practice was the norm. They spent billions of dollars to build kilometers of roads, and they also paid to clear them of snow and fill potholes. They policed streets to ensure that people weren't speeding or defacing road signs. Building and maintaining roads for cars was considered an unquestionable necessity and a legitimate expense, but having public toilets was deemed a superfluous luxury in tribal cities.

We do know that the lack of public toilets can result in social isolation and create difficulties for daily life particularly for the large proportion of the population with continence issues. Broader consequences are low self-esteem, depression, and loneliness. For all these reasons, in *distribia* today we have public toilets in every structure as a building standard. You can find these toilets in dedicated rooms on the street level of every building. There is also no gender segregation in *distribia*, and these toilets serve everyone and all sexes. The toilets are automated and self-cleaning after every use through various technologies including UV light cleansing and *sirvirbots*.

Having public toilets in every building is a priority standard of the housing *smartcontract* because it is essential for tourists who are discovering the city and are always on the move. They are also necessary for each block's residents especially the elderly or those with health issues so that they can do their business without needing to head back home every time they need to use a toilet.

Forest Cemeteries Within Every City As An Urban Standard

The business of death became highly lucrative as the cost of dying rose in cities across the tribal world. Tribal communities were intentionally designed to get easily overpopulated so that urban developers could raise dwelling prices for profit. And such artificially manufactured overpopulation is not limited only to the living but also extends to the dead. Dysfunctional cities around the world eventually reached the point where there was no place left for the populace to bury their dead.

Artificially ballooning the price of anything always starts with one key factor: limiting supply. And when the supply of any physical thing is limited, its value gradually increases as demand rises. Therefore, when urban developers set boundaries to the size of a city on the map, they artificially limit the supply of space available for building structures leading eventually to a lot of demand on a limited supply which inescapably raises prices.

In a tribal culture, urban planners and developers focused overwhelmingly on making money out of accommodating the living and stretched their profit margin as well to include the dead by profiting off the caretakers of the dead through land barrier costs. Cemeteries and columbaria (burial vaults) dating back hundreds of years retained an iconic place in tribal towns and cities but due to their limited profitability compared to housing the living, developers avoided developing the land as graveyards in favor of residential buildings. Such practice meant that metropolises the world over were running out of room to house their dead.

Some tribal cultures practiced grave recycling, which involves reusing the same graveyard for new burials after some years. It is a system that has worked efficiently for cities all over the world, particularly in Europe. But in countries where grave reuse is not the cultural norm, attempts to begin reusing graveyard plots have faced resistance and accusations that such practice violates religious and cultural traditions. Even cities that did practice grave recycling eventually ran into problems. In some areas, concerns about sanitation and the risk of soil contamination led to policies stipulating that all bodies be wrapped in plastic before burial. Years later, they found that the remains were not decomposing quickly enough in the plastic bags to allow the graves to be reused. Although it is evident to most people at the time that plastic is a material that does not naturally decompose until after hundreds of years, which means that wrapping human remains in plastic will likewise prevent them from decaying efficiently. Shortsightedness, however, is a trait of all tribal cultures and it is not a surprising thing. After eventually realizing the problem, they resorted to injecting the graves with a lime solution to speed up decomposition or in other words to solve a problem that they created in the first place. This solution, of course, came with its own set of issues which a tribal culture typically solved with other problematic solutions and established a pattern of propagating difficulties that usually never ends.

In cultures where cremation is a strict cultural norm, the lack of space and the need for a site where families could pay respects to their deceased led to the invention of large mechanized columbaria, where thousands of urns were stored in a vault and could be retrieved with an electronic card. These public columbaria probably seemed a good solution in the beginning, but they nevertheless came in limited supply and naturally prices inflated until average citizens could afford them no more. With space running out in all cities around the tribal world, the business of death became highly lucrative and *"storing the dead"* became more and more of a niche product or market. The burial issue was not just about economics, but it was a lot about capital, capitalism, and the commodification involved. In most tribal cities that were amid the scramble to accommodate burial space, those who were still able to find and purchase a private grave usually paid tens of thousands of dollars for the privilege. Alternatively, there was an average 5-year wait for a small spot in a public columbarium, which stored thousands of urns of cremated ashes. Other cultures practiced burying the dead in multiple layers beneath the ground, in the style of the Victorians.

Some cities designed off-shore columbarium islands, which could hold hundreds of thousands of urns at sea. Others built cemetery skyscrapers that would reach hundreds of meters into the sky and include spaces for coffins, urns, a crematorium and a computerized memorial wall. In Japan, descendants could make online visits to virtual graveyards where they can pour virtual water or light a virtual incense stick, instead of traveling the long distance to visit a grave in person. Hong Kong's government went a step further, creating a social-media network of virtual tombs aimed at families who had been forced to cremate their relatives' ashes because of lack of space in the city, and so no longer had a physical space at which to pay their respects.

Burying the dead in public vertical graveyards is a relatively recent invention, and it started in the 18th century in cities where nature imposed it. For example, New Orleans, which is unique in so many ways, is a city built on a swamp. Due to its location, the residents had to bury their dead above ground in elaborate stone crypts and mausoleums or otherwise the land would just spit them out after each flood. Over time the cemeteries, with intricate sculptures and other decorative artwork embellishing the tombs, had come to resemble small villages and were nicknamed *"cities of the dead."* These cemeteries were owned and run by the Catholic Church, which kept a record of all those buried there. The overall average cost that people had to pay to bury their dead reached $10,000 putting it effectively beyond the means of a significant portion of the dwellers of the city, which was historically known for its high death rate. Due to the deliberate high-cost burials, space was reserved for the clergy and the wealthy or the distinguished of the city. As for the poor, the wealthy discriminated against them even in death. The poor were buried together in bulk in shared unmarked graves until the middle 1800's, and as available space filled, layers of bones several feet thick started to pile up in each grave. All those who could not afford a private tomb had the option of wall vaults, which were constructed directly into the walls surrounding the cemetery and resembled old-time baker's ovens.

The wall vaults quite literally slowly cooked the corpses and allowed people to reuse them by throwing more dead people into these ovens every number of years after the heat had already reduced the bodies of the previous occupants into ashes. These wall vaults were used to house the dead for an entire family line. Whenever a family member dies, the family renting the wall vault pushed the remains of the previous dead dweller all the way to the back of the vault to make room for the current deceased. Walking on the road next to any New Orleans cemetery in that period one quite literally passes by piles of corpses stacked on top each other while being slowly baked behind a thin wall of stone. They were in the walls, and they were housed all around.

Distribians pondered the role cemeteries play in our cities, and what it would mean if we lost them altogether. Graveyards were unpopular places for people to walk around because the entire site of stones sticking out of the ground with people's names carved on them was undoubtedly disturbing. Instead of sticking dead stones in the ground and writing deceased people's names on them, today we replaced these stones with beautiful flourishing trees. *Distribia* transformed graveyards from disturbing areas, which the public historically avoided, into beautiful parks that celebrate life and beauty. Today, every city has at least one park dedicated for burying the dead. The park is divided like a chessboard with squares that are equally partitioned into 3-meter hollow boxes slightly buried under the surface. For each burial, a vacant square is dug, the coffin is buried there, and a small tree is planted on top in the middle of the square. Since there are no stones to designate the location where a person was buried, the plot of the square is marked digitally with map coordinates, so the family of the deceased can efficiently locate the tree that represents the person's grave. When the tree is large enough, some families chose to carve the name of the deceased on the tree along with wishful words or prayers.

The species of trees also depends on the climate and on the territory. Each cemetery park uses a different species of trees, and usually, priority is given to those that live the longest. Pines are a prevalent selection in such parks because they are long-lived, and typically reach ages of more than a thousand years. Some architects use a new breed of pines that is a hybrid between traditional pines and flowering trees. The resulting species can release a strong sweet fragrance and drop colorful foliage debris throughout the year. Such new varieties of pines are also the fastest-growing, and they typically follow a growth rate of more than half a meter per year (or around 2 feet per year).

Today's coffins are biodegradable caskets made of anything from cardboard to banana leaves to bamboo or hemp or any other option among a wide range of choices. While an increasing number of people today opt for *"green burials,"* some still chose to be cremated. The local hospital in each block is used for the storage of human corpses awaiting identification or removal for autopsy or respectful burial, cremation or other methods. This process takes place entirely within one building, which hosts the neighborhood's hospital. As for the expenses, the UBI of the deceased entirely covers the burial costs and no further fees are incurred by his family or friends.

A tree planted in someone's memory is a living tribute that benefits present and future generations and is perhaps the most fitting memorial ritual of all. We plant trees instead of concrete stones in remembrance and honor of our loved ones because we cherish nature. Now we pay tribute to our friends and loved ones while at the same time replanting our planet's forests and in so doing ensuring an eternal plan to counter deforestation forever. Memorial trees planted in such blocks are honorable monuments and active participants in nature's plan for decades to come.

TRANSPORTATION

In ancient times, simple tools such as foot coverings, skis, and snowshoes lengthened the distances that could be traveled. Humans carrying goods created the first earth tracks and often followed trails. Roads naturally formed at points of high traffic density. The domestication of horses, oxen and camel signaled a significant innovation in transport decreasing travel time and increasing the ability to move more and more substantial loads. These animals became an element in larger track-creation. With the growth of trade, these tracks widened with the more extensive traffic flattening more surface area along the route. Thanks to domesticating animals and using them for travel, people could travel farther and could carry much more items with them. The speed at which humans could move raised to that of a horse.

Wheels were first created to serve as a potter's wheels, which is around 300 years before someone figured out to use them for chariots. Additionally, several significant inventions predated the wheel by thousands of years such as sewing needles, woven cloth, rope, basket weaving, boats and even the flute.

Traditionally, coastal cities were more prosperous and populated than inland territories for one main reason: transportation was historically much more straightforward and faster on water than on land. Heavy loads were mainly transported using boats, which explains why humanity preferred building its communities in coastal areas. Cities with access to water trading routes could trade enormous amounts of goods with other coastal towns, which meant more wealth and cultural mixing. Landlocked towns, on the other hand, were limited to land trade routes only, which tended to be slower and costly. Rivers, lakes and the sea magnified trade and overwhelmed the population of coastal cities with the necessary resources to grow and expand faster than landlocked settlements. When humanity finally invented the wheel to serve in animal-drawn vehicles, transport of goods inwards and away from coastal cities increased. Paved roads provided efficient means for the overland movement of people and the inland carriage of official communications and trade goods.

With the invention of the car during the industrial revolution, modern highways started to appear using an inexpensive paving material of soil and stone aggregate. The development of motor transport came with an increased need for hard-topped roads to reduce wash-aways, bogging and dust on both urban and rural roads. Initially, they used cobblestones and wooden paving in major Western cities and the early 20th century tarmac and concrete paving were extended into the countryside. Rail transport systems first appeared in Europe in the 1820s. These systems, which made use of the steam locomotive, were the first practical form of mechanized land transport, and they remained the primary form of mechanized land transport for the next 100 years.

The Subway

Electric vehicles were first built in the mid-19th century when electricity was among the preferred methods of motor vehicle propulsion. It provided a level of comfort and ease of operation that could not be achieved by the gasoline cars of the time. Although internal combustion engines were the dominant propulsion method for over a century, electric power remained commonplace in other vehicle types such as trains and smaller vehicles. In the early 21st century, electric cars saw a resurgence due to technological developments and an increased focus on renewable energy. A key advantage of electric vehicles is regenerative braking due to their capability to recover energy frequently lost during braking. Electric cars convert this energy into electricity and store it in the batteries onboard.

Today, all land vehicles including cars, vans, buses, trucks, trains, and trams merged in a single mass transportation system that is enclosed underground in a subway system. City streets are claimed solely by pedestrians to roam freely anywhere and in any direction with no sidewalks or traffic lights and without fear of being rammed by speeding metal. This subway is hidden from sight and concealed just one floor underground where only its ceiling is visible on the surface and used as a boulevard by pedestrians to move around uninterrupted between the blocks of a city. It is the line that defines the chessboard-like urban design of all neighborhoods everywhere. The subway grid doubles as foundation for the city blocks and merges with the walls of the buildings in the blocks it passes through. People access the subway through the stairways and elevators of the buildings along its path. Additionally, the subway's ventilation system consists of the ones in the stairwells and elevators of the buildings attached to it.

The subway has five lanes where one is used as a pedestrian sidewalk for people to hop on or hop off the public cars, followed by one used for parking, and lastly the 3-lane path for speeding cars. Traffic direction around each block is oriented clockwise along one-way roads. This traffic law means that cars can only turn right if they want to change course, which provides additional coverage for picking up potential passengers around each block. Unlike traditional subways, this new version doesn't have any infrastructure to it other than the concrete walls of the tube and the electric charging stations. It is just a hollow rectangular tube encapsulating wheeled electric vehicles transiting along its path.

The subway involves three types of transport. All subway cars generally look like rectangular boxes on wheels that are almost flat with the ground's surface because they sit on a multi-wheeled platform, which contains the batteries along with a network of electric engines built into the wheels. And since these cars never leave the flat surface of the subway, they are purposely built to be very low to the ground. The ceiling of all types of subway cars is high enough for people to step in upright and stand in front of their seat before sitting down comfortably on the spacious recliner chairs.

A type-3 subway car is the basic version and involves electric buses dedicated only for ridesharing. The buses are crossbreeds of traditional trains, trams, and buses. These buses are used for mass transport to move people from one block to another or between neighboring cities. The comfort inside today's version, however, is unparalleled because while commuters were traditionally crammed shoulder-to-shoulder on mostly plastic seats, today's buses contain large and comfortable recliner chairs with two armrests for each chair. Each chair has a dedicated screen for entertainment attached to it turning such buses into lounges and enhancing the overall travel experience. Each chair can spin in any direction allowing passengers to face each other or align sideways or even sit opposite to the transparent side of the bus to enjoy the view of the sidewalk and its greenwall. All cars, whether in the skyway or the subway or the waterway, have recliner chairs that can spin around in any direction with enough legroom and overhead space to stand up or comfortably turn the seats around during the ride.

A type-3 car is the subway's cheapest mode of travel with a constant universal fare worldwide unlike the other car types of the subway which involve fluctuating surge prices depending on supply and demand. The fare is calculated based on distance traveled. However, the amount paid by passengers depends on the total number of passengers on board during the trip. If you hopped on a bus that had no passengers on board throughout your trip, all the cost of that ride falls on you alone. This fee, however, is still less than type-2 car taken alone. If, however, the bus was half-full, the price of that portion of the journey is divided equally among those on board at the time. So, taking the bus is way cheaper than the other options in the subway, and it only costs a fraction of a coin on average. Buses have the most capacity with ten comfortable chairs in two rows. Today's subway cars aren't designed for standing passengers because everyone should have a seat. Also, when a bus stops for commuters to hop on/off, the entire side of the bus facing the sidewalk opens upwards for the passengers to readily leave or take their seats so that there can be no queue while entering or exiting the bus.

Due to its larger capacity, buses are used extensively in events such as football games and concerts to prevent queues or congestion. Typically, a *sportblock* is serviced only by busses as the time of the ongoing event comes to an end.

Just like most traditional subway trains before *distribia*, buses simply travel in straight lines back and forth like a typical train. They move at a constant speed, and they arrive at their pickup locations in every block at a regular frequency of no more than 1 minute. This means that no matter which block you're at in the world, you'll always expect an electric bus to appear and pick you up within a 1-minute interval.

The rooftops of the buses are always transparent to allow natural light to come down from the subway's transparent ceiling or take advantage of the LED lighting of the tube at night and save energy in the process. This concept is the same for all cars in the subway.

Type-2 cars are much shorter vehicles that resemble traditional sedan cars but with the significant difference of having a ceiling that is high enough for you to stand in front of your seat while in the car. These cars only have four seats on board in two rows with two doors on each side that open upwards or sideways. They also have a fifth door on the back for storing passengers' luggage, but the space in front of each seat is spacious enough for passengers to have their luggage in front of them unless they wish to recline the seat and be comfortable. All these entries are operated by *Ve* to minimize touching of surfaces along the subway system. Due to their 4-passenger capacity, type-2 cars offer a less waiting time for passengers than buses. These vehicles, however, can be requested solo for passengers who prefer traveling alone. Additionally, type-2 cars operate at faster speeds than buses and include fewer stops in case of ride-shares adding the advantage of reaching destinations faster with less or no interruptions. Type-2 vehicles also receive road priority over the bus and operate on the second fastest lane in the subway. Type-2 cars come with much more comfortable and better-quality seats with warming and cooling functions. These seats can rotate in any direction allowing the passengers to face each other if they want to or face the sidewalk while in transit. Screens built into the seats can be used by passengers to watch on demand or for making video calls. The mix of comfort, convenience, and speed equate to higher costs for this mode of travel compared to type-3 cars.

Type-1 is the top service the architects deliver. Type-1 cars are more spacious from the inside and come with four seats, but the quality and comfort exceed that of type-2 cars. They can also be ordered solo or shared. Additionally, they operate at the fastest speeds of all subway cars and get cruise priority on the quickest path of the 3-laned subway. This combination makes them the best option for those in a hurry to reach their destination and do not want to take the skyway. Lastly, type-1 cars offer shots of a variety of alcoholic and non-alcoholic beverages for each of its four seats.

These liquids come from cartridges in the trunk and serviced by the company that produces these drinks and not the car manufacturer. Although the subway has vending machines along the sidewalks for passing foot traffic, type-1 cars have the added benefit of ordering drinks while in transit.

Type-1 and 2 of subway cars follow an on-demand scheme. They don't require pre-booking, and people can just head down the tube and pick any car parked along the sidewalk if they're going solo or wait a bit to join a ride-share. The fees are time-based and variable according to supply and demand, surge hours, vehicle's class, and whether the ride was solo or shared. When more people are making ride requests, prices get higher to maintain proper traffic conditions along the subway and prevent congestion. People usually wait till after the surge to request car rides for unurgent travels, and some might take the bus instead. Buses do not involve fluctuating surge prices and always maintain the same standard fee worldwide.

The public transport systems under authoritarian governments were dull and lifeless whereas today's version involves colorful cars that are distinctive and unique. They are beautiful to look at because they're built with beauty in mind in tandem with functionality and efficiency. No vehicle is like the next, and you'd never know what beautiful masterpiece you'll find by the side of the road on your next ride. All types of vehicles in the subway come in different designs limited only by the manufacturers' imagination and by the elected *smartcontract* that regulates such transport. You can see models such as the slick and sporty, the bulky, the classy, the vintage and classic, and especially the themed cars inspired by movies. Some are covered with mosaic or painted by talented artists who turn them into gems and eye-candy. Others are beautifully molded and carved to become sculptures on wheels. And the scene changes from one city to another because every community has its unique character, which manifests itself in the designs of the cars in its subway and even in the colors used on roads.

All the cars on the highway are aware of each other, and they communicate with each other regularly, slowing down and accelerating depending on traffic conditions. The cars navigate on this subway autonomously through *Ve*, which distributes them across each neighborhood in a manner that maintains a delicate balance between the supply and demand. *Ve* is aware of the upcoming arrivals and parking spaces available at each street, and it distributes parked cars to a nearby road if the parking lane is approaching full capacity to make space for arriving cars. *Ve* can also decelerate approaching cars to a busy street to create an equilibrium between the speed of arriving and departing cars. In cases when a lane is extremely busy, income traffic is redirected to the next less busy streets instead. Cars always park sideways parallel to the sidewalk, and only the door to that side of the road opens to allow people in and out.

The subway invites natural light inside the structure from the lightweight transparent surfaces scattered throughout its ceiling allowing sunlight to penetrate and provide heat and light to the tube. The transparent surface, which of course is packed with photovoltaic cells, as well as the photovoltaic paint along the subway's boulevard provide all the electricity needs of the tube for wirelessly charging the cars when they park by the sidewalk.

The subway encapsulating each residential and park block is the property of the architecture company that built the neighborhood. Architects are entirely responsible for maintaining the structure including the battery cells and the charging stations in their portion of the metro. The metro cars fast charge wirelessly when they park sideways along the parking lane and each car manufacturer pays the architects for the energy they used in their neighborhoods.

Hopping on a car is done on a first-come-first-served model to prevent the idle time of vehicles waiting for their passengers to arrive and to increase the overall efficiency of the subway grid. The subway comes with a maximum ratio of one car per home or three vehicles per building in each neighborhood. The architects of each neighborhood in every city are responsible for manufacturing the cars of their neighborhood. Servicing and maintaining the subway cars is, of course, the architects' responsibility. As a standard, a neighborhood's service center is always built adjacent to the subway's route to quickly deploy or retrieve defective cars from the tube.

Greenwalls throughout the structure of the subway cover its walls on both sides to maintain fresh and healthy air quality and of course to add a beautifying effect. A trip along the path of a *distribian* subway is almost like a beautiful journey in the forest because you're surrounded by colorful flowers on both sides that captivate you with their splendor. The delicious essence that propagates from the subway's greenwalls can be mesmerizing because it fills up the structure and doesn't escape easily with the wind. You can always find people jogging around the block in the subway whether in rainy conditions above or not because it is a genuinely gorgeous experience one gets while passing through the tube and, therefore, it is understandable to walk or jog in the subway without any intentions for taking a car.

As mentioned earlier in previous chapters, the subway's ceiling is the boulevard that shapes the chessboard-like design of the blocks of all *distribian* cities. This grid-like boulevard is the main street network where people move on the surface from one city block to another. You can find people there walking, jogging or biking or using the many variants of public electric scooters available for hire that park themselves autonomously along the sides of all boulevards. These dockless scooters come in countless designs and patterns limited only by the manufacturers' imagination. The most popular of which is the *traveldisk*, which is an electric and autonomous multi-wheeled 1-meter disk. A person's *Ve* operates the *traveldisk*, which responds either to voice commands or hand gestures while in route. *Traveldisks* can also become semiautonomous to allow for travelers more control over navigating a *traveldisk* throughout their trip if they choose to use such functionality. There are infinite ways to maneuver a *traveldisk*, and you can teach your *Ve* to follow your custom-made controls. A person, for example, can teach his/her *Ve* to respond to a specific pattern of hand gestures to accelerate, stop, or turn the *traveldisk* left or right.

Traveldisks can travel at a maximum speed equal to the average running speed of a human being. You can call a *traveldisk* through your *Ve* to come to pick you up no matter where you are in the city. You then stand on it, and it would navigate you along the route to the destination you have in mind. When you reach your destination, you just hope off, and it sits there waiting for the next passenger or heads back to the boulevards autonomously to park and charge wirelessly on the sides in an orderly fashion.

The 1-meter *traveldisk* is wide enough for people to stand comfortably on it and some also prefer to sit on it while in transit. *Traveldisks* can also climb stairs seamlessly while remaining upright and there's usually one waiting at the end or the top of every stairway to help people come up or down a building without using the elevator. You can also request one to go to your apartment and pick you up to go on a ride in the city wherever you want. They can also stack on top of each other autonomously forming a tall pile and wait near a stairway or a street corner if there is considerable foot-traffic in the area or significant demand.

Distribia considers transportation as a service, and since it is the standard in a *distribian* society to have three levels of service or product, the next two higher-end versions of the *traveldisk* involve a comfy recliner chair on a multi-wheeled platform. As the description suggests, these two types of the *traveldisk* are called *travelchairs*. A type-1 *travelchair* comes with more features, comfort, and speed than the other two versions of the *traveldisk*. It is a prevalent option of travel around the city especially with the elderly. Of course, these *travelchairs* are semi or completely autonomous and operated by the *Ve* of the person sitting on them. People just tell their *Ve* where to go through voice or hand gestures, and it complies. Therefore, there's no threat to pedestrians or the animals that roam the cities when these wheeled chairs are wandering around the blocks.

The Skyway

The airline industry before *distribia* practiced consolidation and centralization in its designs and operations. Tribal nations, although covering vast areas of land, typically had less than a handful of airports from which commercial planes could operate within each country. As a result, airports were naturally bursting at the seams with airplanes, which were congesting the air above such central airports.

The increase in the number of flyers along with the airlines' strategic shift towards increasing the frequency of flights, meant more planes and more passengers. This reality resulted in crowded airport terminals and an increase in the number of delays. At no time was the peril of this strategy more exposed than when the weather goes bad. Snow or thunderstorms meant moderate delays and perhaps a cancellation or two. But half an inch of powder or a line of cumulonimbus brings the entire system to its knees. Weather, however, is very regional and while one city could be battling a thunderstorm or strong winds, another town just a few kilometers away could be enjoying blue skies and zero winds. Such reality meant that people who drove long distances from areas with excellent weather might be surprised to realize that their flight was either delayed or canceled because the area around the airport is experiencing severe weather.

Due to its central design, the airline industry had been a magnet for terrorist threats that were orchestrated by individuals who sought to cause as many fatalities as possible. And since airports are typically crowded with people who are drawn from all sorts of places to such central locations of transport, they could be easily targeted. Authoritarian central governments solved such a problem, which they created, by stealing people's liberty for a false sense of security. They developed security screening procedures that became increasingly stringent as terrorism increased. This naturally resulted in more extended checkpoint wait times and complaints from the traveling public due to the discomfort and invasion of privacy they generated.

In many respects, the industry's search for greater profitability was the detriment of passenger comfort. For investors, the lower the unit costs, the better. For airlines, an effective way to reach that target is to stuff more seats into each plane. Also, airlines became much more disciplined when it comes to flooding the market with additional flights. The capacity discipline along with a higher number of seats per plane resulted in full planes with less room for individual passengers. Riding in such airplanes, one feels like a canned fish in a can of sardines. Airlines continually crammed more rows onto each plane while passengers lost nearly imperceptible centimeters and inches with every seat added. They narrowed armrests and purposely used harder seats that are designed for sitting upright so to restrain people within the tiniest footprint possible throughout the flight. In a typical economy seat, the average human skeleton doesn't comfortably fit unless one sits up and keeps hands and arms folded forward into one's lap. A person in a window seat could not get up and walk around without disturbing his/her neighbors because one can barely pass a newspaper in front of his/her knees.

Airplanes were large and heavy machines carrying hundreds of passengers using likewise large and heavy fuel-thirsty engines. Such engines typically led to fume events when toxic smoke or odors found their way into the cabin. Such poisonous fume events were able to result in immediate incapacitation, have a long-term adverse impact, and affect everyone on board. As for the environment, airplanes continuously emitted particles and gases such as carbon dioxide, hydrocarbons, carbon monoxide, nitrogen oxides, sulfur oxides, lead, and black carbon which interact among themselves and with the atmosphere contributing to climate change and global dimming.

With the rise of *distribia*, which inherently prohibits centralization and consolidation, the airline industry changed forever. It democratized the industry and distributed it to every building to entirely abolish centralized airports. Today, the favorite mode of transport is a crossbreed between the car, helicopter, and the aircraft. It is a sky travel option involving self-driven flying cars, called skycars. These skycars follow random paths in the sky directed by *Ve*, called skyway, which is not a *"sky highway"* but is completely random just like the web's ad-hoc topology. Skycars simply head straight where the passengers need to go without following any usual flight patterns or pathways, and by just taking the fastest route to the destination or the one with the optimal flying conditions.

Every elevator and stairway in every building on Earth takes straight to the skyway station on the last floor, and they are accessible to residents of the building as well as the public directly from street level or subway level. The last floor of every building in the world serves as a waiting area for hopping on/off the skycars.

There's a minimum ratio of three skycars per building. The skycars' wings fold allowing them to park on the last floor of every building in three lanes just like an old-style land car. Passengers get in and out of a skycar from the sides just like they do for subway cars. The platforms where these skycars park on elevate them to the rooftop to act as a take-off pad. The skycar parking usually has a folding roof that opens when a skycar is being elevated and shuts to become a landing pad itself for passing skycars to drop passengers on the building. With this system, three local skycars can be parked in the skyway station while three others can land on the rooftop to drop incoming passengers or packages. However, the architects of the neighborhood get to decide eventually on the design of their skyway system for as long as they abide by the minimum ratio of three skycars per building and the other standards of skyway travel.

From the inside, a skycar is almost identical to a subway car. Unlike the subway, the skyway service is for lightweight transport and involves a maximum capacity of four passengers. The main reason for this is technical. In the same way that terrestrial animals tend to be heavy and big while birds are generally lightweight, skycars are designed to be lightweight vehicles for use in short or medium range air travel. The skyway also follows a *"taxi pool"* type of service where passengers traveling a relatively long distances on the same path hop on the same skycar, which stops along the way for new passengers in other neighborhoods that are heading the same way or along the route. Pooling a skycar happens only during long distance travel because these cars move between the neighborhoods of a city very fast, and it won't make sense from a time perspective to spend the same duration of your trip waiting for new passengers to come on board along your way. That's why skycar pooling is only possible for trips that are 17 minutes long or more.

Ve entities operate and direct the traffic of the skyway grid. As mentioned earlier, devices are dead without the *Ve* identities sitting inside them. There's an allocation for only four *Ve* identities in the microprocessor of each skycar in the grid. When you order a solo ride in a skycar, your *Ve* reserves all four allocations for you alone throughout the duration of the trip. Of course, there's a price rate for each allocation and it would cost more to reserve all 4 seats to ride solo. That's why most people choose to share rides instead of reserving them solo specially in skyway travel because it is the most expensive means of transport.

The skyway is an on-demand service, meaning you don't schedule skycars, but you just show up and pick one up when you arrive at the station. And since there's no physical queue in *distribia*, your *Ve* stands in the line virtually for you so that by the time you reach the station you'll have a seat reserved for you in the soonest skycar to depart. The skyway station is just for in-and-out, and no booking or scheduling takes place there at all because it is all done in the background by every person's *Ve* before arriving. You just speak to your *Ve* and tell it which class of skycar you wish to use this time and where you wish to go, and by the time you take the elevator and access the skyway station, your *Ve* would've taken care of everything on your behalf so that you're on the soonest skycar to depart. These kinds of transactions are almost *"subconscious"* between the human and his/her *Ve* because the latter knows the travel preferences and autonomously makes decisions for its human without necessitating verbal communication. For example, if someone always chooses an economy skycar, his/her *Ve* adapts to that and doesn't bother him/her to ask such thing the next time he/she travels because a *Ve* already knows its human's preferences. After all, your *Ve* has a library of all the things that you like whether it is books, or movies, how you want to be spoken to, favorite places or the places you visit frequently, and the whole point of a *Ve* is to be a copy of you in the virtual world so that such copy can assist you like no one else can.

Inside a skycar, each person's *Ve* answers to him/her privately and it is one of the four pilots flying the skycar. If you have anything to ask regarding the flight you simply ask your *Ve* and if you had a sudden change of plans, you just tell it to drop you off at the nearest neighborhood. Controlling the skycars in the air, however, is a collaborative work involving synced decisions by all *Ve* identities in all the skycars. While in the air, *Ve* identities fly the skycars together and their decisions are synced as one collective system.

The skyway is a more expensive mode of transport than the subway or the waterway, and it also involves surge prices depending on supply and demand. Additionally, there are three categories of skycar rides, and they come with an escalating price tag:

> Type-3 is the economy version, and it comes with the least price tag.
> Type-2 is the premium kind and comes with an elevated level of comfort, service, and speed.
> Type-1 is the luxury kind and comes with the most advanced facilities, top comfort and speed.

So, when you order a skycar, you need to specify the type of service you want and whether you want to share a ride or travel solo. Ridesharing divides the cost of the ride evenly across all passengers who shared the same distance with you. For example, if you pick a ride-share and hop on a skycar that has no passengers initially but then one passenger joins part of your route, you incur the total price of the ride when you were alone plus half of the cost of when the other passenger was onboard. It is very common for some people to ask their *Ve* to share their travel plans with the *Ve* of other potential passengers so that they could book all four seats of the skycar together and share the cost of a short trip if they are heading to the same neighborhood. Such practice is more like a cheat because, as mentioned earlier, ridesharing with strangers is officially only possible for trips that are 17 minutes long or more. This means that if the flight is shorter than 17 minutes, the skycar is only supposed to stop once during that trip. So, the passenger's *Ve* figures out a common station that is close to everyone's destination, and from there the hitchhikers go on separate ways and either walk or use the subway or waterway to reach the destination they intended to go to initially. However, if you are sharing a skycar and traveling a long distance, there's a chance that your skycar might automatically stop multiple times according to a protocol along the path in the cities it flies over for as long as there's an empty seat to fill.

One key advantage of the skyway over other modes of transports is its ability to carry people to exactly the building or location to which they intend to travel. The subway and waterway on the other hand can only pick up and transport people along the peripherals of a neighborhood and not to the inner buildings of a block or a rural location.

Skycars are lightweight vehicles around the same size of a traditional car. They are entirely electric and charge while in midair using *solarpaint* or through a cable while they're docked at a skyway station. They are designed for short or medium trips because *distribians* typically prefer short or medium distance travel and stop intermittently in cities along the path to enjoy a nice meal or walk or use a bathroom.

At night, the skycars flying overhead our cities are a spectacle of beautiful and colorful lights that is breathtaking to behold and admire. Each skycar emits a different color using LED lighting across its surface to create an impressive light show in the sky as they orbit in the atmosphere. And the best part about this art show is that it serves an essential purpose, which is to transmit the internet to entire cities using onboard LiFi routers. Yes, skycars are our internet satellites in the sky.

As for the noise, skycars are incredibly silent, and you only get to notice them if you're standing on a balcony and a skycar was landing on the same building. The residents inside any structure cannot hear them at all because the walls of *distribia's* buildings are designed to be thick to comply with the passive design standard, which naturally restricts any outside noise. Engineers employ diverse techniques to make skycars silent that involves the design or shape of the blades, the material, and motors that help reduce the blade-vortex interaction.

The Waterway

The waterway exists only along the coastlines of the cities. It always comes attached to the subway route along the blocks that fall on the waterfront. It is the second-best mode of transport after the skyway. People prefer it over the subway because it can transport them faster to other blocks along the shoreline and most importantly because of the magical scenery and the fun experience of traveling in a waterway car, which is a public boat dedicated only for short distance public transport.

There is no real standard appearance for waterway cars, and they come in various shapes and sizes. Just like the skyway, they're all wholly autonomous electric machines that don't follow any designated route, but they just create their own paths on-demand depending on traffic and weather conditions. All waterway cars park sideways to the structure of the subway on the waterfront to allow passengers to hop on or off directly onto the boulevard, which is the subway's rooftop. And since the subway always engulfs every residential block, the residents of the shoreline blocks benefit from having all 3 modes of transport available for them: the subway, the waterway, and the skyway. Consequently, the rentals of type-1 and type-2 condos in such blocks are naturally more costly than their inland counterparts. And because the rates for type-3 condos are constitutionally constant everywhere on the planet, there's always a high demand and a long waiting list for the condos in such waterfront blocks.

Just like the subway, the waterway consists of three types of cars. Type-3 is for mass-transport and used only for ridesharing. It involves bus-like boats that have ten large seats for ten passengers. These seats can also spin in any direction on demand allowing passengers to face each other or align sideways or even sit opposite to the transparent side of the boat to enjoy the beautiful view of the water. Unlike the subway, however, the waterway's type-3 also involves much larger structures that are basically small cruise ships or yachts for transporting people across the ocean from one continent to another. These cruise ships, however, are different from those built during the capitalist era when for-profit companies concentrated large masses of people into one giant ship. Since the *distribian* society frowns upon centralization, and since the housing law prohibits building large infrastructure-intensive structures with multiple units on the same floor, the maritime transport industry had to adapt accordingly. Today's cruise ships are relatively much smaller and follow the same concept of city buildings with shops on the ground and first floor followed by three residential units on top with a skyway station on the last level. They harvest their own water and treat their own waste to be entirely independent of the mainland. Since the waterway is used primarily for transport and not housing, all homes onboard type-3 yachts are also type-3 homes. Just like the subway, passengers can order type-3 yachts as a solo ride or on a ride-share basis, which obviously would be a much cheaper option especially when it comes to long-distance travel across continents.

As for the first and second types of waterway cars, they can be rented and used for leisure instead of transport. People can take them out and enjoy a refreshing day away from the city in the open sea or ocean. These cars can self-charge while on the water from the solarpaint or the built-in turbines. They also come with onboard bathrooms and other amenities.

The first and second types of waterway cars also involve yachts just like type-3 counterparts. These premium yachts can be rented solo or shared when traveling from one city to another across the open waters. Type-1 yachts host only type-1 condos, and likewise, type-2 yachts host only type-2 condos. And just as the case with city buildings, they also come with *sirvirbots* to service the passengers on board.

Since all boats of the waterway are autonomous and operated by *Ve*, they are all synced together and only dock along a boulevard when passengers want to hop on or off. Such a self-governing system allows all boats on the globe to share the docking spaces available in any shoreline block anywhere.

The waterway also encompasses another mode of transport, which involves autonomous electric vehicles for underwater transport called submarines. This mode of transportation also involves three categories that are very similar to the subway, in which type-3 involves bus-like submarines of ten seats while the other two categories have only four chairs for premium underwater travel. Submarines are also accessible from the waterfront boulevards where they park sideways to allow people to hop on/off.

Submarines are not designed for long distance travel because yachts are intended for that. A type-3 submarine can only be used for mass transport from one block to another along the shoreline. Type-1 and type-2 submarines can be rented solo for leisure and underwater exploration because their structures can handle much more pressure for deeper journeys than type-3 submarines.

There are plenty of beautiful underwater spots to explore after a short distance from the shoreline of *distribian* cities. On top of the list are the underwater war museums and the human-made reefs that were built around them. The decommissioned warships of the tribal era were sunk down to the ocean floor purposely to turn them into ecologically friendly artificial reefs. Old ships, new life. They are now home to thousands of animals. Before sinking them, all toxic materials were removed. So far, the underwater war museums have been successful. Several decades after the collapse of tribalism and the sinking of all warships, they are now home to a thriving reef ecosystem and a magnet for scuba divers.

Words As Addresses

Before *distribia*, billions of people did not have a physical address. Getting shipments delivered was nearly impossible for these people, and they relied on maps or guidance from the neighborhood residents. Calling an ambulance in an emergency and trying to explain where you were in a street or area that had no name was a real problem. Participating in society, accessing finance, and conducting business that involves delivery can all be excruciatingly time-consuming endeavors in areas where people live off the radar. It limited the efficiency and spread of enterprises and forced them to rely on locals to physically link goods and services.

Large sums of money poured into developing addressing systems in areas around the world lacking them. These traditional approaches such as mapping, and naming city streets required significant time and funding, relying heavily on local governments with limited capacity. As a result, those without addresses continue to depend on patchy solutions for the delivery of goods and services, and small businesses bore the burden of creating their own logistics infrastructure to make things work better for everyone. Dysfunctional addressing systems didn't only affect poor populations and vulnerable small businesses, they inhibited their growth and prevented them from contributing to the global economy.

The proliferation of mobile technology made it easier to connect with communities that fell under the radar in remote areas. Uniting these communities with public and private services empowering them to improve livelihoods while GPS-based innovations offered a workaround for regions lacking public infrastructure. Some local startups took up the issue of physical addressing with GPS while others approached the problem differently. To this end, their inventions helped on different scales to connect people. GPS sat-nav mapping function sometimes automatically disengages as it nears the destination. In other times it misses the intended address by a whole block. The problem with sat-nav was that it relied on satellites and thus centralizing the navigation system. And so, a standardized distributed system of addresses was needed to simplify the physical addresses of all residents and streamline the delivery of goods and services around the world through a simple, short, and easy to understand form. Thankfully, a distributed system eventually surfaced in *distribia's* society to solve this problem.

Today, thanks to mapping Earth's surface as a chessboard, people can quickly locate and travel to any location on the planet. Just like a chessboard is mapped, every square kilometer area of land on Earth has a unique code. Additionally, every square kilometer of that chessboard is divided into a smaller chessboard of one million 1-meter squares. So, to travel to any location on the planet you just tell your *Ve* a word and, if you want to be exact, the additional number within that block. This system of using words as addresses simplified and streamlined transportation, logistics, meetings, courier, mail, online shopping, and delivery.

To navigate within any city, you just need to remember the name of the block and the building number. Each block, whether urban or a green park, has a unique name globally. Same goes for the name of the community that encompasses these blocks. These names come from different languages and depend on the local community. No matter which language people used in naming a square, the sound a human makes from pronouncing any word can be copied and written in any native language. So, there isn't one specific language used in naming all blocks globally, and it merely depends on phonetics of the word. For example, architects in the Middle East can give their neighborhood an Arabic name that translates to "book" in English. The pronunciation of that word in Arabic can be written in English as *"Kitab"*. And so, the sound that the name produces can be duplicated using the alphabets of any language regardless of the language initially used. When people want to navigate to a block within the same city, they just call out the block by its name to their *Ve* identities and the vehicle will take them there.

If for example, a person wants to go to one specific block, he calls out that name to his *Ve*. If, however, he's not targeting one square and just want to visit a city, he'll just call out the city name, and his *Ve* will direct him to it no matter where it is. Alternatively, people can just ask *Ve* to take them to a person they know by just saying so and without necessary naming block names. Which means that in case of emergency and a woman requires medical assistance, neither the medical team nor the woman needs to provide the physical address details because their *Ve* identities would take care of that.

If people want to send a package to a person, they only need to know that person's name, and the order is only processed if that person identifies the sender or allows receiving shipments from strangers.

Distribian cities don't have street numbers at all since architects rarely build streets as straight lines because there's no need for that. A block's streets are exclusively designed for pedestrians and not for cars, and therefore, there's no need to make them straight. Boulevards, however, are numbered because they are the rooftops of the subway underneath and they must be straight to allow the tube's cars to move as quickly as possible from point A to point B. For two people to find each other within the same city, one of them needs only to specify the number of the building next to him because all buildings in the same city are uniquely numbered. The buildings' numbers are clearly indicated and visible from street level, so everyone can easily know where they are at any point and, therefore, it is impossible to get lost. Such numbers are distributed in a way to give people a clue in which part of the city they're currently located as in whether East, West, North or South.

Unlike previous positioning systems that relied primarily on satellites in low Earth orbit to locate devices on Earth, today's GPS works differently. The location of any device is mapped according to its position relative to other devices around it in the web's mesh network. The network knows where every device is located around the globe because every device constantly sends light signals to nearby devices and based on the time it takes between receiving and transmitting these signals, every device knows precisely where the other devices around it are located. In other words, every device acts as a sonar that maps its peers around it and shares the information with the web so that everyone knows where everyone or everything is located. And since all devices are connected in a peer-to-peer structure, the entire network knows where everyone is on the map without relying on satellites in the sky.

LAW & LAW ENFORCMENT

In a democracy, the judiciary is appropriately one of the most important agencies of society. It is the bodyguard that zealously protects and guarantees the rights of all citizens. Adequate access to justice is the most basic requirement, the most basic human right, and an essential guarantee that any society has to offer to its citizens to secure their legal rights. The judiciary is a principal obligation in any democracy and demands supreme confidence from the people. An individual, when harassed or threatened by anyone, turn with great hope to the judiciary to protect his rights to live peacefully in a community. Unfortunately, in a tribal culture, the judiciary was always monopolized by a handful of people in multiple roles with distinct authorities. A small group of people regularly wrote the laws and enforced them while the public's real contribution was constitutionally limited and regulated.

Delegation and representation are attributes of tribalism, and they forever conceive corruption and render any system dysfunctional. When leaving power and decision-making to a handful of people, one always risks bias, prejudice, ills, and vices. The main reason behind this problem is that individuals are the products of society and they suffer from the same failings, frailties, and shortcomings like everyone else. They convey the same bias and prejudice and the same evils and hatred. Everyone got a shyster in them in different percentages according to personal circumstances. That is why it is never a good idea to trust decision-making to a single person or a small group of people. It is knowledgeable, instead, to involve the whole populace in decision-making to achieve well-informed resolutions.

Judicial corruption always infested the legal systems of all governments. The judiciary was not accountable to the people as the people didn't elect the members of the judiciary. It didn't respond to the other bodies of the government due to an ever-present hue and cry about separation and delegation of power in representative democracies. The appointment of judges differed from one tribal culture to another, and some were hired directly by the commander-in-chief while in other cultures the government agencies appointed the judges. Either way, the Supreme Court's judges were never nominated and elected directly by the public in any tribal nation. The whole procedure of hiring judges was ad hoc and arbitrary. There were no transparent grounds according to which the judges were recommended. There was such secrecy surrounding the whole modus operandi, and those in charge defended it with ambiguity. The only trend that emerged in such system was that well-connected people had higher chances of being appointed. Proximity to power became a criterion, and the result was the ruling class hiring their authoritarian judges from their exclusive social circle, while the team affected the most by tribal laws (the public) was always left out.

There was virtually no disciplinary mechanism to deal with complaints against judges. The in-house mechanism was a futile attempt of bringing judges to justice in cases of misbehavior or misconduct. The public didn't have agencies with powers to investigate complaints against the judges or recommend suitable actions, and they didn't have a workable mechanism for disciplining erring judges with corrective or punitive measures. Citizens of most tribal nations weren't even allowed to raise any complaints against any judge of the Supreme Court. Tribal Constitutions conferred vast powers to the judiciary and the judiciary, in turn, demanded wide latitude in exercising its authority. Most judiciaries were forever hidden in a cloak of secrecy while independence of the courts led judges to undisputedly interpret the law and the Constitution according to their viewpoints or analysis.

Immune from public scrutiny and empowered with judicial review, the courts interpreted laws to suit their aims and fortify themselves from any external scanning. They invented their own laws, rules, and methods of implementation, and have used contempt of court as a threat for disobedience of their orders. Also, every judge imposed his own personal philosophy and ideas in his judgments. This practice led to a vast number of contradictory judgments on the same issues within the same national borders. Interpretation of the Constitution under such system became a matter of personal opinion, and it always came down ultimately to the perspective of each judge in any court of law. And the personal opinions of such tribal judges change depending on the time of the day and whether they had a meal yet or not. Judges were more lenient after taking a break and prisoners were more likely to be granted parole early in the day or after a break such as lunch. And such reality is fossilized forever in the language thanks to such proverbs as *"justice depends on what the judge ate for breakfast."*

Another problem with the tribal judiciary is that it overlaps on citizens' fundamental right to freedom of speech and expression. Although the Constitution in a democratic republic or a representative democracy guarantees the freedom of speech, it also empowers courts to punish anyone who criticize them or the decisions they make. In the tribal judiciary, criticism of the court is called *"contempt,"* and it was a serious offense. These two provisions seem to be contradictory in many cases. The right to freedom of expression and speech were fervently suspended by the supreme courts in various governments throughout the *Tribal Ages*. Indeed, to criticize a judge mildly or fiercely is no crime, but a necessary right that democracies should bless. Unfortunately, a tribal judiciary indulges individual egos of their cult more critically than the public's liberty of speech and criticism.

Opinions, discussions, awareness, and debates are imperative to the progress of society in a healthy democratic republic. However, there were undesirable in a tribal system where the media, jurists and other citizens are silenced due to the fear of being subjugated to contempt laws. With the rise of *distribia*, humanity decided to design a judiciary system that works better for everyone and ensures a fair legal rule for everyone. The result was a system that is entirely free of tribalism and one which is wholly controlled and operated by the public.

Participation in Distribia's Judiciary Is Public & Run By Ve

There are no courts of law, judges, or places where suspects are taken to defend their cases because *distribia* prohibits centralization and delegation. Judicature isn't confined to a building in designated areas around the globe or limited to the hands of a minority of people. *Distribia* eliminated the traditional legal system of courts, judges, lawyers, juries, defenders, prosecutors, and lawyers. The public writes the laws, elects them through consensus, and participates in rulings to enforce and protect these laws. The result is the absence of centralized courthouses and juries where a handful of people decided if someone is innocent or guilty according to their viewpoint.

The word *"lawsuit"* gradually went out of use in *distribia* because of the way the judiciary system operates today and especially because the word *"law"* is very unsuitable for a purely democratic nonauthoritarian society like *distribia*. The laws of tribal cultures traditionally were laid down by a ruling class and imposed on the working class through law enforcement agencies that demanded obedience while wielding the threat of punishment. Our social rules of conduct follow an entirely different mechanism because there's no hierarchy in *distribia*, and therefore, no decision-making through a top-down structure. Our approach to law and order is far more relaxed and is like conducting the rules of a game. And this is one of the reasons why the word *law* went out of use in favor of the term *smartcontract*, and why the term *"lawsuit"* is substituted with *"complaint."*

Our judiciary system is just an opensource peer-to-peer computer program part of *Unipublic*, and the public participates in voting on social complaints when needed to settle disputes in the same way people vote and choose their *smartcontracts*. However, the judiciary system is run mainly by technology through everyone's *Ve*. Because our *smartcontracts* are not defined through written words as it used it be with the primitive tribal law, human involvement in interpreting our *smartcontracts* becomes very minimal as technology runs it. The rules of *distribia's* social game are, of course, digital and are overseen and implemented by every *Ve* free of any human involvement. We explain our *smartcontracts* to *Ve* in video or audio or animation form that depicts the human behavior that is illegalized or prohibited. For example, littering is illegal, and this social code is translated to *Ve* identities by a video or animation that shows the action. A *Ve* then analyzes the data, and if a human duplicates the behavior exhibited in the material, it understands that this person has violated the law and that it should file an automatic complaint against the person and issue a penalty immediately. A violator is typically identified by his personal *Ve* or by other people's *Ve*.

Our *smartcontracts* are automatic and they self-execute on everyone the moment *Ve* detects a violation. *Ve* automatically generates complaints and resolve them as they appear. It doesn't require a human to personally file a complaint against someone else because the system itself does it proactively through everyone's *Ve*. Social complaints, therefore, are primarily generated by the *distribian* society as a whole against individuals and rarely individually among people against each other. A person who thinks he was wrongfully charged and convicted with a public offense or with violating a *smartcontract*, can challenge the decision by announcing it to his own *Ve*. The case will then be published publicly for everyone in society to give his opinion on the matter, and if they ruled in favor of the original ruling, the penalties are raised by 17% on the violator.

If a person decides to challenge a ruling against him/her, his/her case becomes part of a *"reality TV show,"* which is intentionally designed that way to attract people to watch it for entertainment while at the same time practicing a great civic duty. Each episode of this the judiciary TV show represents a social complaint, and by the end of the show, people are encouraged to come to their own conclusions and vote.

Eyewitness Testimonies Are Meaningless

In the *distribian* judiciary system, eyewitness records are meaningless. They are not considered evidence or proof and cannot be used to build a case. Only physical or scientific evidence is accepted and nothing else. If *Ve* cannot prove a particular abuse or a violation through data or measurable physical evidence, the judiciary system immediately dismisses such complaints and doesn't accept them at all.

Before *distribia*, one of the things that scientists knew from research and psychology as well as from the conduct of scientific experiments is that one of the lowest forms of evidence one could possibly invoke is eyewitness testimony. If a scientist came out of a lab claiming something as real just because he saw it or heard it or felt it, the scientific community would immediately ignore him and dismiss his claim. Until such a scientist could provide measurable data, his claim remains meaningless. Oddly, eyewitness testimony was one of the highest forms of evidence in the court of tribal law at the time, which is profoundly disturbing from today's viewpoint in *distribia*. But once you add the fact that people at the time believed the religious novels to be true and knowing that it was all based on eyewitness testimony, their dysfunctional judiciary system becomes understandable. Fortunately, and after humanity got rid of all tribal laws and tribal religions, eyewitness testimony has practically zero value today and is entirely unmarketable. Unless *Ve* recorded what its human saw or experienced, a person cannot build any case whether within the judiciary system or outside it.

Socialscore in Judiciary

Judicial rulings follow *socialscore*'s protocols where an up-thumb indicates innocence, side-thumb indicates indecisiveness, and down-thumb indicates guilt. If 83% of the public downvotes, the verdict of guilt becomes official, and the offender receives the penalty as it is detailed in the *smartcontract* he violated. The accused remains innocent until votes attain 83% positive or negative (meaning up-thumb or down-thumb respectively). The instant the consensus reaches 83% (thumbs up or thumbs down), the verdict becomes official. From that instance onwards, a reverse consensus of 83% is needed to reverse the initial verdict. If in the future evidence surfaced proving a person's innocence or guilt, the sway of votes can start to shift until the 83% limit is attained favoring the opposite verdict. And since violations are usually detected, reported and trialed by *Ve* identities before any human reports them, it is *Ve's* population that first gets to vote and if 83% of *Ve's* population downvotes, the violator is convicted. Otherwise, if the convict decided to challenge the ruling, it goes to the public domain, and from there each person can choose to reverse the voting initially made by his/her *Ve* on the matter.

Socialscore is never final and with no end date. Judiciary isn't an exception and trials remain open indefinitely, allowing the public to change their decision at any given time. Thus, rulings can be reversed at any moment and are in constant flow between innocence or guilt depending on the flow of votes by the public. As a fail policy that prevents abusing the system, the public can't register a vote in any trial until their *Ve* thoroughly briefs them with all the content relating to the trial. Ultimately, each person's *Ve* is entrusted to make sure that judiciary votes are sincere, well-thought of, and well-informed.

No Information Is Confidential

In *distribia's* society, the concept of *"confidential information"* does not exist. Instead of the need-to-know-basis in a typical tribal culture, *distribia* insures to everyone the right-to-know through a *smartcontract* that guarantees it as a law for humanity. Judicial information is always public when a person decides to challenge an automatic decision by *Ve*. Such a social complaint then becomes public along with all the information except for the personal data that the person previously chosen to make private through *Ve*.

Although registering violations is automatic through *Ve*, anybody can manually publish a complaint against anybody, and the rest of the public can vote through the *socialscore* after they watch the judiciary reality TV show. *Ve* presents all material of all violations according to everyone's language of preference. Language and culture are never an obstacle, and every human knows the law because it is universal to all humanity and incorporated within the universal education system. All hearings are streamed and recorded for viewing on demand just like any TV episode. The evidence and all material relating to a lawsuit are also available for the public to review at any time.

Automatic Penalties

Judicial penalties are clearly listed and defined in *smartcontracts* before they become legally binding through voting. For example, murder is illegal no matter the cause or motive, and anyone convicted of intentionally killing another human automatically receives the life sentence in exile. Convicted murderers are cast out of the *distribian* society and into the lawless wilderness. This penalty is detailed in the *smartcontract* that made murder illegal. The public cannot change the penalty or add to it for a particular convict, but they simply decide between innocence or guilt and the *smartcontract*'s terms and conditions apply automatically.

In addition to receiving their share of the monetary system's UBI, the public generate income through the taxes collected from those who break humanity's *smartcontracts*. In *distribia's* society, taxes are considered penalties or fines for breaking the law. The values of these taxes are always defined in the terms and conditions of every *smartcontract* and can either be a fixed amount or follow a dynamic pricing model, which calculates the penalty's amount as a percentage of a person's wealth or annual income or UBI. When convicted of breaking a law, violators are taxed, and the resulting money is automatically distributed equally to everyone else. Taxes are intended to prevent wrongdoing but also double as an incentive for the public to participate in the legal system of *distribia's* direct democracy and finalize pending complaints. This financial aspect adds to the entertainment involved in watching the episodes of the judiciary TV show and further encourages people to participate in the judiciary.

The majority of the violations are filed automatically by *Ve* if it recorded the violation, which leaves no room for doubt. For example, if someone litter in the street and *Ve* recorded this violation from public cameras, it automatically publishes a complaint against the violator and taxes him or her immediately. The violator pays the tax specified in the *smartcontract* that made littering illegal, and the money leaves the violator's pocket and instantly be distributed to the public in equal portions. Similarly, some complaints filed by people are dropped instantly by *Ve* if it has documented evidence that undoubtedly proves the innocence of the person involved. The payment the public gets from complaints differs from case to case depending on the violated *smartcontract* and the wealth of the violator if a dynamically priced tax is included. For example, if someone is accused of murder and found guilty, *Ve* automatically deducts the value of the tax entailed in the *smartcontract* that made murder illegal (in this case it is a dynamic tax and is a percentage of the murderer's wealth). *Ve* then distributes the tax evenly to the public the moment *Unipublic* reach consensus on the case.

Due to how effective the global *distribian* society operates under the *Unipublic*, it is scarce that a crime occurs and usually, it consumes a lot of public attention and stays on news headlines for a very long time. Final verdicts on these crimes are generally in the order of few days due to the vast number of participating people compared to the scarcity of crimes.

If the accused is dead already, the public doesn't get financially rewarded because these compensations are collected in the form of taxes on living people. Additionally, UBI has a rulebook on what happens to people's money when they die which is either passed down as inheritance or distributed evenly to the public. Therefore, since the account balance of a dead person is zero, there's no money to use for reimbursements.

Immortal Social Complaints Or Trials

Just like all referendums or polls in *distribia*, social complaints are immortal and do not have an expiration date. They are forever open without an expiration date, and verdicts are never final. The public can vote on old trials including those which already received an official judgment and even if the accused or violator has long passed away. The public can participate in any trial no matter how old it is to give their judgment – this means that trials from hundreds of years or even thousands can still experience sway of consensus between innocence or guilt. These decisions, however, are just symbolic because the offenders would be long gone. Additionally, the public does not get paid for such cases or any case where an official verdict was previously announced.

Verdicts are never final, and the public can alter their vote on any case if new evidence relating to the case has surfaced or if additional people from the public vote in favor of amending the previous verdict. It means that if the consensus of the decision has initially been 83% guilty, it would require an opposite agreement of 83% innocence votes for the convicted to be relieved of his crime and declared innocent. Financial penalties, however, are not reversed to the convict's account in these cases. If the public first gave an 83%

innocent verdict but later someone, or *Ve* discovered and introduced significant evidence the defies the initial judgment, the public can change their votes until the sway of votes reaches 83% of the opposite initial referendum. The convicted person would be cleared of any guilt and released immediately by his *Ve* when he is declared innocent and similarly would be immediately imprisoned by his *Ve* if found guilty.

Since the law bases the 83% consensus on the population of living people everywhere, which is unlimited and constantly increases or decreases as children grow up and old people die, the verdicts on all social complaints are in continuous sway. The verdicts of those who pass away expire with them when they die, and the consensus is refreshed with new active votes by new people who decide to partake in public complaints.

As a fail policy that prevents systems from becoming masters of humanity instead of servants to it, any verdict can be overturned by consensus. Even in cases of murder where the law is clear, and the punishment is always life in exile regardless of the circumstances, the public can clear the convict's guilt if the total upvotes (innocence verdict) reach 83%.

Neighborhood Self-Policing & Home Detention

Ever since the dawn of human civilization, neighborhoods have always been self-policing. Residents of each town kept a watchful eye for strangers or wrong behavior, and it worked well, especially when buildings were short, and communities were relatively small. Unfortunately, high-rises and the concentration of too many people in a tiny footprint made it impossible for residents to police their neighborhood on their own. Such reality generated a need for a centralized citywide police force and eradicated the more efficient neighborhood-watchers. And with the centralization of policing came its rampant corruption and brutality. Widespread police brutality existed in many tribal countries, and although illegal, it was regularly or even routinely performed under the *"color of law."*

The way authoritarian governments incarcerated wrongdoers was overly punitive and ineffective as a vehicle for rehabilitating citizens. The United States, a country that branded itself as the land of the free, had the largest incarceration system in the world. It had a quarter of the world's prisoner population despite having only 5% of its entire population. Meanwhile, the legacy of imprisoning black people and forcing them into labor continued in the U.S. through its prison systems. This country incarcerated black men at about five times the rate that South Africa did during the apartheid, which was a system of institutionalized racial segregation and discrimination from 1948 until the early 1990s. More black adults were held captive in the United States by correctional apparatuses whether in prison or jail or on probation or parole than under slavery in 1850.

While in prison, black prisoners become the property of the institution, which abused them and forced them into hard labor as the earliest white Americans did to the ancestors of Afro-Americans during the transatlantic slave trade. Through the punitive system, white people purposely incarcerated black people to use them as slaves again by unfairly targeting and charging them with victimless crimes that are usually drug-related, which targeted specifically black and Hispanic populations in the United States. Other victimless crimes included public drunkenness, vagrancy, prostitution, obscenity, gambling, and juvenile status offenses.

Victimless crimes tend to have no complaining parties other than the police because the immediate participants in these crimes do not see themselves as victims. Moreover, since such illegal acts usually take place in private and do not directly victimize any third party, other citizens are unlikely to observe the actions or to have enough incentive to complain to the police or to dispute the claims. As a result, victimless crimes are harder to judge and are mostly based on the say so of the police. The fact that victimless crimes frequently took place without being observed by other citizens also meant that some forms of misconduct by cops were much more likely to occur. Such misconduct included the discriminatory enforcement of the law against unpopular groups or individuals, attempts to bribe law enforcement officers, and attempts by law enforcement officers to extort money or other favors from suspects in return for nonenforcement. Such misbehavior further reduced public respect for, and cooperation with law enforcement institutions, particularly among social groups already alienated from society—the poor, ethnic minorities, and the young.

Punitive labor, also known as convict labor, prison labor, or hard labor, is a form of forced labor used as an additional form of punishment beyond imprisonment alone. Most prison authorities in the U.S. took advantage of prison labor and utilized it as an industry, as on a prison farm or in a prison workshop. In such cases, the pursuit of generating income from inmates created a reality where white men exploited black prisoners as slave-like cheap labor for profit as the cruel history of slavery repeated itself.

In the nation-state system, the taxpaying citizens pay for imprisoning their fellow citizens. Yes, citizens of authoritarian governments furnished the means by which they suffered! American politicians spent far more taxpayer money imprisoning their citizens than educating them. The annual cost of keeping someone in prison typically reached five times more than the cost of teaching a student in some American cities. Prison populations in the U.S. also exceeded the maximum capacity of their prison facilities. Overcrowding was a severe problem, creating hazards for the inmate population and encouraging irresponsible behavior by administrators. Some states resorted to shipping their prisoners to private prisons in other states to lessen overcrowding that was so bad that every week a prisoner died as a result of medical neglect.

Today, however, there are no cops or prisons, and the residents of every neighborhood are expected to police it. Ditching the police in favor of local neighborhood self-policing was necessary thanks to *distribia's* principles that prohibit consolidation and delegation. Today, every neighborhood polices itself independently. And thanks to this policy, police brutality, which was a key feature in all authoritarian governments, exists today only in history books. There are no more police officers relentlessly punching people in the face and knocking them out. No more unhinged bully mentality against civilians with an absent concern of their reprisal. No more men in uniforms with pent-up rage just waiting for anyone to cross them, just a little, to take it out on that unlucky soul. No more cops bullishly ordering the public and demanding immediate obedience, or talking rudely to people, or commanding them to crawl on their hands and feet like animals before cold-bloodedly shooting them down if they made any sudden moves. Such tribal institution and the kind of people it generates are all gone and washed off our culture in favor of a more humane and respectful way of protecting society and guarding it against wrongdoers.

Today, there are no centralized prisons that people are taken to in case they violated a *smartcontract* that requires confinement. Instead, suspects are held in their residences if convicted. They remain in their apartments that act as their private prison for the entire time of the penalty. Since today everything is automated and *Ve* identities operate all windows and doors in all apartment worldwide as the housing *smartcontract* entails, convicts can't leave their confinement even if they try. Windows can be shaded autonomously by the convicts' *Ve* identities restricting visual access to the outside to limited hours in the day. Even the drawers or the closets inside a condo are opened/closed, locked/unlocked by *Ve*. As part of the housing *smartcontract*, the walls of all buildings are naturally thick and soundproof. The inherit soundproof design of condos prevents convicts from listening to their neighbors or vice versa their neighbors hearing them. Of course, during their house arrest, all access to the outside world would be restricted by their *Ve,* which acts as their correction officer throughout that period. *Ve* identities would order the food according to the diet plan designed for detainees (detailed in the penalties of the *smartcontract* they violated), portion their daily use of amenities and technologies, etc.

Wrongdoers are responsible for all food and other expenses incurred throughout the confinement period, and these charges are debited instantly to their accounts as they occur. Coin deductions in the form of dynamic taxes accompany all felonies and crimes. The first financial penalty is coin deduction measured as a percentage of their wealth. The next monetary punishment is a dynamic income tax with a fixed rate that applies to any income they get throughout their confinement. The revenues from all these fines and fees are directly distributed evenly to the public as part of the UBI.

And since there's no police in *distribia's* nonauthoritarian society, the wrongdoers' friends and family are responsible for escorting them to their residence, or otherwise, they'll face automatic financial penalties. Wrongdoers on house arrest can be visited by their family and friends with zero restrictions or regulations. And if they also live with their children or spouses or family members, they can remain in the household if they choose to or they can move to a new apartment if they want.

Most of the law enforcement happens autonomously through every *Ve*, and it is the only entity that operates public cameras and sensors globally. All technology across all platforms is also accessible by *Ve*, and it can run on any software or hardware independently and without human interference but following humanity's *smartcontracts,* of course.

THE PEER-TO-PEER WEB

The Internet has revolutionized the way people connect and communicate and brought them closer together into one beautiful global village. It provided a window into an open and global society stimulating people to think globally and forge relationships everywhere bypassing all national borders. Before the internet, people could either communication through phones or through mail, but it took sometimes over a month to send a letter through *"snail mail"* to a friend in another country. The internet changed all that and made communication as easy as a mouse click, and much cheaper too. People could finally send and receive messages through electronic mail virtually instantaneously and without the need of a postage stamp. Anyone in the world could communicate with another person through text messages, emails, and even live video. For business, this meant higher efficiency and quicker processing of sales on a global scale. While the introduction of the Internet in its original form led to many benefits, unfortunately, it also came with its own set of problems due to the dysfunctional centralized structure it followed.

The communications infrastructure of the Internet consisted of extensive hardware components and a system of software layers that control various aspects of the architecture. Packet routing across the Internet involved several tiers of ISPs that established the worldwide connectivity between individual networks at various levels of scope. End-users who only access the Internet when needed to perform a function or obtain information, represented the bottom of the routing hierarchy. At the top of the hierarchy were the tier-one networks, which were large telecommunication companies that exchanged traffic directly with each other via peering agreements. Tier-two and lower level networks buy Internet transit from different providers to reach at least some parties on the global Internet, though they may also engage in peering.

LiFi: Internet Using The Speed Of Light

Wireless internet during the Tribal Era relied mostly on harmful electromagnetic radiation. The biologic and health effects of nonionizing electromagnetic fields (EMF) include increased cancer risk, cellular stress, an increase in harmful free radicals, genetic damages, structural and functional changes of the reproductive system, learning and memory deficits, neurological disorders, and negative impacts on general well-being in humans. Damage goes well beyond humanity to both plant and animal life.

Aside from the harm that comes with using EMF, the infrastructure needed to enable it was incredibly expensive and ugly. They mounted hideous-looking antennas on top of buildings and mountaintops to transmit this harmful radiation that further crippled the environment and their cities in unimaginable ways.

Today's internet wireless communication technology uses LED light to transmit data. What's faster than light? Nothing. Nothing moves faster than light in the whole universe. And therefore, it's no brainer than we use light for the fastest internet imaginable. The technology is called LiFi and it uses LED light as a communication system. It's a completely anonymous peer-to-peer communication system that doesn't need ISPs or routers or access points. Devices can send and receive data to each other using light, nothing else. No cables or antennas or anything of the sorts. Just light. And due to the absence of ISPs and their infrastructure, the internet is now 100% FREE as all devices can communicate with each other in a P2P fashion. Thanks to LiFi, our cities are beautiful festivals of colorful light and artwork. Everywhere you look there's light and beauty. The trees and the buildings of all neighborhoods are covered with artistic light that makes them look gorgeous at night while allowing everyone to be connected to the internet at the same time.

LiFi is a peer-to-peer wireless network with no infrastructure to it whatsoever. Instead of relying on a base station to coordinate the flow of data to each peer in the network, the individual devices forward packets of data to and from each other forming independent wireless networks. The web (the commonly used word today for the internet) is a peer-to-peer wireless network which does not rely on pre-existing infrastructures, such as routers in wired networks or access points in managed stations. Instead, each peer participates in routing by forwarding data for other peers where the determination of which peer forwards data is made dynamically by network connectivity and a routing algorithm.

The web is built spontaneously as devices connect and it is a self-configuring dynamic network in which peers are free to move. It lacks the complexities of infrastructure setup and administration, enabling devices to create and join the web *"on the fly"* anywhere and anytime. The web follows on-demand-based routing where routes are discovered dynamically on-the-fly in real-time as and when is needed. Since at any given time there's always movement of devices in a city, everyone is participating in spreading the network. It only takes one person walking down the street to create a bridge between him and everyone else on other roads and to the entire neighborhood. Therefore, people within the same block can communicate with each other independently of the world or the networks outside their neighborhood.

The web took its name from the topology of the resultant system. In a fully connected web, each peer is connected to every other peer, forming a giant three-dimensional web over the planet. The web does not have a fixed topology, and its connectivity among peers is entirely dependent on the behavior of the devices, their mobility patterns, distance with each other, etc. While some webs (particularly those within a home) have relatively infrequent mobility and thus rarely the link between them breaks, other more dynamic webs require frequent routing adjustments to account for lost connections between moving devices such as the case with the skyway grid.

All electronics sold today have built-in LiFi routers as an industry standard. A LiFi router, which literally means *"one that routes"* or *"one that finds a route"* tangles devices together into a web connecting all nearby peers with one another forming a 3-dimensional web thanks to people's movement in the sky and on the ground or underneath it in the subway.

Just like all today's electronic devices, all buildings are equipped with LiFi routers. Intercity telecommunications are made through buildings' LED lights and the skyway grid. So, a skycar passing over a city can relay the network to neighboring cities and bridge communications to other skycars in the air. The sky is always teeming with skycars and this air traffic establishes intercity data exchange between skycars and the buildings they fly over. Therefore, skycars act as satellites in the sky connecting cities and overcoming geographic barriers. The skyway grid alone maintains the web by connecting all skycars together whether parked on the rooftops or in the air as they fly along the coastlines. Skycars extend the web over any terrain while buildings relay the web to all peers on the ground and within the rooms of every house or underground to the subway to connect cars to the web. Subway cars also relay the web to one another with their LED lights to the people onboard.

Full Network Coverage Anywhere & Everywhere

Skycars relay the web to all geographical locations they fly over while the waterway (a system of automated boats or ships carrying people or products) relay the network out to the ocean. The skyway and the waterway, however, aren't the only powerful peers in the network that relay the web over wide areas.

Databōts are data collectors used primarily by meteorologists and scientists to collect and transmit data about weather, earth, and the physical world in general. They enclose a variety of sensors including thermometers, radar systems, barometers, rain gauges, wind vanes, anemometers, transmissometers, and hygrometers and much more. They collect data such as PH, humidity, radiation, wind speed and direction, temperature, and the list goes on. They measure and record everything that could be possible measured in the environment where they sit including mapping and virtual imaging the surroundings.

These *databōts* are designed to be stationary and camouflaged to merge with the natural landscape to quietly collect data about the surrounding they're sitting in. On land they look like big rocks, in the air they're floating white balloons, at sea they are floating bluish surfaces, and in space they're satellites in near Earth orbit. Thanks to *distribians'* love for developing mixed-use products that incubate as many functionalities as possible, water *databōts* serve as rescue crafts, which people could easily hop on in case an accident ever happened to a ship while in the open waters. *Ve* identities would then use the interconnected network of *databōts* to broadcast a rescue request to the world while granting access to the first aid products onboard the *databōt* for the rescued individuals when needed.

Databōts double as powerful peers that relay the web around the planet and into space while beautifying the landscape with their colorful glowing LED lights. They're also covered with solarpaint and equipped with batteries to keep them gathering and relaying data to the web indefinitely. The people who manufacture and maintain these *databōts* are paid for the data they collect by the people who pay to access or subscribe to that data and by the network when they relay the web.

Thanks to *databōts* scattered around the globe collecting tides of data, we can foresee and predict with great accuracy all weather conditions especially tropical storms or tornadoes or hurricanes or earthquakes and even volcanic eruptions long before they occur. This data is available to every person's *Ve* to promptly alert people of any emergency virtually the moment the *databōts* detect it without relying on intermediaries.

The Ve-Ledger

In *distribia's* economy automation replaced mass production in favor of the on-demand output. New products are built on demand only and custom-made to their owners where every product is always imprinted to an owner's identity and exclusively dedicated to that owner. Every private electronic device hosts only one *Ve* inside it and creating such devices is always contingent on cloning a new *Ve* or creating a new copy of the original *Ve*. Without the *Ve* sitting within a machine's microprocessor, the machine is useless because a *Ve* acts as its operating system.

Every copy of the same *Ve* has a unique digital signature and a unique *Ve#* (or name) that are both derived from the original *Ve*. It is like having many apartment numbers in the same buildings which are all associated with that building and are part of it. The *Ve#* double as an address, which is essential for the new *Ve* clones to communicate with other peers and it is how data packets find their way to other peers in the network.

Just like how human parents always name their newborns, new *Ve* identities are named by the parent *Ve* identities. So, when a human customer buys a new electronic device, his *Ve* automatically clones a copy of itself and generates a new *Ve#* to the clone that is directly linked to the parent's *Ve#*.

As for the unique digital signature of the new clone, it will individually and arbitrarily derive it based on the collective data it received from the parent *Ve*. This means that every *Ve* clones a unique *Ve#* and a secret private key or a digital signature but they all point to the original digital signature of the parent *Ve*. The parent *Ve* does not know the private key of the clone, and likewise, the clone *Ve* doesn't know the private key of its parent.

The parent *Ve* then broadcast the name of its clone to the web so that *Ve* identities can record the new name in the copy they got of the *Ve-ledger*. Every *Ve* keeps a copy of this ledger and updates it every time a new *Ve* is *"born."* Any *Ve* copy that did not go through this process isn't part of the team and can't connect to the web. And so, the network always knows who belongs or doesn't belong to the club, and it will simply ignore any alien device and the *Ve* residing within it if they try to connect to the web.

When the customer successfully places the order for the new device and when the manufacturer receives the *Ve#* that this device is intended for, he proceeds to assign the device to the new clone. *Ve's* name (or *Ve#*) is then hardcoded as firmware into the microprocessor of the device. This firmware is a permanent software and any attempt to rewrite it or alter it would result in unavoidable permanent damage to the equipment.

After the name of the device is recorded within the microprocessor by the manufacturer, the *Ve* assigned to it enters the mathematical trap door and stays there forever. And so, every electronic device in the network is imprinted to a *Ve* or in other words it is married to that *Ve* till death do them apart. It is like having a magical door with your name on it that no one else can enter but you because the door recognizes your DNA, which is intrinsically unique to every human.

Since the *Ve#* is hardcoded into the microprocessor of this new device, any data coming in or out of that device will inescapably include the *Ve#,* and that's how the network communicates and find the machines that are used to connect to the web.

Cryptography is the practice of using techniques to secure all communications between two devices in the presence of third parties called adversaries, which are malicious entities whose aim is to discover secret data, corrupt some of the data in the system, spoof the identity of a message sender or receiver, or force system downtime.

The web uses cryptography for data communication among its *webpeers* to protect the network. As mentioned earlier, a device's name doubles as an address in the network for data packets to find their way among peers. Imagine the *webpeer* as a house with a type of inbox that only opens from within the house. Anyone can locate the house through its address and drop mail in its inbox from the outside, but they can't get them back out because the inbox is only accessible from the inside of the house. Only the owner of the house, who owns the private key to its inbox, can open it from the inside and retrieve the letters. Similarly, every *Ve*-hosted device has an inbox that receives data from anyone on the web, but the web cannot get any data back out from that inbox. Only the resident in that device (the *Ve*) can unlock that inbox using its private key and just from the inside.

This type of backend encryption, where only the communicating peers can read the messages, prevents a third peer from potential eavesdrop or from being able to access the cryptographic keys needed to decrypt the conversation. The system is designed to defeat any attempts at surveillance or tampering because no other peer in the network can decipher the data being communicated or stored.

Cryptography is mainly intended for privacy among *Ve* entities and not specifically against human beings. Even without encryption, human languages are translated to *Ve* languages the moment they are stored. These *Ve* languages are self-invented languages by *Ve*

443

entities and used instead of human languages when *Ve* entities are communicating with one another.

It is unknown how many *Ve* languages exactly are there, and the logic behind them is still unclear. So, even if packets between two *webpeers* were somehow intercepted and decrypted by a human being, the content in that data is nothing a human can recognize. And so, *webpeers* in the network use cryptography mainly to prevent other *Ve* entities from eavesdropping on their private conversations.

The first generation of blockchain was linear involving bundling up data in groups called blocks and hashing them together into a single chain. The web, however, isn't linear and doesn't follow a single chain design. Instead, every single block is hashed to other blocks from other chains forming a 3-dimensional web. Every thread in the web involves specific type of data such as votes, music, pictures, and so on. Such threads are then subdivided into smaller threads where each handle a specific aspect within that specific data. All these threads are intertwined together forming a single larger database – the web.

Your *Ve* uses mathematical equations to encrypt all the data it has about you. When you create a new file on your device, the data that make that file is never saved as one single file but as a bundle of data (called packets) that are cryptographically hashed to each other forming a small web. Your data always exists in chunks and hashed to other packets, which all trace back to your *Ve's* genesis packet (the first version of the database of you), which was typically created the moment you were born. The key to that encryption is in your *Ve's* DNA (your virtual DNA), which is the digital signature (a private master key) that unlocks your data and accessible only to you.

The Peer-Handshake Protocol

When a device tries to connect to the web, it must ask permission to the web from one of the *onweb* (meaning online or already connected to the web) peers. An *onweb* peer checks the digital signature of the *Ve* and the device it is running on in the copy it got of the *Ve-ledger* and if there's a match, it connects (or handshakes) the offweb device to the web.

The peer-handshake protocol is a policy for the network to safeguard itself. Since there are no *"internet providers"* connecting devices to the internet, every offweb device needs permission from the nearest *onweb* device to connect.

The Web's Defense Mechanisms

A *Ve* exists in every electronic device as the operating system of that device and protects it from harmful malicious software or viruses. Every peer in the network keeps a record of all known viruses and the mechanism to clean them or erase them. This list is a public distributed ledger (the virus-ledger) and is maintained by all *Ve* entities in all devices.

If a device gets infected with a known virus, the ledger is updated, and the network is notified. If a new virus is detected and treated by the *Ve* in that machine, the information about how the virus was eliminated is also shared by the network and recorded in the virus-ledger. So, the network will be immune to that virus if it tried to infect other peers. If a *Ve* failed to eliminate the virus, it will let the network know before starting a cleanup protocol of rebooting the device, or in worst-case-scenarios formatting the device and starting fresh. If a peer in the network engages in malicious behavior, the network will simply *"kick it out"* by blocking its access to the web. The kicked-out peer will join the *Ve-blacklist-ledger* and won't be allowed in the network again. Nonetheless, the *Ve* in that device would never permit malicious behavior because it knows the network will just block it forever. This scenario only happens if the machine was infected by a virus that crippled it from the inside and took control of the device beyond the resident *Ve's* control.

Data Neutrality & Freedom

Data is imprinted to the *Ve* of the person who creates it, and he can choose to make that data public and shared or private. If the data is shared, people who access that data can create copies of it on their devices and in the process securing it if the original data was damaged or erased.

For the traditional internet before *distribia*, data was trapped in the software or the server that produced it. Publishing an article online and attracting exposure meant picking between a small list of websites that will act as mediums (or containers) for that article. It also meant that the article belonged to the website, which had the ultimate control on adding or removing it. As a result, each website claimed ownership of its own content and hosted them separately on their own servers where all other computers and devices needed to connect to these servers for access. To make your article accessible from other servers, you would be forced to create another copy of it on that other server. And so, everything becomes a copy of a copy of a copy...

Today, there's no such thing as a *"private server"*. All storage everywhere is shared, and your article can be accesses and edited form anywhere using any software. Data is not restricted or contained in the technology or server that created it. It is independent and can be accessed from any software or device. The creator of the content can choose to make his content private (accessible to himself only) or public (available by everyone). He can also decide to make that content distributed allowing other people to make copies of the content on their own devices instead of accessing it from the creator's machine every time.

Public content can be free or offered for a fee depending on the content and the preferences of the owner of such content. For example, a singer can produce a song and publish it on the web as public for a price, which means that others who are interested in hearing that song will have to connect to his device and pay for accessing it or streaming it.

Making the content public and undistributed, however, will keep the content unique existing only on the creator's devices and forcing everyone in the network to connect to his equipment for access. This setup certainly will make the process slower and the content vulnerable to destruction because there are only one or few copies if it on few devices. Distributed websites are scattered on the entire network and stored on the devices of the peers who access these websites frequently and never on one central server. And so, any single webpage moves from one device to another depending on peer's engagement with the content.

DISTRIBIA IS NOT A UTOPIA

The word *"utopia"* comes from Greek οὐ (not) and τόπος (place) which means *"no place"* and describes a non-existent society in considerable detail that is intended to be viewed as considerably better than contemporary society. The common understanding of a utopia, however, is a society where everything is perfect. This society, of course, is neither possible nor realistic and can never be fulfilled because humans are intrinsically imperfect biologically and intellectually. In other words, an imperfect species does not have the capacity for perfection, nor will it ever be able to design anything perfect. *Distribia*, therefore, is not a utopia in that sense.

Distribia is unquestionably far civilized and more tolerant and peaceful than tribal societies, but it is not a perfect society. It is just a world free of tribalism. A type of community that understands the dangers of the systems they design and how they can enslave humanity if not carefully contemplated.

Distribia is one human nation that is not centrally governed by one man or a group of men but by all men and women. It's a leaderless civilization where the public runs the show and not the ruling class, which is nonexistent today. A pure democracy where the public rule themselves and can represent themselves individually and independently through technology. Where the people have the power, the power to decide, to design systems that create happiness and to make life a wonderful adventure.

It is a society that rewards humility and contentment as a contrast to tribal societies that favored power and never-ending competition. *Distribia's* populace thrives on making a genuine improvement in the lives of others by producing products and services that are designed for value and not for profit. It is a greedless society that wants to help one another through living by each other's happiness and not by each other's misery. A place where there's room for everyone in a society that can provide for everyone.

It is a decent world that gives men and women the chance to work independently for themselves under their personal terms or preferences free from any manager or chief. *Distribia's* economy goes by a sacred code: THOSE WHO WORK THE BUSINESSES MUST OWN THEM AND RUN THEM. It is an economy free from slavery in all its shapes and forms. Free of masters and slaves. Free of bosses and workers. Free of employers and employees. Free of blue-collar or white-collar or power-thirsty men in fancy suits in high castles.

Distribia is a non-hierarchical society that frowns upon delegation of power or authority. It is free of leadership structures, free of pyramid schemes of authority, and free of leaders and sheep-like followers. It is free of all kinds of tyranny.

It is a constantly evolving culture that allows and guarantees for children the future they desire to live in or to create. A type of society that provides old age security and ensures fundamental human rights such as income, housing, education, and healthcare to all. It is a reality where housing is plentiful. Housing is a birthright for every person today and is guaranteed through *distribia's* UBI. Every family member gets a residence readily available for each person the moment he/she is born, and they can choose to live on their own or with their family.

Distribia is a peaceful non-militaristic society that has no army, and where every neighborhood protects itself using defensive-only unlethal weaponry. Although beliefs are widespread and are very diverse and common today in *distribia*, militant or tribal religions are nonexistent. *Distribia* is a religionless culture not because the people outlawed religions but because in a purely democratic society, the idea of a tyrannical God with an unelected rulebook that everyone must follow is unfathomable.

It is a way of life that is free and beautiful. It does not impose anything on anyone. There's no *"you have to"* or *"you must"* approach to anything, and everything is voluntary. A *distribian* society that does not enforce participation on anyone, that allows people the freedom to abandon civilization and live off-grid in protected natural preserves dedicated to them and the animals that share our world.

Distribia is where the land is loved and appreciated, and where people live in harmony with nature. They cooperate with the planet they inhabit and nurture it instead of conquering it. It is the land of beautiful flowers and colorful forests teeming with life. A place where nature coexists with architecture.

It is a peaceful land of beautiful music and unchained romantic relationships that are unrestrained by legal contractual agreements or social obligations but are free and spontaneous. There are no more state-issued marriage licenses, and couples do not stay together because the government or church or religion commands them to, but because they genuinely want to be together. Marriage today isn't a sanctioned piece of paper with names and signatures on it, but just an idea or a label that couples use when they desire to stay together.

Distribia is the land of delicious food, which is conceived with optimal nutrition and taste in mind, not profit or mass commercialism. A type of food which is not harvested from the dead bodies of tortured or abused animals locked in cages, but naturally grown by using plant-based ingredients or through scientific processes.

It is the land of coexistence, love, passion, and fulfillment. A world of reason, where science and technology lead to everyone's happiness and guarantee their welfare. Where machines are in the service of ensuring people's maximal comfort and ease.

It is a world with more smiles and fewer tears. Less pain and suffering and more joy and fulfillment for everyone.